Medicalising borders

RETHINKING BORDERS

SERIES EDITORS: SARAH GREEN AND HASTINGS DONNAN

Rethinking Borders focuses on what gives borders their qualities across time and space, as well as how such borders are experienced, built, managed, imagined and changed. This involves detailed and often richly ethnographic studies of all aspects of borders: finance and money, bureaucracy, trade, law, new technologies, materiality, infrastructure, gender and sexuality, even the philosophy of what counts as being 'borderly,' as well as the more familiar topics of migration, nationalism, politics, conflicts and security.

Previously published

Migrating borders and moving times: Temporality and the crossing of borders in Europe
Edited by Hastings Donnan, Madeleine Hurd and Carolin Leutloff-Grandits

The political materialities of borders: New theoretical directions
Edited by Olga Demetriou and Rozita Dimova

Border images, border narratives: The political aesthetics of boundaries and crossings
Edited by Johan Schimanski and Jopi Nyman

Medicalising borders

Selection, containment and quarantine since 1800

Edited by

Sevasti Trubeta, Christian Promitzer
and Paul Weindling

MANCHESTER UNIVERSITY PRESS

Copyright © Manchester University Press 2021

While copyright in the volume as a whole is vested in Manchester University Press, copyright in individual chapters belongs to their respective authors.

An electronic version of chapter 9 is also available under a Creative Commons (CC-BY-NC-ND) licence, thanks to the support of the Wellcome Trust, which permits non-commercial use, distribution and reproduction provided the editor(s), chapter author(s) and Manchester University Press are fully cited and no modifications or adaptations are made. Details of the licence can be viewed at https://creativecommons.org/licenses/by-nc-nd/4.0/

Published by Manchester University Press
Oxford Road, Manchester M13 9PL
www.manchesteruniversitypress.co.uk

British Library Cataloguing-in-Publication Data is available

ISBN 978 1 5261 5466 8 hardback
ISBN 978 1 5261 7457 4 paperback

First published by Manchester University Press in hardback 2021

This edition first published 2023

The publisher has no responsibility for the persistence or accuracy of URLs for any external or third-party internet websites referred to in this book, and does not guarantee that any content on such websites is, or will remain, accurate or appropriate.

Typeset by Sunrise Setting Ltd, Brixham

Contents

List of figures — vii
List of tables — viii
Notes on contributors — ix
Preface and acknowledgements — xvi

Introduction: medicalising borders — 1
Sevasti Trubeta, Christian Promitzer and Paul Weindling

Part I: Quarantine

1 Habsburg border quarantines until 1837: an epidemiological 'iron curtain'? — 31
  Sabine Jesner

2 Cholera at the junction of maritime and land routes in nineteenth-century Trieste — 56
  Urška Bratož

3 Uses of quarantine in the nineteenth century until the Crimean War: examples from south-east Europe — 78
  Christian Promitzer

4 Weak state-controlled disease prevention in peripheral border regions: Austrian Bukovina and Dalmatia in the late nineteenth century — 100
  Carlos Watzka

Part II: (Dis)connections – containment

5 Lazarettos as border filters: expurgating bodies, commodities and ideas, 1800–1870s 129
John Chircop

6 Sealing borders and containing prisoners: from free movement of migrants to containment in concentration camps 155
Paul Weindling

7 Locating disease: on the coexistence of diverse concepts of territory and the spread of disease 178
Sarah Green

8 Fear and panic at the borders: outbreak anxieties in the United States from the colonies to COVID-19 199
Amy Lauren Fairchild, Constance A. Nathanson and Cullen Conway

Part III: Selection

9 'Suspect' screening: the limits of Britain's medicalised borders, 1962–1981 227
Roberta Bivins

10 A question of hygiene or nationality? Exclusion and non-Jewish labour migrants, refugees and asylum seekers in Israel, 2006–2017 256
Robin A. Harper and Hani Zubida

11 Medicalised borders and racism in the era of humanitarianism 287
Sevasti Trubeta

Index 310

Figures

1.1	Habsburg Military Border with quarantine stations (approximately mid-eighteenth century). Source: Sabine Jesner	36
4.1	The border regions of Bukovina and Dalmatia within the Austro–Hungarian Empire. Source: Wikimedia Commons/Public Domain	104
4.2	Annual smallpox death rates in the whole of Cisleithania, Bukovina and Dalmatia, 1880–1909. Source: Carlos Watzka	112
5.1	Lazaretto at Mahon. Source: G. Bussolin, *Delle Istituzioni di Sanita' marittima nel bacino del Mediterraneo* (Trieste, 1881)	133
5.2	Lazaretto at Naples. Source: G. Bussolin, *Delle Istituzioni di Sanita' marittima nel bacino del Mediterraneo* (Trieste, 1881)	133
5.3	Lazaretto at Trieste. Source: G. Bussolin, *Delle Istituzioni di Sanita' marittima nel bacino del Mediterraneo* (Trieste, 1881)	134
5.4	Plan of the Manoel Island lazaretto (Malta). Source: A. Ghio, *The Cholera in Malta and Gozo in the Year 1863* (Malta Government Printing Office, 1867)	139
10.1	Local pamphlet. Source: Hani Zubida and Robin Harper	270

Tables

10.1 Number of refugees/asylum seekers entering
    Israel in recent years   260
10.2 Refugees and asylum seekers in Israel by country
    of origin   261
10.3 Appendix: Framing table   278

Notes on contributors

Roberta Bivins is Professor of the History of Medicine at the University of Warwick. Her work has focused on Britain as a node in extensive global networks of migration and exchange from the late seventeenth century until the present day. Bivins' first two books examined the cross-cultural transmission of medical expertise, particularly in relation to global and alternative medicine (*Acupuncture, Expertise and Cross-Cultural Medicine*, 2000; *Alternative Medicine? A History*, 2007). Since 2004, funded by the Wellcome Trust, she has studied the impacts of immigration and ethnicity on post-war British health, medical research and practice. In 2015, she published findings from this research as *Contagious Communities: Medicine, Migration and the NHS in Post War Britain*. This continuing work has formed the basis of scientific presentations to a WHO Europe Summer School on migration and health; the UK Parliament (under the auspices of the Industry and Parliament Trust); and the UK NHS Research and Development Forum. She is currently a Principal Investigator on the five-year Wellcome Trust funded project, The Cultural History of the NHS, which has included work on the visual culture of race and a study of state and public attitudes towards self-quantification in the NHS era.

Urška Bratož, PhD (Koper) graduated in 2005 in Cultural Studies and Social Anthropology at the University of Primorska (Faculty of Humanities in Koper, Slovenia). In 2010 she was awarded her PhD degree, after finishing the postgraduate course on History of Europe and Mediterranean at the same institution. Since 2005 she has been working at the Science and Research Centre of Koper (ZRS Koper), currently as a research fellow. Between 2010 and 2017 she also collaborated with the Faculty of Humanities of the University of Primorska as Assistant and Assistant Professor at the Department of History.

John Chircop is resident professor in social and economic history at the Department of History, and chairperson of the Mediterranean Institute, the University of Malta. His principal research and publications focus on poor relief, social welfare, hospitalisation, colonial medicine, public health and quarantine, during the nineteenth and early twentieth centuries. Most of this work is set in the British colonial domains of Cyprus, Ionian Islands, Malta, Gibraltar and Egypt. He is now shifting interest beyond the Mediterranean towards British and other western European colonies in other regions, including the Caribbean, within a comparative historical approach. John is co-founder of the international *Quarantine Studies Network*. He chairs the editorial board of the *Journal of Mediterranean Studies* and sits on the editorial boards of *Mediterranean Review* and *Mediterranean Knowledge*. He has just started coordinating a new research project *Body Health and Food*. His latest book (co-edited with F. X. Martinez) is *Mediterranean Quarantines, 1750–1914: Space, Identity and Power* (Manchester University Press, 2018).

Cullen Conway is a Research Associate at Oregon Health and Science University where he collaborates with primary care clinics throughout Oregon to enhance their quality improvement infrastructure and capacity. He received his MPH degree in the History and Ethics of Public Health from Columbia University, where he worked with Amy Fairchild and Connie Nathanson on the politics of panic and crisis.

Amy Lauren Fairchild is a historian who works at the intersection of history, public health ethics, and public health policy and politics. Her work has helped establish public health ethics – which is concerned with the well-being of populations – as contextually rooted and fundamentally distinct from either bioethics or human rights. Whether exploring the tension between privacy and surveillance, immigration and border control, or paternalism and liberty, Fairchild assesses the social, political and ethical factors that shape not only the potential and limits of the state to intervene for the common good but also what counts as evidence. Fairchild has written two books, *Science at the Borders: Immigrant Medical Inspection and the Shaping of the Modern Industrial Labor Force* and *Searching Eyes: Privacy, the State, and Disease Surveillance in America* (with Ronald Bayer and James Colgrove). In addition, she has published in leading journals including the *New England Journal of Medicine*, *Health Affairs*, the *American Journal of Public Health*, *Science*, and the *JAMA*. The National Endowment for the Humanities is funding her current book project: a social history of fear and panic. She is currently the Dean of the College of Public Health at The Ohio State University.

Sarah Green is Professor of social and cultural anthropology at the University of Helsinki. She focuses particularly on the anthropology of space, place and location, not only in terms of border regimes, but also many other spatial aspects of social existence, including the spatial implications of digital technologies, gender politics and monetary exchanges. Regionally, she has carried out fieldwork in the Greek–Albanian border region, southern Greece, the Aegean, London, Manchester and, in wider terms, on the Mediterranean region and the European Union. She has recently begun new research to explore border regimes established for controlling the movement of animals and the spread of zoonotic diseases in the Mediterranean region. That work is part of her European Research Council Advanced Grant called Crosslocations, and an Academy of Finland project called Transit, Trade and Travel. She is author of *Notes from the Balkans* (Princeton University Press, 2005), *Urban Amazons* (Macmillan and St Martins Press, 1997), and joint author of *Borderwork* (Jasilti, 2013) with Lena Malm (photography; additional written contributions by Robin Harper and Markus Drake).

Robin A. Harper is Professor of Political Science at York College (CUNY). Her research focuses on comparative citizenship policy and issues of inclusion/exclusion in Germany, Israel and the United States. She is especially intrigued by questions of meaning in citizenship, belonging, borders and temporary labour migration. Formerly, she was the Deputy Director of Immigrant Affairs and Language Services for the New York City Mayor's Office and Policy Supervisor for Social Services and Immigrant Affairs at the NYC Office of Management & Budget. She served as a Policy Analyst as a Robert Bosch Fellow in the Berlin, Germany, Office of Integration Affairs and the Ministry of Labor in the Immigrant Integration Department. She was a Project Supervisor for a cross-border social service/public health programme in Pakistan and Afghanistan. Recent publications include: 'The meaning of doing: reflective practice in public administration education', *Teaching Public Administration* (April 2018), 1–20; 'Deconstructing naturalization ceremonies as public spectacles of citizenship', *Space and Polity*, 21:1 (2017), 92–107; 'Being seen: visibility, families and dynamic remittance practices', *Migration and Development* (March 2017), 1–21 (with Hani Zubida). Her research focuses primarily on topics from social history and the history of medicine. She has investigated the appearance of several infectious diseases (plague, cholera, variola) in the Upper Adriatic region, including preventive health measures, and health in particular population groups. In 2017 she published her scientific monograph, entitled 'The pale intruder from the east: cholera in north-western Istria (1830–1890)', in which she deals with different aspects (approached by demography, medical and social history) of cholera outbreaks in the Austrian Littoral.

Sabine Jesner is an early modern historian and postdoctoral researcher at the department of Southeast European History and Anthropology located at the University of Graz. Her main research interest is in the Habsburg rule in Southeast Europe in the eighteenth century. Her work explores issues such as the Habsburg battlefield medicine, the Habsburg prevention and defence strategies in the Transylvanian Military Border, the personnel management of the Habsburg Monarchy in the Banat, and the functioning of quarantines at the Habsburg cordon sanitaire.

Constance A. Nathanson holds a PhD in sociology from the University of Chicago and is currently a Professor in the Departments of Sociomedical Sciences and Population and Family Health at Columbia University's Mailman School of Public Health in New York City. She has over forty-five years of experience in research on sociological dimensions of health and health policy. Her work over the past twenty years has focused on the history, politics and sociology of public health policy and policy change in the United States and in its peer developed countries. Recent publications include articles on tobacco and gun control policy, the role of social movements in policy change, and essays on health inequalities, as well as a book, *Disease Prevention as Social Change* (2007), that describes and interprets public health policy shifts across time in the United States, France, Great Britain and Canada. Her current project, *Blood, Politics, and Death*, is a cross-national comparison of the very different responses to HIV contamination of the blood supply in the United States and France, grounded in extensive archival research and oral history interviews with actors in this drama of the 1980s and early 1990s, a tragedy now largely forgotten, at least in the United States.

Christian Promitzer is Assistant Professor at the Department of Southeast European History and Anthropology (SEEHA), University of Graz. Since his doctoral dissertation on the history of unsettled border and minority issues between Austria and Slovenia he has worked on the history of small ethnic groups in south-eastern Europe as well as with the social history of medicine in the Balkans. In this latter field he has concentrated on individual epidemics and the history of racial science and eugenics. Promitzer was the project leader of 'Hidden minorities between Central Europe and the Balkans', in 2001–2004, and 'Infectious diseases and public health in southeast Europe', in 2013–2017, both projects funded by the FWF Austrian Science Fund. He has published several papers in the aforementioned research fields, most of them in the English language. He is co-editor of several books, including *Health, Hygiene and Eugenics in Southeastern Europe to 1945* (CEU Press, 2011), published by academic presses.

Sevasti Trubeta is a sociologist and has a temporary professorship at the University for Applied Sciences Magdeburg-Stendal, in Germany. From 2009 to 2015 she was professor for Sociology of Migration and Globalisation at the Institute of Sociology at the University of the Aegean (Lesvos, Greece) and from 2015 to 2017 a visiting professor at the Free University Berlin. Prior to these appointments she had research positions at the Free University Berlin and Albert-Ludwigs-Universität, Freiburg im Breisgau, in projects funded by the German Research Society (DFG). She has been a visiting researcher and fellow at various universities including Princeton University (2003) and Kosmos-Excellence Initiative, Humboldt Universität Berlin (2015). The focus of her research addresses the fields of diversity, borders, migration, refugees and minorities (especially Roma), eugenics, medicalisation and racism. Her latest book is *Physical Anthropology, Race and Eugenics in Greece, 1880s–1970s* (Brill Academic Publishers, 2013). Other publications include 'Vaccination and the refugee camp: exercising the free choice of vaccination from an abject position in Germany and Greece', *Journal of Ethnic and Migration Studies* 2018; '"Rights" in the grey area: undocumented border crossers on Lesvos', *Race & Class* (2015); and joint editorship (with Christian Promitzer and Marius Turda) of *Health, Hygiene and Eugenics in Southeastern Europe to 1945* (Budapest & New York: CEU Press, 2011).

Carlos Watzka studied sociology and history at the University of Graz and in 2004 concluded his doctoral studies in social and economic sciences with a study on the hospital system and the treatment of the mentally ill in early modern times. In 2008 he finished his habilitation in sociology with a study of the regional differences of and social risk factors for suicide in contemporary Austria. From 2006 to 2011 he was head of an FWF-funded, Graz-based research project, examining charitable catholic orders in Central Europe during the seventeenth and eighteenth centuries. From 2009 to 2013 he functioned as vicarious professor at the University of Eichstaett. From 2014 to 2019 he conducted several research projects concerning the history of health and illness in modern Central Europe at the University of Graz, the Institute for the History of Medicine of the Robert Bosch Foundation, Stuttgart, the Austrian Academy of Sciences and the Sigmund Freud Unversity, Vienna. His research focuses on medical and health sociology; social, cultural and religious history; and the history of health and illness.

Paul Weindling is Research Professor in History of Medicine at Oxford Brookes University. He has researched the life histories of the victims of coerced experimentation under National Socialism. Since 2017 he has been part of a group researching the life histories and brain tissue histories of victims of brain research as held by the Kaiser Wilhelm Gesellschaft and post-WW2 Max Planck Institutes for Brain Research, Psychiatry and Neurology. He is co-president (with Florian Schmaltz) of the Commission of the Université de Strasbourg to research the medical faculty of the Reich University Straßburg 1941–1944. Publications include *Health, Race and German Politics between National Unification and Nazism* (1989), *Epidemics and Genocide in Eastern Europe 1890–1945* (2000), *Nazi Medicine and the Nuremberg Trials: From Medical War Crimes to Informed Consent* (2004), *John W. Thompson, Psychiatrist in the Shadow of the Holocaust* (2010), and *Victims and Survivors of Nazi Human Experiments: Science and Suffering in the Holocaust* (2014). As editor: *From Clinic to Concentration Camp: Reassessing Nazi Medical and Racial Research, 1933–1945* (Abingdon: Routledge 2017); with Herwig Czech, *Österreichische Ärzte und Ärztinnen im Nationalsozialismus. DOEW Jahrbuch* (Vienna: DOEW, 2017). Between 2018 and 2019 he presented a series of papers on the eightieth anniversary of the Kindertransport to the UK.

Hani Zubida, PhD, is a Senior Lecturer, Department of Political Science, The Max Stern Yezreel Valley College and social activist. His research interests include: immigration, labour migration, Israeli politics and society, citizenship, borders, and social identities.

His latest publications include: 'Being seen: visibility, families and dynamic remittance practices', *Migration and Development*, 7:1 (2018), 5–25 (co-authored with Robin Harper); 'Voting locally abstaining nationally: descriptive representation, substantive representation and minority voters' turnout', *Ethnic and Racial Studies* (2017), 1–19 (co-authored with Rosenthal Maoz and Dave Nachmias); *Stop – No Border in Front of You! About Borders and the Lack of Them in Israel 2017* (in Hebrew, co-edited with Raanan Lipshitz). He serves on the board of the Arteam NGO which operates the Open Library at the old central bus station in Tel Aviv, the CEC – Community Education Center in south Tel Aviv – and offers various classes and occupational training to migrant labourers, asylum seekers and refugees. He also anchors a television show on public TV on socio-political issues.

Preface and acknowledgements

This volume emerged from the conference 'Border Crossing and Medicine: Quarantine, Detention and Containment in History and the Present' which was organised by the editors of this volume. The conference was funded by the Fritz-Thyssen-Foundation and took place in February 2017 at the Free University of Berlin, hosted by the Centre for Modern Greece where Sevasti Trubeta at that time held a DAAD visiting professorship.

Neither when we organised the Berlin conference, nor when we started editing the book chapters could we have imagined that the end of this long road would coincide with the outbreak of a pandemic like COVID-19, which has led to lockdowns and the closing of borders worldwide – developments that have become part and parcel of our own lives. Indeed, in an ironic way, the authors of this volume wrote the last lines of their revised chapters while in home quarantine. Because of the timing, with the finalisation of the revised manuscript coinciding with the emergence of COVID-19, our volume considers only a few developments related to the time of the coronavirus.

There are several institutions and colleagues to whom we are indebted for their support and collaboration. We would like to express our thanks to the Centre for Modern Greece at the Free University Berlin for hosting the conference and to the Fritz-Thyssen-Foundation for the generous funding which made possible both the realisation of the conference and the copy-editing of this volume. A supplementary grant from the Austrian Science Fund (FWF), allocated to the project P 25929 (Infectious Diseases and Public Health in Southeast Europe), allowed us to polish an earlier version of the texts of the Austrian authors. We are much obliged to the

Acknowledgements

anonymous reviewers whose constructive comments and recommendations on the first submitted version of the book manuscript induced us to rethink some conceptual aspects. We gratefully thank the editors of the Manchester University Press series 'Rethinking Borders' for accepting the manuscript for publication. Tom Dark accompanied the publication process with competence from the first communication up to the final submission of the revised manuscript. For the careful, professional and outstanding copy-editing we are indebted to Dr Philip Jacobs.

Our warm thanks go also to the authors of this volume for their engaged collaboration, their openness and patience, and for imparting the sense that we work for the same objective. This book is the result of joint efforts, even though each chapter represents the views of the author(s).

Sevasti Trubeta
Berlin, May 2020

Introduction: medicalising borders

Sevasti Trubeta, Christian Promitzer and Paul Weindling

At the beginning of the outbreak of the COVID-19 pandemic, the statements of the Italian philosopher Giorgio Agamben triggered controversial debates when he suggested that coping with the COVID-19 pandemic had been reduced to a biomedical issue: it is through such reductionism that societies implement biopolitics of 'bare life'. In his own words: 'The problem is not to give opinions on the gravity of the disease, but to ask about the ethical and political consequences of the epidemic. The first thing that the wave of panic that has paralysed the country obviously shows is that our society no longer believes in anything but bare life'.[1] Indeed, in the rhetoric of governments and politicians there is an obvious shift from political rights to medical diktat. However, the scientists show epistemological disagreements, and the politicians are not in the front line when it comes to shortages of resources. Epidemics 'operate as a form of "dramaturgy"', as Alex Langstaff has recently discussed with historians on the occasion of COVID-19.[2] Medical reasoning and the goal of decelerating the spread of the pandemic became the basis for imposing control and surveillance measures and a 'state of emergency' in which social life, civil rights and mobility rights were widely affected by restrictions.

Given that shutting down borders was one of the first measures in counteracting the spread of the pandemic, some political and other agents saw themselves confirmed in their previous demand to consolidate border controls, and beyond this to close borders, as for example President Trump has voiced on several occasions in the United States. In the same vein, a US press report remarked: 'We are all restrictionists now. In the coronavirus crisis, everyone realizes the importance of borders, even the people who not long ago were ideologically hostile toward them'.[3] The worldwide 'state of emergency' has increased not necessarily the importance of the borders, but certainly their visibility and the imposed restrictions on movement have effected their multiplication. Starting with shutdowns of state borders, notably those between the EU member states, restrictions on mobility were extended to regions of a single country and started to paralyse public life as soon as 'social distancing' and 'home quarantine' were prescribed. Among the most affected by the current management of the pandemic are refugees and migrants, those who are residing in the mass accommodation centres and those trying to cross borders. Sandro Mezzadra and Maurice Stierl point to how '[r]estrictive border measures endanger the lives of vulnerable populations for whom movement is a means of survival'.[4]

The coronavirus emergency has highlighted the sanitary significance of borders, and therefore reinforced the need for turning the spotlight on the medical dimension as essential to border studies. A critical perspective emerges from the synthesis between the interdisciplinary field of border studies and longer-term historical studies of quarantine, contagion and sanitary controls on migrants and those who cross borders. These historical studies derive ultimately from a historical approach to public health, which represents a critique of bacteriology in that even if there is a uniform pathogen, there are historically contingent forms and demarcations. One might see an academic pedigree from Rudolf Virchow (1821–1902) as a pathologist and public health reformer, continuing on to Charles Creighton (1847–1927) and Arthur Newsholme (1857–1943) in the UK, to the American public health historian George Rosen (1910–1977) – all prioritising sanitary innovations, whether local or national, over any microbial Blitzkrieg, sweeping across borders and sanitary defences.[5] Borders and associated sanitary controls thus become crucial points of tension in terms of the cross-border movements of human mobility and commerce. Our studies presented in this volume focus on multifaceted dimensions of borders and medical zoning and illustrate how medical zoning operates as sanitary and medical foci of tension and transition.

The control of human mobility and border surveillance by biomedical means was the subject of a conference, 'Border crossing and medicine: quarantine, detention and containment in history and the present', held 2–4 February 2017 at the Freie Universität Berlin, from which this volume emerged. We discuss here borders as sites where human mobility has been and is being controlled by biomedical means, both historically and in the present. The central aim of the volume is to raise cutting-edge questions in the research on biomedical techniques and borders, and to revisit contemporary interdisciplinary approaches to the deployment of medicine and sanitary surveillance in controlling the crossings of borders and the drawing of boundaries. We consider three types of control technologies for preventing the spread of disease by means of controlling human mobility: quarantine, the biomedical selection of migrants and refugees, and containment; all of these have a long-standing tradition in western countries, especially on the European continent and its maritime and inland borders. The idea that prompts us to explore these different types of border control technologies under one heading is that they are not exclusive of one another, nor do they necessarily lead to total restrictions on movement. Rather, the lines of demarcation between them are often blurred, requiring composite methodologies. The objectives of this volume are served by two methodological decisions: taking a broader time frame (from the nineteenth century up to the present) and an interdisciplinary approach. Indeed, this volume is a collection of such cross-discipline approaches arising from the multidisciplinary backgrounds of the authors who cover a wide range of academic disciplines including humanities, social sciences and public health sciences. The authors retrace historical shifts in governing human mobility, the implementation of medical knowledge, and the understandings of disease. They revisit historical and social-scientific studies which have shed light on the crucial role of public health policies in governing human mobility by the medical screening of immigrants, and they point out the political and medical (in)effectiveness of these measures.

A core argument of this volume is that the consideration of border controls through the lens of a bipolar scheme of 'inclusion–exclusion' is not a capable tool for grasping and explaining the multiple dynamics of action that are revealed in actual border regimes; nor do public health concerns alone provide a sufficient framework for understanding the complexity of controlling the spread of disease across places and in bordering processes. Certainly, a considerable body of historical and social-scientific studies have shed light on the crucial role of public health policies in governing human mobility; such studies have contributed a great deal to an understanding of the intertwining of medicine, power and mobility across places with respect to empires, colonialism, national states, international relations and globalisation.[6] The authors of this volume revisit such sources, using as a vehicle different case studies to pursue historical shifts in governing human mobility through implementing medical knowledge and different perceptions of disease.

Framing the intersection of disease concerns and border crossings

The questions addressed in this volume are situated at the point of intersection of approaches to medicalisation and borders. Crucial to the convergence of these two fields of research was the 'spatial turn' in the 1980s, which threw the spotlight on the cultural signifiers of space and gave rise to epistemological paradigm shifts in the understandings of both borders and medical control technologies. With respect to borderwork, the consideration of boundary-generating practices and symbolic significations of borders led to a revision in the scholarly view, which previously had seen borders as predominantly geographical and state-territory demarcations.[7] In the social sciences, borders are increasingly understood in relational (rather than in exclusionary) terms and in conformity with 'a relational understanding of space as an arrangement of objects, places and (groups of) people';[8] but in turn, this very understanding challenges relational concepts given that borders may still 'have a highly exclusive character'.[9]

A further important implication of the epistemological shifts deriving from the spatial turn was a subsequent boom in publications which were based on Michel Foucault's approaches to territory, power and disease discourses. In several studies, and especially in 'Surveillance and Punishment', Foucault pointed out the connection between the transformed norms of social control and the spatial order in urban administration systems, using the example of combatting disease. Foucault considers this development to be the historical moment in which the surveillance disposition was incorporated into power techniques and the same context in which public health and hygiene acquired their semantics and were integrated into health policies.

Along with Foucauldian theory, a remarkable trend in the social sciences and humanities challenged the normative role of medicine in defining health and disease. Moreover, this scholarly trend approached medicine as a control system and considered both health and disease as societally constructed in processes that were described as 'medicalisation'.[10] Nikolas Rose portrays the essence of the idea of medicalisation in its important role in shaping social relations in the modern state as follows: 'medicine has been bound up with the ways in which, since the end of the eighteenth century, the very idea of society has been brought into existence and acquired a density and a form'.[11] These approaches were mostly framed in terms of the nation state and its institutions. The establishment of the interdisciplinary field of the cultural history of medicine in the 1980s contributed a great deal to reframing medicalisation phenomena in broader contexts, challenging grand narratives of health and disease as determined by state or supranational authorities. In so doing, attention was called to the agency of actors other than state authorities.

In terms of historiography there was in the 1990s a shift from person to pathogen in the contrasting analyses of Michel Foucault and Bruno Latour's disembodied perspective in the 1990s, the latter developed in a reading of Pasteurian microbes. Both Foucault and Latour have articulated theoretically engaging, and respectively contrasting, analyses which have been immensely influential, but they lack context and specificity, qualities which give social history its cutting edge in terms of behaviours, regulations and practices. Latour's philosophically deductive vision meant a change from writing the history of border regimes as a set of procedures to a pathogen-focused historiography in terms of power and preventive regimens of eradication by means of pesticides, vaccines and pharmacological interventions.[12] This results in a change in the history of medicine as less one of Foucauldian institutional repression towards an ecology of pathogens – bacterial, rickettsial and viral, as they evolve and interact with animals and the human species.

The field of research with which this volume deals is shaped by the conjunction of new understandings of medicalisation and borders. In fact, Alison Bashford's research is pioneering in drawing sharp outlines and pushing forward this research field.[13] In several studies, Bashford has illuminated multifarious aspects of the correlation between medical knowledge, its power across time to define societal relations, and bordering processes: in historical forms of quarantine, in international relations, and in the global era of epidemics and pandemics. Furthermore, over the last two decades, publications have provided important insights into medical controls in the recruitment of (would-be) labour forces.[14] Others highlight the link between migrants/refugees and the allegedly emerging threat of the dissemination of diseases that have disappeared in the western world, especially the revival of TB.[15] While challenging a predominantly biomedical explanation of immigrant health as an exclusively medical problem, scholars suggested including the migratory process and the restrictions to legalisation (the illegal paths for fleeing and the poor hygienic conditions in the camps and settlements) as risk factors for the re-emergence of contagious diseases. Critical scholarship looks for historical continuities in the logic of the threat of disease when it comes to the association of immigrants and the spread of contagious diseases in the host societies of the global North.[16]

The concept of medicalisation was revisited by the political theorist Stefan Elbe[17] who used it as a theoretical vehicle for approaching health policies in the much discussed topic of global security. Indeed, a large number of studies in the last two decades have addressed the entanglement of the health–disease issue with the logic of biosecurity in international and national securitisation regimes. Especially with respect to the period from the 1990s up to today, such studies call attention to the linking of biomedical border control with global health regimes: the fusion of global health concerns with security regimes culminates in 'global health security'.[18] As de Bengy Puyvallée and Kittelsen[19] suggest, the phrase 'disease knows no borders' encapsulates the essence of these internationalising regimes. Most recently, at his speech before the UN security council on 9 April 2020, the Secretary General of the UN, Antonio Guterres, warned of threats to security and opportunities for bioterrorism in association with the COVID-19 pandemic.[20] For all restrictions to human mobility and the shutdown of state borders, in the logic of the global health security regimes, borders remain porous. In the light of the security regime and the implementation of biometric surveillance technologies, borders become deterritorialised *and* multiplied.[21]

Medicalising borders: towards new research questions

Beyond a simplifying logic of disease prevention as a matter of exclusion/inclusion, the authors of this volume direct their focus at the multilayered entanglement of medical regimes in the attempts to manage the porosity of the borders. Consistent with a remarkable trend among scholars, who are inspired by Étienne Balibar's post-Marxist social philosophy,[22] we consider both border and disease preventive measures as filtering systems. But, over and above the perception of 'filter' as a mere metaphor, the chapters of this volume illustrate how borders pose filtering systems in that they become topoi for the design and implementation of technologies of selection. We explore how containment for medical reasons operates as bordering process in different historical periods and different socio-historical contexts: in 'classical quarantine' and the lazarettos of the nineteenth century; in the sanitary screening of migrants, for example on the German–Russian border prior to World War II; with respect to models of selection in port and frontier procedures, for instance at the UK's external and internal borders in the postcolonial era; and in the reception of refugees and migrants in contemporary Israel and in Europe.

In so doing, the authors scrutinise ways in which concerns and policies of disease prevention shift or multiply borders, connect and disconnect places; how understandings of disease and the selection of migrants and refugees impact the drawing of borders and boundaries and what factors put limits on selection technologies.

During the intensive and fruitful exchange we had in February 2017 at the Berlin conference, the participants underlined the need for future research to place a stronger emphasis on both the local level of action and the actors other than the authorities, especially the border-crossers themselves, grass-roots agents and those who implement the decisions made by policy stakeholders. Even though these aspects are gaining more and more attention in recent research about the crossing of borders and the refugee issue,[23] their consideration in historical paradigms has still not been adequately investigated.

In general, research has bestowed only limited consideration on border-crossers and their agency, and their reactions to selection procedures by medical means, quarantine and containment. A relative exception may be studies that pay attention to what is called 'medical humanitarianism':[24] the appeal to medical reason by unsuccessful asylum applicants, of undocumented migrants, in order to avoid expulsion and secure a longer stay in a country.

Besides shedding light on actorship, a further specific interest of this volume is to address the need for a strong focus on the limits of control technologies on border crossing. A close consideration of a possible failure reveals important societal dynamics. Control plans can founder for various reasons related to the resistance by those who were/are subject to such technologies or/and their lobbyists in the civil society, but also to local circumstances or the inappropriate and (at times) controversial cost calculations, and many other factors.

The chapters in this volume address key questions which define the medicalisation of borders in breaking down a hitherto unquestioned nation state approach. The focus on interstitial borders represents a shift from policy in a single country to an interactive approach that may bring to the light transnational, regional and local dynamics. A demarcating border becomes an interactive location of cultural intersections, and transformative processes of cleansing and disinfection. What factors different from, or complementary to, public health concerns (including economic and professional interests) do health control techniques at borders depend on? In which ways are such factors interwoven with a goal of constantly increasing scientific knowledge? How do (designed or/and implemented) medical controls at the borders connect or disconnect places by means of the containment, quarantine, detention and selection of migrants, refugees and border-crossers?

Medical control of borders by way of quarantines

The 'carceral architectures' of quarantines are remnants of the oldest medical techniques at state borders.[25] In pre-modern times they formed an essential component of medical prevention, based on the observation that after forty days of isolation suspicious persons and goods would no longer communicate the plague. Chase-Levenson describes quarantines as 'both bureau and barrack'[26] which indicates the connection between the various boards of health as administrative steering bodies (which since the Napoleonic Wars cooperated in a continent-wide and later global network, and the individual lazarettos as venues of detention. The power and principle of quarantines proceed from contagionism, a theory that explained epidemics by the transmission of invisible pathogens adhering to bodies and goods.[27] In practice, quarantines were no panacea against plague, yellow fever and cholera. Thus they became targets for propagators of free trade, not to mention political uses other than sanitary ones.

With his sharp eye on spatial structures, Michel Foucault would have described a quarantine station as a model for a *heterotopia*. For Foucault *heterotopias* are nested spaces – different from the outside and with relationships to other places which are not visible at first glance – like the provenance and the destination of a person suspected to be ill. Lazarettos, quarantine stations and isolation wards are therefore institutional spaces which contain undesirable bodies, belonging to the variant of 'crisis heterotopia' which according to Foucault is 'reserved for individuals who are, in relation to society and to the human environment in which they live, in a state of crisis'.[28] As isolated spaces, quarantines were not publicly accessible – they could be only entered with authorisation. Thereby obligatory rituals and procedures of purification – reception, medical inspection, constant observation, fumigation or spraying of the quarantined persons with disinfectants during their stay, and, finally, discharge – had to be performed. Thus, quarantines belonged to 'heterotopias of ritual or purification'.[29] These 'rituals of passage and purification' bore the meaning of a 'performative sanitation', whereby the inmates were not kept in ignorance about the circumstance that they had to endure under a distinct legal regime which put the lazaretto into 'a permanent state of emergency.' According to Chase-Levenson, the latter was 'a permanent locus of Giorgio Agamben's "state of exception"', and therewith – contrary to the critique of the anticontagionist contemporaries of the nineteenth century – 'a harbinger, not an anachronism'.[30]

From our perspective, now shaped by the experience of COVID-19, among quarantine regulations of the eighteenth and nineteenth centuries we can detect instructions for *social distancing*. Thus, at terrestrial borders a so-called 'parlatorio' allowed for interlocution between persons from both sides of a border without undergoing quarantine, since they were separated from one another by a double wooden barrier. Within a quarantine station a person in an advanced stage of quarantine should otherwise never come into physical contact with a person in an earlier stage, or he or she had to start the whole procedure over.

The emergence of quarantines as preventative measures against the Black Death in the late medieval period forms an important landmark: for the first time, medical knowledge controlled human mobility. The port cities of Venice and Dubrovnik erected the first quarantines, and inland towns would follow suit. Not only whole towns, but in an elementary form of a selective *lockdown,* even contaminated town quarters or single houses, whose doors were marked with chalk crosses, could be put under quarantine.

Prevention of plague on a large scale, however, would be only possible with the development of the modern territorial state. Research on the historical development of such structures is concentrated on maritime quarantines in the Mediterranean and western Europe. In the first half of the eighteenth century a chain of permanent terrestrial quarantine stations was established along the borderline of the Habsburg Empire with the Ottoman Empire, which counted as a hotbed of plague. In her chapter, Sabine Jesner thoroughly reviews this first system of terrestrial quarantines with its institutional practices and its embeddedness in contemporary medical theories.

From the late eighteenth century, but certainly after the Congress of Vienna in 1815, medical control of state borders in Europe was an affair based on informal interstate arrangements. The boards of health in the individual ports constituted a joint 'European sanitary system', in fact a 'transnational biopolity', which accepted that the state of health within the single polities depended on their cooperation, while 'the presence of even one plague-ridden body outside the lazaretto gates in any single European state could compromise the sanitary integrity of the whole Contintent'.[31] The failure of quarantines to protect Europe from the second pandemic of cholera in the early 1830s was a decisive impetus for the adherents of rising global trade to put an end to their annoying traffic limitations. They gained support from anticontagionist physicians. But only the ensuing establishment of a network of lazarettos in the southern Mediterranean, the Levant and in south-east Europe protected central and western Europe from the evils of plague and cholera from these regions.[32] By introducing a geoepidemiological perspective which acknowledged the duration of the passage to European destinations as part of quarantine, Peter Baldwin was among the first to solve this apparent contradiction – the reduction or even abolition of quarantines in Europe was compensated for by the establishment of quarantines in the contaminated 'Orient'.[33] As a by-product of these developments, new states in the Balkans which had seceded from the Ottoman Empire considered quarantines a tool to demonstrate their autonomy vis-à-vis their suzerain's power, as Christian Promitzer shows in his chapter. Consequently, the chapter by Urška Bratož deals with the implications of these developments in the northern Mediterranean, by focusing on the Habsburg port town of Trieste and the threat of cholera.

In the late nineteenth century, germ theory and bacteriology reinforced attitudes towards medical controls which Baldwin, in contrast to classical quarantines, calls 'neoquarantinism',[34] an approach with an empirical assessment of incubation times and making use of modern disinfection methods, bacteriological examinations and other preventive measures. In his chapter Carlos Watzka examines the coverage of this approach in two remote border regions of the Habsburg Empire in the late nineteenth century.

The transition from an informal system of 'universal quarantine' towards one with formal international standards was increasingly endorsed by several International Sanitary Conferences beginning in the mid-nineteenth century.[35] They led to interstate sets of regulative procedures, by which the dual system of easing European quarantines by their enforcing medical control in the Middle East and Northern Africa was confirmed. This was the case in particular, after cholera had reached Europe in 1865 by transmission via Indian Muslims pilgrimaging to Mecca. Consequently, Muslim pilgrims became a 'risk group' who were subjected to quarantine measures in the Red Sea and the eastern Mediterranean.[36]

The Office Internationale d'Hygiène Publique (1907–1946) was essentially regulative, to oversee quarantine procedures in the years before the First World War. By way of contrast, the foundation of the Health Organization of the League of Nations in the early 1920s had not only to deal with the threat of typhus epidemics from eastern Europe, but also with the dissolution of the previous quarantine system of the eastern Mediterranean due to the demise of the Ottoman Empire.[37] The issue about the starting point of the international era of public health is therefore rather one of how to define 'international', a term which up to the end of the Great War was mainly used to designate European and Mediterranean medical affairs thereby including the sanitary implications of the Suez Canal, while the USA in 'their' hemisphere started to organise specific pan-American sanitary conferences in the early twentieth century both in the run-up to the opening of the Panama Canal and in the wake of it.[38] A key issue is whether an international health organisation had critical autonomy to address inadequacies of state provisions towards citizens, and to look beyond state interests that could be authoritarian and restrictive.

(Dis)connecting places and shifting borders

Sanitary borders become displaced in terms of procedures and functionality. For Étienne Balibar, health control, quite similarly to security control, is a paragon for the shifts or displacement of geographical borders in that 'some borders are no longer situated at the borders at all in the geographico-politico-administrative sense of the term. They are in fact elsewhere, wherever selective controls are to be found, such as, for example, health or security checks.'[39] Indeed, medical control over human mobility generates or corroborates borders that do not necessarily coincide with geographical or state territorial demarcations, even though the rules of surveillance are imposed by state or supranational authorities. This observation applies as much to the globalised surveillance of mobility as to other historical eras in which medicalised borders may be situated outside the territory of the state that has imposed the rules of control, or even may be internal to it. The former happened, for example, with respect to the Jewish migration to Palestine during the British Mandate when immigration agencies located in Eastern Europe examined and certificated the health and fitness of the Jewish settlers.[40] This was the case with Ellis Island as well; although considering the paramount historical paradigm of medical control for those who were entering the United States, Ellis Island was more than a gate to the United States or a 'camp'. As Paul Weindling argues in this volume, it was the culmination of a chain of medical controls which connected European countries which were crossed by migrants (especially those coming from eastern Europe) as transit places on their way to the United States. In the post-war transfer of

Introduction

guest-workers (*Gastarbeiter*) to western Europe and especially to Germany,[41] medicalised borders were situated outside the receiving countries in that medical controls of potential labour immigrants took place in their countries of origins where the health certifications were in fact issued.

The controlling and managing of the spread of infectious disease connects or/and disconnects places conducive to the drawing, shifting or even multiplying of borders and boundaries. The interconnection of political regimes and scientific knowledge in such bordering processes takes central stage in Sarah Green's chapter, which throws the spotlight on the Mediterranean area over time, starting from empires of the nineteenth century up to the twentieth-century regimes of supranational and international stakeholders such as the EU and WHO and the current context of biosecurity. Green uses as a theoretical vehicle the notion of 'location', which reflects the level at which the spatial dimensions of place acquire their significance in the interweaving of political, epistemological and moral understandings of disease and also the understandings of how disease moves across places and transgresses borders.

The dissemination of panic and fear of disease is a condition able to connect or disconnect places and multiply borders and boundaries. This is the argument at the heart of the chapter by Amy Lauren Fairchild, Constance A. Nathanson and Cullen Conway in this volume. While scholars have tended to illustrate exclusionary practices based on the dissemination of a public health panic and fear,[42] this chapter turns the spotlight on a neglected issue in the history of public health: the consideration of panic and fear of disease as impactful factors for framing public health politics with respect to drawing borders and boundaries. The authors show how changes in the interconnections between public health structures and the scientific understanding of disease altered the language of threat, fear and panic in the US public over time; and, in reverse, how shifts in the understanding of fear and panic accompanied alterations in US public health policies. Fairchild, Nathanson and Conway frame these questions in different historical periods starting with the 'quarantine era' in the 1880s. This is the period in which the miasma theory still determined the understanding of disease; public health policies and the language of threat addressed the geographic and internal borders. The subsequent 'bacteriological era' starts in the 1880s when germ theory came to predominate the understanding of disease, and is earmarked by the utilisation of the threat of disease for the drawing of internal boundaries in US society by means of processes of othering. This era stretches up to the Second World War and coincides with the period which is indeed in the spotlight of a great deal of historical and social scientific studies that have scrutinised the population and health politics in the United States, shedding light on repressive hygiene and eugenic measures towards nationals, minorities and migrants. The 'international era' in the aftermath of World War II was marked by the Cold War, the threat of nuclear war, and the attempts to control pandemic threats. Fairchild, Nathanson and Conway argue that in this era, the focus of the US institutions charged with civil defence and security was more so now on the porosity of the borders and its consequence internally for US society. In the current era of biowarfare the porosity of the borders has the primary focus. The reaction to the risk is the multiplicity of the borders and their shifting into the interior of the country. Framing in this analytical scheme, the authors reflect the new challenges for US society deriving from the handling of COVID-19.

Selection technologies and their limits

The selection of migrants by means of medical screening has been applied to refugees in Europe as well. Indeed, humanitarianism has drawn boundaries along the lines of the physical and health condition of those in need, broadly considered as refugees, in diverse historical contexts. This has been explored in several cases, also with respect to Holocaust survivors and displaced persons who were subject to a triage based on their physical and mental health as regards onward migration.[43] The UK Movement for the Care of Children from Germany (the 'Kindertransport') in 1938–1939 (and here the UK was no different from the United States, which in sharp contrast admitted only very few unaccompanied child refugees) excluded mentally or physically handicapped children and those children suffering from an infection. The exclusions resulted in the children becoming racial victims of Nazi genocide (see Paul Weindling's chapter in this volume). National states had a strong interest in using border controls to exclude the oppressed, persecuted and deprived.

With respect to the uses of the disease argument in the screening, inspection and 'welcoming' of immigrants and refugees, the authors of this volume show how societal dynamics in the fields of action prove to be challenging for the implementation of the selection. Moreover, technologies of selection may not result in solely the exclusion or inclusion of migrants and refugees; they can also result in a labelling of those who are not expelled but are allowed to stay either permanently or temporarily in a country. The arguments of disease, poverty and criminality appear interlinked in ways in which the symbolic meanings of disease contribute to drawing internal boundaries in societies when the newcomers are viewed as dirty, uncivilised, illiterate, dangerous and destined for poverty.

Robin A. Harper and Hani Zubida argue in this volume that the disease and cleanness argument is employed in the contemporary migration policies in Israel, as a filter in the selection and separation of refugees who are 'worthy of welcome' from those who are not thought to be so. The argument using disease, dirtiness and lack of hygiene is currently being invoked with respect to refugees and asylum seekers, especially those coming from Sudan and Eritrea. Harper and Zubida trace the history of the refugee discourse in the Israeli state across time and identify similar arguments in the treatment of other groups who are constituents in the country's population today: Arabs, but also peoples of Jewish origin and their descendants who originated in Asia and Africa. The historical perspective allows for recognising dynamics related to interaction between diverse actors with different attitudes and possible conflictual interests; this all renders selection a matter of negotiation. In the Israeli case discussed by Harper and Zubida such actors include civil servants, mainstream media and doctors who use the media to disseminate ideas about the alleged threat from diseased immigrants and refugees, but also solidarity networks, medical initiatives and individual doctors expressing themselves against populism.

The conflicts among experts and authorities about cost calculations and expenses have impaired the efficiency of medical screening at the borders in postcolonial UK. Roberta Bivins' timely chapter demonstrates how the borders at the entry points to the UK became contested, even 'suspect', and the power of the authorities was challenged, because of the costliness of control measures. Furthermore, the effectiveness of the medical screening has been challenged several times and even abolished by postcolonial UK immigrants – or would-be immigrants – from the Commonwealth who took action negotiating their situation with regard to the imposed restrictions for medical reasons.

What is the role of race and racialisation in the bordering processes of selection by medical means, and how does the disease argument link race with medicalisation? This question becomes particularly important with respect to the alleged race-neutrality of the medical screening of Commonwealth migrants, in the vein of the political correctness of the postcolonial context. Bivins argues in this volume that the racialisation of the medical screening of immigrants became a point of contention between border officers and medical experts, on the one hand, and the Select Committee on Race Relations on the other.

The tacit racialisation in bordering processes in the context of the current humanitarian era takes centre stage in the chapter by Sevasti Trubeta, who raises the question as to how racialisation is possible in the current humanitarian engagement and rescue operations, especially at the European maritime borders, given that refugees and border-crossers become associated with the threat of contagious disease? What might render a possible association of racialisation and humanitarianism to appear paradoxical is that anti-racism is the politically correct ideology in European societies. Still, the rescue operations at the borders reveal quite contradictory attitudes, and transnational and international medical stakeholders insist that refugees and immigrants do not pose any threat to the public health of host/receiving countries. How much racism is at play behind such attitudes? Trubeta argues that the treatment of refugees and migrants as carriers of contagious disease (including the ritualised visual inspection of the rescued border-crossers) is a manifestation of absolutising the biomedical perception of disease; moreover, it brings to the fore a racism that writes the narrative of migration in terms of pathogenic germs originating in the global South that threaten the global North.

Controlling mobility through containment and encampment for medical reasons

In his essay on a lazaretto in the Red Sea, Saurah Mishra has suggested that it 'is tempting to liken quarantine camps to prison and other total institutions'.[44] Indeed, such a comparison is quite

Introduction

17

reasonable and is abreast of current scholarship which proposes 'encampment' as a generic term for the diverse types of camps, including concentration camps, protection zones at the borders, detention centres and reception facilities for border-crossers, refugee camps, and many other types of camps in different historical eras.[45] As soon as scholars revised Agamben's idea of the Nazi concentration camp as the archetype for the camp concept, attention was called to a framing of encampment into broader societal relations.[46] The camp is not (necessarily) determined by the condition of total isolation, but rather by its 'extra-territoriality', and its property of being an emergency site out of (but not absolutely detached from) the established order of the surrounding society.[47]

For all its character as a place of isolation, the camp is still integrated into institutional, political and scientific networks and operates as a site of selection in the processes of bordering or drawing internal boundaries. How far are these general characteristics of a camp applicable in the case of lazarettos and especially Nazi concentration camps – two camp types which were sealed and with different logics of encampment regimes? The former represent places for isolation and simultaneously 'border filters', as John Chircop shows in this volume based on a consideration of the different lazarettos in the Adriatic Sea. Being located at the interface of land and sea lazarettos were thought to operate as a bulwark against the spread of contagious disease, counteracting the extreme porosity of the maritime borders. Most importantly, their operation exceeded the prophylaxis of the spread of disease across places; rather, they constituted a multifunctional filtering apparatus that separated, classified and treated travellers according to their social status, religion and class. One therefore can come to the conclusion that Mediterranean lazarettos only partly fulfilled their role as warrantors of 'universal quarantine', as recently proposed by Alex Chase-Levenson.[48] Chircop's research provides evidence that in the Mediterranean, racial and classist stereotypes against foreign and suspected bodies of colonial subjects, Muslim pilgrims and immigrants already played a prominent role in the first half of the nineteenth century (the period considered by Chase-Levenson as the 'universal' era of quarantine), and this was long before such individuals would in the end became the focus of attention, figuring as 'risk groups' in the period of imperial quarantine and colonial global health during the second half of the nineteenth and early twentieth centuries.[49] Thus, Chircop shows that in the first half of the nineteenth century, well-off white people of European origin were able to fare considerably better, whereas certain groups of lower social ranking at that time were subject to a process of being exfiltrated.

The lazarettos were spatially sealed and severely surveyed institutions, but still an integral part of institutional networks and broader border structures. A property the lazarettos seem to share with the generic concept of camp is that they operated as 'ambiguous places',[50] given that for all their isolation and 'extra-territoriality' they still were stopovers and 'venues for new beginnings'[51] for those who came successfully through the controls that enabled them to transfer into the surrounding society.

In terms of their conception and operation, the lazarettos were multifunctional systems; they were disciplining mechanisms, places of disinfection that could work as a technology of surveillance over the transfer of humans, animals and ideas (for example, using the access granted by postal disinfection as a way to filter ideas);[52] and as sites where new scientific knowledge was generated. The observations derived from a close look at the interior of the lazarettos, as John Chircop does in this volume, reveal a further camp-like property, that is, the creation of organisational structures which support their potential transformation from emergency places into 'relatively stable ghettos' or 'town-like formations'.[53] With respect to their internal organisation the focus on the multiplicity of the actors brings to the fore the interaction between the controlling authorities and those who did not participate in policy-making but instead were engaged in the execution of measures, such as the hygiene guardians, or the priests who acted as stakeholders in the internal religious–moral order. A particular contribution of Chircop's chapter to the scholarly debate about borders and medicalisation is its specific focus upon the 'expurgators' and their central role in the disinfection of people, animals, transport-media (ships) and the material belongings of the travellers. The expurgators were charged with tasks which they executed in the form of 'purifying cross-border rituals'. This seems to be generic for the characteristic of the border, as Michel Agier describes it, as 'a place, a situation or a moment that ritualizes the relationship to the other […] the border always functions with mediations, such as tutelary and protective divinities, bearers or translators'.[54] 'Expurgators' acted as mediators in the

Introduction 19

bordering processes and in the same moment, as Chircop shows, it so happened that they became objects of medical observations.

The consideration of medical barriers with respect to restrictions on human mobility, containment and encampment in a historical nexus, as Paul Weindling suggests in this volume, sheds a new light on the Nazi concentration camp as well. Weindling regards containment in Nazi camps as an inverting of the liberal notion of free movement (to a better quality of life) with racially exploitative medical research. For all the restrictions on movement in the later nineteenth century, regimes of migration nevertheless still allowed the persecuted and starving to escape distress. Yet, in the liberal notion of free movement, with the imposed disease screening mechanisms (including quarantining), the idea was for people to pass through hygienic controls, rather than be subject to containment. The welfare state became a rationale for exclusion at borders and for a new regime of visas and border control. Weindling argues that the greater the welfare benefits, the greater the incentive to exclude from welfare entitlement. The post-Versailles principle of national self-determination meant the multiplication of borders (at times contested) in interwar Europe, and a new system of visas and migration quotas effectuated the containment of populations who were stigmatised or even persecuted because of their nationality or ethnicity. The guarantor system for refugees from Nazi oppression covered the welfare issue, but it was both a facilitator and obstacle. Whereas in the window of time before the Nazis imposed new regimes of segregation and deportation to a ghetto or death camp 'in the East', efforts were made by assistance organisations to extract as many of the persecuted as possible. Within a short period of time after war broke out, the fateful deportations 'to the East' began.

A further consequence of the closure of borders to the starving and oppressed was a fundamental reshaping of international relief after World War I. The new procedure was relief at the point of distress. This meant containment of diseased and starving populations while large-scale international relief agencies were mobilised. This was just at the time of severe distress after World War I when new borders were imposed, culminating in the containment of the 'iron curtain' after World War II.

The observation that Auschwitz – as an endpoint – was the inverse of the human processing centre of Ellis Island shows a chilling dimension in the processes when fitness to work is the key issue in border crossing. Mengele's role in selecting from incoming trainloads a quota of persons who were fit to work (or more accurately to be worked to death) exposes a profoundly dismaying aspect to border regimes. Mengele and his SS colleagues on the ramp policed what was meant to be a final border before a shorter or longer route to death. The procedures of persecution were permeated by the routines of quarantine with the capacious poison gas chamber designed to process and kill batches of several hundred people at a single functioning. The barbed wire compounds that held stateless Jews exposed the vulnerability of persons now excluded from their homelands by virtue of the deprivation of their status as citizens and denied welfare benefits by the state. It resulted in being deported to a concentration camp, ghetto, forced labour camp, or (after 1941) to an extermination camp. Increasingly, the Nazi concentration camp came to represent the inverse of an open migration system: the sealed borders, and the designation of population groups as 'surplus' and 'pathogenic' meant that hygiene provided rationales and technologies of destruction. 'Resettlement in the East' was a genocidal fiction when all that awaited the 'resettled' was a severely overcrowded and underprovided ghetto, or a gas van, or (after 1941) a carbon monoxide or Zyklon gas chamber with a fake shower, or a firing squad in an isolated wooded area in the Ukraine or Belarus.

Conclusions

Closing borders to people but allowing goods to pass echoes contemporary issues with erecting new medical barriers across previously open European spaces. COVID-19's uneven spread has resulted in new borders and sanitary controls with personal spacing, home quarantine, internal borders in a country, city, or between regions and politically devolved federated states. The result is – once again – multiple 'spaces of crisis' and multiplication of borders.[55]

Our volume is a contribution to the scholarly debate about borders and boundaries, which are fluid in response to the ebb and flow of pathogens. What emerges are long lines of different understandings of disease by political regimes. This is a book about policies of disease prevention, and about interconnections between policies against the spread of disease with the creation of filtering systems at border crossings, along with the drawing of internal boundaries in the societies.

The contributions to this volume illustrate medicalised borders, seeing them as fields of interaction between diverse actors who include (but are not limited to) state and international agents, medical experts, and state and public health officials. The focus of these reflections is also on the general public, local societies, NGOs (in recent times) and transnational (humanitarian) agents.

As an alternative to their being considered through the lens of a bipolar scheme of exclusion–inclusion, border regimes, once established, have often been used by border-crossers as zones of transition in continuing their journey. Border-crossers use the opportunities to seek to regulate their legal status of residence, even though they do so in the absence of alternatives. The case studies here reveal that the control over human movement by medical means can design selection technologies or containment, and operate both towards purposes of total isolation as well as a means of recruiting labour forces, citizens, and new members of the nation.

In the meantime, there is a considerable body of relevant publications dealing with the screening of immigrants (mostly in migrant detention and the camps), pointing to ethical issues, or even the medical effectiveness of these measures. Our volume shows that instead of viewing a border as a value-neutral space between states, it can be perceived as a constellation of constructed procedures; viewing it in this way helps to open up new perspectives on migration, welfare and refugees. Raphael Lemkin, the genocide theorist saw during the 1930s that ethnic and cultural minorities within states were inherently vulnerable. The studies here show how borders have represented increasingly complex procedures in which sanitary controls, rather than being a passage to health or at least value-neutral, could themselves become a process of stigmatisation and ultimately genocidal.

Notes

1 G. Agamben, 'The invention of an epidemic', *European Journal of Psychoanalysis*, Special Issue: Coronavirus and philosophers (22 February 2020): www.journal-psychoanalysis.eu/coronavirus-and-philosophers/ (accessed: 21 May 2020).

2 A. Langstaff (ed.), 'Pandemic narratives and the historian' (discussion with Simukai Chigudu, Julie Livingston, Debroah Coen, Nayan B. Shah, Paul Weindling, Richard Keller, Alison Bashford), *Los Angeles Review of Books* (18 May 2020), https://lareviewofbooks.org/article/pandemic-narratives-and-the-historian/ (accessed: 27 May 2020).
3 R. Lowry, 'We are all restrictionists now', *National Review* (3 April 2020), www.nationalreview.com/2020/04/coronavirus-pandemic-nations-realize-importance-borders (accessed: 21 May 2020).
4 S. Mezzadra and M. Stierl, 'What happens to freedom of movement during a pandemic?', *openDemocracy* (24 April 2020), www.opendemocracy.net/en/can-europe-make-it/what-happens-freedom-movement-during-pandemic/ (accessed: 21 May 2020).
5 A. Labisch, *Homo Hygienicus: Gesundheit und Medizin in der Neuzeit* (Frankfurt am Main; New York: Campus Verlag, 1992).
6 A. Bashford (ed.), *Medicine at the Border: Disease, Globalization and Security, 1850 to the Present* (Basingstoke: Palgrave Macmillan, 2006); A. Bashford, *Imperial Hygiene: A Critical History of Colonialism, Nationalism and Public Health* (Basingstoke: Palgrave Macmillan, 2004); A. Bashford (ed.), *Quarantine: Local and Global Histories* (Basingstoke: Palgrave Macmillan, 2016); L. Marks and M. Worboys (eds), *Migrants, Minorities and Health: Historical and Contemporary Studies* (London; New York: Routledge, 1997); A. L. Fairchild, *Science at the Borders: Immigrant Medical Inspection and the Shaping of the Modern Industrial Labor Force* (Baltimore, MD: The Johns Hopkins University Press, 2003); M. Harrison, *Contagion: How Commerce Has Spread Disease* (New Haven, CT; London: Yale University Press, 2012); J. Booker, *Maritime Quarantine: The British Experience, 1650–1900* (Aldershot: Ashgate, 2007); K. Maglen, *The English System: Quarantine, Immigration and the Making of a Port Sanitary Zone* (Manchester: Manchester University Press, 2014); J. Chircop and F. J. Martinez (eds), *Mediterranean Quarantines, 1750–1914: Space, Identity, and Power* (Manchester: Manchester University Press, 2018).
7 For comprehensive overviews see D. Newman, 'On borders and power: a theoretical framework', *Journal of Borderlands Studies*, 18:1 (2003), 13–25, https://doi.org/10.1080/08865655.2003.9695598; G. Orsini, A. Canessa, L. G. Campo and J. B. Pereira, 'Fixed lines, permanent transitions: international borders, cross-border communities and the transforming experience of otherness', *Journal of Borderlands Studies* (2017), 1–16, https://doi.org/10.1080/08865655.2017.1344105; T. Nail, *Theory of the Border* (Oxford: Oxford University Press, 2016); O. Demetriou and R. Dimova (eds), *The Political Materialities of Borders* (Manchester: Manchester University Press, 2019); H. Donnan, M. Hurd

and C. Leutloff-Grandits (eds), *Migrating Borders and Moving Times: Temporality and the Crossing of Borders in Europe* (Manchester: Manchester University Press, 2017); J. D. Sidaway. 'Decolonizing border studies?', *Geopolitics*, 24:1 (2019), 270–5; H. van Houtum, O. Kramsch and W. Zierhofer (eds), *B/ordering Space* (Aldershot: Ashgate, 2005), pp.17–32.
 8 G. Weidenhaus and M. Löw, 'Borders that relate: conceptualizing boundaries in relational space', *Current Sociology Monograph*, 65:4 (2017), 553–70, at 566.
 9 Ibid., at 558.
10 Initially these approaches drew on Talcott Parsons and the labelling theory. See indicative works I. K. Zola, 'Medicine as an institution of social control', *The Sociological Review*, 20:4 (1972), 487–504; I. Illich, *Medical Nemesis* (London: Calder & Boyars, 1974); P. Conrad and J. Schneider, *Deviance and Medicalization: From Badness to Sickness* (St Louis, MO: Mosby 1980); P. Conrad, 'The discovery of hyperkinesis: notes on the medicalization of deviant behavior', *Social Problems*, 23:1 (1975), 12–21.
11 N. Rose, 'Medicine, history and the present', in R. Porter (ed.), *Reassessing Foucault: Power, Medicine and the Body* (London: Routledge, 1994), p. 54.
12 B. Latour, *Les Microbes: guerre et paix, suivi de Irréductions* (Paris: A.-M. Métaillé, 1984). B. Latour, *The Pasteurization of France* (Cambridge, MA: Harvard University Press, 1988). For a contrasting approach looking at institutional power structures and the state: P. J. Weindling, 'Scientific elites in *fin de siècle* Paris and Berlin: the Pasteur Institute and Robert Koch's Institute for Infectious Diseases compared', in A. Cunningham and P. Williams (eds), *Laboratory Medicine in the Nineteenth Century* (Cambridge: Cambridge University Press, 1992), pp. 170–88.
13 A. Bashford and C. Hooker (eds), *Contagion: Historical and Cultural Studies* (London; New York: Routledge, 2001); Bashford, *Medicine at the Border*; Bashford, *Quarantine*; Bashford, *Imperial Hygiene*.
14 S. Topp, 'Medical selection in the recruitment of migrant workers ("Gastarbeiter")', in I. Ilkılıç, H. Ertin, R. Brömer and H. Zeeb (eds), *Health, Culture and the Human Body: Epidemiology, Ethics and History of Medicine, Perspectives from Turkey and Central Europe* (Istanbul: Betim Center Press, 2014), pp. 19–38; N. Molina, 'Borders, laborers, and racialized medicalization: Mexican immigration and US public health practices in the 20th century', *American Journal of Public Health*, 101:6 (2011), 1024–31.
15 R. Bivins, *Contagious Communities Medicine, Migration, and the NHS in Post War Britain* (Oxford: Oxford University Press, 2015). For the

elaboration of such a connection see P. Cosman, 'Illegal aliens and American medicine', *Journal of American Physicians and Surgeons*, 10:1 (2005), 6–10; M.-J. Ho, 'Migratory journeys and tuberculosis risk', *Medical Anthropology Quarterly, New Series*, 17:4 (2003), 442–58.

16 H. Markel and A. Stern, 'The foreignness of germs: the persistent association of immigrants and disease in American society', *The Milbank Quarterly*, 80:4 (2002), 757–88. See an overview in S. Trubeta, 'Vaccination and the refugee camp: exercising the free choice of vaccination from an abject position in Germany and Greece', *Journal of Ethnic and Migration Studies*, 2018, DOI: 10.1080/1369183X.2018.1501269.

17 S. Elbe, *Security and Global Health: Towards the Medicalisation of Insecurity* (Cambridge: Polity, 2010).

18 Elbe, *Security and Global Health*; D. Fassin, 'That obscure object of global health', in M. C. Inhorn and E. A. Wentzell (eds), *Medical Anthropology at the Intersections: Histories, Activisms, and Futures* (Durham, NC: Duke University Press, 2012), pp. 95–115; A. Lakoff, *Unprepared: Global Health in a Time of Emergency* (Oakland, CA: University of California Press, 2017).

19 A. de Bengy Puyvallée and S. Kittelsen, '"Disease knows no borders": pandemics and the politics of global health security', in K. Bjørkdahl and B. Carlsen (eds), *Pandemics, Publics, and Politics: Staging Responses to Public Health Crises* (Singapore: Palgrave Macmillan, 2019).

20 'COVID-19 threatening global peace and security, UN chief warns', *UN-News* (10 April 2020) https://news.un.org/en/story/2020/04/1061502 (accessed: 9 May 2020).

21 B. Muller, *Security, Risk and the Biometric State: Governing Borders and Bodies* (New York: Routledge, 2010); P. Adey, 'Facing airport security: affect, biopolitics, and the preemptive securitisation of the mobile body', *Environment and Planning D: Society and Space*, 27 (2009), 247–95, DOI:10.1068/d0208; L. Amoore, 'Biometric borders: governing mobilities in the war on terror', *Political Geography*, 25:3 (2006), 336–51.

22 E. Balibar, *Politics and the Other Scene* (London: Verso, 2002); Nail, *Theory of the Border*; A. Sager, *Toward a Cosmopolitan Ethics of Mobility: The Migrant's-Eye View of the World* (Cham, Switzerland: Palgrave Macmillan, 2018).

23 In the last decade (2010–2020) there has been a boom in publications on solidarity with respect to refugees and migrants which consider the agency of the latter; for example, K. Rygiel, 'Bordering solidarities: migrant activism and the politics of movement and camps at Calais', *Citizenship Studies*, 15:1 (2011), 1–19, DOI: 10.1080/13621025.2011. 534911; A. Kallius, 'Solidarity in transit', in T. Birey, C. Cantat,

E. Maczynska and E. Sevinin (eds), *Challenging the Political Across Borders: Migrants' and Solidarity Struggles* (Budapest: Center for Policy Studies, Central European University, 2019), pp. 246–67.
24 M. Ticktin, 'Medical humanitarianism in and beyond France: breaking down or patrolling borders', in A. Bashford (ed.), *Medicine at the Border.* pp. 116–33. M. Ticktin, 'How biology travels: a humanitarian trip', *Body & Society*, 17:2–3 (2011), 139–58, https://doi.org/10.1177/1357034X11400764.
25 A. Bashford, 'Maritime quarantine: linking Old World and New World histories', in A. Bashford (ed.), *Quarantine*, pp. 1–12, at p. 1.
26 A. Chase-Levenson, *The Yellow Flag: Quarantine and the British Mediterranean World, 1780–1860* (Cambridge: Cambridge University Press, 2020), p. 123.
27 J. K. Stearns, *Infectious Ideas: Contagion in Premodern Islamic and Christian Thought in the Western Mediterranean* (Baltimore, MD: Johns Hopkins University Press, 2011); M. DeLacy, *The Germ of an Idea: Contagionism, Religion, and Society in Britain, 1660–1730* (Basingstoke; New York: Palgrave Macmillan, 2016); M. DeLacy, *Contagionism Catches On: Medical Ideology in Britain, 1730–1800* (Basingstoke: Palgrave Macmillan, 2017).
28 M. Foucault, 'Of other spaces,' *Diacritics*, 16 (Spring 1986), 22–7; see the farther-reaching explorations of heterotopias in A. Faramelli, A. Hancock and R. White (eds), *Spaces of Crisis and Critique: Heterotopias Beyond Foucault* (London: Bloomsbury, 2018).
29 Foucault, 'Of other spaces'.
30 Chase-Levenson, *The Yellow Flag*, pp. 96–9.
31 Chase-Levenson, *The Yellow Flag*, p. 124; A. Chase-Levenson, 'Early nineteenth-century Mediterranean quarantine as a European system', in A. Bashford (ed.), *Quarantine*, pp. 35–53.
32 D. Panzac, *Quarantaines et lazarets: l'Europe et la peste d'Orient (17–20 siècles)* (Aix-en-Provence: Edisud, 1986); B. Bulmuş, *Plague, Quarantines and Geopolitics in the Ottoman Empire* (Edinburgh: Edinburgh University Press, 2012); S. Chiffoleau, *Genèse de la santé publique internationale: de la peste d'Orient à l'OMS* (Rennes; Beirut: Pr. Université de Rennes, Institut français du Proche-Orient, 2012), pp. 19–82.
33 P. Baldwin, *Contagion and the State in Europe, 1830–1930* (Cambridge: Cambridge University Press, 2005 [1999]), pp. 211, 242, 340, 344, 557–63.
34 Baldwin, *Contagion and the State*.
35 N. Howard-Jones, *The Scientific Background of the International Sanitary Conferences, 1851–1938* (Geneva: WHO, 1975); M. Harrison, 'Disease, diplomacy and international commerce: the origins of

international sanitary regulation in the nineteenth century', *Journal of Global History*, 1:2 (2006), 197–217; V. Huber, 'The unification of the globe by disease? The International Sanitary Conferences on Cholera, 1851–1894', *The Historical Journal*, 49:2 (2006), 453–76; A. Velmet, *Bacteriology and Politics in France, its Colonies, and the World* (Oxford: Oxford University Press, 2020).

36 See, for example: F. E. Peters, *The Hajj: The Muslim Pilgrimage to Mecca and the Holy Places* (Princeton, NJ: Princeton University Press, 1996); M. C. Low, 'Empire and the hajj: pilgrims, plagues, and pan-Islam under British surveillance, 1865–1908', *International Journal of Middle East Studies*, 40:2 (2008), 269–90; S. Mishra, *Pilgrimage, Politics and Pestilence: The Haj from the Indian Subcontinent, 1860–1920* (New Delhi: Oxford University Press, 2011); Chiffoleau, *Genèse*; V. Huber, 'International bodies: the pilgrimage to Mecca and the emergence of international health regulations', in E. Tagliacozzo and S. Toorawa (eds) *The Hajj: Pilgrimage in Islam* (Cambridge: Cambridge University Press, 2015), pp. 175–95.

37 P. Weindling (ed.), *International Health Organisations and Movements, 1918–1939* (Cambridge: Cambridge University Press, 1995); I. Borowy, *Coming to Terms with World Health: The League of Nations Health Organisation, 1921–1946* (Frankfurt am Main: Peter Lang, 2009); R. M. Packard, *A History of Global Health: Interventions into the Lives of Other Peoples* (Baltimore, MD: Johns Hopkins University Press, 2016).

38 Harrison, *Contagion*, pp. 134–8.

39 Balibar, *Politics*, p. 84, emphasis in original; see also E. Balibar, *We, the People of Europe? Reflections on Transnational Citizenship* (Princeton, NJ: Princeton University Press, 2004).

40 N. Davidovitch and R. Zalashik (guest editors), 'Medical borders: historical, political, and cultural analyses', *Science in Context*, 19:3 (2006), 309–16.

41 Topp, 'Medical Selection'.

42 S. I. Wallace, *Not Fit to Stay: Public Health Panics and South Asian Exclusion* (Vancouver; Toronto: UBC Press, 2017); A. Fairchild, R. Bayer, S. Green, J. Colgrove, E. Kilgore, M. Sweeney and J. Varma, 'The two faces of fear: a history of hard-hitting public health campaigns against tobacco and AIDS', *American Journal of Public Health*, 108:9 (2018), 1180–6.

43 Davidovitch and Zalashik, 'Medical borders'.

44 S. Mishra, 'Incarceration and resistance in a Red Sea lazaretto, 1880–1930', in A. Bashford (ed.), *Quarantine*, pp. 54–65, at p. 56.

45 I. Feldman, 'What is a camp? Legitimate refugee lives in spaces of long-term displacement', *Geoforum* 66 (2015), 244–52, DOI:10.1016/j.

geoforum.2014.11.014; C. Minca, 'Geographies of the camp', *Political Geography*, 49 (2015), 74–83; E. Engin and K. Rygiel, 'Of other global cities: frontiers, zones, camps', in B. Drieskens, F. Mermier and H. Wimmen (eds), *Cities of the South: Citizenship and Exclusion in the 21st Century* (London: Saqi, 2007), pp. 170–209.

46 A. Robinson, 'Giorgio Agamben: the state and the concentration camp', *Ceasefire Magazine* (7 January 2011), https://ceasefiremagazine.co.uk/in-theory-giorgio-agamben-the-state-and-the-concentration-camp/ (accessed: 16 May 2020).

47 B. Diken and C. Bagge Laustsen, *The Culture of Exception: Sociology Facing the Camp* (London: Routledge, 2005); M. Agier, *Managing the Undesirables. Refugee Camps and Humanitarian Government* (Cambridge: Polity Press, 2011); D. Martin, 'From spaces of exception to "campscapes": Palestinian refugee camps and informal settlements in Beirut', *Political Geography*, 44:1 (2015), 9–18; M. Fresia and A. von Känel, 'Beyond space of exception? Reflections on the camp through the prism of refugee schools', *Journal of Refugee Studies*, 29:2 (2016), 250–72.

48 Chase-Levenson, *The Yellow Flag*, pp. 6–7.

49 Ibid., pp. 24, 243, 245–6.

50 S. Turner, 'What is a refugee camp? Explorations of the limits and effects of the camp', *Journal of Refugee Studies*, 29:2 (2016), 139–48.

51 Trubeta, 'Vaccination'; Fresia Von Känel, 'Beyond space of exception'.

52 On postal disinfection see R. Ellis, 'Disinfecting the mail: disease, panic, and the post office department in nineteenth-century America', *Information & Culture*, 52:4 (2017); K. F. Meyer, *Disinfected Mail* (Holton, KS: Gossip, 1962); V. D. Vandervelde, E. R. Gunter and W. A. Sandrik, 'USA: New Orleans epidemics, 1769–1909', *Pratique*, 24:3 (1999), 82–100; M. Carnevale-Mauzan, 'The study of communications in times of epidemics', *Postal History Journal*, 21:45 (1977), 47–55, and 21:46 (1977), 27–36.

53 Agier, *Managing the Undesirables*.

54 M. Agier, *Borderlands: Towards an Anthropology of the Cosmopolitan Condition* (Cambridge: Polity, 2016), p. 7.

55 Faramelli et al., *Spaces of Crisis*.

Part I

Quarantine

1

Habsburg border quarantines until 1837: an epidemiological 'iron curtain'?

Sabine Jesner

Introduction

Over the last two decades the tendency and the will to limit border controls and entry checks to a minimum is tangible. Missing infrastructural elements such as border crossing points or the no-longer required use of a passport are signs of such developments. This has changed drastically in the last two years, from 2018 to 2020, as migrant flows have had to be managed by the state. Border crossings have again become linked with surveillance and control. In spring 2020, this process has been accelerated again by the COVID-19 pandemic and is reviving public interest in medicalized borders. This chapter focuses on the installation of medical quarantining as a new technological surveillance strategy at border entry points in the Habsburg Empire. Although the politics of health and combatting diseases are not new subjects of research, it has been recently shown in the anthology *Epidemics and Pandemics in Historical Perspective* (edited by Jörg Vögele, Stefanie Knöll and Thorsten Noack) that it is necessary to shift the focus to specific case studies, which allow more in-depth questions with precise foci to be addressed.[1] However, examining mandatory and historical quarantining systems done for medical reasons in the context of border crossings in early modern times remains a research niche. Asking critically for an epidemiological 'iron curtain' means looking for both an ideological–medical conflict concerning the necessary application of preventive measures for controlling plague between the Habsburg and Ottoman spheres of influence as well as a physically sealed border.

In this chapter I will address some questions about the implementation of quarantines at the external border of the Habsburg

Monarchy in south-eastern Europe as the primary method of medical control over human movement and border crossing. The established cordon sanitaire functioned until the nineteenth century as an early-warning system, with the objective of containing infectious diseases. I argue that a significant motive for implementing intensified measures on medical grounds was linked with the Peace Treaty of Passarowitz in 1718 which formally ended the Austro–Turkish War (1716–1718). Six days after its ratification, a separate Commercial and Shipping Treaty was signed on 27 July 1718 between the Emperor and the Sultan to regulate prospective trading terms between the empires, granting merchants more freedom and protection from abuse. From the Habsburg point of view, the intensified entrepreneurial spirit, which is tangible in the declaration of Rijeka and Trieste as free ports in 1719 as well as the inception of the Imperial Privileged Oriental Company, led to more intense points of contact with both Ottoman subjects and thereby also with the Levantine plague. Simultaneously, the interest of the Habsburg state in protecting its domestic population gained in importance. This development was intermingled with the central idea of an emerging mercantilism, where human labour had been rediscovered as an economic motor within a prosperous state. The resulting care by the state for its subjects presupposed that an established state territory would be ruled by a legitimate sovereign and defined by an external border. The formation of the territorial state laid the foundation for the legal enforceability of state-based regulations, which would remain valid for all inhabitants. The spatial aspects of the body politic, tightly linked to a stable central administration, functioned as a prerequisite for implementing effective sanitary measures on a state level. The historian Ute Frevert stresses that these measures became visible in the formation of public health institutions, standardized sanitary procedures and educational institutions, as well as the training and employment of properly qualified medical staff supervised by state officials.[2] Consequently, in the course of the eighteenth century, reforms were implemented and with increasing medical knowledge, health care was regulated in more detail to improve the health of the inhabitants. This marked the beginning of a comprehensive medicalization of the population.

One element of these sanitary innovations was the establishment of specific quarantine facilities as permanent institutions on the Habsburg

Military Border in southeastern Europe. These quarantine facilities[3] (*Contumaz* in contemporaneous German) served as a health bulwark against bubonic plague and will be a focal point of interest in this chapter. These facilities were constructed to offer a framework for medical inspections to see if those transiting the border, as well as animals and goods, had been in contact with any epidemic disease.

Erna Lesky has authored the pivotal historiography of the quarantines at the Habsburg cordon sanitaire. She took a pioneering role in the history of medicine within the Habsburg Monarchy of the eighteenth century.[4] In her study *Die österreichische Pestfront an der k.k. Militärgrenze,* published in the journal *Saeculum* in 1957, Lesky demonstrated a multifaceted insight into the practical procedure of plague prevention at the external border.[5] Moreover, the design of the sanitary cordon featured was in Gunther E. Rothenberg's 1973 paper, 'The Austrian sanitary cordon and the control of bubonic plague 1710–1871'.[6] Gheorghe Brătescu picked up the issue with a focus on the Transylvanian part of the military border in his survey 'Seuchenschutz und Staatsinteresse im Donauraum (1750–1850)' in 1979.[7] All these works addressed the growing interest within the Habsburg state in establishing plague-preventive measures as well as the motivation underlying it, which oscillated between sanitary and economic interests. Recently, Bora Bronza has scrutinized preventive medical strategies on the Habsburg–Ottoman border during the eighteenth century.[8]

The position of the central state as the organizer and originator of quarantining techniques at external borders builds on the ideas of surveillance and permanent registration. This intertwining was stressed by the French philosopher Michel Foucault in his book *Surveiller et punir: Naissance de la prison* in 1975 in which he describes plague containment measures in an urban area in the course of an outbreak during the seventeenth century. The rising fear of plague led the population to follow disciplinary mechanisms, which had been initiated by authorities, and which culminated in an extensive monitoring of individuals. The effectiveness of quarantining was responsible for the new techniques of control and the distribution of the exercise of power, a model of inclusion and surveillance as it is described by Foucault, and it was accepted by society.[9]

The interaction of protection and obedience as well as the subordination of personal freedom have formed part of the scholarly debate since Thomas Hobbes published his work on the state, *Leviathan, or, the Matter, Forme and Power of a Common-wealth Ecclesiasticall and Civil* in 1651.[10] As Francesca Falk[11] has outlined in her essay 'Hobbes' "Leviathan" und die aus dem Blick gefallenen Schnabelmasken' (Hobbes' "Leviathan" and the masks of the plague doctors that escaped critical attention). Hobbes framed the publication with a frontispiece, where two plague doctors are included in the pictorial composition wearing the typical bird-like masks. Taking the plague doctors on Hobbes' book as a starting point, Falk argues that the plague policy was responsible for new urban and state structures, whereby the city functioned as a model for the state. New forms of border control accompanied this process. Falk emphasizes that both the implementation of quarantines as well as the introduction of individual permits of entry (*Pestbrief*) were forms of a 'new boundary' that culminated in a restriction of mobility.

However, this chapter investigates the importance of the sanitary cordon from a medical point of view. The questions raised rest on the assumption that the structural frame for the cordon was based on the concept of the Habsburg Military Border. The military border was essential for the establishment and consolidation of terrestrial quarantine stations. These were responsible for the implementation of sanitary checks at border crossing points located along arterial roads to control border-crossers. A further issue relates to the understanding of the intertwining of surveillance techniques and entry conditions as well as contemporaneous medical theories and their effect upon the quarantining procedure. Finally, it can be reasonably assumed that the procedure of compulsory quarantining gave rise to criticism and reluctance among border-crossers.

Fear of the bubonic plague was the most important reason to establish quarantine stations. The prevailing perception within the Islam-dominated Ottoman Empire of seeing illness as divine purpose while neglecting precautions in the case of plague both supported the spread of the plague within the territory of the Ottoman Empire. Birsen Bulmuş notes the intention of learned men to implement preventive measures, but then puts this assessment in doubt.[12] On the other hand, Daniel Panzac has shown that during the eighteenth century the city of Istanbul was afflicted by the bubonic plague for sixty-eight years, Aegean Anatolia for fifty-seven years, Egypt for forty-four years, Albania-Epirus for forty-two years, Bosnia for forty-one years, Syria for thirty-three years and Bulgaria for eighteen years, which casts doubt on the efficacy of available measures.[13] The Ottoman Empire started effective quarantine reforms in 1838, which marked a turning point in the history of plague prevention in southeastern Europe.[14]

In contrast, at the beginning of the second half of the eighteenth century the Habsburg Monarchy introduced rigorous penalties for illegal border crossing that illustrate the growing fear caused by the plague. The punishments were outlined in the so-called 'Renewal of the Quarantine Order' (*Erneuerung der Kontumaz-Ordnung*) of 1766. Everyone, regardless of social status, who illegally crossed the border, thereby ignoring the binding quarantine stay (a universal precondition for legal entry into the Habsburg Monarchy) was sentenced to death by hanging. Supporters who knowingly assisted illegal border-crossers likewise could expect prosecution.[15] These measures reflect the exceptional zeal of the Monarchy in inflicting punishment for illegal border crossing.

The plague early-warning system

The Habsburg Military Border

The Ottoman–Habsburg border in the eighteenth century was about 1,800 kilometres long and reached from the Adriatic Sea to the northeast Carpathian Mountains. The area included parts of present-day Croatia, Serbia, Hungary and Romania. The border zone stretched inland and spread over 50,000 square kilometres and was guarded by 4,000 to 11,000 border soldiers.[16]

The historian William O'Reilly describes the Military Border as a sort of buffer zone.[17] The spatially defined belt of land was organized as an individual administrative unit of the Habsburg Empire. The origin of this institution can be traced to the first half of the sixteenth century. At that time a group of peasants was granted privileges in exchange for performing military service. These privileges included land ownership and exemptions from certain taxes.[18] These privileged border soldiers cultivated the borderland. The defence concept is based on the scope of the duties of the involved peasants, ambiguously referred to by Karl Kaser as 'free peasant and soldier'. The system was successively expanded to adjacent regions until it achieved its largest expansion in the second half of

Figure 1.1 Habsburg Military Border with quarantine stations (approximately mid-eighteenth century)

the eighteenth century.[19] At that point in time the Habsburg Military Border was structurally divided into three main sections: Croatian–Slavonian, Banatean and Transylvanian. The aforementioned dual concept of land ownership and military service was responsible for the development of the special social characteristics in the family structure of the soldiers in the Military Border (*Grenzer*, *Grenzsoldaten*), leading them to follow adapted military logic and needs. Military service among the male inhabitants functioned as a cornerstone of the defence system, because their primary function included the surveillance of the Habsburg–Ottoman border zone. This was manifested in their constant and regular time-consuming patrols directly along the frontier, day and night, from one military post to another, to prohibit illegal border crossings. The tilling of soil in exchange for military service was a lucrative deal for the Viennese authorities, as it both guaranteed the regular monitoring of the external border against potential Ottoman invasions and garrisoned a cheap and operationally ready corps of soldiers.[20]

The terrestrial quarantine stations

The ever present fear of contagion and insufficient precautions against communicable diseases were responsible for the introduction of wide-ranging efforts at the end of the 1720s by the Habsburg Monarchy to erect permanent sanitary controls on the external border in south-eastern Europe with the Ottoman Empire. On 22 October 1728 the Imperial Court issued a groundbreaking decree with the instruction: 'to initiate as soon as possible countermeasures toward the Ottoman territory and countries, because of the incessant threat and risk of infection, and making them permanent in so far it is possible in terms of the circumstances.'[21]

In view of this complexity, it seems necessary to emphasize that temporary controls including border closure were practised well before the introduction of the decree.[22] It is known that since the Middle Ages quarantine stations or lazarettos had been established to prevent plague spread. The use of quarantine concepts was reinforced by a range of regulations enacted by towns as well as governments.[23] As far as the Habsburg Monarchy is concerned, we can refer to the first relevant state laws enacted by the Lower Austria Government at the end of the seventeenth century, which paved the way for further corresponding schemes and the institutional framework. The first known Austrian sanitary commission was the *Consilium sanitatis* in Lower Austria, which was transformed in 1719 into the *Commissio sanitatis aulica*. Finally, a centrally organized institution, the Court Sanitary Deputation (*Sanitätshofdeputation*), became the highest public health body of the Monarchy in 1753 until its abolishment in 1776. Afterwards its responsibilities were divided between the Aulic War Council (*Hofkriegsrat*) and the Bohemian–Austrian Court Chancellery (*Böhmisch-Österreichische Hofkanzlei*). Thereafter the Aulic War Council was responsible for quarantine stations on the Military Border.[24]

The military's administrative responsibilities for preventive sanitary measures began in the 1730s, concurrently with the official formation of the permanent quarantine network. On 24 December 1737 Emperor Charles VI enacted an instruction which invested the military with a predominant role.[25] This consequently led to a sort of militarization of plague prevention. Even back in the seventeenth century we can observe cases of systemic border closure by the military; limited, but burdensome, military cordons in the light of plague prevention were drawn in 1647 in Spain, in 1668 around Paris, in 1708 in Transylvania and in 1720 around Marseilles.[26] The well-known quarantine legislation of the Venetian seaports influenced the plague prevention policy and consequently the development of accompanying legislation. The sanitary regulations introduced by the Viennese Court built upon such maritime regulations. The establishment of a forty-day quarantine in 1726 at the Austrian Littoral followed the Venetian model and was adopted by the Habsburg authorities for Trieste.[27]

The first permanent quarantine stations on the south-eastern border of the Monarchy were installed in the early 1740s, with the quarantine station in Zemun established before that.[28] Throughout the rest of the eighteenth century, the network consisted of the following quarantine stations: Rudanovac, Slunj, Kostajnica, Gradiška, Brod, Mitrovica and Zemun in the Croatian–Slavonian section, Pančevo, Mehadia and Jupalnic in the Banatean section, and Buzău, Turnu Roşu, Bran, Predeal, Vulcan, Biritzke (replaced by Tulgheş), Tihuţa (replaced by Rodna), Ghimeş and Oituz in the Transylvanian Military Border.[29]

Practical measures and concepts of control

Surveillance techniques and entry conditions

In order to ensure an effective monitoring mechanism, specific forms of individual identification became a functional control instrument in cross-border traffic. This was implemented by the introduction of various forms of passports by both the Ottoman and Habsburg authorities. The aim of this measure was clear: track the places of departure as well as determine the travellers' itineraries. We have to assume, however, that entry registers about Ottoman subjects were not compiled solely for medical reasons.[30] Consequently, we can find rubrics in these documents which portend economic and other interests among groups of border-crossers, as the Habsburg authorities also asked for the kind of trade and possible changes of nationality.[31]

Medical surveillance strategies, in turn, made no exceptions regarding class; thus, the entry procedure as requested by the Viennese Court did not discern between the treatment of princes from the Danubian principalities, Ottoman pashas, or even high-ranking Habsburg officials.[32] All travellers and peasants had to spend a defined time span in quarantine, with the duration specified by the authorities in Vienna.[33] During quarantine, diverse purification methods, based on contemporaneous medical knowledge and proficiency were applied. The focus was laid on airing and washing. We can assume that during the eighteenth century the entry conditions for border crossing were familiar to the concerned parties. In the archival sources, we rarely find documents about missing passports and bureaucratic hurdles, which could create complications during the entry check. In contrast, there were many regulations enacted which addressed abuse.[34] Ottoman pashas, who were in charge of provincial affairs for the Empire, were obliged to issue permits for Ottoman subjects, which included the complete first name and surname, and had to be shown at the border crossing points, i.e., at the quarantine stations.[35]

These surveillance techniques at the border were reflected in the establishment of quarantine stations. Architectural plans for different quarantine stations reveal huge structural variety among the facilities. According to such plans, these largely relate to the envisioned size. For each constructional change or major repair work, a permit from the Viennese Court had to be obtained. This administrative procedure allows us now to monitor the technical development of the quarantine stations.[36] Those plans offer an insight concerning the distribution of buildings and the infrastructure needs. In addition, some details about the practical life and spatial circumstances within the quarantine area can be derived from them. Unfortunately, autobiographical notes and descriptions by both staff and those quarantined are rare.

The quarantine stations were situated near major transport and trading routes, which served simultaneously as entry points. According to the mentioned architectural plans, it becomes clear that a typical quarantine area comprised accommodation facilities for the staff and individuals undergoing quarantine, as well as storehouses and stables. A geographical reference point for selecting the quarantine terrain was the availability of water resources. Therefore, we can find a river or at least a stream at every quarantine station.[37] In 1770 an idealized plan for quarantine stations was elaborated and sent to the directors who headed the facilities, including the order to give an overview of what kind of modifications were necessary to match the proposed plan as closely as possible. The most important objective of this plan was to guarantee a strict segregation between healthy and suspected people, animals and goods. This thought is reflected in the spatial conception of the whole quarantine area and the functioning of it as an isolating safety facility.[38]

Contemporaneous medical theories and their effect on quarantining procedure

Contemporary theories on infection were undeniably responsible for the strict organizational procedure, in particular the miasma theory which dates from classical Greece. According to this theory, disease causation relates to environmental emanations (gases) or miasmas. Miasma was considered to be a noxious form of 'bad air'. Hippocrates postulated that bad air was the cause of pestilence and Galen expanded the theory, tracing individual susceptibility to the balance of humours in the body. Exhalations from swamps, marshes, stagnant water and winds were some of the causes for the corruption of air. On the other hand, the contagion theory was part of the medical discourse, which was based on the assumption that contagion was carried by unknown adhering particles or *animalcules* as Girolamo Fracastoro (1476/8–1553) stressed in the sixteenth century. Especially during the nineteenth century, supporters of the contagion theory promoted quarantine measures, while proponents of the miasma theory assessed quarantine as inefficient, because in their approach pestilential air was the pathogen and remained unaddressed. The measures undertaken in Habsburg quarantine stations encompassed a combination of both theories, anticontagion or miasma as well as contagion. For example, the miasma theoretical approach is visible during the purification method of fumigation or the simple airing of personal belongings and commercial goods,[39] while the contagion theory appears in isolation and the prevention of physical contact under any circumstances.

Teodora Daniela Sechel (2011) outlines the fact that the concepts of miasma and contagion coexisted in the writings of doctors and plague physicians in the Habsburg Monarchy, which is an important revelation.[40] Another key insight from Sechel's study is that specially employed doctors in the border regions generated new knowledge about contagion and the spread of disease.[41]

The entire staff of a quarantine station fulfilled a medical monitoring function. This refers to the positions of the director, at least one doctor and the purification assistants. On 2 January 1770 the most important comprehensive sanitary regulation for the Monarchy for the eighteenth century was issued with the name *Generale Normativum In Re Sanitatis*.[42] The second part of this regulation laid its focus on the terrestrial quarantine stations in the Military Border within the context of disease control.[43] The obligations of the quarantine staff were duly specified, which partly allows us to reconstruct the daily routine and the procedural arrangements in the stations. The director had to monitor and supervise all administrative activities. He conducted in-depth interviews with new arrivals at the station, controlled their passports, monitored the sanitary checks and the cleaning procedure, maintained correspondence with the local and central authorities, created specific records relating to the entry and exit of people, animals and goods, and finally, was responsible for formal discharges from the quarantine station. The latter was completed with the issuance of a health certificate, the so-called *Sanitätsfede*. The *Sanitätsfede* had to be signed by both the director and the physician of the quarantine facility. The doctor fulfilled a key function because he decided if individuals were contaminated or not. Before putting someone suspected of disease, as was the case with all travellers, under quarantine, the physician undertook a medical examination. The regulation of 1770 stipulated that the position of a quarantine doctor required a medical degree from a university, part of a new strategy initiated to professionalize public health care and to guarantee a clear distinction from barbers or surgeons with a craftsman's background (*Wundarzt*).[44] The third occupational group, the cleaning servants, fulfilled an important role in the course of the quarantine procedure, because they functioned as assistants who monitored the isolation and carried out the purification measures.[45]

The medical investigation of border-crossers, who were all categorized as suspect, was carried out in a separate room designed for the purpose. The room possessed two entrances and was divided in the middle by a wooden barrier. This precaution illustrates how fear could run rampant. One door was reserved for the physician and the other for the suspect, because physical contact had to be prevented under any circumstances.[46] All risks had to be minimized and hazards of a possible infection contained. According to the contagion theory, the physician used specially designed medical instruments and accessories with extended grips to prevent unwanted physical contact. Such contact would have necessitated a quarantine for the physician too.[47]

That the incubation period for bubonic plague, calculated from the day of infection, should be a maximum of seven days is today scientifically established and well understood. However, this important fact was not recognized during the eighteenth century, and this provoked extraordinarily long quarantine periods. Based on the regulation of 1770, the sanitary treatment and duration of quarantine depended on the degree of danger expected: forty-two days, if neighbouring provinces were infected, twenty-eight days if there was an outbreak somewhere else in the Ottoman Empire, and twenty-one days under normal circumstances. Additionally, total entry travel bans were possible and enforced in very precarious times.[48] The length of quarantine depended upon the assessed level of danger, the latter also influencing the manpower of border soldiers along the cordon, which increased when there was an enhanced risk of epidemic.[49]

It should be pointed out yet again that the source of disease infection and transmission was incompletely investigated, and the rat–flea nexus was unknown. However, some contemporaries, like the physician Adam Chenot (1722–1789), did possess the right instinct to clarify how the infection and the zoonotic path of transmission functioned. Chenot's expertise rested primarily on his experience while fighting the bubonic plague in Transylvania as well as his own suffering from plague in Braşov.[50] Chenot recognized that such long periods of quarantine were responsible for the obstruction of commerce. Chenot achieved great success with his elaboration *Die Einleitung zu den Vorbauungs-Anstalten wider die Pest* that was announced on 4 May 1785 as an official instruction (but not on a legal footing) for the General Command of the Military Border. The instruction included the abolishment of the first quarantine period. This meant in effect that when hitherto no cases of the plague had occurred in neighbouring provinces, then no quarantine was necessary when crossing the border.[51]

Contemporary perception and difficulties

While the cordon sanitaire was in force in south-eastern Europe, this early-warning system of the Habsburg Monarchy was described in highly contradictory terms by historians, contemporaries and the state. In the older historiography of the first half of the twentieth century, terms such as 'protective wall' or 'bulwark' were used as vivid descriptions of the sanitary cordon, often with a political flavour in order to distinguish the 'Western' from the 'Occident' Ottoman world.[52] Among contemporaries, negative as well as positive sentiments were in evidence. The varying needs or interests of individuals as well as the state were responsible for the predominant perception patterns and the assessment of the epidemiological 'iron curtain'. It is easily comprehensible that a long and forced stay during a journey did not elicit joy and consent.

Perception

It seems necessary to consider which main categories of border-crossers were involved and how they experienced the sanitary checks and the quarantine itself. These questions are difficult to answer, but several trends can be discerned from autobiographic travelogues as well as the correspondence between the personnel in quarantine stations and their local contact at the provincial government or the competent bodies in Vienna. Distinctive categories of individuals such as simple travellers, war refugees, soldiers, merchants, seasonal workers and border zone residents all crossed the Habsburg–Ottoman border for a variety of reasons. The Viennese Court classified the border-crossers as: required, permitted, suspect or even unwanted. This classification notwithstanding, all had to stay in quarantine. Sabine Sutterlüti recently determined that some border-crossers in Mehadia, for instance servants or maids, perhaps went through quarantine anonymously.[53]

Those under quarantine had to bear the costs themselves for the enforced stay. The aforementioned architectural plans show that within most quarantine areas was an inn. Peasants, in turn, brought their own alimentation to the quarantine station, which presupposed good self-organization.[54]

The Reverend Robert Walsh (1772–1851), who travelled in the 1820s from Constantinople to England, authored an in-depth narrative. In Constantinople he was appointed chaplain at the British Embassy. In his 1828 book *Narrative of a Journey from Constantinople to England* he gives a brief insight into his experiences during his twenty-one-day period at the Turnu Roşu quarantine station in Transylvania:

> The quarantine establishment is situated at the bottom of a deep romantic glen on the banks of the Olt. It consists of about twenty houses, with a chapel, and a little inn, forming a village embosomed in high wooded hills. [...] six of these houses are intended for the incarceration of travellers passing from Turkey, and the rest for the accommodation of persons attached to the establishment, which consists of a Director, a Doctor, two Secretaries, a Comptroller, an Inspector, twelve Domestics, and forty Soldiers. The houses intended for quarantine are huts detached from the rest: they are built of wood, plastered, and originally whitewashed. Each of them stands in a little dirty yard, surrounded by a paling of wood eight or nine feet high. Nothing can be more revolting than the manner in which the traveller is received, or more dismal and disgusting than the place in which he is shut up.[55]

In his writing, Walsh described his personal interaction with the quarantine staff, who considered him *a person actually infected with pestilence, and treated him in every respect as such*.[56] He wrote further that 'every person, who has the misfortune to be shut in, is taught to believe that he is an infected person, and a proper object of danger and terror.'[57]

Walsh even underlined the lack of adequate medical treatment regarding the medical procedure related to his departure. Walsh noted that 'the doctor came by candle-light in the morning; his man brought a pan of charcoal, on which he threw a few pinches of nitre; he then walked round me in a circle, like a magician, and so I was purified.'[58]

Walsh's description offers some points of reference concerning the structural weaknesses of the Habsburg cordon sanitaire. Reading his autobiographic lines one can reconstruct the inconvenient circumstances he was in. He experienced his stay in Turnu Roșu under permanent surveillance which restricted his daily routine while in quarantine.

One of the main critical points of the method of quarantine was the loss of time, which depended on the length of the period of quarantine, even after Chenot's amendment. Merchants, in particular, relentlessly complained about the loss of time and as a consequence the rotten goods. In contrast, some groups managed to gain significant economic advantages from the system.[59]

Errors of the system

The complete closure of the border facing the Ottoman Empire seemed hardly practicable and it is reasonable to assume that a certain degree of permeability possibly reduced the effectiveness of the medical control. Although Military Border soldiers patrolled the external border 4,000, 7,000, or 10,000 strong, depending on the level of plague risk, some loopholes existed.[60] A comprehensive collection of documents of the magistrate of Zemun was published in 1973 by Tanasije Ž. Ilić.[61] This rarely used source material offers several case studies about the handling of illegal border crossings. Quite often, we can read about the so-called *Contumazübertreter* (illegal border-crossers intending to circumvent quarantining) and the resulting death penalty or corporal punishment exacted on them. The illicit phenomenon of smuggling appears repeatedly in the collection and was of growing concern to the Habsburg state. Contraband and smuggling were seductive, owing to the long quarantine times as well as the purification costs.[62] In addition, the Viennese Court used the entry regulations that were originally decreed for sanitary reasons to impose import prohibitions for special product groups, which were deemed to have a negative effect on Habsburg economic development.[63]

The regulations addressed to the border soldiers included many instructions and detailed references concerning the manner in which the border region should be more effectively controlled. Paragraph five of the instruction from 1770 demanded that soldiers intensely watch out in the morning for traces which would hint at clandestine border crossings during the past night.[64] Finally, we cannot dismiss the idea that various forms of corruption among border soldiers and officials in quarantine stations as well as in the nearby customs offices existed.[65]

It is worth mentioning that the cordon sanitaire was not a lucrative business for the Viennese Court, even though it was based on a self-financing system, which meant that the expenses for the quarantine stations, staff salaries and maintenance costs were to be covered by the purification taxes (*Reinigungssteuern*) demanded for the cleaning of commercial goods.[66]

Concluding remarks

Deliberating about quarantine and border control implies thinking about the importance and possibilities for the state in the eighteenth century to provide a protective framework in order to fulfil a protective function. In our case, we have concentrated on protective measures at the external border of the Habsburg Empire. The surveillance of each individual became part of all legal border crossings from territories under the Ottoman sphere of influence. The addition of medical components to the purely military design of the Military Border allowed more effective containment of the *Pestzunder* or *Pestgift* (plague tinder or plague poison), because the guarded external border opened the possibility for concentrated entry at specific border checkpoints. The intertwining of constant control by the border soldiers enabled the installation of permanent quarantine stations. As argued above, it was those functional elements which allowed the physical cordoning-off of the border and facilitated quarantine as the method of medical control over human movement.

The illustration of the infrastructural needs of a quarantine station as well as the purification methods was intended to highlight the impact of contemporaneous medical infection theories. The quarantine procedure was influenced by both the miasma and contagion theories of the time – with a slight preponderance of contagion over miasma theory. Actually, both theories were prevalent in the minds of the local medical staff. Walsh's autobiographical chapter about his stay in the quarantine station at Turnu Roşu clarifies this approach. At that point in time Walsh was not the only one displeased with the 'purification-arrest' (*Reinigungshaft*), to use a contemporaneous term, and a growing resistance against the method of quarantine was perceptible among all kinds of border-crossers. The medical debate by both supporters of the contagionist and anticontagionist theories, however, remained controversial. The anticontagionists became more influential in the 1820s and fought for less-strict sanitary regulations and against quarantining. They denied direct pestilential contagion as well as the efficacy of quarantine and criticized the expensive maintenance of quarantine stations and the resulting trade restrictions.[67] It is an indisputable fact that plague epidemics spared most parts of Europe after the erection of the cordon sanitaire in south-eastern Europe.[68]

Incidentally, other factors influenced the impact of the cordon sanitaire in the 1830s: first, the change in opinion of the Sublime Porte which now supported the establishment of a quarantine system on its own territory, and second, the recently installed quarantine measures in the Danubian principalities.[69] Some of those Ottoman measures were implemented with Habsburg knowledge as Marcel

Chahrour has outlined, stressing the input of Habsburg physicians including their 'self-conscious and missionary approach' for the reform of medical structures.[70]

In addition, the quarantine facilities in the adjacent Danubian principalities (the Ottoman vassal states Moldavia and Wallachia, which were occupied by Russia from 1828) relieved the Habsburg sanitary cordon.[71] The Treaty of Adrianople (1829) concluded the Russo–Turkish War of 1828–1829 and governed the declaration of quarantine in the region. In 1830 quarantines were established in Wallachia at thirteen stations and at one, namely Galaţi, in Moldavia.[72] In his paper 'Between Polizeistaat and cordon sanitaire: epidemics and police reform during the Russian occupation of Moldavia and Wallachia 1828–1834', Victor Taki emphasizes that it was not the lack of practical models to follow, but rather the lack of determination which was responsible for the delayed erection of quarantines at the border in the beginning of the 1830s.[73] Finally, quarantines were erected along the Danube on the order of Russian Plenipotentiary President Pavel Dmitrievich Kiselyov (1788–1872).[74]

On 30 June 1837 the *Pest-Polizey-Ordnung* (Plague Law) was a new regulation enacted within the Habsburg Monarchy.[75] From a medical point of view we cannot find any innovative changes in this Plague Law when comparing it with the last comprehensive regulation in 1770. Rather, the quarantine procedure remained the same, even though it was described more comprehensively and multifariously. The purification methods that were proscribed highlighted that the use of water and simple airing of products had been pushed into the background. Greater effectiveness can be attributed to the reduction of quarantine periods. Initiated by Adam Chenot in the 1780s, the graduated periods of 0–10–20 days of quarantine – according to the epidemic situation – became official. For the first time an instruction on how to contend with plague rumours was published, since such hearsay was a phenomenon used quite frequently by merchants to influence pricing or by peasants to keep tax collectors away from their villages. This was facilitated by the gathering of information about the plague via physicians or specially employed agents, who were sent to the Ottoman Empire to investigate such plague rumours.[76] The Military Border structure continued to function as an essential framework for quarantine at the border until well into the nineteenth century.

Despite the quoted objections, the Habsburg cordon sanitaire was of great importance until the signing of the *Donauschifffahrts-Acte* (Danube Shipping Protocol) by Turkey, Bavaria, Württemberg and the Habsburg Monarchy on 7 November 1857 (article XXX). This contract included the agreement that for all ships on the Danube no quarantine measures were necessary, if during the last twelve months no sign of plague had been recognized in European Turkey or on the riverside of the Danube.[77] Along with this regulation, the 'epidemical iron curtain' lost its compelling necessity. This was intensified by the extension of this provision for shipping traffic to include land traffic in December 1857, when for years no signs of plague had been noticed.[78] In the Military Border, the *Contumaz* had been replaced by the *Rastell* from the 1860s. This term describes a wooden boom barrier, which made a simplified and less strictly controlled exchange where no bodily contact of goods and animals was possible.[79] This gradual downgrading implies that the Habsburg sanitary cordon lost much significance and, with the final abolishment of the Habsburg Military Border in 1881, it appeared that terrestrial quarantines would disappear. This was long after the Habsburg 'epidemical iron curtain' in south-eastern Europe had lost its preventive relevance for the rest of Europe.

Notes

1 J. Vögele, S. Knöll and T. Noack (eds), *Epidemien und Pandemien in historischer Perspektive. (Epidemics and Pandemics in Historical Perspective)* (Wiesbaden: Springer 2016).
2 U. Frevert, *Krankheit als politisches Problem 1770–1880. Soziale Unterschichten in Preußen zwischen medizinischer Polizei und staatlicher Sozialversicherung* (Göttingen: Vandenhoeck & Ruprecht, 1984), pp. 23–7.
3 The term quarantine is used to refer to a restriction on the movement of people who were exposed to a contagious disease in order to see if they became sick.
4 Important studies are E. Lesky, 'Österreichisches Gesundheitswesen im Zeitalter des aufgeklärten Absolutismus', *Archiv für österreichische Geschichte*, 122:1 (1959), 1–228; E. Lesky, 'Die josephinische Reform der Seuchengesetzgebung', *Sudhoffs Archiv für Geschichte der Medizin und der Naturwissenschaften*, 40:1 (1956), 78–88; E. Lesky, 'Das Wiener

Allgemeine Krankenhaus: seine Gründung und Wirkung auf deutsche Spitäler, *Clio medica, acta Academiae Internationalis Historiae Medicinae*, 2 (1967), 23–37 and E. Lesky, *Arbeitsmedizin im 18. Jahrhundert: Werksarzt und Arbeiter im Quecksilberbergwerk* (Wien: Verlag des Notringes der wissenschaftlichen Verbände Österreichs, 1956).
5 E. Lesky, 'Die österreichische Pestfront an der k.k. Militärgrenze', *Saeculum*, 8 (1957), 82–106.
6 G. E. Rothenberg, 'The Austrian sanitary cordon and the control of bubonic plague 1710–1871', *Journal of the History of Medicine and Allied Sciences*, 28 (1973), 15–23.
7 G. Brătescu, 'Seuchenschutz und Staatsinteresse im Donauraum (1750–1850)', *Sudhoffs Archiv*, 63:1 (1979), 25–44.
8 B. Bronza, 'Austrian measures for prevention and control of the plague epidemic along the border with the Ottoman Empire during the 18th century', *Scripta Medica*, 50:4 (2019), 177–84.
9 M. Foucault, *Überwachen und Strafen. Die Geburt des Gefängnisses* (Frankfurt am Main: Suhrkamp, 1977), pp. 251–6. With regard to Foucault, see M. Foucault, 'Die Politik der Gesundheit im 18. Jahrhundert', *Österreichische Zeitschrift für Geschichtswissenschaften*, 7:3 (1996), 311–26; M. Foucault, 'Die Geburt der Sozialmedizin', in M. Foucault, *Schriften in vier Bänden: Dits et Ecrits, III 1976–1979*, edited by D. Defert and F. Ewald (Frankfurt am Main: Suhrkamp, 2003), pp. 272–98; M. Foucault, 'The politics of health in the eighteenth century', in M. Foucault, *Power: Essential Works of Foucault 1954–1984* (New York: New Press, 2000), pp. 90–105.
10 T. Hobbes, *Leviathan, or, the Matter, Forme and Power of a Common-wealth Ecclesiasticall and Civil* (London: Andrew Crooke, 1651).
11 F. Falk, 'Hobbes' "Leviathan" und die aus dem Blick gefallenen Schnabelmasken', *Leviathan*, 39:2 (2011), 247–66, at 254.
12 B. Bulmuş, *Plague, Quarantines and Geopolitics in the Ottoman Empire* (Edinburgh: Edinburgh University Press, 2012).
13 D. Panzac, 'plague (veba; waba)', in G. Ágoston and B. Masters (eds), *Encyclopedia of the Ottoman Empire* (New York: Facts of File, 2009), pp. 462–3.
14 K. L. Sigmund, *Die Quarantäne-Reform und die Pestfrage. Beobachtungen und Anträge, geschrieben nach einer, im Auftrage der k.k. österreichischen Staatsverwaltung unternommenen, Bereisung der Donauländer, des Orients und Egyptens* (Wien: Verlag Wilhelm Braumüller, 1850), pp. 31–3.
15 The 'Renewal of the Quarantine Order' is dated 25 August 1766, Austrian National Archives Vienna (hereafter OeStA), FHKA SUS Patente 159.31. Some years later, in 1769, the regulations were mitigated and

that made processing with trials possible. See the letter of the Court Sanitary Deputation to the Transylvanian Sanitary Commission from 9 February 1769. OeStA, KA ZSt HKR, 719, 1769/94/11.
16 Lesky, 'Pestfront', at 89.
17 W. O'Reilly, 'Border, buffer and bulwark: the historiography of the military frontier, 1521–1881', in S. G. Ellis and R. Eßer (eds), *Frontiers and the Writing of History, 1500–1850* (Hanover: Wehrhahn, 2006), pp. 229–44.
18 Concerning the Military Border see, among others, C. Göllner, *Die Siebenbürgische Militärgrenze. Ein Beitrag zur Sozial- und Wirtschaftsgeschichte 1762–1851* (Munich: Oldenbourg, 1974); K. Kaser, *Freier Bauer und Soldat. Die Militarisierung der agrarwirtschaftlichen Gesellschaft an der kroatisch-slawonischen Militärgrenze 1535–1881* (Vienna; Cologne; Weimar: Böhlau, 1997); K. X. Havadi-Nagy, *Die Slawonische und Banater Militärgrenze. Kriegserfahrungen und räumliche Mobilität* (Cluj-Napoca: Academia Română, Centrul de studii Transilvane, 2010); C. B. von Hietzinger, *Statistik der Militärgrenze des österreichischen Kaiserthums. Ein Versuch*, 3 vols. (Vienna: Carl Gerold, 1817–1823) and F. Vaniček, *Specialgeschichte der Militärgrenze. Aus Originalquellen und Quellenwerken geschöpft*, 4 vols. (Vienna: Kaiserl.-Königl. Hof- und Staatsdruckerei, 1875).
19 Kaser, *Freier Bauer und Soldat*.
20 With a focus on the Transylvanian Military Border section, see S. Jesner, 'Habsburgische Grenzraumpolitik in der Siebenbürgischen Militärgrenze (1760–1830): Verteidigungs- und Präventionsstrategien' (PhD dissertation, University of Graz, 2013). Concerning the Habsburg cordon sanitaire see Lesky, 'Pestfront' and G. E. Rothenberg, 'The Austrian Sanitary Cordon and the Control of the Bubonic Plague: 1710–1871', *Journal of the History of Medicine and Allied Sciences*, 28:1 (1973), 15–23.
21 Lesky, 'Pestfront', at 84.
22 O. Briese, *Angst in den Zeiten der Cholera. Über kulturelle Ursprünge des Bakteriums* (Berlin: Akademie Verlag, 2003) pp. 242–3; A. Huttmann, 'Zur Geschichte der wichtigsten Seuchen in Siebenbürgen' in A. Huttmann, *Medizin im alten Siebenbürgen. Beiträge zur Geschichte der Medizin in Siebenbürgen*, edited by R. Offner (Sibiu: Editura hora, 2000), p. 262.
23 M. Dinges, 'Süd-Nord-Gefälle in der Pestbekämpfung: Italien, Deutschland und England im Vergleich' in W. U. Eckart and R. Jütte (eds), *Das europäische Gesundheitssystem. Gemeinsamkeiten und Unterschiede in historischer Perspektive* (Stuttgart: Steiner, 1994), pp. 19–51; F. Mauelshagen, 'Pestepidemien im Europa der Frühen Neuzeit (1500–1800)' in M. Maier (ed.), *Pest. Die Geschichte eines Menschheitstraumas* (Stuttgart: Klett-Cotta, 2005), pp. 237–65, at p. 261; E. Rodenwaldt,

Die Gesundheitsgesetzgebung des Magistrato della sanità Venedigs 1486–1550 (Heidelberg: Springer, 1956) and Z. Balžina Tomić and V. Balžina, *Expelling the Plague. The Health Office and the Implementation of Quarantine in Dubrovnik 1377–1533* (Montreal: McGill-Queen's University Press, 2015).

24 Lesky, 'Österreichisches Gesundheitswesen', 11–20 and the note of the Aulic War Council to the Transylvanian General Command from 6 January 1776, Romanian National Archives, Sibiu County Service (hereafter RNA), Comandamentul general al armatei austriece CC din Transilvania, 9/1776, folio (fol.) 109.

25 Lesky, 'Pestfront', at 86.

26 Briese, *Angst in Zeiten der Cholera*, pp. 242–3.

27 Lesky, 'Österreichisches Gesundheitswesen', at 34.

28 Lesky, 'Pestfront', at 92–3.

29 D. Panzac, *Quarantines et Lazarets. L'Europe de la peste d'Orient (XVIIe–XX siècles)* (Aix-en-Provence: Édisud, 1986), p. 77 as well as the report of the Transylvanian Sanitary Commission regarding a meeting of 9 December 1768, OeStA, KA ZSt HKR, 701, 1769/47/22.

30 J. Pešalj, 'Some observations on the Habsburg–Ottoman border and mobility control policies', in M. Wakounig and M. P. Beham (eds), *Transgressing Boundaries: Humanities in Flux* (Münster: LIT, 2013), pp. 246–56.

31 *Der führende Handel, und Gattung der Waaren* and *Sich für diesseitig Kaiserl. Königl. Unterthan erkläret und dessentwegen, ihme der Erlaubnuß-Schein abgenommen worden*. For the form see RNA, Comandamentul general al armatei austriece CC din Transilvania, 14/1769.

32 This was the case for the Prince of Wallachia, Constantin Ipsilanti, who stayed in the quarantine station of Tömös in the year 1806 with his family and royal household, totalling around 300 people, RNA, Comandamentul general al armatei austriece CC din Transilvania, 10/1806.

33 For case studies, see T. Ž. Ilić, *Beograd i Srbija u dokumentima arhive Zemunskog magistrata od 1739 do 1804 god., Knjiga I, 1739–1788* (Belgrade: Istorijski arhiv Beograda, 1973).

34 Such as the regulations included in the Renewal of the Quarantine Order in 1766.

35 *Ferman* from 1768. See the comments regarding *Praecautiones contumaciales intuitu Mercium ex Turcia* (No. 1222) in F. X. Linzbauer (ed.), *Codex Sanitario-medicinalis Hungariae*, 1. Sectio (Budae: Typis Caesareo-Regiae Scientiarum Universitatis, 1853), pp. 541–2.

36 Some of these plans are stored at OeStA, KA ZSt MilKom Sanitätshofkommission Akten 3 (1763–1775), Contumazpläne aus der Militärgrenze.

37 For comparison, see the medical considerations regarding the importance of water during the purification process in quarantine stations in

1769 by Adam Chenot. Note of Adam Chenot of 21 July 1768. OeStA, KA ZSt HKR 641, 1768/27/September 644.
38 'Ideal Normal Plan zu Erbau oder Verbesserung der Contumaz Gebäude', 6 June 1770, OeStA, KA ZSt MilKom Sanitätshofkommission Akten 3 (1763–1775), Contumazpläne aus der Militärgrenze, 1770/12.
39 M. Lindemann, *Medicine and Society in Early Modern Europe* (Cambridge: Cambridge University Press, 1999), pp. 62–5.
40 T. D. Sechel, 'Contagion theories in the Habsburg Monarchy (1770–1830)', in T. D. Sechel, *Medicine Within and Between the Habsburg and Ottoman Empires: 18th–19th Centuries* (Bochum: Winkler Publishers, 2011), pp. 55–78, at p. 59.
41 Ibid., at p. 58.
42 See the full regulations printed by J. N. Hempel-Kürsinger, *Handbuch der Gesetzkunde in Sanitäts- und Medicinal-Gebiethe*, vol. 2 (Vienna: Hof- und Staats-Aerarial-Druckerey, 1830), pp. 410–90.
43 'Von den Vorsichten, welche die Besorgung der Gesundheit von fremden Gränzen her betreffen'. See Hempel-Kürsinger, *Handbuch*, pp. 433–90.
44 L. Himmelmann, 'From barber to surgeon – the process of professionalization', *Svensk medicinhistorisk tidskrift*, 11: 1 (2007), 69–87.
45 Hempel-Kürsinger, *Handbuch*, pp. 478–82.
46 'Ideal Normal Plan zu Erbau oder Verbesserung der Contumaz Gebäude'.
47 J. Gerlitt, 'Die Entwicklung der Quarantäne', *Ciba-Zeitschrift*, 2:24 (1935), 805–40, at 812.
48 The existence of outer quarantine stations (*Vorkontumazen*), which were mostly closer to the border and upstream to the main quarantine station, proscribed periods of eighty-four days in the middle of the eighteenth century, such as in the Banat in 1763, OeStA, FHKA NHK AB 184, fol. 437, 451.
49 For example, the list of military posts in the Transylvanian Military Border in 1803, which depended on the season as well as the pestilential risk, RNA, Comandamentul general al armatei austriece CC din Transilvania, 4/1803, fol. 1–26.
50 In 1766 Chenot published significant observations and medical findings, including a description of his own plague infection in the book *Tractatus de Peste*. See for the German translation A. Chenot, *Abhandlung von der Pest* (Dresden: Michael Gröll, 1776).
51 S. Jesner, 'The physician Adam Chenot – reshaping plague control in the Austrian cordon sanitaire (approx. 1770–1780)', *Banatica*, 25 (2015), 283–300. For the papers see OeStA KA ZSt HKR HR Akten 1430, 1784–50–134 and A. Chenot, 'Die Einleitung zu den Vorbauungs-Anstalten wider die Pest', in Linzbauer (ed.), *Codex Sanitario-medicinalis Hungariae*, 1, pp. 151–79.

52 See H. Kerchnawe, *Die alte k.k. Militärgrenze: ein Schutzwall Europas* (Vienna: Wiener Verlag, 1943); K. Wessely, *Die österreichische Militärgrenze: der deutsche Beitrag zur Verteidigung des Abendlandes gegen die Türken* (Kitzingen: Holzner, 1954) and R. von Schumacher, *Des Reiches Hofzaun: Geschichte der deutschen Militärgrenze im Südosten* (Darmstadt: Kirchler, 1942).
53 S. Sutterlüti, 'Die Kontumaz in Mehadia. Mobilitätskontrolle und Seuchenprävention im 18. Jahrhundert' (Master's thesis, University of Vienna, 2016), 8–9 and 79.
54 In the 1820s Robert Walsh described the quarantine station in Turnu Roşu: 'Groups of these peasants, from the Wallachian side, were frequently shut up in large huts in the quarantine below, during our detention. The meat they brought with them for their support was hung round the building, so that they resembled shambles; and much of it seemed so stale as to be unfit for food […].' R. Walsh, *Narrative of a Journey from Constantinople to England* (London: Frederick Westley and A. H. Davis, 1828), pp. 284–5.
55 Walsh, *Narrative of a Journey*, pp. 269–70.
56 Ibid., p. 270.
57 Ibid., p. 272.
58 Ibid., p. 285.
59 This was the case with the well-organised Greek merchants, who had franchises on both sides of the border. See M. Lange, 'Von der Glaubwürdigkeit der meisten Pestberichte aus der Moldau, und Wallachey' in P. J. von Ferro, *Nähere Untersuchung der Pestansteckung, nebst zwey Aufsätzen von der Glaubwürdigkeit der meisten Pestberichte aus der Moldau, und der Wallachei, und der Schädlichkeit der bisherigen Contumazen von D. Lange und Fronius* (Vienna: Verlag Joseph Kurzbek, 1787), pp. 149–76, at pp. 155–6.
60 Lesky, 'Pestfront', at 89.
61 Key insights into the daily routine of a border city were part of the selection of Ilić, *Beograd i Srbija u dokumentima*.
62 Ilić, *Beograd i Srbija u dokumentima*, pp. 198–9, 387, 524.
63 The import ban from 8 March 1787 regarding specific product groups, RNA, Comandamentul general al armatei austriece CC din Transilvania, 6/1787, fos. 1–8.
64 J. T. Edler von Trattnern, *Supplementum Codicis Austriaci*, vol. 6 (Vienna: Johann Thomas von Trattnern, 1777), p. 1246.
65 In 1817, the director of the quarantine station in Oitoz named Jonak was under suspicion of illegal trading with subjects from Moldova. See the note from 13 November 1817, OeStA, FHKA NHK Caale Sieb. Akten 253 (1801–1820), Sanitäts- und Kontumazwesen (6), 1817/9/November, fol. 976.

66 Report about financial expenses concerning quarantining in Transylvania, Banat, Hungary and Croatia in 1776, OeStA, FHKA NHK Kaale U Akten 1053 (1775–1779), Sanitäts- und Kontumazwesen (15), in genere (15.1), 1776/92/May, fol. 111–12.
67 E. H. Ackerknecht, 'Antikontagionismus zwischen 1821 und 1867', in P. Sarasin, S. Berger, M. Hänseler and M. Spörri (eds), *Bakteriologie und Moderne. Studien zur Biopolitik des Unsichtbaren 1870–1920* (Frankfurt am Main: Suhrkamp, 2007), pp. 71–110; C. Hamlin, 'Commentary: Ackerknecht and "anticontagionism": a tale of two dichotomies', *International Journal of Epidemiology* 38:1 (2009), 22–7, and F. Mauelshagen, 'Neuerfindung einer medizinisch-politischen Kontroverse. Johann Jacob Scheuchzer und die Debatte der Kontagionisten und Antikontagionisten während der Pestepidemie von 1770–1722', in A. Holenstein, M. Stuber and G. Gerber-Visser (eds), *Nützliche Wissenschaft im Ancien Régime. Akteure, Themen, Kommunikationsformen* (Heidelberg: Palatina, 2007), pp. 149–85.
68 E. A. Eckert, 'The retreat of plague from central Europe, 1640–1720: a geomedical approach', *Bulletin of the History of Medicine*, 74:1 (2000), 1–28.
69 C. Promitzer, S. Trubeta and M. Turda, 'Introduction. Framing issues of health, hygiene and eugenics in southeastern Europe', in C. Promitzer, S. Trubeta and M. Turda (eds), *Health, Hygiene and Eugenics in Southeastern Europe to 1945* (Budapest; New York: Central European University Press, 2011), pp. 1–24, at pp. 4–6; A. Robarts, *Migration and Disease in the Black Sea Region: Ottoman–Russian Relations in the Late Eighteenth and Early Nineteenth Centuries* (London; New York: Bloomsbury Academic, 2017), pp. 116–30.
70 M. Chahrour, '"A civilizing mission"? Austrian medicine and the reform of medical structures in the Ottoman Empire, 1838–1850', *Studies in History and Philosophy of Biological and Biomedical Sciences*, 38:4 (2007), 687–705.
71 Robarts, *Migration and Disease,* p. 121 and C. Promitzer, 'Stimulating the hidden dispositions of south-eastern Europe – the plague in the Russo–Turkish War of 1828–29 and the introduction of quarantine on the Lower Danube', in Sechel, *Medicine Within*, pp. 79–110.
72 Sigmund, *Die Quarantäne-Reform und die Pestfrage*, pp. 12–23.
73 V. Taki, 'Between Polizeistaat and cordon sanitaire: epidemics and police reform during the Russian occupation of Moldavia and Wallachia 1828–1834', *Ab Imperio*, 9:4 (2008), 75–112, at 89.
74 Taki, 'Polizeistaat and cordon sanitaire', at 98–100.
75 Rothenberg, 'The Austrian sanitary cordon', at 21 and J. Bernt, *Ueber die Pestansteckung und deren Verhütung* (Vienna: J. B. Wallishausser, 1832).

76 Regarding the Plague Law, see F. X. Pichl (ed.), *Sammlung der Gesetze im politischen, Cameral- und Justizfache*, 3. Bd. (Vienna: J. B. Wallishausser, 1839), pp. 192–326.
77 For the Danube shipping file from 7 November 1857 see *Reichs-Gesetz-Blatt*, Stück IV, 1858.
78 Briese, *Angst in Zeiten der Cholera*, p. 243.
79 Concerning the *Rastell*, see J. H. von Benigni-Mildenberg, *Handbuch der Statistik und Geographie des Großfürstenthums Siebenbürgen* 2 (Sibiu: Thierry Buchhandlung, 1837), p. 161 and for the restructuring of the quarantines, the annual published volumes of the *Militär-Schematismus des österreichischen Kaiserthums* (Vienna: k.k. Hof- und Staats-Druckerey, 1815–1871).

2

Cholera at the junction of maritime and land routes in nineteenth-century Trieste

Urška Bratož

Many examples from the history of western medicine show that responses to events of contagious diseases generally involved taking steps on several levels. First, the incursion of a disease had to be prevented; second, a possible locus of infection (the first cases) had to be contained; and lastly, measures had to be taken if there was an outbreak of an epidemic. Focusing on the first level, one inevitably has to consider concepts such as inspection, containment, isolation and quarantine. In the centuries following its establishment as a system, the concept of quarantine became increasingly imbued with different connotations that – in association with forcible physical removal and restrictions of movement for a certain period of time – evoked different emotions and viewpoints.[1] In particular this was an issue of whether such measures that placed people, animals or objects (only merely potentially exposed to the source of infection) under scrutiny, were efficient and necessary in the first place.

Even though their institution was associated with plague epidemics, quarantines had been preserved as a prophylactic construct up to the period when Europe was threatened by other epidemic diseases, particularly cholera. By dealing just with the example of cholera between the 1830s and 1880s in the Habsburg port of Trieste (an important mercantile centre vibrant with the movement of people and goods[2]), this chapter[3] will focus on the prevention of the spread of contagious diseases. This period saw numerous changes[4] happening in the European (and broader) political, social and economic sphere, which had certain consequences in an epidemiological sense – from the expedited development of international commerce and transport, which underwent revolutionary improvements (for example, steamers and railway networks), as well as in modes of communication (for example, telegraphy). On the one hand, all these contributed to faster and shorter routes for the spread of disease and its wide-ranging geographical reach, and, on the other, to the unification of the world public in terms of the issue at hand, for it was the period in which epidemic diseases began to bring about international perspectives on these issues.[5]

Due to its location on the maritime border of the Habsburg monarchy, Trieste was, at the time of cholera, both a gateway for and a bulwark against the disease and, concurrently, of great importance owing to its immediate proximity to the Italian border. Trieste's important role in the Habsburg Empire's navigation had already begun in the period of the introduction of free navigation (1717), a free port (1719) and individual commercial contracts that opened Trieste to the east.[6] In the scope of economic mercantilist policy and administrative changes aimed at centralization, the monarchy attempted to gain access to international maritime trade, which was a process that deliberately promoted the immigration of merchants and tradesmen.[7]

Trieste saw an intense growth of its population, which more than quadrupled in the course of the eighteenth century. At the beginning of the nineteenth century, it numbered more than 21,000 inhabitants and, subsequently, after exponential growth, exceeded 152,000 people in 1886.[8]

By entering the international maritime market, Trieste (and with it the monarchy) came into almost direct contact with countries in which many infectious diseases, particularly the plague, were endemic. Additionally, Trieste risked becoming a key epicentre for the further spread of contagious diseases. As the monarchy had just begun to establish its maritime trade, it still lacked a maritime health system, which had yet to be established in the second half of the eighteenth century.[9]

Rules on contagious diseases in maritime transport

The regulation of maritime health, which initially focused on containing the plague, began in the reign of Maria Theresa – particularly with the Austrian Health Code of 1755, and later with the Regulations of the St Theresa Lazaretto of 1769.[10] They also served as the basis for provisions in the first decades of the nineteenth century (for example, the Port and Sanitary Offices Code of 1764 was reprinted in 1831 with the first threat of cholera).[11] The legacy of the anti-plague measures also provided guidance in the period when Trieste was faced with cholera for the first time; but as they failed, a new and systematic set of regulations – a general state regulation concerning maritime health for the Austrian Littoral[12] (*Regolamento generale per l'amministrazione della sanità marittima nell'Impero austriaco*) was adopted in 1851. The rules defined prevention of the spread of the plague and yellow fever; even though cholera was not mentioned, its articles were also applied in the event of this disease or served as a basis for a string of amendments issued by the competent ministry and the Maritime Government. This set of provisions led to the formation of rules that were in force until the 1870s–1880s.

In 1850, the Maritime Government in Trieste, which was (up to the formation of the Dual Monarchy – thereafter an additional Maritime Government in Rijeka was established) the central authority for the entire Littoral, was placed at the helm of services in charge of the administration of Austrian maritime affairs (with the exception of the military), merchant navy and navigation, the fishing industry, maritime health, correspondence with Austrian consulates and foreign ports, and the supervision of the port's operation. It thus replaced the former Health Magistrate – an eighteenth-century remnant.[13]

The Maritime Government, which was overseen by the Minister of Commerce, represented an intermediary between the Ministry on the one side and all port offices, maritime health offices, and lazarettos on the monarchy's coastline on the other.[14]

The vibrancy of Trieste's maritime transport is indicated by the data from, for instance, 1883, when thirty-six ships with a tonnage of 6,602 called on a daily basis, with 81 per cent of the tonnage being either from Austro–Hungarian, Italian, Turkish, Egyptian, Greek or Indo-Chinese ports. Most imports were agricultural produce or raw materials (e.g. minerals, charcoal, cotton, figs, oil, oak, wine, grain, skins, coffee, rubber); exports, on the other hand, mainly consisted of goods or finished products.[15]

Health inspection of vessels in the port of Trieste was supervised by the Maritime Government. Ships demonstrated their crews' health or possible health risk by means of bills of health (*fede di sanità*) containing one of the following possible labels: 'unsuspicious' or 'suspicious' (*netti, brutti* or *brutti aggravati*).[16]

Ships, crew and cargo arriving from 'suspicious' locations had to be quarantined in a broad sense. This implied one of two quarantine measures: a) the vessel, including its cargo and passengers, was detained for a fixed period of time for observation, or b) the observation of persons' health and the unloading of cargo along with specific treatment of potentially risky objects.[17]

Here, we should draw attention to a difference in meaning; the term quarantine denotes spatial containment of *potential* carriers of disease where there is *risk* of their becoming a carrier, unlike isolation, which involves containment of subjects whose infection has already been confirmed and involves the actual containment of disease transmission.[18]

Vessels with unfavourable bills of health were forced to call in ports with appropriate structures for inspection – lazarettos.[19] Trieste obtained its first lazaretto under Charles VI (San Carlo Lazaretto, 1730). It was followed by a more spacious one during the reign of Maria Theresa, namely the St Teresa Lazaretto in 1769, which was later demolished due to the construction of the railway and the new port. In 1867 the two city lazarettos were replaced by a lazaretto at San Bartolomeo, in the proximity of Muggia.[20] For its time, this was a very modern complex, divided into 'dirty' and 'clean' wards. Within it, a single large building was intended for isolation. Several smaller buildings were intended for sorting and treating goods and merchandise,[21] to which the most attention was paid (provisions concerning inspection of persons were scarcer).[22]

A rather detailed list of materials and goods that were regarded as susceptible to transmission of disease was already included in the Theresian Lazaretto Ordinance. Even thereafter, all substances and manufactured goods produced by or from them – as it was reasoned at the time – to which germs could easily get stuck due to their features, especially roughness and permeability, and could not be easily removed using mechanical means[23] were regarded as suspicious or susceptible to disease and 'germ-bearing'. By contrast, it was maintained that substances (given that their smooth, compact or powdery structures prevented germs from sticking) were viewed as unsuspicious.

A newly devised nineteenth-century list of (non-)susceptible objects was roughly based on a distinction between animal and plant-based origins of goods, whereby the latter was not necessarily subject to 'purgation'. Based on different risk levels of the contagious germ transmission (in the case of the plague, in particular) the code of 1851 divided goods into: 'highly suspicious' (cloth, used objects, particularly if they belonged to the sick or the dead); 'suspicious' (linen, flax, wool, cotton, leather, skins, feathers, silk, cocoons, rugs, paper, etc.); 'less suspicious' (ship equipment, items intended exclusively for personal use in quarantine); 'unsuspicious' (salt, sugar, powder, pottery, items made of stone, glass, wood, metal, plant material, seeds, medicines, liquids, resin, tar, rubber, etc.).[24]

The methods of 'disinfection' (understood as the removal of 'germs') were chosen with respect to the material and its level of "suspiciousness" or susceptibility. They included drying or airing (*sciorino*), heat treatment, fumigation using chlorine vapours, wiping with damp cloths or sweeping with straw brooms, rinsing with fresh water, saltwater or vinegar, and tarring. If items were used by patients, they were burnt in the lazaretto.[25] The list of goods to be sanitized in San Bartolomeo Lazaretto between 1871 and 1880 for instance included animal skin, leather, wool, entrails, bones, horns and cloth, with the major suppliers of these goods being the Levant, Albania and Thessaly.[26]

General prophylactic measures and their theoretical underpinnings

Vessels that could transmit one of the three 'importable and transmissible' diseases – i.e. the plague, yellow fever and cholera (as defined in the first international sanitary convention that resulted from the first International Sanitary Conference in Paris in 1851)[27] were subject to quarantine. The process of preparing the convention clearly also had a direct impact on the formation of the Austrian code that was issued shortly before its adoption. Every state could choose freely; consequently, cholera was excluded from the Austrian monarchy's code, most probably due to strong tendencies to reject its contagiousness (which were favoured also by the Austrian representatives at the conference).[28]

If the Austrian maritime health code defined the plague and yellow fever as contagious diseases, cholera, which Europe was facing a new during this period, aroused controversy. Despite the famous dichotomy between contagionists and anticontagionists, the boundary between them could often be slightly blurred.[29] These doctrines were analytically discussed by E. Ackerknecht,[30] who tried to draw a clear polarization between contagionism, quarantine and authoritarian states on one side and anticontagionism, sanitary measures and liberalism on the other. Here, we can agree with recent remarks about his statements that the contagionist versus anticontagionist conflict was not as divergent as it appeared.[31] Similarly, the simplification and underestimation of the complex national responses to epidemics by Ackerknecht has been criticized by Baldwin, and even more recently some other critical assessments have been proposed[32] to this framework for understanding the epidemics in their 'broader political, social, cultural, economic and geographic contexts'.[33]

The dominant contagionist perceptions in the first decades of the nineteenth century were deduced from the plague-logic, with which cholera was also addressed (quarantines, cordon sanitaire), but since it appeared to be useless in facing cholera, the anticontagionist position strengthened, inclining towards milder strategies of environmental and social reform.[34] At the time, when this 'antique doctrine (…) had not been proven by epidemiological or experimental data' (yet),[35] contagionists were regarded as obsolete, reactionary, conservative and even antisocial; on the other hand, anticontagionists' opinions were considered more in line with the principles of the bourgeois and, as such, mercantile and socially responsible.[36] With respect to available evidence, it could be claimed that (at least 'contingently') the contagionistic standpoint was also represented in the mid-century Triestine medical establishment. According to local treatises of the time,[37] cholera took on various characters (contagious, sporadic, epidemic). A predisposed person could catch the disease one way or another (infection or atmosphere). The difference between a 'contagious' (direct contact transmission) and an 'epidemic' disease (simultaneously affecting many people, influenced by specific atmospheric, climatic or edaphic conditions, often paired with poor hygiene, which together supposedly form an 'epidemic constitution') seems to be another form of the contagionism versus anticontagionism divide. Concepts, such as contagion (implying direct contact) and infection (indirect contact with a medium, such as water, air or contaminated articles), are also crucial to understanding this logic, although they underwent modifications and simplifications, which resulted in ambiguities and notional confusion.[38]

The aforementioned assumptions were in accordance with the standpoint of the Austrian representatives at the Conference in 1851, who described cholera as 'merely an epidemic', not a contagious disease; moreover, it selectively chose its victims, particularly on the basis of social circumstances and moral premises (such as intemperance). Daring but well-founded theories on the transmission of cholera by water (Snow in 1849, then in 1855) and on the existence of organisms[39] that supposedly caused cholera (Pacini) were completely ignored at the following conference (1859) as well.[40]

In the third International Sanitary Conference, influenced by Max von Pettenkofer, the opinion took root that the disease was spread through the movement of people if all conditions[41] were met for the epidemic to develop; cholera thus was ascribed the status of a transmissible, albeit not a directly contagious, disease.[42] The prevalence of certain theories on the spread of contagious diseases was supposedly closely related to economic interests, which set the tone for health measures;[43] anticontagionism (in the case of cholera) dominated in the period of liberalism and free trade (during Pettenkofer's period which was averse to quarantines), while Koch's influence (and the scope of bacteriological discoveries) was greatest in the period of protectionism,[44] which somehow saw the revival of contagionism.

The first decades of the nineteenth century, on the other hand, saw contagionist theories that came up against the plague as the first major threat from the 'East'. Owing to the fact that in 1838 the central shipping company Austrian Lloyd sought to play the prestigious role of transporter to Alexandria within the scope of the British postal route to India, the company received state support, as Austria was competing with France for dominance over maritime communication with the Levant. In the 1840s, the period of isolation (twenty-eight days for plague) was shortened. In the worst-case scenario, a ship with *patente brutta* that called into the Austrian port was quarantined for fifteen days; for ships with a clean bill of health the quarantine was abandoned altogether.[45] As for cholera, the tendency towards reducing quarantine measures grew at the time as well. It is no coincidence, then, that the book by the Triestine physician Alessandro De Goracuchi (1807–1887), who argued for anticontagionistic or even miasmatic approaches, was published by Austrian Lloyd in 1850.[46] In comparison, during the last quarter of the nineteenth century, in the event of cholera, a seven-day observation was proscribed for ships with *patente brutta* that had arrived from foreign lands (suspicious or infected).

Land routes and the spread of cholera across the border

Prophylaxis of contagious diseases, such as cholera, was not entirely contingent upon the prevention of its entry from the outside. The contemporary Triestine authorities were well aware that appropriate conditions were required for its spread. These included, inter alia, living conditions in overcrowded parts of the city with poor hygiene and a lack of adequate infrastructure. The Triestine population was most densely concentrated in the city centre, where a hectare was populated by up to 700 people.[47] Even in Trieste the then-current trends of urbanization were outpaced by the city's growth as it lacked a proper sewage system during the last cholera outbreak in 1886.[48] This is why preliminary measures in the 1860s, obviously partly under Pettenkofer's influence, included examining hygienic conditions, water and victuals in particular. Even two decades later the final report on the cholera epidemic closely analysed physical, meteorological and hygrometric conditions in the city.[49]

Statistics on cholera in Trieste, showing the extensive dimensions that these epidemics reached, were a part of risk justification and planning measures to be taken. The quantitative data, even though subjected to some methodological limitations, indicates large casualty figures, mostly in the outbreaks of 1836, 1849 and 1855 (with more than 7 per cent morbidity). The mortality rate varied between 35 and 60 per cent, a level exceeded only in the case of smaller epidemics, when it was mostly the army[50] that was affected.

It has also been demonstrated clearly by such data, for example in the case of the 1855 epidemic that, at state level, morbidity was highest in the Littoral, which was an area in direct contact with the disease.[51] It is evident from all epidemics that cholera spread from Trieste to the nearby Istrian cities (where morbidity was even up to 13 per cent), as they were connected by a network of provision-related routes traversed daily, by both land and sea. In the next phase, the disease also spread to the neighbouring provinces, particularly Carniola,[52] a process expedited after the construction of the southern railway branch between Ljubljana and Trieste (1857).

Cholera did not always arrive in Trieste directly by ships from the Levant or Egypt, if at all, but could enter indirectly via Italy (Venice, Ancona), and not necessarily by sea. From the outset of the regulation regimes, the monarchy's central administration paid attention to both maritime and terrestrial disease control and prevention.[53] If sea routes were to a great extent controlled by the Maritime Government (linked with the provincial authorities, but eventually also subject to international sanitary rules[54]), measures related to land routes were adopted exclusively by the municipal authorities, whereby the provisions of both bodies were always in line with state legislation.

It should be emphasized that it is not evident that quarantine-related measures (particularly concerning maritime health) in the period under discussion acted selectively in any way (for example through social, national, ethnic or other categories); instead, the passengers were to be separated in the quarantine only by the vessel on which they arrived.[55] However, research in this regard has been rendered even more difficult as some precious historical sources have been lost, such as the archives of the terrestrial and maritime border posts, through which the transit of emigrants occurred, and also the archives of the Harbour Office and Maritime Health Office in Trieste.[56]

Quarantine (in the sense of detention of potentially infected people) was carried out solely in maritime transport; passengers travelling by land were merely subject to fumigation, and required to isolate only in case of an actual infection, indicating that overland transport was only minimally hindered. Particularly in the second half of the century, isolation rooms were set up at key railway stations in the north-western Triestine territory (Aurisina, Monfalcone). Despite the repeatedly mentioned ideas about a militarily guarded cordon sanitaire that would encircle the broader city territory, this was believed to be an infeasible and costly endeavour, which would necessitate systematic control of the entire overland transport system (railway, roads and footpaths), and that was never undertaken.[57]

It appears that the cosmopolitan city of Trieste was rather open and tolerant of the influx of immigrants due to its great labour needs. However, the inspection (without detention), particularly in terms of preventing the spread of cholera by land routes, focused on all newcomers (but only after their arrival in the city). Proprietors of accommodation facilities had to report each arrival of foreigners and their health status to the local police authority.[58] Concurrently, in the last quarter of the century municipal officers met passengers at railway stations and gathered data on their journey. Subsequently, for a short period of time,[59] a physician was also engaged to 'inspect the arrivals and take necessary measures' if a passenger manifested symptoms. After collecting data, the physician visited newcomers in their temporary residences and examined them for three consecutive days in order to ascertain the absence of the disease.[60] Here, a parallel could be drawn with 'neoquarantinism', as the new approach (not implying a return to the 'old' quarantinism; rather, its ideas were closely related to those of Pettenkofer) is referred to by Peter Baldwin for Britain at the turn of the 1860s and 1870s. This system included inspection, isolation, disinfection and surveillance, by means of which it sought to replace the medical inspection of passengers who did not manifest any symptoms (traditional quarantine) and reduce the duration of the necessary sequestration.[61]

With almost unlimited movement on land routes, the question was raised of the (ir)relevance of maritime quarantines. An anonymous 'letter from lazaretto', published in 1865 in one of the Triestine newspapers, for instance, indicates several examples of how cholera (despite the rigorous control of sea routes) could easily reach the city: a passenger arriving directly from (cholera-afflicted) Ancona by railway could reach Trieste with ease after being subjected to merely a cursory fumigation, while a passenger arriving in Trieste by sea from the much-feared Alexandria, without travelling through infected cities, was quarantined for seven days.[62]

'Public opinion' was clearly the target of such writings,[63] and they seemed to drive the implementation of certain measures. The general population viewed them as a guarantee that active efforts were being made to prevent the epidemic. In general, quarantines, which represented a 'tangible' method of prophylaxis,[64] were particularly popular with the general population.[65] If the authorities refused to take certain measures, they had to justify their decision well. Here newspapers played an important role, as did official announcements, in which the mayor listed anti-epidemic measures in order to calm the population and give the impression of the municipal authorities' active involvement.[66] The abandonment of measures, such as quarantine or the cordon sanitaire, was in these cases presented as a decision that would benefit the population. Alongside excuses related to the inability to control a large and busy territory, the discourse on the economic damage showed quarantines as particularly harmful to the small-scale economy, rather than justifying the merchant elite's more general economic interest.[67]

It is evident that the dialogue between the public on one side and the competent inspecting institutions or executive organs on the other took place through the network of public roles. Confidants (*caposestiere*) and district delegates, who were well informed on the situation in their city quarters (and could thus be viewed as intermediaries between the city inhabitants and the institutions), were members[68] of ad hoc 'perlustrative committees'. These organs performed domiciliary visits and demanded particular hygienic improvements, where needed. The press and private individuals both helped the municipal authorities, for example by identifying questionable hygienic conditions within the city or drawing their attention to similar problems to be solved. One of the key mechanisms for informing on someone seems to have been denouncements, which were also read and discussed at the Sanitary Commission's[69] meetings and thereafter handed over to the magistrate.[70] In order to avoid public discontent, many complaints were actually reflected and considered in the implementation of measures.

The increasing 'danger'? Unequal newcomers and the risk of infection

Even though there were no specific formal provisions that would, by and large, limit the influx of foreigners, public prejudice could somehow affect the adoption of specific provisions at the local level, which meant that the competent institutions could justify their decisions on sanitary measures partly with 'general contentment'. It is in this sense that we are to understand the episode indicating the fear[71] of 'the dangerous other' which was strengthened by the awareness of cholera as a disease that always arrives 'from outside' (this perception started to play a more visible role from 1866 onwards, when its spreading via pilgrimage was mentioned at the International Sanitary Conference, and was eventually confirmed by the international community of scholars at the Conference of 1874).

In 1865, the Montenegrin Senator Pejović's ten-member family arrived in Trieste by steamer to take refuge. Meanwhile, his wife fell ill with cholera and the house in which they resided became the first (civilian) focus of infection on the outskirts of Trieste. The authorities distanced themselves from these assumptions. Nevertheless, the 'public' (presumably referring to the local inhabitants of the city quarter in question) viewed them with mistrust, believing that they had brought cholera to the city.[72] The prospect of Montenegrins moving freely around the city might have brought additional fear to the city's population. The 'dangerousness' of these newcomers, as was recognized by the official report of the City Sanitary Commission, lay in the assumption that they distinguished themselves from the domestic population in certain cultural features, to which great importance was ascribed in those sanitary circumstances. In particular they were associated with a 'lack of hygiene', and further, they refused to accept some implemented health measures and modern (western) hygienic norms, pursuant to which the symbolic mark of their ethnic group, their national clothes, were removed. The authorities were afraid that this might bring about severe conflicts, so they segregated the entire family in the temporary San Giacomo hospital. Eventually, the family was given a clean bill of health and handed over to the police directorate, who saw to their swift 'removal' from Trieste to Rijeka.[73]

Actually, the cholera-related fear of arrivals from the east intensified only later on.[74] It was not until the end of the nineteenth century that in Trieste fifty-eight Bosnian pilgrims, returning from Mecca by steamer in 1890, caused an outbreak of fear. These individuals were placed in the San Bartolomeo lazaretto for a week, as prescribed by the Austrian Ministry of Commerce. The pilgrims and their luggage were medically examined, whereupon they were released from quarantine.[75] This measure reflects the mindset that had materialized in conclusions related to Mecca pilgrims (who were at the time 'recognised' as representing the greatest risk for transmitting cholera) at the International Sanitary Conference two years later and in 1894;[76] the Suez Canal thus became an entry point to Europe that had to be monitored even more closely.[77]

Even before 1894, Mecca pilgrims featured on the International Sanitary Conference's agenda. In 1866 discussion arose around the key presumption, namely, that one should not simply wait for cholera to arrive, but instead must stop it before it even reached the continent. The more quarantine and other prophylactic measures were taken against cholera near the original focus of the disease, the less costly these measures would be, and the more effectively they could serve in the preservation of Europe.[78]

Additionally, the convention that stemmed from the International Sanitary Conference in 1893 added new categories of suspicious carriers of cholera: habitually itinerant individuals, Roma, immigrants and people who crossed the border for professional reasons.[79] In Trieste and elsewhere, at a much earlier stage, attention was paid to wanderers who roamed (freely) over the area, particularly specific mobile groups. The state code of 1848 stipulated actions in the event of epidemics, and these required that the local authorities take care of the poor (within the community) while preventing the entry of pedlars and beggars from outside.[80] As Promitzer has shown in the case of Bulgarian Turks and Roma[81] and the discourse on hygiene, infectious disease (typhus, in particular), the ethnic differences which surrounded them were embedded within a nation-building context as ideas, and helped define the contours of a (sedentary) national community.

The first state act in 1870 on the regulation of health-care services also stipulated that peddling, rag-and-bone men, and door-to-door begging were to be prevented with rigour in the event of disease, and that control over Roma and vagabonds[82] must be exercised in the event of an epidemic outbreak in the nearby municipality.[83] If the commercial exchange of fabrics and other problematic materials was directly associated with a fear of the transmission of germs, the attitude towards other aforementioned groups stemmed from a long tradition of incrimination and stigmatization. Measures in the sphere of public security, associated with issues related to begging and poverty,[84] were from the eighteenth century onwards intended for the social control of the population's mobility, which posed a threat as a potential carrier of disease.[85] Several eighteenth-century imperial acts, for instance, attest to the image of beggars as carriers of disease.[86] In the rhetoric of disgust and contempt in the period of bourgeois hygiene, this connotation applied even more to Roma.[87]

'Epidemic' often represented an additional lever for the escalation of existing social conflicts and the limitation of various undesirable contacts between people co-inhabiting a nationally diverse environment, such as the case in Trieste.⁸⁸ The emergence of cholera – along with the fear of biological infection – also meant an additional circumstance for emphasizing the existing cultural, social and national contrasts, which were not necessarily the result of being faced with newcomers from somewhere else.⁸⁹ It is in this sense that we can understand the fear of other forms of social, national and symbolic 'infection' that found their expression in circumstances in which public health was faced with a serious threat. It was at this point that the closure and sensitivity of boundaries that were not necessarily of a physical or geographical nature were strengthened, and contrasts and definitions of 'the other/different' were outlined even more clearly. Although they were not an objection to institutionalized quarantine practices, these 'internal others' were sometimes labelled scapegoats for disease transmission, especially through the press. Here, national identity and/or social background played their roles in making different 'border-crossers' (even insiders) dangerous.

Conclusion

This chapter has sought to examine the image of the control over movement of goods and people in the period when Trieste, as a major Austrian port and situated close to both maritime and terrestrial political borders, was threatened by cholera and other infectious diseases. One might remark generally that the focus of the maritime quarantines and isolation practices was mainly on the inspection of goods, which to a great extent stemmed from the city's and monarchy's commercial interests. The accepted medical theories of the day as well (the prevalence of anticontagionism or contingent contagionism) seem to have been driven by commercial ends that resulted in concern with goods instead of ('directly contagious') people. On the other hand, protective measures against disease also encompassed the defence of terrestrial borders.

If quarantine practices (the preventive detention of risky subjects) were much more characteristic of maritime transport, it could hardly be identified with controlling the land routes, over which the municipal authority had more autonomy. Instead, inspecting was a more common practice than detaining (the latter was carried out only when isolating the presumed epicentre of the epidemic). General sanitary measures, including control over hygienic conditions, was the main prophylactic alternative to quarantine. Besides, measures taken against new arrivals (at their entrance to the city/state) were not particularly selective, but their presence in the city at the moment of epidemic crisis was controlled. Provisions which emphasized the importance of controlling specific mobile groups, such as pedlars, were to a certain extent associated with goods and objects (or with fear of their role in spreading disease), but it was not until the end of the nineteenth century that new directives concerning those who were subject to a stricter preventative health inspection in the event of contagious diseases (for example, Muslim pilgrims) came into being, which brought new dimensions to this issue.

Finally, in order to continue research in this regard, one should take a closer look at the actual implementation of quarantine-related provisions, which is, in the absence of significant subjective testimonies that were unrelated to institutional interests, an extremely difficult task.

Notes

1 G. F. Gensini, M. H. Yacoub and A. A. Conti, 'The concept of quarantine in history: from plague to SARS', *The Journal of Infection*, 49:4 (November 2004), 257–61; on these notions see in particular: M. Pelling, 'The meaning of contagion: reproduction, medicine and metaphor,' in A. Bashford and C. Hooker (eds), *Contagion: Historical and Cultural Studies* (London: Routledge, 2001), pp. 15–38; A. Bashford (ed.), *Quarantine: Local and Global Histories* (Basingstoke: Palgrave Macmillan, 2016).
2 Situated in the Upper Adriatic, Trieste played the role of the main Austrian port. The monarchy's contact with the sea implied its connection within the Mediterranean, which turned out to be a 'shared European frontier against the forces of the outside world' (A. Chase-Levenson, 'Early nineteenth-century Mediterranean quarantine as a European system', in A. Bashford, *Quarantine*, p. 37).
3 Partly financed by the ARRS research programme P6–0272 (B).
4 See V. Huber, 'The unification of the globe by disease? The International Sanitary Conferences on cholera, 1851–1894', *The Historical Journal*, 49:2 (2006), 453–76, at 455.
5 See Huber, 'The unification of the globe'; N. Howard-Jones, *The Scientific Background of the International Sanitary Conferences 1851–1938* (Geneva: WHO, 1975).

6 See for example F. Gestrin, 'Pregled pomorstva v Slovenskem Primorju', in G. Novak and V. Maštrović (eds), *Pomorski zbornik* (Zagreb; Zadar: JAZU, 1962), [1489]–1515 and F. Gestrin, 'Pomorski promet v Trstu leta 1760', *Kronika*, 37:1–2 (1989), 46–9. See also Jesner in this volume.
7 A. Kalc, 'Politika priseljevanja v Trstu v 18. stoletju', *Annales: Series historia et sociologia*, 17:1 (2007), 1.
8 Municipal territory included. On data, see Kalc, 'Politika priseljevanja'; B. Benussi, *Manuale di geografia, storia e statistica del Litorale* (Pola: Bontempo, 1885); V. De Giaxa and A. Lustig (eds), *Relazione sul colera nell'anno 1886* (Trieste: Municipio, 1887).
9 See C. Simon, 'La sanità marittima a Trieste nel Settecento (da Carlo VI a Maria Teresa – 1711–1780)', *Archeografo Triestino*, 64 (2004), [263]–359; U. Bratož, 'Zamejevanje epidemij kuge v pristaniških mestih severnega Jadrana: primerjava med beneško Istro in Avstrijskim primorjem v 18. stoletju', *Povijesni prilozi*, 32:45 (2013), 313–31.
10 Simon, 'La sanità marittima'; P. Balázs and K. L. Foley, 'The Austrian success of controlling plague in the 18th century: maritime quarantine methods applied to continental circumstances', *Kaleidoscope*, 1:1 (2010), 73–87.
11 *Regolamento delle provvidenze e rispettive istruzioni per gli uffici di sanità*, quoted after C. I. Lorinser, *Die Pest des Orients, wie sie entsteht und verhütet wird* (Berlin: Enslin, 1837), p. 374.
12 The term is used here to denote the *Österreichisches Küstenland* or *Litorale Austriaco* as one of the crown lands existing since 1815 within the Austrian Empire. It comprised the imperial free city of Trieste (its capital), the province of Istria and the districts of Gorizia and Gradisca.
13 On the subject see especially Simon, 'La sanità marittima'.
14 See for example N. Terčon, 'Organizacija pristaniške in pomorskosanitetne službe v avstrijski monarhiji', *Annales*, 3:3 (1993), 243–56. The Maritime Government was helmed by a provincial governor (*luogotenente*) and *Luogotenenza*, his office and administration, was (from 1850 to the end of World War I) the highest provincial administrative body for the implementation of direction and control in practically all matters within the Austrian Littoral (see G. Tatò, 'Prestigio e politica del potere economico a Trieste nelle carte della Deputazione di Borsa poi Camera di commercio', *Acta Histriae*, 7 (1999), 609–18).
15 Benussi, *Manuale di geografia*, p. 167.
16 *Regolamento generale per l'amministrazione della Sanità marittima nell'Impero austriaco* (Wien, 1851); *Raccolta delle leggi ed ordinanze concernenti il servizio della sanità marittima nei litorali austro-illirico e dalmato*. Vol. I–II (Trieste: Lloyd austro-ungarico, 1879–1880), pp. 30–1;

see also G. Bussolin, *Delle istituzioni di sanità marittima nel bacino del Mediterraneo* (Trieste: Governo marittimo, 1881), p. 17.
17 Bussolin, *Delle istituzioni*, p. 44.
18 See Gensini et al., 'The concept of quarantine'. In sources, *contumacia* is often used as a synonym for quarantine.
19 Additional lazarettos on the Austrian coast were located in Poveglia, up to Austria's loss of Veneto, in Martinščica, Gruž and Meljine.
20 On Triestine lazarettos, see for example C. Visintini, *I lazzaretti della città di Trieste: rilievi e ricerche sulle architetture dei centri di controllo sanitario e commerciale tra Settecento e Ottocento* (Trieste: Italo Svevo, 2008); E. Metlikovitz, *I Lazzaretti marittimi di Trieste* (Trieste: Club Touristi Triestine, 1904); E. Ponte, 'Un lazzaretto dell'Ottocento nell'Alto Adriatico', *Acta medico-historica Adriatica*, 4:2 (2006), 235–46. On Mediterranean lazarettos see also Chircop in this volume.
21 See Bussolin, *Delle istituzioni* and G. Bussolin, *Dell' I.R. Lazzaretto Marittimo in valle San Bartolomeo presso Muggia e della sua operosità durante l'anno 1878: cenni* (Trieste: Governo marittimo, 1879).
22 Mediterranean quarantine as primarily centring on goods and merchandise (A. Bashford, 'Maritime quarantine: linking Old World and New World histories', in Bashford, *Quarantine*, pp. 1–12, at p. 5), is a significant point which has been elaborated in D. S. Barnes, 'Cargo, "infection", and the logic of quarantine in the nineteenth century', *Bulletin of the History of Medicine*, 88:1 (Spring 2014), 75–101, who argued that the nineteenth-century quarantine (which was more concerned about cargo than people) rested more on the conceptualization of infection rather than on contagionist medical doctrine.
23 *Raccolta delle leggi ed ordinanze*, p. 59; *Regolamento generale*.
24 *Regolamento generale*.
25 Bussolin, *Delle istituzioni*.
26 Ibid., pp. 183, 196–203.
27 On this subject, in particular, see A. Cappello, *Sul sanitario congresso internazionale aperto a Parigi nel di' 23 luglio 1851 e chiuso 19 gennaio 1852. Cenni storici* (Roma: Belle Arti, 1852); Howard-Jones, *The Scientific Background*.
28 Howard-Jones, *The Scientific Background*, p. 15.
29 See ibid., p. 25.
30 E. Ackerknecht, 'Anticontagionism between 1821 and 1867', *Bulletin of the History of Medicine*, 22 (September 1948), 532–93.
31 Huber, 'The unification of the globe', at 457. See also Pelling, 'The meaning of contagion', pp. 25–6.
32 P. Baldwin, *Contagion and the State in Europe 1830–1930* (Cambridge: Cambridge University Press, 1999), pp. 529, 563; C. Hamlin,

'Commentary: Ackerknecht and 'anticontagionism': a tale of two dichotomies', *International Journal of Epidemiology*, 38:1 (2009), 22–7; C. E. Rosenberg, 'Commentary: epidemiology in context', *International Journal of Epidemiology*, 38:1 (2009), 28–30; A. M. Stern and H. Markel, 'Commentary: disease etiology and political ideology: revisiting Erwin H Ackerknecht's classic 1948 essay "Anticontagionism between 1821 and 1867"', *International Journal of Epidemiology*, 38:1 (2009), 31–3.

33 Stern and Markel, 'Commentary: disease etiology and political ideology' at 31.
34 Hamlin, 'Commentary', at 22.
35 Rosenberg, 'Commentary', at 28.
36 K. F. Kiple (ed.), *The Cambridge World History of Human Disease* (Cambridge; New York; Melbourne: Cambridge University Press, 1994), p. 648; M. Pelling, 'Contagion/germ theory/specificity', in W. F. Bynum and R. Porter (eds), *Companion Encyclopedia* (London; New York: Routledge, 1993), pp. 309–34, at p. 310.
37 Prominent physicians of Trieste took quite different positions, from anticontagionist–miasmatic, for example A. De Goracuchi, *Studi sul cholera asiatico con ispeciale riguardo all'epidemia che regnò in Trieste l'anno 1849* (Trieste: Lloyd Austriaco, 1850) to contagionist, for example G. Castagna, *Intorno alla coléra in Trieste nel 1849* (Trieste: G. D. Pagani, 1850) and 'contingent' contagionist, such as A. Guastalla, who was sharply criticized by the latter.
38 Pelling, 'The meaning of contagion', p. 16.
39 During the epidemic of 1849, several physicians from the Trieste and Koper districts subscribed to the contagionist view; however, scepticism and ridicule were expressed when referring for example to the theories of Bristolian microscopists (Budd, Brittan, Swayne), who observed 'tiny beings' or 'animals' in patients' excreta that were believed to propagate by air, partly also by water and objects (Castagna, *Intorno alla coléra*, pp. 54–5).
40 Howard-Jones, *The Scientific Background*, pp. 12, 20.
41 These include: a specific germ propagated predominantly by patients' excreta, local/seasonal preconditions (ground, soil that is porous to water and air), and individual predispositions (see Baldwin, *Contagion and the State*, p. 143).
42 Baldwin, *Contagion and the State*, p. 143.
43 See Balázs and Foley, 'The Austrian success', at 80.
44 R. J. Evans, *Death in Hamburg: Society and Politics in the Cholera Years* (New York: Penguin Books, 2005), p. 269.
45 R. E. Coons, 'Steamships and quarantines at Trieste, 1837–1848', *Journal of the History of Medicine*, 44:1 (1989), 28–55, at 39 and 55.

46 De Goracuchi, *Studi sul cholera asiatico*.
47 De Giaxa and Lustig, *Relazione sul colera*, pp. 7–8.
48 See for example F. Braulin, *La questione sanitaria nella Trieste di fine '800: i caratteri antropologici della medicina ospedaliera sul Litorale austriaco* (Milano: Franco Angeli, 2002), p. 114; M. Remec, *Podrgni, očedi, živali otrebi: higiena in snaga v dobi meščanstva* (Ljubljana: INZ, 2015), p. 111.
49 See *Provedimenti sanitari della città di Trieste nell'anno 1865. Relazione publicata per incarico della commissione sanitaria centrale* (Trieste: Lloyd Austriaco, 1866); De Giaxa and Lustig, *Relazione sul colera*.
50 The spread of cholera was very closely related to armies' movements, see L. Loy, *Relazione e documenti della Commissione sanitaria centrale di Trieste sul cholera morbus nel 1866* (Trieste: Municipio, 1867), p. 9.
51 G. Krebs, 'Die geographische Verbreitung der Cholera im ehemaligen Oesterreich-Ungarn in den Jahren 1831–1916', in *Veröffentlichung aus dem Gebiete des Volksgesundheitsdienstes* (Berlin, 1941), p. 26 (474).
52 See K. Keber, *Čas kolere: epidemije kolere na Kranjskem v 19. stoletju* (Ljubljana: ZRC SAZU, 2007).
53 See Balázs and Foley, 'The Austrian success', at 85. Quarantine, not necessarily being a maritime practice, could also be connected to territorial borders and isolation hospitals or inland lazarettos among others (Bashford, 'Maritime quarantine', p. 2).
54 As pointed out by Chase-Levenson, this was the reason lazarettos were usually outside the purview of local authorities. See Chase-Levenson, 'Early nineteenth-century Mediterranean quarantine', p. 51.
55 See Bussolin, *Dell' I.R. Lazzaretto Marittimo* and *Delle istituzioni*.
56 P. Dorsi, 'Emigrazione italiana verso l'Austria (1870–1914): Trieste come luogo di destinazione e di accoglienza', in *L'emigrazione italiana 1870–1970*. Vol. I (Roma: Ministero per i beni e le attività culturali, Direzione generale per gli archivi, 2002), pp. 364–77, at p. 372.
57 The only implementation of this measure in the time of cholera, albeit with a broader regional note, dates back to 1831 when the cordon sanitaire was located on the border between Carniola and Croatia, and transport was diverted to the port of Trieste (see K. Keber, 'Kranjski obrambni mehanizem za zaščito pred prvo epidemijo kolere v Evropi', *Kronika*, 53:3 (2005), 351–64).
58 Archivio di Stato di Trieste (hereafter AST), Luogotenenza, Atti generali (hereafter LAG), b. 520, Poduk o koleri, 5 August 1886, n. 14067; De Giaxa and Lustig, *Relazione sul colera*, p. 16.
59 In 1885, physicians were no longer involved in this protocol. The municipal administration believed the data concerning passengers' health en route from the (Italian) border to Trieste, acquired by their

deputies, to be sufficient; a physician was summoned only in the event of a possible infection (De Giaxa and Lustig, *Relazione sul colera*, p. 17).
60 De Giaxa and Lustig, *Relazione sul colera*, p. 17.
61 Baldwin, *Contagion and the State*, p. 164. On the British preventative system, which avoided quarantines (particularly due to the principles of free trade), preventative health inspection by means of isolation and disinfection were favoured. See also A. Hardy, 'Cholera, quarantine and the English preventive system, 1850–1895', *Medical History*, 37 (1993), 250–69. We can probably also agree with Baldwin's assertion that Austria partly modelled its cholera-related measures on the British system (Baldwin, *Contagion and the State*, p. 213), naturally, taking into account the contemporary economic guidelines and scientific findings of bacteriology and medical prevention.
62 *Il Diavoletto*, 29 August 1865.
63 The question is, however, who exactly spoke in the name of the public through the press; although usually hidden behind pseudonyms or anonymity, the authors supposedly belonged to the city's mercantile elite.
64 See Baldwin, *Contagion and the State*, p. 200.
65 It should be pointed out that, despite changing attitudes towards the question of contagiousness, the 'contagionist' attitude prevailed in popular belief (see Pelling, 'Contagion/germ theory/specificity', p. 322).
66 For instance, in *Provedimenti sanitari*, p. 76. In this context, the imposition of quarantine symbolizes the responsibilities of a government to its citizens and its duties to the international community and is an important sign in times of crisis, which can be important as such (M. Harrison, 'Afterword', in Bashford, *Quarantine*, pp. 251–7, at p. 254).
67 On the Triestine mercantile elite and its embeddedness into municipal administrative bodies and institutions through which it represented the city's economic interests see Tatò, 'Prestigio e politica'.
68 Besides being magistrate functionaries, physicians, engineers etc.
69 At the time this body was not yet a permanent one; its members were, apart from the mayor, the police counsellor, magistrate representatives, city chief physicians and construction inspector.
70 *Provedimenti sanitari*.
71 Beside considering fear within the context of the cultural history of emotions, such as proposed by J. Bourke (*Fear: A Cultural History*, London: Virago, 2005), fear has also been recognized as a constitutional element of contemporary politics and particularly foreign policies as well, see R. Taras, *Fear and the Making of Foreign Policy: Europe and Beyond* (Edinburgh: Edinburgh University Press, 2015).
72 *Provedimenti sanitari*, p. 43. It should be noted, however, that these newcomers were not under suspicion as border-crossers with mere

regard to their provenance (after all, Trieste was a multi-ethnic city); they attracted attention only after the actual manifestation of cholera symptoms, once they had already been accommodated in the city suburbs.

73 *Provedimenti sanitari*, pp. 43–6.
74 We can agree with historians who connect this with Europe's increased 'vulnerability' after the opening of the Suez Canal (for example Huber, 'The unification of the globe', at 465) and, in general, with improvements in transport.
75 AST, LAG, b. 520, m. 39/30, Trieste, 6 November 1890.
76 On this subject, see Howard-Jones, *The Scientific Background*, pp. 64–5, 71–7.
77 In 1874, at the first conference following the opening of the Suez Canal, its role in the spread of epidemics is not mentioned at all. It was only at the international conferences in the 1890s (particularly in connection with examination of pilgrims) that the introduction of a specific control regime over the Canal is pointed out. See Howard-Jones, *The Scientific Background*, p. 64.
78 *Procès-verbaux de la Conférence sanitaire internationale ouverte à Constantinople le 13 février 1866*. Tome II (Constantinople: Imprimerie centrale, 1866).
79 Huber, 'The unification of the globe', at 468.
80 *Regolamento sulla procedura da osservarsi dai Capitanati circolari, Domini, Autorità locali, Parrochi, Medici circolari, distrettuali ed ausiliari, nonché dai Chirurghi nei casi di Epidemie in generale ed in particolare del Colera epidemico* (Wien, 1848).
81 C. Promitzer, 'Typhus, Turks, and Roma: hygiene and ethnic difference in Bulgaria, 1912–1944', in C. Promitzer, S. Trubeta and M. Turda (eds), *Health, Hygiene, and Eugenics in Southeastern Europe to 1945* (Budapest; New York: Central European University Press, 2011), pp. 87–126.
82 The mode of implementation was not specified.
83 Instructions on law implementation in G. Waller, *Manuale delle leggi e regolamenti comunali e provinciali nonchè delle varie altre leggi ed ordinanze ai medesimi attinenti valevoli per la contea principesca di Gorizia e Gradisca e pel margraviato d'Istria* (Innsbruck: Libreria Accademica Wagneriana, 1886).
84 For instance, one of the first preventive measures, taken in 1865, was control over spaces where the poor moved around, as well as the 'dispersion of the working class' from the tight lodgings they lived in. See *Provedimenti sanitari della città di Trieste nell'anno 1865*, p. 3 and Pelling, 'The meaning of contagion', p. 21.
85 A. Studen, *Neprilagojeni in nevarni: podoba in status Ciganov v preteklosti* (Ljubljana: INZ, 2015), p. 85.

86 On issues regarding attitudes towards migration and travelling groups, see in particular L. Lucassen, 'Eternal vagrants? State formation, migration and travelling groups in western Europe, 1350–1914', in L. Lucassen, W. Willems and A.-M. Cottaar, *Gypsies and Other Itinerant Groups: A Socio-Historical Approach* (Basingstoke: Palgrave Macmillan, 2015), pp. 55–73; cf. D. Čeč, 'Odnos do mobilnega dela prebivalstva od 18. stoletja dalje na primeru glavnih deželnih vizitacij', in P. Štih and B. Balkovec (eds), *Migracije in slovenski prostor od antike do danes* (Ljubljana: ZZDS, 2010), pp. 191–207, at p. 197.

87 See, for example, Lucassen, 'Eternal vagrants?'; Promitzer, 'Typhus, Turks, and Roma', pp. 87–126; Studen, *Neprilagojeni in nevarni*.

88 Such conflicts between the Italian and Slavic (Slovenian) populations were particularly noticeable in the period of Taaffe's government, when demands for linguistic rights and efforts for Slovenian national affirmation solidified.

89 Alongside the aforementioned conflict between the Italian and Slovenian nationalities, other levels of conflicts were manifested as well, for instance, between the urban and rural spaces, the civilized and uncivilized, the bourgeois and peasant mentalities. For examples see U. Bratož, *Bledolična vsiljivka z Vzhoda: kolera v severozahodni Istri (1830–1890)* (Koper: Založba Annales ZRS Koper, 2017).

3

Uses of quarantine in the nineteenth century until the Crimean War: examples from south-east Europe

Christian Promitzer

During the nineteenth century the classical system of maritime and terrestrial quarantines in the Old World increasingly came under stress and would consequently become subject to extensive modifications. These changes pertained to the length of time that travellers spent in isolation, to the infrastructure, and to the underlying sanitary doctrine itself. Since this process has already been examined for western Europe and the Mediterranean,[1] this chapter focuses on the situation in south-east Europe. Despite initial work by various scholars,[2] developments connected with quarantines in these regions, in particular with respect to the nineteenth century, await closer historiographic examination.

The arguments against the system of classical quarantine in the nineteenth century were at least twofold; first, the economic interests of manufacturers, wholesale companies, haulage contractors, ship owners and their customers, who considered quarantines in the era of rising industrial capitalism unnecessary barriers to trade, now clashed with traditional medical theories about the transmission of deadly epidemics such as plague and cholera (or more exactly, whether either or both of them were considered contagious at all). And, second, according to the then fashionable miasma theory, not all diseases were deemed contagious, but were transmitted instead via a so-called miasma which comprised all kinds of 'bad air' or fetid vapours from the soil; for these reasons they could not be combatted by means of quarantines.

This chapter will try to show, however, that quarantines still played a prominent role in a period when they were put under rigid scrutiny and proved to be more flexible than expected. Thus, one can observe a palliative function of quarantines in situations of panic when they at least provided for a precarious, yet still palpable sense of security. The authorities could grant this protective function of quarantines only as long as they were kept orderly and functioning. Thus, the sense of security was always offset by threats and fears of failure, the 'worst case' of a 'sanitary disaster' being an epidemic that would pass unnoticed over a quarantine line and consume the entire continent. This was the case during the second pandemic of cholera which easily vanquished all sanitary cordons and quarantine lines in Europe from 1830 to 1832. In this respect, one has to keep in mind that quarantines formed a complex ensemble of customary technologies and rituals, sharing a commonality with the modern industrial machinery of the early industrial capitalist period. For these reasons the historical failure of quarantines is closely connected with the conceptual history of the notion of technological hazards.

Nevertheless, another aspect is also critical; it appears that some of those who advocated quarantines on medical grounds allied themselves with non-medical entities in order to retain this specific institution of sanitary prevention. In order to recognize the flexible uses of quarantines one has only to visualize their spatial organization; terrestrial and maritime quarantines thereby followed different geometrical patterns. In the first case, one has to think of an uninterrupted chain of terrestrial quarantines which were envisioned as protecting a border stretching several hundred kilometres. A continuous cordon of patrolling soldiers had to connect each of the adjoining stations in order to guarantee that no person or consignment of goods could cross the border uncontrolled and bypass the quarantine stations. Such strings of quarantine stations and cordons, as they existed alongside the southern boundaries of the Habsburg Monarchy, Russia and the Danubian principalities at least up to the Crimean War, claimed to render the borderlines hermetic and to protect the health of the territory behind it. They could also be used, however, to make real other forms of demarcations, not for sanitary purposes but for political or economic reasons. Some of the newly founded states in south-east Europe and even the time-honoured Ottoman Empire used classical quarantines in order to underscore their claims to sovereignty. Terrestrial quarantines were arranged subsequently alongside a border *line*; maritime quarantines, on the other hand, were organized *pointwise* and limited to individual harbours at which vessels with a foreign provenance had to call. Maritime quarantines therefore were also suitable for extended uses, although the level of control was not as high as in the case of terrestrial quarantines, which in turn were afforded far more resources and manpower for their effective maintenance.

By the nineteenth century at the latest, quarantine had become 'at once part of the world forged through connections of capital, trade and empire, and one of the responses perceived to hinder those connections', as Alison Bashford has written recently.[3] Alex Chase-Levenson has shown that after the Napoleonic Wars, Mediterranean quarantines up to the first International Sanitary Conference of 1851 in Paris functioned as a universal and shared system of cooperation among the European ports that split the sea into zones of health and disease, so that ships coming from the contaminated ports in the Ottoman Empire, Egypt and other parts of North Africa had to undergo detention.[4] Attempts to establish continent-wide cooperation also existed with regard to terrestrial quarantines, insofar as they were not only supposed to protect the state on whose borders they had been established, but also the neighbouring states located behind it.

This chapter deals with examples that touch all the aspects mentioned above and thus seeks to show the transformability of an old institution that was based on the temporary arrest of suspected persons in the name of disease prevention during an age of burgeoning global trade. The first example deals with the inspection trip of a doctor in Prussian service along the plague front at the southern border of the Habsburg Monarchy in the winter of 1828/29. His journey was instigated by a fear among Prussian authorities that the plague, then rampant in the Balkans and the two Danubian principalities of Wallachia and Moldavia, would intrude into central Europe. The second part covers the entanglement of quarantines against the backdrop of power politics, with examples from the Danubian principalities, the estuary of the Danube, Greece and the Ottoman Empire. It shows that sanitary issues often did not play the most important role when the establishment of quarantines or the imposition of quarantine measures were at stake.

The chapter partly draws on material from the 'Secret State Archives Prussian Cultural Heritage Foundation (Geheimes

Staatsarchiv Preußischer Kulturbesitz)' in Berlin (Dahlem). The Prussian perspective shows that sanitary issues of foreign states and their quarantines, in particular, were an important sub-field within issues of trade policy. In the second half of the nineteenth century, which is not the topic of this chapter, these activities would increase, evolving into outright sanitary diplomacy.

Along the Carpathian Mountains and the Danube (1829–1830)

During the Russo–Ottoman war of 1828–1829, both banks of the lower Danube were rife with a plague-like epidemic. It gripped many among the advancing Russian army but did not stay to haunt the soldiers at least during their advance from Eastern Wallachia across the Danube into north-eastern Bulgaria and even across the Balkan mountain range into Rumelia before their final encampment at the gates of Adrianople in September 1829. It was only after the campaign had concluded that the general staff and the army's sanitary service declared that the plague was widespread, and that Russian soldiers would have to undergo severe measures of quarantine before they could return home. These measures did not, however, prevent the outbreak of the plague in the Russian Black Sea port of Odessa. Altogether the epidemic took the lives of 9,500 Russian soldiers from a total manpower of 150,000. Military experts, such as the German Helmuth von Moltke (1800–1891), assessed that the number of plague deaths among the Russian army from spring 1829 until the end of the year could even have reached 60,000.[5]

In the first half of September 1829, Austrian and German newspapers worryingly wrote about the approach of the plague from the direction of Odessa.[6] Already in late August the Prussian government had received a private letter from Kraków which claimed that the Austrian authorities were going to establish a sanitary cordon along their border with Russia. Additional news that the plague had allegedly caused the death of a Jewish woman in the Galician town of Brody further startled the authorities in Berlin.[7] Hermann von Staff-Reitzenstein (1790–1867), then a major in the Prussian Army and someone who had observed the Russian military operations first-hand, returned to Berlin before the end of the campaign. He became concerned about the rumours and informed his superiors that on a Russian ship across the Black Sea a plague victim had touched his belongings, which he then left behind on his subsequent return from the theatre of war. The two servants of Staff-Reitzenstein, who monitored his belongings, had already undergone thirty-eight days of quarantine before they reached Berlin. The Prussian authorities therefore decided that the two men were not contagious anymore, but for good measures had their clothes and the belongings of Staff-Reitzenstein incinerated. Meanwhile the Prussian Ministry for Religious, Educational and Medical Affairs gave the governors of the provinces of Silesia, Posen and Prussia the option to decide whether it was necessary to establish military sanitary cordons along the borders with Russia and Austria.[8]

A council of Austrian physicians meanwhile declared that the death of the Jewish citizen of Brody had not been caused by the plague.[9] This notwithstanding, the Prussian authorities were disturbed and wanted to be sure that the 'plague front' – the ensemble of quarantine stations and sanitary cordons controlled by military authorities and located at the southern border of the Austrian Empire vis-à-vis the two Danubian principalities and Serbia, all of whom were vassals of the Ottoman Sultan (see also the chapter by Jesner in this volume) – would deflect an incursion of the plague and therewith also safeguard the Prussian lands. On 23 September 1829 the Prussian Ministry of the Interior suggested that the physician Karl Ignaz Lorinser (1796–1853) should conduct an inspection of this protective institution which, apart from the region of Bukovina, was located in the Hungarian parts of the Habsburg Monarchy, that is, in Transylvania, the Banat and along the Croatian border with the Ottoman province of Bosnia and Herzegovina.[10]

Lorinser was of Austrian origin and his father had been a surgeon (*Wundarzt*) in Bohemia. After a short spell at the University of Prague, he had completed his medical studies at the University of Berlin. He soon became an unsalaried lecturer and thereafter councillor and medical officer of health in the town of Oppeln/Opole in Upper Silesia, where he was active in the fight against various epizootics.[11]

The state councillor Johann Gottfried Langermann (1768–1832), who was Lorinser's mentor, was mandated to work out the itinerary and procedures for the inspection trip. Langermann indicated that

Robert Walsh (1772–1852), the chaplain to the British Embassy in Constantinople, had on his voyage home in autumn uttered severe criticism about the Austrian quarantine facilities at the mountain pass of Rothenturm/Turnu Roşu in Transylvania at the border with the Danubian principality of Wallachia, where he had had to undergo twenty days of quarantine. Walsh, among others, argued that his personal belongings and clothes had never been cleaned by the staff during his stay in this facility, so the whole procedure of incarceration had been in vain.[12]

By the end of October the Prussian Ministries for the Interior and Religious, Educational and Medical Affairs had signed the instruction for Lorinser. He was asked to collect all Austrian legislative texts and regulations concerning human and animal plague and 'to journey to the quarantine facilities along the [Austrian] border and to examine in how far the employed officials possess the necessary knowledge, carefulness and integrity, so that foreign countries could also rely on the strict and exact execution of the laws'. The end of the instruction is indicative: 'The signed ministries are persuaded by your preparedness to accept the assignment and by doing so are trusting your expertise and solicitude in this affair, which is a question of protecting Germany and the whole of western Europe ('die Sicherung Deutschlands und des ganzen Westens von Europa') against the terrible evil from the Orient.'[13]

This assessment is important for two reasons. First, it confirms that the border between the Habsburg Empire and the vassal states of the Ottoman Empire, as well as with Russia, was in general considered a civilizational border or 'fault line' between a zone of health and an unhygienic contaminated one, where plague and other epidemics would be endemic. Not only the Austrian but also the Prussian authorities shared this perception of the land mass east and south-east of the Habsburg Monarchy, which not by accident corresponded with the already mentioned bisection of the Mediterranean into healthy and unhealthy halves. The second important issue was the fact that, at the time, terrestrial quarantines could no longer be reduced to an issue solely of the state which had established them and was responsible for their function. Consequently, the Prussian government claimed it was ensuring not only its own welfare, but the common good of foreign countries and the 'whole west of Europe' as well.

Lorinser's posthumously published autobiography included a retrospective account of the trip and excerpts from his diary from that period. He left Oppeln on 25 November and first travelled to Kraków, before pressing on to the Galician towns of Lemberg/Lviv and Brody. By Christmas he had reached Czernowitz/Chernivtsi, the administrative centre of Bukovina. Shortly after the turn of the year he went to Suczawa/Suceava. From there he entered Transylvania and reached the huge quarantine facilities at Rothenturm/Turnu Roşu on 24 January. Due to the bad weather he had to abandon his wish to visit the quarantine facility of Zsupanek/Jupalnic (Zsupanek) close to the Danube. He reached the town of Panczova/Pančevo in the Banat and its quarantine by 8 February. From there he went to the town of Semlin/Zemun and its quarantine facility which was the largest in the region and was also responsible for the sanitary examination of correspondence and post, including diplomatic communications, from the Ottoman Empire to central and western Europe. From Semlin, Lorinser went to the quarantine at Mitrowitz/Sremska Mitrovica and further to the Croatian town Esseg/Osijek, which he reached on 14 February. On his return journey, he passed Pest and Vienna and arrived in Oppeln on 12 March 1830. Therewith he had covered a set of regions which, from Lemberg to Mitrowitz, are now located in Ukraine, Romania, Serbia and Croatia. His personal account did not contain the results of his findings, but does unveil additional insightful observations which were absent from his official report:

> During the winter of 1829/1830, which by its harshness has not been matched by any other as long as anyone could remember, I visited the borders of the Russian and Turkish Empires; I crossed the countries of Galicia, Bukovina, Banat, Slavonia and Hungary; I had to socialise with the highest and the lowest, with civilized and barbarian people, with Poles, Ruthenians, Wallachians, Moldavians, Serbs, Slovaks, Hungarians, Russians, Armenians, Turks, Jews and Gypsies; I had to confront innumerable dangers, namely freezing to death, dying from exhaustion or from malignant fever, being ripped apart by wild animals, being looted or murdered by bandits, having my bones broken along the terrible trails, plunging from the heights into an abyss, and finally, suffocating from the smoke of stoves or being drowned by flooding.[14]

On 24 April 1830 Lorinser submitted his report. It bore the title 'Reise-Bericht über die in den Kaiserlich-Königl. Österreichischen

Staaten gegen die orientalische Pest vorhandenen Anstalten und Einrichtungen' ('Travel report on the institutions against the Oriental plague, existing in the Imperial and Royal Austrian States'). The manuscript comprises 283 sheets, of which the report itself entails sixty-four, while the remaining more than two hundred feature reproductions of various Austrian measures and quarantine regulations against the plague and epizootics, as well as individual reports of local epidemic outbreaks in Bessarabia and the Danubian principalities.[15]

At the outset of his report Lorinser states that 'the result of my investigations does not correspond with our usual notion about the functionality of the Austrian institutions against the plague'.[16] With respect to the military cordons between the separate quarantine facilities, Lorinser was dubious about the morality of the soldiers. Illegal traffic and clandestine transits of the Danube and the Sava rivers regularly occurred in wintertime, when the ice formed a natural bridge, as Lorinser witnessed himself when he visited the quarantine of Semlin. But illegal border crossings also happened during the warm season close to ship mills and aided by fishermen.[17]

With respect to the quarantine facilities, Lorinser criticized the outdated regulations from the eighteenth century. He also viewed recent suggestions (which at the time were under discussion by an official commission of physicians in Vienna) as too permissive; cotton, in particular, should stay longer than twenty days under quarantine.[18] He concluded:

> Located at the outer most border of a huge empire, in provinces where civilization is hardly halfway accomplished, partly in inhospitable regions, which are distant from the eye of the supreme authorities of the state [...] the quarantine departments appear to be abandoned and isolated; they are only loosely associated with the military authorities, of whom nobody can expect scientific interest and real expertise. [...] In such isolation and due to the low interest, it is not surprising that the quarantines have lagged behind the other medical institutions of the imperial state and that the already long overdue and dead formalism has prevailed over every vital principle.[19]

Lorinser additionally criticized the location and construction of the quarantine buildings along the border. Some of them had not been renovated for three or four decades, and had become ramshackle. Due to lack of room, often twenty to thirty people were confined together, so that if one fell ill from the plague, the others were at great risk of infection and would have to undergo a whole period of quarantine anew. Apart from that, the rooms were fumigated every day in the presence of those quarantined.[20] Lorinser was also critical of the shortage of staff and of the low wages of the officials at the quarantine facilities, something which opened the door for bribery. The physicians at the quarantines, in turn, did not even possess the necessary technical literature on the plague.[21] About the second physician at the quarantine station of Semlin, Franz Xaver Minas, Lorinser wrote: 'Quarantine doctor Dr Minas, formerly in military service, is an intelligent young man who will do his job if he does not neglect himself in the scientific respect and does resist opportunities for bribery. His procedure during the admission of strangers seemed very superficial to me.'[22] This assessment is important, because from 1838 onwards Minas, who had meanwhile become director of the quarantine station in Semlin, would stay in Constantinople for one-and-a-half years as the leading figure in the construction of the Ottoman quarantine system.[23]

Another problem was the uncertainty surrounding the respective state of health on the other side of the border. In the Danube principalities unverified stories about the occurrence of plague were often used by landlords ('Boyars') and princely officials to compel travellers to pay a ransom for not being held in arbitrary quarantine or to prevent the timely arrival of merchants at certain marketplaces. These uncertainties led to inconsistencies in the periods of quarantines. Lorinser quotes the example of an imposed quarantine period of ten days in Panczova, while at the same time in Semlin it lasted twenty days.[24]

Lorinser did not visit the quarantine facilities of Croatia. But even so he felt competent enough to give a verdict on the entire Austrian quarantine system and to warn of the erroneous belief that 'Germany during the last century has been protected from the plague by these facilities, and that they will provide constant and sufficient protection for the future.'[25] They had reduced the danger of contagion, but had not eliminated it totally. Apart from the quarantine system on the Austrian border other reasons 'must have contributed to avert an invasion of this most frightening of all diseases from Central Europe'.[26] And even so, the plague repeatedly made incursions into Austrian territory – the last time in 1828, when several members of a merchant's family had died in the Transylvanian town of Kronstadt/Braşov because the officials at the quarantine station of Tömös had not considered it worthwhile to examine a wardrobe trunk which was in their custody for the twenty days of the quarantine.[27] The only consolation Lorinser could provide was the prospect of the imminent introduction of additional quarantine sites at the border of Serbia, Wallachia and Moldavia with the Ottoman Empire.[28]

From the lower Danube to the Aegean Sea: the entanglement of quarantines with power politics (1830–1857)

Lorinser's second thoughts about the efficiency of the Austrian terrestrial quarantines were trivial compared with the second cholera pandemic, whose first climax in Europe was from 1830–1832. Individual European governments had initially resorted to measures formulated around the existing plague regulations, nearly all of which failed. This failure – easy to read by the huge toll of lives this initial assault of the pandemic took – empowered adversaries of quarantine measures in western and central Europe to point out its futility. But in south-east Europe this sentiment did not pervade. In the same time period, the two Danubian principalities, which after the 1829 Peace of Adrianople had come under Russian influence, actually established a sanitary cordon and quarantine stations along the lower Danube.[29] What is more, in the wake of its recent victory against the Ottoman Empire, Russia had gained almost the whole estuary of the Danube, and one of the most important measures in this respect was the establishment of a Russian quarantine station for ships at the Danube estuary of Sulina in 1836. It seems that the conceived purpose at the heart of this costly project was not so much a sanitary one, but rather related to economic–political considerations. Having also defeated the Ottoman Empire previously in 1829 in a series of similar wars, hawkish elements within the Russian government sought to utilize the institution of quarantines for the realization of two geopolitical aims. First, along the Danube, to help sever as many contacts as possible between the Ottoman Empire and the two Danubian principalities of Moldavia and Wallachia, which had come under Russian influence but whose nominal suzerain still remained the Ottoman Sultan;[30] and second, to inhibit the economic penetration of the lower Danube both by British ships seeking to sail upstream along the river from the Black Sea, as well as vessels from the Habsburg Empire which moved downstream and wanted to pass the estuary in order to reach Black Sea ports. In this respect one has to keep in mind that the 1830s were an important period for the proliferation of the first steamships and thereby also for the intensification of global trade.[31]

Actually, the sanitary cordon on the left bank of the Danube proved to be a stroke of luck, for when a deadly epidemic of plague spread in 1836 from the centre of the Ottoman Empire across Bulgaria to the Danube, it did not cross the river and enter the Danubian principalities, as had been the case several times before the establishment of the quarantines.[32] The epidemic on the right bank of the Danube would last at least until 1840, killing approximately 86,000 people in Ottoman Bulgaria.[33] From February 1836 to June 1840 one can read the dispatches of the Prussian consul in Bucharest, the capital of Wallachia, which continually emphasize the state of good health in both principalities, cast against the progression of the epidemic and the number of its victims beyond the Danube, as communicated to him by the Wallachian quarantine committee.[34]

The epidemic accelerated the already ongoing establishment of quarantines in the principality of Serbia.[35] In 1837, a new Plague Law, the *Pest-Polizey-Ordnung*, was enacted in the Habsburg Empire. It relied on the quarantines of its neighbouring states to the south as a first line of defence and therefore to provide for facilitation of border traffic with respect to the length of quarantine (see the chapter of Jesner in this volume). Around 1838 the Ottoman Empire followed suit after Sultan Mahmud II had overcome the religious resistance of the Ottoman Grand Mufti. The Austrian physician Karl Ludwig Sigmund (1810–1883) would later record that the spatial organization of the quarantine system of the Ottoman Empire differed from that of the other states in one essential aspect: it could not adopt the customary linear shape of a 'chain' ('Kette') which was supposed to isolate unhealthy alien territories from its own healthy country. The Ottoman Empire was in a different situation because the plague at the time was still endemic at various places in its own territory. It had to resort, therefore, to the shape of a 'web' ('Netz') across the entirety of its domains, with the quarantine facilities – both maritime and terrestrial – placed at its nodal intersections.³⁶ This organization atomized the polity, isolated the Ottoman provinces from each other, and had the effect that in times of plague and cholera, the Ottoman Empire's internal traffic was more severely afflicted than the foreign trade of European states with the Levant. With the introduction of its own quarantines, the Ottoman Empire now had to shoulder most of the negative economic and political consequences of local plague and cholera epidemics, while other states had the advantage of reducing their quarantines accordingly. This organization – and its contemporaneous Egyptian equivalent – now ensured that the entire eastern Mediterranean, Asia Minor, the Levant, the Black Sea and the Balkans were protected by an extensive structure of maritime and terrestrial quarantines. Therewith, the conditions demanded by Karl Ignaz Lorinser for the protection of central Europe from the plague were fulfilled. Consequently, more and more voices were heard questioning the role of the Austrian quarantine system as an obsolete and unnecessary obstacle to trade.³⁷

Moreover, the establishment of the Ottoman quarantine system was not entirely autonomous. Western doctors were involved in its construction. The aforementioned Dr Franz Xaver Minas had the chance to be one of the pioneers in this labour, because the Sublime Porte asked the Austrian diplomatic representative in Constantinople to send a doctor specifically from its quarantine station in Semlin, as that installation had the only Austrian doctors who were able to understand Turkish.³⁸ Also representatives of the European states, whose merchant ships had to pay a tax in Ottoman ports for the quarantine, oversaw the system. The Ottoman delegates accounted for the majority of representatives in the International Sanitary Council in Constantinople which was the highest competent body for every aspect of the Ottoman quarantines. In the event of a disagreement, the majority of the Sanitary Council could even overrule the will of the Sultan and his divan.³⁹

The establishment of quarantines and sanitary cordons in southeast Europe, the Ottoman Empire and Egypt entailed another issue, however. The governments of these states soon detected that quarantines could also be employed to strengthen their role in the field of international politics. This was the case, in particular, in the quarantine conflict between Greece and the Ottoman Empire in the 1840s and 1850s.

It must be said that since the Greek War of Independence, three informal parties had dominated the political system in Greece, the so-called French, Russian and English parties, which – as shown by their names – followed the directives of the respective diplomatic representatives of the Great Powers concerned. They were not only competing with each other but also had to deal with the powerful figure of King Otto (1815–1867), who had come from Bavaria and ruled the country from 1832.

In 1846 the Greek government under the leader of the French party, Ioannis Kolletis (1773/74–1847), enacted a new regulation for its quarantines. Thereafter it also decided not to approve the good health of ships and their crews arriving from Ottoman ports if such could not produce bills of health signed by a Greek diplomatic Consul or by a Consul of an allied power. This meant that these ships, their crews and the passengers had to undergo twenty-one days of quarantine. As a result, in early 1847 the Sublime Porte succeeded in persuading the International Sanitary Council in Constantinople to pass a retaliatory measure which subjected to a quarantine of twenty-one days not only Greek ships, but all ships which most recently had called at a Greek port. Within the International Sanitary Council, the Prussian delegate was the only member to protest against this measure, while the other delegates believed in vain that they would be able to negotiate exemptions from this measure for the ships of their states.[40] According to Wilhelm Perponcher-Sedlnitzky (1819–1893), the Prussian chargé d'affaires in Constantinople, one of the authors of this 'misuse of quarantines for reasons other than sanitary ones' ('Mißbrauch … Quarantainen aus anderen als Sanitätsgründen anzuwenden') was the British Foreign Secretary Henry Viscount Palmerston (1784–1865). The latter allegedly wanted to disadvantage Kolletis politically with this countermeasure, which actually used both the Sublime Porte and the International Sanitary Council in Constantinople as proxies for his own purposes.[41] To understand this better, one also has to add that Kolletis had ousted Alexandros Mavrokordatos (1791–1865), a member of the English Party, from government in 1844.

One has to keep in mind that these measures of the Greek and Ottoman governments affected British, Austrian, French and Prussian merchant ships if their captains could not produce the required document. It is ironic that the measures, imposed by the Greek government in particular, did not impact the Turks or other Muslims the most severely, but instead mainly other Greeks, since a considerable portion of the owners, captains and crews of ships under Ionian, Ottoman and Russian flags in the Black Sea and the eastern Mediterranean in that period were in fact Greek.[42]

In mid-1848 these measures remained in force, although Kolletis had died in September 1847. It would take until late 1849, before Antonios Kriezis (1796–1865), a member of the English party, would occupy the post of Greek Prime Minister. Actually, the label of 'English' did not mean that much anymore, as Kriezis proved to be a loyal follower of King Otto, whose policy against the Ottoman Empire was followed by Palmerston like a hawk.[43] As a possible sign of détente, in early 1851 the Greek government temporarily eased the duration of quarantine to twenty-four hours for those ships coming from Ottoman ports that had clean bills in hand.[44]

In reality, the sanitary dangers faced by the Greek population did not emanate from the Ottoman Empire (against whom the Greek King Otto wanted to engage his army on Russia's side when the Crimean War started), but rather came from the European troops (French and British) deployed to Greece in 1854 (which consequently thwarted King Otto's plans). The French troops, which occupied the port of Piraeus, also brought cholera along with them. This epidemic disease had surfaced for the first time on Greek soil in 1848, taking about a hundred lives among the 2,000 inhabitants of the Island of Skiathos. But now, during its second outbreak, it took considerably more, in total approximately 40,000 civilians.[45]

After 1851 the original quarantine regulation of Kolletis seemed to have been reinstated and remained in force during the entirety of the Crimean War, despite the exemption of British and French war vessels from quarantine. Only in March 1857 did the Greek government decree that from then on it would also accept health certificates issued by Ottoman authorities and that ships which had them in hand could avoid quarantine altogether.[46] In late April the International Sanitary Council responded to the Greek suspension of twenty-one days of quarantine for ships arriving from Ottoman ports without a health certificate from a Greek or allied consul and announced that the equivalent Ottoman measure (which to that point had applied to ships arriving in Turkish ports from the Greek Littoral) would henceforth be repealed.[47]

The abolition of these harsh bilateral quarantine measures, which had been applied without any presence of a plague epidemic during their period of validity, seems to have been influenced by the *Zeitgeist*, which, after the end of the Crimean War, had become liberal with respect to trade and economy. With regard to sanitary issues, one can detect the counterpart of this kind of thinking in the temporary victory of the miasma theory over contagionism and quarantines. Consequently, the sanitary cordon along the lower Danube was abolished and the river was opened for international trade. This context also seemed to have softened the attitudes of the Greek and Ottoman political elites with regard to maritime quarantines. One cannot, however, observe similar attitudes when terrestrial quarantine stations were at stake. These had been erected along the Greek–Ottoman border, running at the time between central Greece, on the one side, and Epirus and Thessaly (regions which were still in Ottoman possession) on the other. Up to the 1870s more and more quarantines would be erected on the Greek side along the borderline, thus inhibiting border traffic and even mixed Greek–Ottoman detachments cooperating in the pursuit of bandits and smugglers.[48]

Conclusion

This chapter has shown that the use of quarantines is often combined with the sense of security they are able to instil in the face of a potential danger. This sense of security, however, is only as strong as the degree of trust in the proper functioning of this means of prevention. In this respect, Lorinser's findings were sobering. When he returned home in March 1830, the second cholera pandemic was transgressing the Asiatic–European boundary in Russia. The panic, which had grasped the Prussian authorities in the late summer of 1829 due to the plague in south-east Europe, now had a different instigator. This was the reason why Lorinser's careful and detailed report never received the attention it deserved, but it would motivate him to write an entire work on the bubonic plague.[49]

At least the new sanitary cordon along the lower Danube, that Lorinser had anticipated for sanitary reasons, would be put into place. However, its erection was mainly based on geopolitical considerations, which was also the case with the Russian quarantine in the Sulina estuary of the Danube some years later. The continued use of quarantines for purposes apart from sanitary ones can be seen in the quarantine war between Greece and the Ottoman Empire. It showed that in secondary arenas even representatives of the Great Powers, like the British, used quarantines as a tool for ends other than to combat a concrete epidemic, while in the wake of the liberalization of Mediterranean quarantine since the early 1840s between the main European ports '"tit-for-tat" retaliatory quarantines [...] were beginning to sputter'.[50] The entire conflict between Greece and the Ottoman Empire lasted about a decade before it ceased in 1857, one year after the Peace Treaty of Paris which ended the Crimean War.

In the ensuing period, lasting about a decade, anticontagionism would reach its climax, but would stop dead with the arrival of the fourth cholera pandemic in Europe in 1865, which showed that the actual reasons for the dissolution of universal quarantine had been the retreat of the plague in the Middle East and the introduction of quarantines in the Ottoman Empire. The fourth cholera pandemic did not follow the route of its predecessors via the Russian land mass but was spread by Muslim pilgrims infected by their peers from India in the Islamic holy cities of Mecca and Medina. The experiences of the pandemic shattered the anticontagionist optimism, so the International Sanitary Conference of 1866 in Constantinople and that of 1874 in Vienna officially reinstated quarantines as a suitable means of prevention against cholera.[51] Consequently, several locations on the Red Sea and the eastern Mediterranean, particularly since the opening of the Suez Canal in 1869, came to host new quarantine facilities. All of these had Muslim pilgrims returning to Europe as their focus.[52]

At the time, the plague had not reappeared for three decades in Europe. Consequently, the 'plague front' at the southern border of the Habsburg Empire, which Karl Ignaz Lorinser had visited in the winter of 1829/30, was abolished step-by-step after the Crimean War. The employment of quarantines against cholera, however, was different from their universal application in Lorinser's time. In the long run, updated and distinct forms of monitoring 'suspicious individuals and commodities' would become part and parcel of a novel concept of how to prevent epidemic diseases. According to this, persons of concern had to at least obey social distancing or, in more severe cases, were kept in quarantine. This new concept combined the potential quarantining of persons and goods – adjusted to the actual incubation period of the respective disease by offsetting the duration of a journey from the incriminated point of origin – with measures of disinfection (instead of the traditional ritual of fumigation). This coherent approach was also in harmony with the principles of the emerging germ theory and the first findings in the field of bacteriology. Peter Baldwin called this new concept 'neoquarantinism'; it was otherwise known under its contemporaneous name as the 'revision system'.[53]

Notes

1 See P. Baldwin, *Contagion and the State in Europe, 1830–1930* (Cambridge: Cambridge University Press, 2005); M. Harrison, *Contagion: How Commerce has Spread Disease* (New Haven, CT; London: Yale University Press, 2012), pp. 50–106; J. Chircop and F. J. Martínez (eds), *Mediterranean Quarantines, 1750–1914: Space, Identity and Power* (Manchester; Manchester University Press, 2018); A. Chase-Levenson, *The Yellow Flag: Quarantine and the British Mediterranean World, 1780–1860* (Cambridge: Cambridge University Press, 2020).

2 For recent works, see B. Bulmuş, *Plague, Quarantines and Geopolitics in the Ottoman Empire* (Edinburgh: Edinburgh University Press, 2012); S. Jesner, 'Habsburgische Grenzraumpolitik in der Siebenbürgischen Militärgrenze (1760–1830): Verteidigungs- und Präventionsstrategien' (PhD dissertation, University of Graz, 2013); A. Robarts, *Migration and Disease in the Black Sea Region. Ottoman–Russian Relations in the Late Eighteenth and Early Nineteenth Centuries* (London; New York: Bloomsbury Academic, 2017); C. Promitzer, 'Quarantines and geoepidemiology: the protracted sanitary relationship between the Habsburg and Ottoman empires', in W. Göderle and M. Pfaffenthaler (eds), *Dynamiken der Wissensproduktion: Räume, Zeiten und Akteure im 19. und 20. Jahrhundert* (Bielefeld, transcript, 2018), pp. 23–56.

3 A. Bashford, 'Maritime quarantine: linking Old World and New World histories', in A. Bashford, *Quarantine: Local and Global Histories* (Basingstoke: Palgrave Macmillan, 2016), pp. 1–12, at p. 11.

4 Chase-Levenson, *The Yellow Flag*, pp. 7–8, 18, 124–5; A. Chase-Levenson, 'Early nineteenth-century Mediterranean quarantine as a European system', in Bashford, *Quarantine*, pp. 35–53, at p. 37.

Uses of quarantine in the nineteenth century 95

5 C. Promitzer, 'Stimulating the hidden dispositions of south-eastern Europe: the plague in the Russo–Turkish War of 1828–29 and the introduction of quarantine on the Lower Danube', in T. D. Sechel (ed.), *Medicine Within and Between the Habsburg and Ottoman Empires 18th–19th Centuries* (Bochum: Winkler Verlag, 2011), pp. 79–110.

6 See for example *Wiener Zeitung* (2 September 1829) p. 845; (5 September 1829) p. 857; (10 September 1829) p. 870; (16 September) pp. 890–1; (19 September 1829) p. 903; *Allgemeine Zeitung* [Augsburg] (6 September 1829) p. 997; (8 September 1829) p. 1004; (13 September 1829) p. 1024.

7 Geheimes Staatsarchiv Preußischer Kulturbesitz, Berlin (hereafter GSTA PK) III. HA Ministerium der Auswärtigen Angelegenheiten II, Nr. 19051, file N 5311, report by N. Schuster, Kraków, presented 24 August 1829.

8 GSTA PK I. HA Rep. 76 Kultusministerium VIII A, Nr. 2896, Pest 1827–1836, Quarantaine-Anstalten und Maaßregeln gegen die Pest, reports by Major von Staff, Berlin, 8 and 11 September 1829, report by Major General von Thile, Potsdam, 11 September 1829, III. HA Ministerium der Auswärtigen Angelegenheiten II, Nr. 19051, file N 6988, instruction by the Prussian Ministry of Foreign Affairs, Berlin, 10 November 1829, file N 7240 B, instruction by the Prussian Ministry of Foreign Affairs, Berlin, 7 November 1829 with attachments, file N 7393 B, report by N. Darrest, Kraków, 15 November 1829.

9 *Lemberger Zeitung* (18 September 1829) p. 563.

10 GSTA PK I. HA Rep. 76 Kultusministerium VIII A, Nr. 2896, Votum ad Nr. 785, copy of a statement of the Prussian Minister for Internal Affairs, F. Schuckmann, Berlin, 23 September 1829.

11 A. Hirsch, 'Lorinser, Karl Ignatius', in *Allgemeine Deutsche Biographie*, vol. 19 (Leipzig: Duncker & Humblot, 1884), pp. 197–8.

12 GSTA PK I. HA Rep. 76 Kultusministerium VIII A, Nr. 2896, Votum ad Nr. 3893, statement of J. G. Langermann, Berlin, 23 October 1829; see R. Walsh, *Narrative of a Journey from Constantinople to England* (London: Frederick Westley and A. H. Davis, 1828), pp. 266–88; Langermann apparently knew the shortened translation of that book: Walsh, 'Reise durch die Türkei', *Ethnographisches Archiv*, 38 (1929), 181–436 with the description of the quarantine of Rothenturm at 369–83. See also Chase-Levenson, *The Yellow Flag*, pp. 95–7.

13 GSTA PK I. HA Rep. 76 Kultusministerium VIII A, Nr. 2896, zu Nr. 3893, instruction by the Prussian Ministry for Religious, Educational and Medical Affairs and that for Internal Affairs, Berlin, 31 October 1829. The author of this chapter has translated this from the German original, which will be the case hereafter.

14 C. I. Lorinser, *Eine Selbstbiographie, vollendet und herausgegeben von seinem Sohne Franz Lorinser*, vol. 1 (Regensburg: Georg Joseph Manz, 1864), p. 198.
15 GSTA PK I. HA Rep. 76 Kultusministerium VIII A, Nr. 2903, Reisebericht des Dr Lorinser zu Oppeln.
16 Ibid., fos. 5a–b.
17 Ibid., fol. 15b.
18 Ibid., fol. 21b.
19 Ibid., fol. 19b.
20 Ibid., fos. 22a–b.
21 Ibid., fos. 22b–4b.
22 Ibid., fol. 56b.
23 K. L. Sigmund, *Die Quarantäne-Reform und die Pestfrage: Beobachtungen und Anträge geschrieben nach einer im Auftrage der k. k. österreichischen Staatsverwaltung unternommenen Bereisung der Donauländer, des Orients und Egyptens* (Vienna: Braumüller, 1850), p. 32; L. Rigler, *Die Türkei und deren Bewohner in ihren naturhistorischen, physiologischen und pathologischen Verhältnissen vom Standpunkte Constantinopel's geschildert*, vol. 1 (Vienna: Carl Gerold, 1852), pp. 407–8.
24 GSTA PK I. HA Rep. 76 Kultusministerium VIII A, Nr. 2903, Reisebericht des Dr Lorinser zu Oppeln., fos. 19a–21a.
25 Ibid., fol. 61a.
26 Ibid.
27 Ibid., fol. 62b.
28 Ibid., fos. 63a–4a
29 See G. Bratescu, 'Seuchenschutz und Staatsinteresse im Donauraum (1750-1850)', *Sudhoffs Archiv: Zeitschrift für Wissenschaftsgeschichte*, 63 (1979), 25–44; S. G. Focas, *The Lower Danube River in the Southeastern European Political and Economic Complex from Antiquity to the Conference of Belgrade of 1948* (New York: Columbia University Press, 1987), pp. 105, 132–5; C. Ardeleanu, *International Trade and Diplomacy at the Lower Danube: The Sulina Questions and the Economic Premises of the Crimean War (1829–1853)* (Brăila: Muzeul Brăilei, Editura Istros, 2014), pp. 67–73.
30 The Russian author Viktor Taki does not deny such an interpretation of the establishment of the quarantines along the Danube, but in view of earlier plague epidemics in the region his focus is more on the 'civilizing mission' of the Russian custodians of Wallachia and Moldavia by way of a German-style 'medical police'. See V. Taki, 'Between Polizeistaat and cordon sanitaire: epidemics and police reform during the Russian occupation of Moldavia and Wallachia 1828–1834', *Ab Imperio*, 9:4 (2008), 75–112.

31 See M. Sauer, 'Österreich und die Sulina-Frage 1829–1854. Erster Teil', *Mitteilungen des Österreichischen Staatsarchivs*, 40 (1987), 185–236; M. Sauer, 'Österreich und die Sulina-Frage 1829–1854. Zweiter Teil', *Mitteilungen des Österreichischen Staatsarchivs*, 41 (1990), 72–137; B. V. Zmerzliy, 'Privatni karantini v institute karantinoy sluzhbi rosiyskoy imperiy v XIX st., na prikladi sulinskogo karantinu', *Chasopis Kiyvskogo universitetu prava*, 2 (2012), 10–14; Ardeleanu, *International Trade and Diplomacy*, pp. 10–12, 133–252; A. Emilciuc, 'The trade of Galaţi and Brăila in the reports of Russian officials from Sulina Quarantine Station (1836–1853)' in C. Ardeleanu and A. Lyberatos (eds), *Port Cities of the Western Black Sea Coast and the Danube: Economic and Social Development in the Long 19th Century* (Corfu: Black Sea, 2016), pp. 63–93, https://books.blacksea.gr/en/15/.

32 See Ardeleanu, *International Trade and Diplomacy*, p. 69.

33 On the number of fatalities see A. Boué, *La Turquie d'Europe*, T. 3 (Paris: Bertrand, 1840), p. 567; 'Conférence sanitaire internationale. No 9. Seance du 18 Septembre 1851', in Procès-verbaux de la Conférence sanitaire internationale ouverte à Paris le 27 juillet 1851 (Paris: Impr. Nationale, 1852), at 7.

34 See the earliest report in GSTA PK III. HA Ministerium der Auswärtigen Angelegenheiten II, Nr. 19053, file N 1545 B, report by Sakellario, Bucharest, 6 February 1837. The last report before the end of the epidemic was GSTA PK III. HA Ministerium der Auswärtigen Angelegenheiten II, Nr. 19055, file N 5839 B, report by Sakellario, Bucharest, 13 July 1840. It is not clear if the dates are using the Julian or Gregorian calendars.

35 I. Duraković, *Serbien und das Modernisierungsproblem: Die Entwicklung der Gesundheitspoliitik und sozialen Kontrolle bis zum Ersten Weltkrieg* (Frankfurt am Main: Peter Land, 2014), pp. 57–8, 172, 178–81; N. Plavšić, 'Porečki kontumac (karantin) i izveštaj o epidemijama iz protokola magistrata nahije Porečke (1828–1832)', *Razvitak: Časopis za društvena pitanja*, 44:217–18 (2004), 103–5.

36 Sigmund, *Die Quarantäne-Reform und die Pestfrage*, p. vii.

37 See Sigmund, *Die Quarantäne-Reform und die Pestfrage*; F. Gobbi, *Beiträge zur Entwicklung und Reform des Quarantainewesens. Nach eigener Anschauung* (Vienna: kaiserlich-königliche Hof- und Staatsdruckerei, 1849).

38 M. Chahrour, '"A civilizing mission"? Austrian medicine and the reform of medical structures in the Ottoman Empire, 1838–1850', *Studies in History and Philosophy of Biological and Biomedical Sciences*, 38:4 (2007), 687–705, at 690; Chase-Levenson, *The Yellow Flag*, p. 250.

39 D. Panzac, 'Tanzimat et santé publique: les débuts du Conseil sanitaire de l'Empire ottoman', in D. Panzac, *Population et santé dans l'Empire Ottoman (xviiie-xxe siècles)* (Istanbul: Isis, 1996), pp. 77–85; S. Chiffoleau, *Genèse de la santé publique internationale: de la peste d'Orient à l'OMS* (Beirut; Rennes: Institut français du Proche-Orient, Presses universitaires de Rennes, 2012), pp. 30–1, 35; A. Robarts, *Migration and Disease in the Black Sea Region* (London; New York: Bloomsbury, 2017), pp. 117–38.

40 GSTA PK III. HA Ministerium der Auswärtigen Angelegenheiten II, Nr. 19058, file II 54, report by W. Perponcher-Sedlnitzky, Pera, 31 May 1848; on the new Greek regulation for quarantines see GSTA PK III. HA Ministerium der Auswärtigen Angelegenheiten II, Nr. 19057, files N 7814 B, N9593 B, N 40006 B.

41 GSTA PK III. HA Ministerium der Auswärtigen Angelegenheiten II, Nr. 19058, file II 95, report by W. Perponcher-Sedlnitzky, Pera, 14 June 1848.

42 G. Harlaftis, *A History of Greek-Owned Shipping: The Making of an International Tramp Fleet, 1830 to the Present Day* (London: Routledge, 1996), p. 30

43 E. V. Nomikos, 'The International Position of Greece during the Crimean War' (PhD dissertation, Stanford University, 1962), p. 108.

44 GSTA PK III. HA Ministerium der Auswärtigen Angelegenheiten II, Nr. 19059, file N 4047, report by L. Wildenbruch, Athens, 10 March 1851.

45 M. M. Ruisinger, *Das griechische Gesundheitswesen unter König Otto (1833–1862)* (Frankfurt am Main: Peter Lang, 1997), pp. 222–30. The figure of 40,000 fatalities is suggested by C. Ponting, *The Crimean War: The Truth Behind the Myth* (London: Chatto & Windus, 2004), p. 61.

46 GSTA PK III. HA Ministerium der Auswärtigen Angelegenheiten II, Nr. 19060, file II 5445, report by ambassador R. Goltz, Athens, 13 March 1857.

47 Ibid., file II 8737, report by Ambassador L. Wildenbruch, Constantinople, 29 April 1857.

48 G. Gavrilis, 'The Greek–Ottoman boundary as institution, locality, and process, 1832–1882', *American Behavioral Scientist*, 51:10 (2008), 1516–37, at 1531.

49 K. I. Lorinser, *Die Pest des Orients, wie sie entsteht und verhütet wird* (Berlin: Enslin, 1837).

50 Chase-Levenson, *The Yellow Flag*, p. 258.

51 A. Drasche, 'Über Cholera-Quarantaine', *Deutsche Zeitung*, 640 (11 October 1873), 1–4; L. Oser, 'Über Quarantaine bei Cholera', *Medizinische Jahrbücher* [Vienna] (1873), pp. 476–95; K. L. Sigmund, 'Die Cholera- und die Quarantänefrage vor den internationalen

Sanitätsconferenzen,' *Deutsche Vierteljahrsschrift für öffentliche Gesundheitspflege*, 8:2 (1876), 230–48.
52 V. Huber, 'The pilgrimage to Mecca and international health regulations', in E. Tagliacozzo and S. M. Toorawa (eds), *The Hajj: Pilgrimage in Islam* (Cambridge: Cambridge University Press, 2016), pp. 175–95; Harrison, *Contagion*, pp. 139–73.
53 See Baldwin, *Contagion and the State*, pp. 141–67.

4

Weak state-controlled disease prevention in peripheral border regions: Austrian Bukovina and Dalmatia in the late nineteenth century

Carlos Watzka

Theoretical perspective, central assumptions and empirical–spatial focus

The following contribution does not primarily address health-related measures employed immediately during border transit, but entails a broad range of medical, hygienic and administrative techniques which were developed by state bureaucracies to minimise the risk of disease proliferation through the traffic of persons and goods across borders of nineteenth-century European empires. These activities are of interest from a border studies perspective as well[1] and were associated with the term 'revision system' which in the current scholarly debate on the history of epidemic prevention is considered an element of 'neoquarantanism'. This expression was introduced, along with a specific geoepidemiological perspective, by Peter Baldwin.[2] His groundbreaking study *Contagion and the State in Europe* focuses on epidemic prevention policies in Great Britain, France, Germany and Sweden. The 'sanitary revision system' for the prevention of plague proliferation emerged as a sort of compromise between the isolationist approach advocated by the continental 'contagionist' school – focusing on the avoidance of infection and public safety in the interior, as embodied in the traditional 'quarantine' – and the progressive, liberal and trade-oriented view of the 'sanitationists', centred in Britain. Although negotiated from the 1860s until the 1890s at the International Sanitary Conferences by all major European powers (and the USA), and finally set in binding international law, the actual implementation of the sanitation revision system of disease control varied considerably from state to state.[3] Moreover, in most instances, its shape varied even within states from region to region. This was particularly the case for the contemporary Great Powers, as they comprised vast territories, heterogeneous in their general socio-economic[4] as well as geoepidemiological conditions.

Opinions on the somewhat conflicting goals of economic prosperity and protection from imported plagues varied significantly within such large states. In particular there were widely differing possibilities and necessities for epidemic prevention within the economically advanced, already industrialised and densely inhabited centres of European 'civilisation' on the one hand, and the more remote, economically 'backward' and rural regions at the margins of the flows that constituted wealth and power, on the other hand, the so-called 'inner peripheries' of Europe.

These differences do not strictly coincide but do highly correlate with the spatial-structural and political differentiations between 'core lands' and 'border provinces' within individual nations or empires. In so doing, they also relate to the quite different meanings of border-crossing processes, whether viewed from a metropolitan or a border region perspective. The term 'border regions', in this contribution, is used in a rather simple manner, and indicates those administrative subdivisions of each 'sovereign state' geographically adjacent to the pertinent country's 'national borders' vis-à-vis those of another sovereign state.[5]

In this manner 'centre–periphery relations', as framed by Immanuel Wallerstein et al. in the 'world-system-analysis' approach, can provide a useful framework for investigating the practices of epidemic prevention in border regions as they occurred within the specific context of diverging interests between the central state's authority over health policy on the one hand, and the manifold regional and local political strategies on the other. World-system-analysis, relying on a broad base of empirical research on the capitalist 'world system', supposes: 1) There are economic processes (in production and in trade) which for various reasons (ecological, technical, logistical etc.) are more apt to be commandeered by oligarchs than other processes and thus prove themselves particularly profitable. 2) Over time such processes tend to concentrate in distinct geographical areas providing local populations, and particularly their upper classes, with comparatively greater wealth. 3) These economic advantages are often converted into political and military advantages which further increase the gap in overall social power and in the potential of organised action between the 'leading' areas – the 'centre' or 'core'– and the rest, the 'semi-peripheral' and 'peripheral' social and spatial sections of the whole system. 4) Far from representing a 'free market', such political–economic system processes are key mechanisms of capitalism, as described by Marx, that equate with concentrative tendencies in accord with an 'economics of scale', an institutionally inherent quest for maximisation of profit, and a tendency to continually appropriate new social and spatial areas into this system.[6] Relations between centres and peripheries therefore can be viewed as 'exploitive', based upon unequal means of power. Yet, this does not imply omnipotence in the case of the former, and powerlessness in the case of the latter. Instead the relatedness pertains to mutual, but not equal dependency, characterised by continuous power struggles and tensions. They do not at all confine themselves to 'purely economic' matters but heavily influence cultural and ideological standpoints and leave their mark on all fields of policy.

Continuing, one can suppose that considerable tensions arise in the field of applied epidemic prevention policies as well, if one scrutinises the interactions between central state health bureaucracies – as agents of the centre's interests – and local self-governing bodies, health officers and other professionals.[7] A distinctive feature of centre–periphery relations is the lower living conditions within the periphery in general, and an accompanying deficiency in general health care. Seen as a consequence of the unequal distribution of wealth, this is generally well in line with the interests of the centre's privileged population. Nevertheless, epidemic prevention presents, to some degree, an exception to this pattern. Effective epidemic prevention on a large scale – even if it grew more feasible with the expansion of biological-medical, technical and administrative skills during the 'hygienic revolution' of the nineteenth century[8] – proved quite costly for most of the dangerous epidemics. Therefore, as the poor could contribute little or no money to fund related health protection measures, expenses had to be covered primarily by the comparatively wealthy, the middle and upper classes, concentrated in the urban centres. Refusing to do so would not only put the health and well-being of the poor at risk – who, of course, represented the majority of the inhabitants in border regions – but also meant a serious menace to the 'worthier' members of the upper classes, some of them inevitably being directly 'exposed' as functionaries operating in those peripheral areas. In the end, the ruling elites and their families, living pleasantly in the cities of the core land and their surroundings, could themselves be threatened by an all too laissez-faire approach to epidemic prevention. This constellation of conflicting aims for the upper class highlights a particular feature of modern epidemic prevention policies, conditioned by the biological nature of infectious diseases, which became increasingly familiar to late-nineteenth-century contemporaries. Proposals and actions intended to solve this problem varied, and were heavily dependent on the cultural context, generating very different approaches towards actual epidemic prevention. Another feature, which obviously contributed greatly to the differences in attitude on public epidemic prevention, rests in the peculiarities of public finance. Similar to other policy issues, central and regional governments regularly allocated sums of money over periods of several years, and in advance. The relevant budgets often left little space for the subordinate administration to meet demands that could vary considerably in time. Regional levels of administration tended to view quickly arising problems as the preserve of the central state's sphere of responsibility. In this, they were often as tenacious as their counterparts in assigning financial burdens, not entirely bound by them, to even lower levels, following an approach of 'subsidiarity', which they practised little in material matters. Moreover, poorer areas had more incentive than richer ones for 'obstructive' behaviour regarding the introduction of new, costly sanitary procedures. Cultural differences, based on past experiences concerning the extent of effective human agency in view of plagues, reinforced internal discrepancies.

These constellations will be examined now by investigating two peripheral border regions of the late nineteenth century Austro–Hungarian Empire, Bukovina and Dalmatia, as related to the actual epidemic prevention measures applied there within the framework of neoquarantanist central state health politics.[9] A primary facet will be to show the particular difficulties the Viennese central authorities encountered when attempting to control infection-relevant behaviour of subjects in such remote border regions. Distance

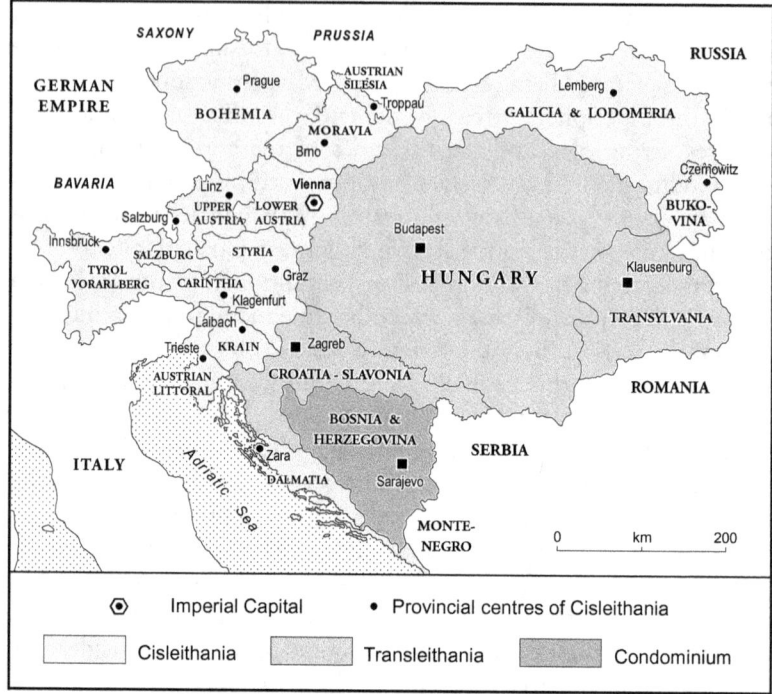

Figure 4.1 The border regions of Bukovina and Dalmatia within the Austro–Hungarian Empire[12]

from central regions, in this context, proved to be a factor not only in slowing economic progress, but also in increasing informational, logistical and therefore financial demands on the centre in exerting somewhat efficient control of local processes, whatever their nature.[10] The two border regions of Dalmatia and Bukovina represent the southernmost and easternmost extremes of what was called 'Cisleithania'. After the Settlement of 1867, the Austrian half of the Austro–Hungarian monarchy, ruled from Vienna, was referred to in this way, while the other 'Transleithanian' part was ruled from Budapest. For nearly all political issues (military and foreign policy excluded), the two 'halves' of the Empire formed autonomous states with separate institutions,[11] even though they refrained from re-establishing permanent inner border barriers, as customs or regular sanitation controls.

Regional and local epidemic prevention in Bukovina and Dalmatia

In the following, first an overview will be given on the topographical, economic, political and legal–administrative conditions and frameworks for epidemic prevention in Bukovina and Dalmatia within the late-nineteenth-century Austro–Hungarian Empire. Afterwards the issue of actual plague proliferation prevention measures is addressed. The text focuses on two major infectious diseases which concerned state authorities and medical professionals around 1900: cholera and smallpox. The argument is based mainly on the evaluation of primary sources[13] – articles from contemporary official journals and bulletins[14] as well as the ample stock of pertinent records at the Austrian National Archive in Vienna.[15]

Traffic between the Austrian core lands and both Bukovina and Dalmatia was particularly laborious and lengthy. Around 1900, rail travel to Czernowitz/Chernivtsi, the Bukovinan capital, from Vienna required eighteen hours. To Zara/Zadar, the seat of the Dalmatian vice-regency, although less distant, travel by the fastest means available took even longer, about twenty hours, because there was no railway connection through Croatia and Slavonia southwards.[16] These mountainous regions were sparsely populated and, moreover, Hungarian-administrated. Therefore, the fastest connection was via the port of Trieste and the Adriatic Sea, using steamboats. Both Bukovina and Dalmatia were somewhat removed from major trade routes and of minor importance for trans-regional commerce. Dalmatia was probably even more affected by being situated in a 'dead end' of international traffic flows.

Income per capita in both regions around 1900 was only about half of the Cisleithanian average, and for Dalmatia, again, considerably lower than for Bukovina. Levels of education were equally low, with about 80 per cent of the population in both territories illiterate, compared with just 6 per cent in Lower Austria or Bohemia. The two regions were also sparsely populated, counting around 730,000 inhabitants in Bukovina and barely 600,000 for Dalmatia, according to the 1900 census. University-trained physicians were in shortest supply there, excluding Galicia, compared with all other regions of Cisleithania.[17] The comparatively poor living standards of the general population in both Bukovina and Dalmatia also resulted in structural similarities with regard to the issue of the prevention and control of epidemics. One has to bear in mind that since the 1860s Austrian health policy had generally relied heavily on the idea of decentralisation, leaving most organisational work as well as financing to the prerogative of individual crown lands and/or the communities.[18]

In the late nineteenth century, the 'war' on epidemics had to some extent already reached the level of international law, particularly as far as plague and cholera were concerned. The possibilities and limitations for sovereign states to control 'international' cross-border traffic were a key issue in these regulations. They provided the state administrations with certain generally recognised faculties to restrict the international traffic of persons and goods, but also forbade some instruments hitherto in practice. The old-style, general land quarantines had already faded away during the 1870s and 1880s, and were officially banned by the Dresden International Sanitary Convention of 1893, which was signed by all major European states, the Austro–Hungarian Empire included.[19] This meant a profound change in the general framework of epidemic prevention, particularly for its eastern and southern borderlands, where the famous 'sanitary cordon' against the Ottoman Empire had existed for centuries.[20]

For some spheres of cross-border traffic, more or less neglected by the Convention of 1893, other binding contracts were drawn up by groups of nations separately. For river traffic on the Danube in particular this had already occurred much earlier. After prior, less comprehensive, treaties, in 1857 the 'Donauschiffahrts-Acte' was agreed to in Vienna by the representatives of all states bordering this river.[21] Thus, for one of the most important inner-European waterways, internationally agreed free navigation was already in force around 1860 and soon it was the impetus for further developments in the areas of international sea law as well as in actual trade flow. Black Sea trade, particularly, was stimulated. Consequently in 1870, a treaty was signed between the governments of Romania, Russia and Austria–Hungary concerning the regulation of navigation on the River Prut, this time directly affecting Bukovina, too. It was apparently inspired by liberal political–economical thought. Although the text mentions possible 'quarantines' in the event of plague danger, it narrowly limits the measures which could be imposed.[22]

Another regulation of particular importance was the bilateral treaty between the Habsburg monarchy and Russia from 1896 regarding 'the application of sanitary provisions on the traffic in the border regions during times of cholera'.[23] It defined a 'border zone' on both sides of the border for the purpose of intensified mutual information exchange and reaction possibilities with regard to local cholera events. Each party was allowed to close parts of the border in the event of an epidemic outbreak, and to facilitate efficient sanitation reviews at some main crossing points, which were to remain open, and through which traffic would then be concentrated. Moreover, this neoquarantinist regulation differentiated between 'normal' foreigners, for whom collective border-crossing prohibitions were declared inapplicable even in the case of a cholera epidemic, and other classes of persons, for whom the prohibitions were allowed, such as 'vagabonds, emigrants, beggars and pilgrims'.[24] Obviously, the authorities associated more significant sanitation dangers with these kinds of people, who often stemmed from the poorest strata of society.

Within this framework of early, internationally established sanitation law, many additional regulations were made at the central state level. Above all, in contrast to the interstate treaties, Austrian state law dealt with many more different infectious diseases, which were made subject to a notification duty primarily for all officials and physicians, but in the end for the entire population. An official list of 'notifiable diseases' in 1888 included 'cholera, smallpox, typhus and typhoid, dysentery, diphtheria, scarlet, and puerperal fever', and this list was even expanded significantly in 1892.[25]

During the last two decades of the nineteenth century, several decrees by the Austrian Ministry of the Interior displayed a clear intent to quicken the reporting system established between the various levels of administration. Clearly, this was intended to facilitate swift and timely decisions on preventive measures imposed by the central authorities, even when remote regions were concerned. Above all, on the occasion of the European cholera epidemics of 1892, a decree was issued demanding immediate dispatching of *telegraphic* notification to the regional authorities and the Ministry of the Interior simultaneously for each incidence of the disease if it had been confirmed by a physician.[26]

The core practical measures to be taken against the spread of the illness, as advised by the new neoquarantinist approach, were, as in other countries, a medical examination, isolation of the infected person and precise disinfection procedures. Particular attention was paid by the authorities to the ability to eliminate any disease from all major means of mass transportation, trains and ships. Corresponding decrees were issued in 1886 for each of the Austrian crown lands.[27]

Relating to the peculiarities of naval traffic, important state regulations were laid down by Imperial Law in 1871, when the 'Hafen- und Seesanitätsdienst' ('port and sea sanitation service') was reorganised by the Austrian Ministry of Commerce.[28] This law related to sea and coastal traffic (but not inland waterways) and therefore applied only to the Austrian territories adjacent to the Mediterranean, but not to the coastline of the Hungarian-ruled part of Croatia. According to this, a particular sea authority ('k.k. Seebehörde') was established at Trieste which became directly responsible to the Viennese central government. For the organising of epidemic prevention in Dalmatia, this sea sanitation service was of utmost importance in the late nineteenth century. By that time, neighbouring Bosnia had already become a de facto part of the Austro–Hungarian monarchy, leaving a small area at the southernmost edge of the country adjacent to Montenegro, the only direct 'international' land border. Moreover, sea traffic – mainly coastal and short-range navigation – played a major role in the flow of persons and goods to and from the Dalmatian region. Due to its many islands and mountainous topography this even came to include its *internal* traffic.[29]

The Trieste sea authority and its sub-authorities were responsible for decisions regarding departing and incoming ships and their sanitation treatment according to the norms set by the Austrian central government. In this regard, long-distance naval traffic to 'foreign' countries, the most important for sanitation issues, was limited largely to only a few major ports, which were equipped with specialised staff to perform the task of sanitation reviews. For this purpose, the relevant district physician was attached to the 'Hafenkapitanat' ('harbour master's office'). For Dalmatia in the late nineteenth century, four such sanitation review centres existed, in Zara/Zadar, Spalato/Split, Ragusa/Dubrovnik and Megline/Meljine (today Montenegro). The latter was not overseen by a district physician, but had a medical doctor attached to the sea lazaretto there. This institution, situated at the very southern edge of the province, was the only regular and major sea lazaretto in Dalmatia during the second half of the nineteenth century. It was responsible chiefly for isolation procedures for all incoming persons and goods, if their provenance was found 'suspect' or 'impure' at the official sanitation inspection.[30] Of course, this caused many delays and additional costs for the parties involved, making it subject to repeated criticism. Sometimes arriving travellers, even if judged 'suspect' or 'infected', were admitted to other isolation localities by local authorities. This was particularly the case for (cholera) lazarettos, which had been established in the cities of Zara, Split, Ragusa and Sinj. A further one was in operation at the land border with Bosnia at Mrcine.[31] In contrast to this, Bukovina's sanitation review stations were all situated along land borders. According to a report sent from the regional government to Vienna in 1885, such institutions were located at the border railway stations of Nowosielitza/Novoselytsia (to Russia) and Itzkany/Iţcani (to Romania), and at the road customs stations of Zurin/Zuren, Unter Sinoutz/Nyzhni Synivtsi, Suczawa/Suceava, Kornoluncze/Cornu Luncii, and Gura Negri, all towards Romania.[32]

As already mentioned, health care within the Austrian Empire was in general made an obligation for the regions and communities from at least 1870 onwards. Although the central state authorities ordered epidemic prevention measures, only a small share of the financial burden so incurred was shouldered by them. In 1890, for instance, the total sum of expenses directly made or reimbursed to lower administration levels by the Ministry of Interior with the particular aim of epidemic prevention, according to the Cisleithanian budgetary statistics, was hardly 300,000 crowns (K). This represented only 1.4 per cent of the Ministry's annual budget. Considering that the population was more than 25,000,000 subjects, this sum corresponded to about a hundredth of a crown per person per year, which in today's purchase power roughly equals 0.1 € annually – a negligible sum.[33] This disjointed structure saw orders being issued from the central state, and the financing, largely left to the regional and local administrations, did not contribute much to an accurate implementation of the Ministry's directives, particularly in cases when an immediate health risk was not perceived as present by the local authorities. This problem was sometimes even acknowledged by the central authorities. During the 1892 cholera panic, for instance, a ministerial decree ordered regional authorities in Galicia to purchase sufficient amounts of disinfectant for community usage, explicitly suggesting a mistrust of the ability and volition of the municipal authorities to take care of these matters on their own. Bukovina fared somewhat better, as the regional self-government had already taken this step autonomously, obviously because of a lack of confidence in the municipal communities' agency.[34]

Particular problems of non-compliance were visible for the so-called 'emergency hospitals', a key element in the planning of the Austrian central health administration during the early 1890s for the prevention of cross-border as well as further internal plague proliferation. The term 'Nothspitäler' referred to small buildings usable as 'isolation facilities' for individuals acutely infected by cholera or other particularly contagious diseases. The sites were slated to be equipped with all means of disinfectants and remedies for persons declared infected. According to the Viennese central authorities, such 'emergency hospitals' were to serve as a core instrument of epidemic prevention everywhere, but particularly in proximity to the Empire's borders. At the introduction of the concept, officials imagined such localities in every community across the Austrian Empire, but at the community's expense. Soon it turned out that this plan was unworkable in many rural areas. A decree in 1893 then explicitly encouraged the common erection of such edifices by several small communities jointly, a task which they would not have been able to fulfil on their own.[35] Nonetheless, in many rural communities they were either not built at all or constructed so poorly that their utilisation became impossible after only a few years, which was something the Viennese sanitation department had to concede.[36]

The establishment of a network of steam disinfecting machines at the most important traffic centres was more successful. This had to do primarily with major cities and border-crossing stations, but also with major railway stations in the interior of the Habsburg Empire. The Ministry of the Interior paid significant attention to this during the early 1890s. Yet, problematic gaps remained, not so much at the prioritised border control stations, but in the hinterland. In 1894, for instance, the central government felt urged to intervene through the vice-regency of Dalmatia to assure the acquisition of such steam apparatus for the largest Dalmatian city, Split. Regional authorities simply had not yet finalised this costly, required purchase. Poor provinces like Bukovina and Dalmatia showed particular lethargy in the acquisition of such devices. While in Lower Austria – the core land of the Empire, including the capital of Vienna – 233 steam disinfection devices had been installed by 1893, Bukovina and Dalmatia each possessed only ten such machines.[37] Although admittedly the population of Lower Austria was four times higher than in Bukovina, this disparity speaks for itself.

Regarding the empire-wide legal and administrative framework of regional epidemic prevention in the late nineteenth century, it has to be pointed out that limiting travel constraints and invoking particular surveillance procedures in the case of serious epidemics were not only scheduled for the external borders of the Habsburg Empire or of Cisleithania, but sometimes internally as well. During the large cholera epidemics, which reached Austria from 1893 onwards, a general 'sanitation supervision' of five days was ordered in July 1894 for all persons crossing from Galicia to Austrian Silesia. This order seriously restricted the only traffic route that led directly from the eastern provinces to the Austrian core lands.[38]

Although health policy was in no way as effective as planned by the central authorities, there was a substantial decline in mortality due to infectious diseases during this period. Apart from other causes, this certainly was also an effect of meliorated hygienic conditions in general and more effective prevention measures against particular diseases. A look into mortality statistics seems appropriate in this context.[39] Cholera cost the lives of more than 165,000 Austrian subjects during the major outbreak of 1866, and about 107,000 during its next appearance in 1873. In contrast with this, the death toll during the subsequent large cholera plagues in 1893 and 1894 – the last in Austria before World War I – was about 10,000. Even if considerable numeric inaccuracies are taken into account, a significant decline is evident. The two regions focused on in this chapter were hit only marginally by cholera; Dalmatia was nearly totally spared in 1873 and in 1893/94. Bukovina in 1873 suffered from a death rate of only a third compared with the Cisleithanian average. Yet, in 1894, registered deaths attributed to cholera in Bukovina were twice as high as the imperial average. On the other hand, in 1886 there was a local cholera epidemic, carried in from Italy, which affected only the Austrian coastland, but not the rest of the Empire. The total number of deaths was comparatively low, and in

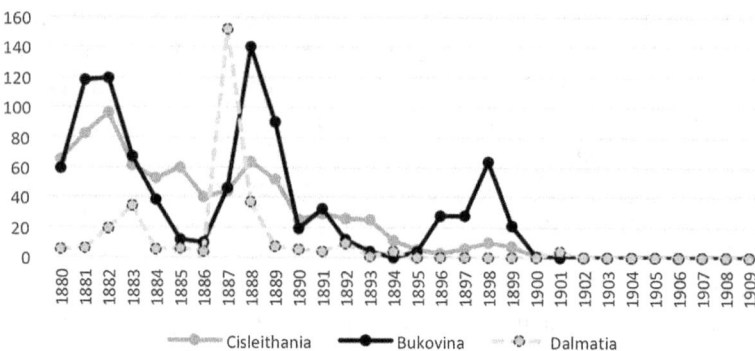

Figure 4.2 Annual smallpox death rates (per 100,000 inhabitants) in the whole of Cisleithania, Bukovina and Dalmatia, 1880–1909

Dalmatia (74) as well. With its irregular appearance, cholera was not a very typical lethal infectious disease. Others, like typhoid, diphtheria, pertussis, measles and scarlet fever, were more or less ever-present within the Habsburg monarchy around 1900, causing tens of thousands of premature deaths per year. Particular successes were made in the late nineteenth century in the rollback of smallpox due to a specific and effective preventative measure at the micro-level: vaccination. A closer look at this seems appropriate. Brought to central Europe in the early nineteenth century, methods of immunisation were improved and proliferated particularly during the second half of the century. The decline in the number of registered smallpox deaths in Austria was dramatic (see the graph in Figure 4.2).

The annual death toll fell from around 14,000 on average for all of Cisleithania in the 1880s to around 3,500 during the 1890s, and finally to less than a hundred during the first decade of the twentieth century. In the case of smallpox, the mortality rate in Bukovina – at least the officially registered one – for most years was similar to the overall average of the Austrian crown lands. It sank annually from an average of seventy in the 1880s to about twenty in the 1890s and then to 0.1 for 1900–1909; for all of Cisleithania the corresponding decline was from sixty-two to fifteen and finally 0.3 deaths per 100,000 inhabitants a year. As one can see, the decline was somewhat slower in Bukovina during the 1890s, but the nearly total extinction of variola was achieved at the same time during the first decade of the twentieth century. Dalmatia in turn was not so heavily hit even during the 1880s, and a reduction to nearly zero registered deaths was archived during the 1890s.[40]

Even if some inaccuracy in the contemporary statistics is factored in, the overall trend of a sharp decline in cases of lethal infection is unquestionable. Nonetheless, the application of epidemic prevention methods, conceptualised by modern medicine and organised by the central state authorities was in no way a simple realisation of top-down directives. Problems for careers of sanitation police affected their abilities in 'backward' regions more than anywhere else. Particular difficulties for Bukovina in 1890 were summarised within the official *Das Österreichische Sanitätswesen* periodical thus:

> Bukovina takes the last place amongst the Austrian crown lands with respect to the distribution of physicians and therefore also with regard to access to medical assistance. The low-level cultural conditions and the shortage of possibilities to make a living [for doctors] in the countryside [...] are regarded as the main causes for this lack of medical practitioners.[41]

The lack of professionally trained medical experts especially in rural areas was a consequence not least because of the massive decentralisation of the Austrian health supply system. Communities were supposed to appoint physicians, at their own expense, responsible for public health issues. This more or less traditional state of affairs was fixed by the *Reichssanitätsgesetz* of 1870. Interference by regional authorities – in particular, contributions to health-care costs for poorer areas from the common regional budgets – was neither prohibited nor demanded explicitly. Arrangements on this issue were left to the regional political processes.

The relevant negotiations in some cases, such as for Bukovina, lasted for about two decades.[42] Even after this, community physicians for small, poor settlements only began to arrive once provincial subsidies for their salaries began. Many small communities still had to form 'sanitation districts' together with some adjacent communities to take on the financial burden of paying a community physician at all, even with some regional subsidies. Planned salaries for such community physicians were not exorbitant at all; a published table from 1895 states sums of 1,000 to 1,200 K as annual wages for most posts.⁴³ This was only about twice or three times the current average wage in Cisleithania.⁴⁴ As a result, 'for some posts it was not possible to find any applicants even with repeated advertisements'. This situation continued until at least 1897.⁴⁵ It has to be added that one community physician would be responsible for the health of nearly 20,000 residents on average. This illustrates the dire situation whereby some of these posts could not be filled at all for years, even up to 1900.

In Dalmatia, a relevant law on community sanitation services was issued much earlier, in 1874.⁴⁶ Nonetheless, problems in the practical hiring of community physicians were considerable and often unresolved up to the 1890s. The regional authority had only partially succeeded in increasing the number of active physicians. When factoring in population increase, in fact a decrease took place, as a sanitation officer at the imperial royal vice-regency in Zara pointed out in a rather critical article in 1892.⁴⁷ But a real improvement had occurred at least in the spatial distribution of doctors through instituting the position of sanitation district physicians. Still, from eighty-four communities established in 1891, only thirty-five actually had such a publicly paid medical professional. Some communities did their best to avoid incurring such expenses.

The spread of cholera in Dalmatia in 1886 serves as an example of the massive difficulties in the actual application of planned sanitation measures. The small and particularly remote town of Metković, situated near to the border with Bosnia, was struck severely. The community, comprising only about 1,500 inhabitants at that time, had experienced a debilitating cholera epidemic in 1855. In 1886, thirty-six people succumbed to the disease there. Regardless of this, the local population did not collaborate with the external medical professionals at all. There was 'a lack of any active participation by the community administration and the population, which did not pay any attention to the advice of the physicians, and could be persuaded neither to isolate the diseased nor to conduct disinfection'.⁴⁸

Preventive measures were then undertaken by force, against the will of the residents. They consisted in the disinfection of all rooms where infected individuals were being or had been treated, in the 'cleaning' of all public localities, the forced isolation of the sick, supervised by guards, the disinfection of all people visiting patients, including physicians and priests, the careful removal of waste and excrement, and, finally, the erection of a cholera hospital and a separate graveyard to bury the victims of the disease. With penalties for offenders, the 'cooperation' of the community was achieved in subsequent years, as the author of a relevant report asserted.

For the case of Bukovina, the sources available document the enormous difficulties that agents of modern epidemic prevention had to face from segments of the rural population. Here, the religious–ethnic group of the so-called 'Lipovans' engaged in fierce resistance against the smallpox vaccination up to 1900. They were so-called 'old-believers' of the Russian Orthodox Church, who had fled the Russian Empire before 1800 because of innovations in religious practice there which they regarded as heretical.[49]

Bukovina and Galicia were the only Austrian provinces where, during the late 1890s, the registered number of deaths due to variola rose again heavily. In Bukovina, numbers increased from nearly zero from 1893–1895 to more than two hundred per year in 1896 and 1897, and to just under five hundred in 1898. Therefore, opposition to vaccination among the Lipovans, once it was recognised by the regional sanitation officials, was regarded as a serious problem. In fact, even the Ministry of the Interior in Vienna paid attention to the development.[50] The smallpox epidemics which hit these vaccination opponents during the late 1890s were described at length in a written report by the district physician of Sereth/Siret, Dr Josef Perl. A summary of this text was published in the official periodical of the Austrian health administration, *Das Österreichische Sanitätswesen.*[51]

Within the district of Siret, of nearly nine hundred infections with variola officially registered in 1898, 667 cases were traced to two small communities of a combined 2,500 inhabitants, while the rest of the district, counting more than 40,000 residents, contributed only 231 official cases. These communities were Klimoutz/Climăuți and Fontina alba/Fântâna Albă/Bila Krynytsia, only about three kilometres distant from one another. Most infections afflicted children, with about a quarter of the afflicted perishing of smallpox. The vast majority of the adult population in turn had acquired immunity as surviving victims of earlier smallpox epidemics, so not by vaccination. The Lipovans not only refrained from medical immunisation, citing religious concerns against it, but generally regarded a consultation with a physician in the event of illness as inappropriate, leaving healing to divine discretion. These attitudes were problematic for the state of health of the surrounding population as well. Lipovans engaged heavily in trade and many of them travelled frequently, crossing over to other districts, provinces and even states, as Romania and Russia were nearby.[52] With respect to these activities, the Lipovans in 1898 had concealed most incidences of smallpox among them, from the first local appearances in July until October, as Dr Perl lamented. The full level of the local sanitation catastrophe thus became visible only in the autumn, when the physicians responsible were ordered to monitor the health of all inhabitants by house visits personally, assisted by temporary rural police outposts installed in both communities. Yet by August 1898, regional health authorities were keeping a special focus on the Lipovans. This can be concluded from the weekly sanitation report for Bukovina sent to the Ministry of the Interior on 19 August. It relates that 'the Lipovans refuse vaccination obstinately with fanatic stubbornness and as a people engaged in commerce, they could easily disseminate smallpox by steady traffic'.[53] The report moreover announces that 'the most extensive measures were conducted to avoid a further spread' – probably an exaggeration and for sure a failure, as even the following official reports show. Dating from September and October, they again refer to attempts to persuade the local Lipovans to 'participate in protection by vaccination'.[54] The head of the provincial sanitation office himself attempted to convince their representatives of the wrongfulness of their views at a theological level, but with little success. The statistical reports sent to Vienna during these weeks remain somewhat vague, as they cite only a small number of newly infected persons, leaving the total number of cases open.[55] This remained the general vague manner of reporting until May 1899.[56]

Starting in late October 1898, the weekly reports disclose twenty-nine acute smallpox infections in Klimoutz and forty-six in Fontina Alba.[57] Children who had already succumbed to the disease were not included in these totals. By the second week of November, the number had risen to fifty-eight in Klimoutz, while for Fontina Alba a moderate decline to forty was listed. Very probably, even at this stage, there were additional non-registered cases. The report sent to the Viennese authorities in November 1898 provides in greater detail the measures taken at the local level, because the provincial authorities were repeatedly urged to do so. They referred to 'emergency vaccinations' in all surrounding communities within the district of Siret, conducted without major opposition, and the application of the same measures to the small numbers of the non-Lipovan population there, in Klimoutz. Vaccination of the Lipovans remained impossible. At this stage of the spread of variola, the regional sanitation officials felt obliged to inform the authorities of other districts, too. Even the vice-regency of Galicia and the Russian and Romanian consulates in Czernowitz were contacted.[58]

In Klimoutz and Fontina Alba at least until August of 1898 the potential for implementing the measures ordered by the provincial authorities must have been limited. There was no permanent police presence in either community up to that point. Once again, it becomes clear that although central state power was immense, the social reality included blind spots and areas where state power was nearly completely lacking. For remote rural areas like these, enforcing state policy regularly meant that staff with police competences had to be deployed from outside in sufficient numbers and for considerable periods. This inevitably required considerable effort and expense for state authorities and therefore, in many instances, it was the last option. In general, political power and compliance rely heavily on a perceived potential to use force, and the sentiment of menace which results from it, more than on actually enforcing distinct measures.

Concerning the state-planned epidemic prevention measures in rural Bukovina before 1900, in the sources the authorities appear rather helpless and slow to act. Undoubtedly, the situation was perceived as a sanitation problem, but for several months it was not regarded as pressing enough to mobilise extraordinary means on a grander scale. In late November 1898, the Ministry of Interior still felt the urge to ask the regional government, 'if and in which manner the isolated accommodation and treatment of the individuals suffering from smallpox was provided, and if peddling trade [...] was prohibited for the period of the epidemic'.[59]

The answer was only indirectly given by the regional authorities, who simply attached to one of the standardised weekly reports a cut-out from the local newspaper. It contained a decree on the issue, which must have been perceived as quite sobering in Vienna. Infected persons and their cohabitants were requested to stay in their homes during the acute period of the disease, and in order to leave the community to travel, inhabitants had to demonstrate their state of health to the local head of the government and the police officer in charge. These seem not too strict and not very effective measures, as no involvement of a physician in the process of issuing such health certificates was called for. Apparently, even at this juncture, no medical doctor was permanently available for the two remote Lipovan communities. Nonetheless, infection numbers there declined, as is typical for variola during winter as a biological consequence of lower temperatures. But the pestilence had already spread further, as feared. The provincial government remained keen not to publicise this directly in its regular reports sent to Vienna, probably with the intent of avoiding discussions about the lack of effectiveness of the measures which it had hitherto ordered.[60] In December 1898 provincial sanitation officials had to report explicitly to Vienna that 'in the Lipovan communities of Klimoutz and Fontina Alba [...] specific isolation locations for the persons infected with variola were not erected, because according to the experiences hitherto one must assume with full certainty that the affected families would have refused to turn over their members to the isolation centres.'[61] General prohibitions on peddling had not been enacted either.

One may question whether this happened out of empathy with the local population, or for economic motives, or due to fear of a violent escalation of the conflict. Probably, it was a mixture of all such. Other official correspondence on the issue even gives the impression that the provincial government in Czernowitz was not well informed about the measures set by its subordinate district authority in Siret. In January 1899, the regional authorities insisted to Vienna that many of the newly registered cases of infections were caused by 'a repeated carrying of smallpox from Galicia, Romania and Russia', thus scapegoating all available neighbouring countries and territories for the persistent trouble at home. The pestilence had been transmitted, among others, to the town of Lukowetz Lipoweny/Lukavtsi, another stronghold of Lipovans in Bukovina. Moreover, it had arrived at the regional capital of Czernowitz too, although not causing large numbers of deaths there. The communications to Vienna also report nearly 5,800 new and over 42,400 repeat vaccinations in the territory during 1898.[62] Subsequently, the vice-regency explicitly requested their subordinate authorities to extend the vaccination campaign to the Lipovans too.[63] Whether this was enforced or not remains unclear. In any case, the provincial government sent a final report on the 1898 epidemics to Vienna in February 1899, including the aforementioned text from Dr Perl. Unfortunately, the report itself was not kept at the Ministry of Interior. A summary of the report, which 'survived' in the record file in Vienna, contains one remark that did not find its way into the published text, but seems particularly worth mentioning. Apart from the small section of non-Lipovans in Klimoutz, there was also a small group of Lipovans there and in Fontina Alba, who had already been vaccinated in 1898: '24 children could participate in the protection against smallpox by vaccination – those children were brought to vaccination by their mothers secretly'.[64]

For twenty of them, the vaccination was judged successful by the physician, and only one child of this group contracted variola afterwards, moreover of a quite benign kind. Dr Perl added that this fact became known to all Lipovans over time and 'had great influence'. He expressed his hope that the 'absolute refusal of vaccination' among them would soften in the near future.

Officially registered deaths from smallpox in Bukovina fell markedly then. In 1900 only nine deaths from variola were officially recorded for the whole territory.[65] Accordingly, there was no further major outbreak, even among the Lipovans.

Conclusion

This discussion has sought to show what was often called 'the peculiarities of circumstances', when general regulations concerning epidemic prevention were issued by the central state and were to be applied regionally. Regarding the empirical material, it focused on the eastern and southern extremes of the empire, Bukovina and Dalmatia. The introduction took up a geoepidemiological perspective, specifically making use of the concept of neoquarantanism of Peter Baldwin. A combination of this approach with that of world system analysis was used to investigate inner centre–periphery relations and their impact on the actual implementation of plague proliferation preventative measures within the complex Austrian system of 'sanitation review'.

The conditions and framework for epidemic prevention in Bukovina and Dalmatia were sketched. The location of both provinces, lying outside major international routes of commerce and travel, and removed geographically from the Austrian core lands were concomitant with having poor economic, education and health conditions within the two regions. An overview of the relevant international treaties revealed that although the old quarantine system had faded away after the 1860s, some important limitations on traffic and transportation remained in force, particularly along the Austro–Russian border, but only for members of the lower social classes and cultural outsiders, regarded as particularly dangerous.

Within the Austrian Empire itself, core practical measures against the spread of contagion, as advised by the 'neoquarantinist' approach, were a medical examination, isolation of the infected people, and precise disinfection procedures. As a prerequisite, the official reporting system on infectious diseases was of particular importance. Even late in 1892 the Viennese government ordered an immediate telegraphic report to the Ministry of Interior of every single case of cholera which had been confirmed by a medical doctor.

Apart from the land borders, for which railway traffic was considered most dangerous, particular attention was paid to the maritime traffic on the Adriatic Austrian coast, including Dalmatia. There, a separate system of sea authorities was established. It had to handle day-to-day decisions on permission or prohibition regarding incoming traffic according to international agreements, and on isolation of persons or goods, revealed, or believed to have been infected during sanitation reviews when disembarking. To facilitate such control procedures, long-distance maritime traffic was concentrated in only a few major ports even in elongated Dalmatia. There, particular 'isolation facilities' were maintained, similar to those at the major land border crossings. Bukovina, as a comparatively small region, possessed only a few such stations.

Regarding the costs of epidemic prevention, the regional and local level was left 'holding the bag' by the central government, which caused problems particularly for indigent communities. As can be gleaned from the budgetary statistics, in 1890 for instance, the Cisleithanian central government spent a sum equalling about 0.1€ per person for specific epidemic prevention measures. Regions and communities therefore were very unequally equipped with staff and material to be used when danger of contagion became visible. While at the end of 1893 the core land of Lower Austria possessed 233 steam disinfecting devices, the two peripheral border regions of Dalmatia and

Bukovina were equipped with only ten such machines each. Of course, this all contributed negatively to regional mortality rates. Nonetheless, for some epidemics, like cholera, a remote geographical location and a 'backward' economy could work as a protective factor, too, as long as an actual spread of the disease did not take place.

For smallpox, as the second illness focused on in this contribution, regional trends of death tolls for Bukovina and Dalmatia were somewhat aberrant from the Cisleithanian average, too. 'Grave sanitation nuisances' – formulated from a 'modern' hygienically informed standpoint – and tenacious resistance by the local rural population against any changes introduced from outside, turned out to have formed the basis of the particular cholera epidemics in Dalmatian Metković in 1886, as well as the smallpox peak the following year. A particular constellation of differing perceptions of epidemics and their eventual prevention by sanitation measures at the local level was found to be an important contributing factor to the Bukovinan smallpox epidemics of 1896–1898.

The religiously defined, rural population group of Lipovans fiercely resisted most of the isolation and disinfection protocols, as well as vaccinations scheduled by central and regional government in the case of smallpox outbreaks. They even continued largely in their peddling trade, which formed a major part of their income. Only after the contagion had already taken the lives of at least a hundred individuals, most of them children, within the two little communities predominantly affected, did some change come about. Some female members of the religious community were willing to endanger their status as respected community members for the sake of protecting the lives of their children and they secretly carried them to the physician for vaccination. Admittedly, at that time, the illness had already spread further to other, mainly non-Lipovan, communities causing several deaths, which probably would have been avoidable. Yet, central and regional authorities had avoided extraordinary costly measures for the protection of the health of a remote and poor rural population, of which a part moreover resisted the sanitation measures for far too long. The regional government did not hesitate then to scapegoat the bordering states of Russia, Romania and Hungary as being the source of new smallpox infections which was probably a selective, rather than completely wrong, interpretation of the real contagion events that had taken place around Bukovina in 1898. Late-nineteenth-century Bukovina and Dalmatia represent typical examples of peripheral regions. Similarly, they were border lands in the geoepidemiologically more sensitive southern and eastern direction. These two aspects, taken together, heavily influenced the extent of exposure to epidemical dangers on the one hand, and the possibilities for medical–hygienic countermeasures on the other. The level and form of their actual application was strongly conditioned by political, economic and cultural considerations. For those living in these border regions this meant, above all, that they were confronted later and to a lesser extent with the imposition of modern epidemic control procedures. Otherwise, the indisputable benefits in modern health care were to a lesser degree (and later) accessible to the populations there, compared with the inhabitants of the Empire's crown lands.

Notes

1 For an overview of this research field see D. Wastl-Walter (ed.), *The Ashgate Research Companion to Border Studies* (Farnham-Burlington: Ashgate, 2011); T. Wilson and H. Donnan (eds), *A Companion to Border Studies* (Chichester: Wiley, 2012).
2 See P. Baldwin, *Contagion and the State in Europe, 1830–1930* (Cambridge: Cambridge University Press, 1999), especially p. 141.
3 See Baldwin, *Contagion and the State in Europe* pp. 139–201; N. Howard-Jones, *The Scientific Background of the International Sanitary Conferences 1851–1938* (Geneva: WHO, 1975), pp. 58–80.
4 See R. J. Evans, *The Pursuit of Power: Europe 1815–1914* (London: Penguin, 2016).
5 For a discussion about the term 'border region' and its several potential meanings, see R. Gua, *Border-Regional Economics* (Heidelberg: Physica, 1996), especially pp. 25–31. Concerning the particular meaning of border regions for Austrian central state authorities in the nineteenth century see H.-C. Maner (ed.), *Grenzregionen der Habsburgermonarchie im 18. und 19. Jahrhundert* (Münster: Lit, 2005). On centre–periphery relations within the Habsburg Empire see E. Hárs (ed.), *Zentren, Peripherien und kollektive Identitäten in Österreich-Ungarn* (Tübingen; Basel: Francke, 2006).
6 See I. Wallerstein, *World-Systems Analysis: An Introduction* (Durham; London: Durham University Press, 2004), pp. 1–59.

7 The importance of health politics for the expansion of nineteenth-century central state bureaucracy is debated in detail in D. Porter, *Health, Civilisation and the State: A History of Public Health from Ancient to Modern Times* (London; New York: Routledge, 1999), pp. 63–162.
8 See P. Weindling, 'From germ theory to social medicine: public health 1880–1930', in D. Brunton (ed.), *Medicine Transformed: Health, Disease and Society in Europe, 1800–1930* (Manchester: Manchester University Press, 2004), pp. 257–83.
9 As introductions to the histories of both regions see: G. Praga, *History of Dalmatia* (Pisa: Giardini, 1993); K. Scharr, *Die Landschaft Bukowina* (Vienna: Böhlau, 2010).
10 See M. Mann, *The Sources of Social Power*, vol. 4 (Cambridge: Cambridge University Press, 1986–2011).
11 See P. Judson, *The Habsburg Empire. A New History* (Cambridge, MA: Harvard University Press, 2016).
12 Basic map: wikimedia commons; corrected, adapted and supplemented by the author. Note that names of regions and capital cities are given here in their contemporary German versions for reasons of simplicity.
13 Research literature on epidemics and their prevention in the Habsburg Empire around 1900 remains sparse. See O. Birkner, *Die bedrohte Stadt. Cholera in Wien* (Vienna: Deuticke, 2002).
14 Particularly the comprehensive periodical *Das Österreichische Sanitätswesen* (hereafter ÖSW).
15 Of course, it is preferable to systematically examine regional and local archives and journals as this provides greater and more refined insights. Several aspects dealt with here have already been scrutinised on such a regional archival base in previous publications, mostly by Romanian and Croatian historians. See especially H. Mareci-Sabol, 'Change your habits! Health and hygiene issues in Bukovina during the 19th century', *Codrul Cosminului*, 21:2 (2015), 357–68; I. Marinović, 'Gesundheitsdienst in Dubrovnik und Dalmatien im 19. Jahrhundert', *Acta medico-historica Adriatica*, 4:1 (2006), 163–70.
16 See K. Bachinger, 'Das Verkehrswesen', in A. Wandruska and P. Urbanitsch (eds), *Die Habsburgermonarchie 1848–1918*, vol. 1 (Vienna: ÖAW, 1973), pp. 278–322.
17 See B. Bolognese-Leuchtenmüller, *Bevölkerungsentwicklung und Berufsstruktur, Gesundheits- und Fürsorgewesen in Österreich 1750–1918* (Munich: Oldenbourg, 1978); R. Sandgruber, *Österreichische Agrarstatistik 1750–1918* (Munich: Oldenbourg, 1978); A. Komlosy, 'Regionale Ungleichheiten in der Habsburgermonarchie', in H. Nolte (ed.), *Innere Peripherien in Ost und West*. (Stuttgart: Steiner, 2001),

pp. 97–111; K.k. statistische Zentral-Commission (ed.), *Österreichisches Statistisches Jahrbuch* (Vienna: Hölder, 1901).
18 See the 'Reichsanitätsgesetz', *Reichsgesetzblatt*, 1870, 25:68.
19 For the wording in German see *Reichsgesetzblatt*, 1894, 23:69.
20 See especially G. Rothenberg, 'The Austrian sanitary cordon and the control of bubonic plague 1710–1871', *Journal of the History of Medicine and Allied Sciences*, 28:1 (1973), 15–23; E. Lesky, 'Die österreichische Pestfront an der k.k. Militärgrenze', *Saeculum*, 8 (1957), 82–106.
21 See N. N., *Die Donauschiffahrts-Frage [...]* (Stuttgart: Metzler, 1858).
22 See *Reichsgesetzblatt*, 1870, 26:69
23 See *Reichsgesetzblatt*, 1896, 26:72.
24 Ibid., p. 248.
25 See J. Daimer, *Handbuch der österreichischen Sanitäts-Gesetze* vol. 2 (Leipzig; Vienna: Deuticke, 1898), p. 203.
26 See ibid., p. 316.
27 For Bukovina see: *Gesetz- und Verordnungsblatt für das Herzogthum Bukowina*, 21:28 (1886); for Dalmatia, *Landes- Gesetz- und Verordnungsblatt für Dalmatien*, 12:35 (1886).
28 See A. von Obentraut, *Systematisches Handbuch der österreichischen Sanitätsgesetze* (Vienna: Manz, 1877), pp. 518–36.
29 See R. Petermann, *Führer durch Dalmatien* (Vienna: Hölder, 1899).
30 See M. Macher (ed.), *Handbuch der kaiserlich-österreichischen Sanitäts-Geseze* vol.4 (Graz: Ferstl, 1853), p. 356.
31 See Marinović, 'Gesundheitsdienst in Dubrovnik und Dalmatien', at 167.
32 Austrian State Archives Vienna (hereafter AT-OeSTA) AVA Inneres MdI SA A 1043, file 17416/1885.
33 See K.k. Statistische Central-Commission (ed.), *Der oesterreichische Staatshaushalt in den Jahren 1889 und 1890* (Vienna: Gerold, 1893), and the subsequent budgetary statistics on the Austrian Habsburg monarchy
34 See Daimer, *Handbuch der österreichischen Sanitäts-Gesetze*, vol. 2, p. 305.
35 Decree, Ministry of Interior, 20 August 1893, Nr. 20581, in ÖSW, 5:35 (1893), 318–19.
36 AT-OeStA/AVA Inneres MdI SA A 2556, file 14332/1906.
37 Ibid., A 1025, file 21001/1894.
38 See 'Cholera-Nachrichten', in ÖSW, 6:29 (1894), at 275.
39 For sources of the data given here see Bolognese-Leuchtenmüller, *Bevölkerungsentwicklung*, especially pp. 152–3, 166–9; pp. 236–55 (tables part); K.k. Statistische Central-Commission (ed.), *Österreichische Statistik* (Vienna: Hof- und Staatsdruckerei, 1883–1918), especially vol. 37:2, 38:2, 40:2, 44:3, 48:3, 49:2, 52:2, 54:1, 55:3, 62:3, 67:1, 72:1, 73:3, 79:1, 84:1, 84:3, 86:1, 881:1, 88:3, 92:1, NF [i.e. new series]

8:1, NF 8:3, NF 14:1; A. Killiches, 'Beiträge zur Sanitätsstatistik', *Statistische Monatsschrift*, 1:10 (1875), 547–63.
40 See the sources cited at note 39 above.
41 N. N., 'Aus den Jahresberichten der Landessanitätsräthe für das Jahr 1888', ÖSW, 2:12 (1890), at 187.
42 See *Landesgesetz- und Verordnungsblatt für das Herzogthum Bukowina* 10:13 (1888), 117–22.
43 Announcement of the Bukovinan Landesregierung, 27 April 1895, Nr. 6788, in ÖSW, 7:31 (1895), 289–94.
44 See T. Cvrcek, 'Wages, prices, and living standards in the Habsburg Empire, 1817–1910', *Journal of Economic History*, 73:1 (2013), 1–37.
45 See N. N., 'Fortschritte in der Organisation des Gemeinde-Sanitätsdienstes', ÖSW 9:52 (1897), at 509.
46 *Landesgesetz- und Verordnungsblatt für Dalmatien*, 5:10 (1874), 49–54, at 49.
47 See C. Vipauc, 'Die Erfolge der Gemeinde-Sanitätsorganisation in Dalmatien', ÖSW 4:1 (1892), 2–6, and ÖSW 4:2 (1892), 10–16.
48 See N. N., 'Assanierungsarbeiten in Dalmatien', ÖSW, 4:29 (1892), 232–4, and ÖSW 4:31 (1892), 251–3, at 233.
49 See R. Kaindl, *Das Entstehen und die Entwicklung der Lippowaner-Kolonien in der Bukowina* (Vienna: KAW, 1896).
50 An impressive number of sources for the issue are available in: AT-OeStA/AVA MdI – Sanitätsakten.
51 See N. N., 'Die Infectionskrankheiten im Jahre 1898', ÖSW, 11:47 (1899), 443–8, and ÖSW 11:48 (1899), 456–61, and ÖSW 11:49 (1899), 467–71.
52 See 'Die Infectionskrankheiten im Jahre 1898', 445–7.
53 AT-OeStA/AVA Inneres MdI SA A 1031, file 27905/1898.
54 Ibid., file 31762/1898.
55 Ibid., files 34689/1898, 33891/1898, 36255/1898.
56 Ibid., SA A 1032, file 8395/1899.
57 Ibid., SA A 1031, file 36255/98.
58 Ibid., file 38300/98.
59 Ibid., file 38300/98.
60 Ibid., file 41662–98.
61 Ibid., file 41974–98.
62 Ibid., SA A 1032, file 3046/99 and 5768/99.
63 Ibid., file 10200/99.
64 Ibid., file 6026/99.
65 See Central-Commission (ed.), *Österreichische Statistik*, 55:3 (1898), 62:3 (1899), 67:1 (1900).

Part II

(Dis)connections – containment

5

Lazarettos as border filters: expurgating bodies, commodities and ideas, 1800–1870s

John Chircop

Introduction

Overlapping solid land and fluid sea, lazarettos marked the countries' borders operating, as Gilles Deleuze and Felix Guattari would put it, to subordinate the immense maritime 'hydraulic force'[1] – considered as the foremost liquid carrier of contagious disease[2] – to the powers of the territorial state. These quarantines, intended primarily as prophylactic institutions came to constrain, regulate and sanitise the movement and influx of individuals and merchandise of every sort. They became increasingly important for the state during the first three-quarters of the nineteenth century, at a time of rapid technological innovation in transport and communication – especially with the coming of the steamship – which intensified speed and human movement, travel and trade, creating greater interconnectivity between all areas of the Mediterranean and beyond. At the same rate, this also accelerated the transmission of contagious disease from one part to the other of the region and between continents.

To properly operate in this way, southern European lazarettos had evolved into complex institutions specialised in governing the porosity of the territorial borders.[3] Such control was achieved through a systematic filtering instrument which selected, separated, disinfected and disciplined alien or returning embodied subjects before these entered the country. This chapter seeks to explore in some depth how this filtering–purifying institution functioned. Rather than accept the conventional description that lazarettos were merely public sanitary institutions protecting society from epidemics, which of course they were, this study adopts a multidimensional perspective, in line with the more recent and innovative historical works.[4] To be able to take on such analysis, this study critically engages with an influential historiographical current of a Foucauldian matrix, not least by drawing from it the key concept of 'dispositif'. More specifically, it employs Giorgio Agamben's more recent articulation of this concept as an *apparatus* which can be described as a 'machine of governance',[5] in the sense that it has 'the capacity to capture, orient, determine, intercept, model, control, or secure the gestures, behaviours, opinions, or discourses of living beings'.[6] Careful employment of this notion helps us investigate, describe and explain more thoroughly the multiplicity of functions effected by the lazaretto according to shifting epidemiological circumstances.

The approach taken here allows the research to proceed beyond the simple acceptance of the fact that lazarettos were prophylactic instruments located on the sea boundaries of a state. Instead, there is an attempt to regard these edifices as inbuilt, as part and parcel of the border structure itself. It therefore makes sense to start the first section of this chapter with an attentive analysis of their internal arrangements – spatial structures, divisions and organisation – conforming to the selection, separation and disinfection of persons, merchandise, animals and mail passing through quarantine. It immediately becomes evident that the most vital zone and apparatus in the entire quarantine process was the disinfection of everyone and everything crossing the border. The chapter continues with a section which deals specifically with the various expurgation operations conducted in these lazarettos, analysing each of these in view of their sanitary as well as social, political and ritualistic aspects.

It stands to reason that one cannot really obtain a thorough understanding of what was involved in these disinfection procedures, as in other phases of quarantine, without taking into consideration the human element involved. This is why at various points of this study, the focus shifts towards those protagonists – from the physicians to the health guardians and the expurgators – who were indispensable to the quarantine operations, but who have been largely forgotten by the historical literature. Accentuating the importance of human agency set against the solid structures of quarantine, the last few pages of this study are intentionally dedicated to the expurgator himself, whose vigorous disinfection performances – which attracted contemporary scientific inquiry – are interpreted not only as crucial sanitary procedures, but also as purifying cross-border rituals.

Such a multilevel inquiry can only be attained from within a comparative framework grounded on solid empirical research employing the widest range of primary and secondary sources possible. This means making ample use of the contemporary literature which includes plentiful quarantine narratives and travelogues. Not only do these provide descriptive accounts of the lazaretto setting, but perhaps more importantly, they express the multiple human experiences of at least a portion of those travellers undergoing quarantine. Equally important is the plethora of written and printed material featuring quarantine regulations and guidelines. This chapter pays particular attention to records concerning the lazarettos in the Adriatic region (Dalmatia), those belonging to the Pontifical states and others under the Kingdom of Two Sicilies, although references to other locations will be made for comparative purposes.[7] Coupled with extensive visual documentation – provided by maps, plans and illustrations of these and other lazarettos[8] – the resulting blend of original sources allows for the construction of a more inclusive picture of the internal structures, sequential procedures and human dynamic involved in the making of quarantine at a time when quarantinism was still prevalent in most of these countries.

Interiors of filter apparatus

Sharing a similar prophylactic purpose, being set up and operating on the principles of the old contagionist medical philosophy that disease was transmitted through contact with infected bodies and objects,[9] lazarettos developed identical interior layouts. Walled – or, in any case, thickly enclosed – and secured, all such quarantines were properly insulated from unwanted external infiltrations. Anyone trying to get in without permission, or caught escaping from quarantine, could be shot on the spot or face severe penalties, which included corporal punishment and public execution.[10]

A comparative analysis of the architectural morphology of some of the principal lazarettos located on the sea borders of southern European countries, and whose sanitary–political regimes adhered to the same contagionist doctrine,[11] makes evident their similar internal structures. Such was the case even when their exterior designs were different,[12] as well as when the actual size of the buildings varied to a great extent. This mainly reflected the geostrategic location of each lazaretto on the trade and travel routes, as well as their nation's preventive strategies which, as Peter Baldwin argues, 'corresponded to their position in the geoepidemiology of disease'.[13]

Regardless of these lazarettos' building aesthetics and dimensions, their underlying function remained that of a filtering apparatus characterised by an identical partitioning of internal space. The effective division of these structures corresponded to each sequential phase and related procedure that individuals had to go through before gaining free authorisation to cross the border. At this juncture, a description of each of these quarantine phases follows:

1. Disembarking from the same ship, passengers lined up for identification and physical examination. A physician separated and isolated those showing signs of disease.
2. Grouped together, travellers from the same ship were allocated a common lodging division.
3. They all passed through disinfection with their belongings in various measures.
4. Having served their imposed period in quarantine and being completely expurgated, persons were granted free pratique and permitted to cross the border into civil society.

Lazarettos essentially constituted what Michel Foucault describes as functional sites, operating not only the 'need to supervise, to break dangerous communications, but also to create useful space'.[14] While acknowledging this, a more empirically informed analysis which specifically focuses on lazarettos indicates the multiple purposes of these structures. It shows that the sequential phases and the various intricacies involved in each of the procedures of filtering and disinfection of bodies, things and ideas in correspondence, made lazarettos unique crossover institutions. They were concurrently effective as detention sites, border checkpoints, isolation/infective hospitals, asylums, sanitary and social-behavioural laboratories, postal and censorship offices, and state intelligence-gathering centres. All this comes to show lazarettos as multifunctional sites operating on and forming part of the sea-territorial border of a country.

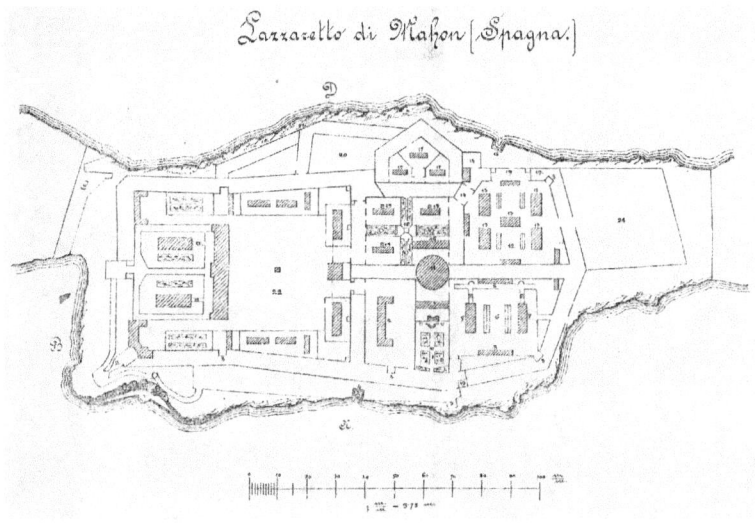

Figure 5.1 Lazaretto at Mahon

Figure 5.2 Lazaretto at Naples

Figure 5.3 Lazaretto at Trieste

Well-defined yet interconnected divisions, rooms, yards, terraces and corridors were configured to expedite the sequence of quarantine procedures in accordance with the basic contagionist principle of strict separation and non-contact. For contagionists such as T. Spencer Wells, selection and segregation practices, starting with that of the sick from the healthy, 'were quite conclusive as to the practical good derived from quarantine'.[15] Each of these separate areas was designed and fitted with utensils and assigned sanitary employees, with the purpose of assuring that procedures at each stage of the quarantine process were properly conducted according to similar regulations and codes of practice. Abiding by these regulations was fundamental for the continued well-functioning of the quarantine system, and hence heavy penalties were imposed for any infringements. For instance, the punishment for the violation of the fundamental rule of not touching or coming in contact – or even exchanging things – with persons from other divisions, and of not touching goods from other shipments, entailed restarting the whole quarantine process anew. More seriously, those caught attempting to take things out of the premises were liable to be sentenced to corporal punishment including death by execution.[16] To really deter people from committing such serious infractions, as well as to mark the state's power over its territorial borders and to maintain discipline and order within the establishment, penalties imposed for the most serious of infringements included public hanging. In one interesting case which occurred at the Manoel Island Lazaretto in Valletta in 1814, gallows were erected on a spot visible to all to hang a certain Felice Camilleri. He was a health guardian sentenced to death for having stolen things from the lazaretto. Although the condemned was reprieved by the governor as a sign of the King's benevolence, the gibbets were kept standing in the same place for all to see and dread until 1839.[17]

Internal order: discipline and a hygiene regime

Compliance with quarantine discipline also included maintaining a hygiene regime. Any sign of contamination in any part of the lazaretto precincts would trigger a nightmarish breakdown of the whole quarantine system, leading to the closure of the country's territorial borders. For this reason, heavy penalties were imposed for infringing hygienic rules – such was considered essential for the proper proceeding of quarantine.[18] The responsibility to keep internal facilities scrupulously tidy lay in the hands of the health guardians (*guardiani*). These were stationed at fixed posts, but also moved from one point to another with caution to avoid contact with quarantined items and individuals. Making use of a lance-like stick or iron grabber, the guardians picked up and burnt any waste or 'polluting matter' they found lying around,[19] and made sure that all furnishings and utensils were clean.[20] To impart both cleanliness and discipline, these guardians and all other personnel had to wear clean and distinct uniforms[21] indicative of their rank in the quarantine occupational hierarchy.[22] All of them, including the physicians, were also expected to conduct themselves in an exemplary hygienic manner. On entering the lazaretto, they were required 'to disinfect [...] every time, and in all cases, to wash their hands and their face with water mixed with *aceto*'.[23]

Deeper still, abiding by the basic quarantine tenets of physical cleanliness, discipline and order implied a certain moral rectitude and a socially respectful behaviour. Quarantine regulations made this connotation explicit by condemning disturbing, noisy, rude, threatening and any other improper and 'corrupt' comportment as offensive and unacceptable – and therefore punishable. Gambling, swearing, quarrelling, infighting and the carrying of arms were among those actions to be most emphatically prohibited.[24] The underlying tone of these regulations was that time in quarantine was to be spent in a physically and morally clean environment, and that all persons undergoing expurgation were also expected to experience moral purification before crossing the border. Priests – be they Catholic or Greek Orthodox – were employed to help uphold this internal moral arrangement. They were to take care of the spiritual affairs of persons in quarantine, as well as being meant to provide moral comfort through the sacraments – including performing extreme unction to the dying.[25] For this purpose, a chapel could be found in all lazarettos. Like the glass rotunda chapel in the Mallorca lazaretto, located on high ground, or the chapel located at the top of the bastions, across the water from the Manoel Island lazaretto in Valletta, each of these places of worship was centrally located for all detainees to be able to follow mass,[26] without leaving their divisions. Bell-tolling from the chapel,[27] not to mention hailing from the town churches nearby, not only helped those in quarantine to keep track of time, but even sustained routine within the lazaretto.[28]

With the first bell tolls at sunrise, and others following throughout the day,[29] all the quarantined could move within their quarters and terraces, always under the constant watch of the *guardiani*. By sunset, all divisions were closed down, with everyone having to remain inside and not be seen out for any excuse whatsoever. During the night, gates were to be closed and passengers were not allowed to disembark.[30] Such regulation of movement and activities responded to security concerns and facilitated the maintenance of a sense of order.

Efficiency, cleanliness and orderliness seemed to characterise the principal lazarettos of southern Europe. Such well-kept conditions caught the attention of contemporary hospital reformer and traveller John Howard (1726–1790), who in 1778 visited the lazarettos of Genoa, La Spezia, Livorno and Malta among others.[31] In truth, Howard also observed that not all other quarantines were kept to the same standards as the above. Like many others after him, he emphasised that having to undergo quarantine nearly always generated a feeling of apprehension[32] which was shared by numerous travellers and triggered by the connotation of quarantine with prison conditions.[33]

Through the filtering arrangement: selection by social class, status and religion

On arrival, disembarkation took place in an 'orderly manner', with passengers held together or cordoned as a group, separated from other travel groups. Landing procedures were considered of utmost importance and were carried out under the direct supervision of the head of quarantine himself.[34] A physician was present to conduct the first medical examination on each passenger. Using non-contact techniques – with the aid of tongs and by questioning his patients – the physician would immediately isolate those who showed symptoms of disease at the infective hospital. Those who died in hospital were buried in the cemetery, which was often located within a zone of the lazarettos' complex.[35]

All other travellers arriving on the same ship with a clean bill of health proceeded to the main entrance gate. These were kept together in a common division, where they would remain separated from others, in accordance with the non-contact regime in place. The duration and intensity of quarantine imposed on each travel group or individual passenger was primarily determined by their ship's bill of health and 'place of origin', as well as the actual state of health found aboard on arrival. To be sure, by and large in all lazarettos, those arriving from Egypt and any other port in the Levant and North Africa marked as 'endemically contagious',[36] had a longer quarantine imposed on them. If these travellers happened to be Muslim hajjis returning from Mecca, they were ordered an even lengthier and stricter detention period.[37]

In other words, the criteria in use by the boards of health for each lazaretto to determine the duration of quarantine generally privileged those vessels originating in Europe, as well as their passengers and cargo, over those arriving from or having touched Egypt, Turkey, or any other port on the North African or 'Ottoman' Levantine coasts.[38] With the adoption of more detailed classification lists by European lazarettos from the late 1850s, the duration and intensity of quarantine came to be fixed according to the degree of 'susceptibility' of their merchandise, coupled with their declared 'port of origin'. In practice, this meant that ships arriving in southern European lazarettos from 'Arab' or 'Ottoman' ports, and carrying indigenous products such as cotton bales (listed as 'highly susceptible'), were usually ordered to undergo rigorous, all-round quarantine. The process also involved having their passengers separated in specific quarters, where they would endure firmer procedures and lengthier detentions.[39]

Above and beyond this strictest quarantine, imposed on those arriving from non-European ports – especially Arabs and Muslims returning from their Hajj – treatment of passengers was also subject to their social class and power status. To begin with, on landing, wealthy and influential individuals could choose their own distinct rooms in allocated divisions.[40] A wide range of privileges, considered appropriate to their socially elevated position distanced them as much as possible from the rest of the people in quarantine. According to Murray's 1840 *Handbook for Travellers,* 'a sitting room is not given if not as a favour' and the same applied for the kitchenettes that were available.[41] Meanwhile in the lazaretto of Piraeus, it was noted that the best rooms were allocated to those who were ready to pay more.[42]

Monied travellers could lodge their servants with them.[43] Local servants were available upon landing – at a fee and on the condition that they would undergo the whole quarantine term together. Accommodated in relatively more comfortable rooms, usually commanding panoramic views, and enjoying better furnishings, these privileged individuals were able to indulge in a good selection of food and wine as well as ice. Books, newspapers and journals[44] were frequently provided on demand, helping these travellers pass the time, which would otherwise feel as if it 'crawl[ed] but heavily along'.[45]

It was not so with the 'common passengers' who had just afforded the passage, and who had to do with what was available and cheap. Most of these were illiterate and left very little writing, if any, behind as a means to record their feelings and experiences during their days in the lazaretto. Occasionally, one may stumble upon a reference of sorts, on the 'several pale and dejected people'[46] who were lodged in dormitories containing the minimum of furniture – a chair, a table and bedstead – at their disposal.[47] All this serves to indicate how separation and treatment was also based on social

Lazarettos as border filters 139

class and status. It also shows how this constituted an internal rift within quarantine, which in turn reflected the social hierarchy and state class ideology of the countries under which the lazarettos were run.

High-profile travellers were also those most likely to meet visitors of their own social station in the *parlatorio* – which they were granted permission to access after undergoing expurgation. This demarcated zone was fitted to operate as a non-contact site of social encounter and negotiation, and especially for the merchants to be able to talk commerce and access local trade networks. Even if held under surveillance, meeting with a variety of people of different languages and cultures rendered the time spent in quarantine bearable and possibly creative, as narrated in various travelogues.[48] In the *parlatorio* or any other zone with the same function,[49] individuals communicated by talking and looking at one another from a distance, with no physical contact or exchanging of objects allowed. These areas were held continuously under the strictest supervision.[50] Moreover, this zone of encounters served as a form of public self-display for the 'socially respectable', allowing them to reassure everyone that they were physically healthy and perfectly purified,

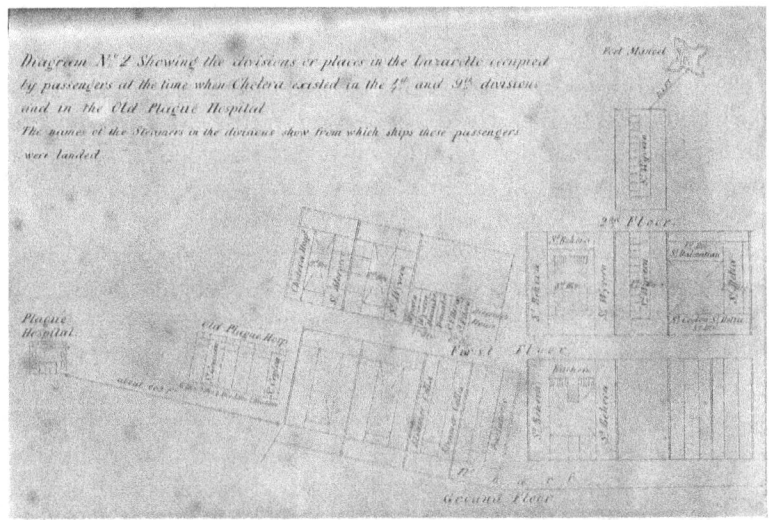

Figure 5.4 Plan of the Manoel Island lazaretto (Malta)

and thus ready to be granted pratique to circulate in society. Found in all lazarettos, the *parlatorio* operated as a social, psychological and emotional safety valve – at least for a number of those in quarantine. It also simultaneously enabled the recuperation of trade which had been inevitably ruptured by the quarantine system itself.

Border purification: bodies, commodities and ideas

Disinfecting bodies, merchandise and animals

Lazarettos were set up to protect countries against the intrusion and spread of disease by filtering and disinfecting inflows of bodies, animals and commodities before these crossed the borders. Passing through quarantine, travellers were detained, physically examined, separated and disinfected, and in the process disciplined into bodies subjected to the state authority of the receiving country. From the sequence of filtering procedures in the lazaretto, the disinfection phase was considered the most crucial for the well-functioning of the entire quarantine operation. During this phase, various forms and techniques of depuration were conducted, which mainly consisted of fumigation – frequently done with sulphuric vapours – and immersion or *spoglio* in baths or seawater. The use of water and fumes was essential in these expurgation procedures, as in all other purification rituals that had been practised from earliest times. Similarly, all cross-border travellers and all their belongings had to undergo meticulous depuration – this was to be conducted step by step and according to guidelines and specific procedures. Indeed, it was carried out under surveillance for fear of contagion. Being performed by a repetition of gestures and manual techniques in proximity to but without touching the body or object undergoing disinfection, the entire procedure left most travellers with a strong sense of having undergone a sort of sacred cross-border ritual of purification.[51]

As they landed, all people were required to let go of their luggage and personal belongings for disinfection.[52] They were also required to pass on any paper material for fumigation, while coins were dipped in vinegar and sea water several times, after which they were given back to be reused.[53] All belongings were marked and registered, with receipts given to their owners to be able to reclaim them. Once all passengers had disembarked and the last cargo had been unloaded, expurgators would be called to disinfect all parts of the ship under the watchful eyes of other sanitary officials.[54] Meanwhile, all the ship's passengers would be separated as a group. Together they proceeded to undergo individual expurgation, while their clothes were ventilated and purified with sulphuric vapour, formaldehyde, or a combination of these, with other chemicals and herbs added in as required.[55] For most passengers, disinfection was a rather unpleasant affair.[56] In most lazarettos, even after having gone through all the phases of quarantine without showing any indication of illness, passengers were called for another medical inspection before being admitted to free pratique. In some cases, as in the lazaretto of Malta, those ready to make their exit were once again ordered to undertake a final 'expurgation with sulphuric vapours' ten hours before being officially permitted to leave the lazaretto.[57] This was done as a matter of extra precaution.

By the late 1830s, travellers who had already spent half of their imposed time with 'no suspicion of contagious disease among them' following disinfection, could opt to end their quarantine by paying for a *spoglio*.[58] One can take the Greek lazarettos as an example of how the *spoglio* worked in practice after it was made legal on the passing of the Hellenic Royal Ordinance on 10 October 1836. Those in quarantine could, being examined by a physician, pay to undergo a *spoglio* by immersing completely nude 'in a warm bath, remaining in the water – with a temperature of 28 to 30 degrees – for at least a quarter of an hour and dip [their] head also.' Once out of the water, they had to wear new clothes '[sent to] them from the town'. If the physician certified them healthy 'they were admitted to free pratique',[59] but their personal clothes and belongings were left to undergo complete fumigation until they reached the end of their officially imposed quarantine period.[60]

Animals, such as those accompanying travellers, also came under strict regulations. Quarantine was enforced on these creatures according to their 'place of origin' and their classification in the 'susceptibility list' which corresponded to their type of skin or fur. Once brought down on land, they were swiftly taken in isolation for a period lasting as long as, if not actually exceeding, that of their owners.[61] They were to be kept confined at all times in cages, or alternatively chained.[62] Their disinfection was usually achieved by repeated immersion in sea water,[63] although other forms of expurgation – including fumigation – were also employed. When it came to large beasts, including livestock, these were herded in a distinctively enclosed area complete with sheds, pans and yards. This would normally be located at one end of the compound at sea level. On showing the first visible signs of disease, an animal was slain right away, and its carcass burned in a location specifically indicated for that purpose. All animals had to do their time in quarantine, passing through repeated immersions and being meticulously scrubbed.[64]

At the same time, large cargo was unloaded in separate yards and warehouses specifically fitted for the 'purification of bulky merchandise'.[65] Upon the presentation of a clean bill of health, expurgators, assisted by a couple of guardians,[66] proceeded to ventilate commodities – a process known as *sciorino* – taking care not to make contact with any other cargo. Commodities such as cotton, wool and skins, classified as susceptible material, were unpacked to be aired and then fumigated. In doing so, great attention was paid to ensure the goods would not be damaged. However, regulations, such as those under which all Dalmatian lazarettos operated, explicitly advised that it was better to damage merchandise – which meant facing protests for indemnities by the owners – than risk leaving any matter not completely depurated. Material considered 'highly susceptible to contagion' such as (Egyptian) cotton, could be unpacked and left to ventilate for a couple of days on board the ship itself before being unloaded to be disinfected with the above method.[67]

Expurgating ideas: filtering knowledge

Paper was another material classified as susceptible to contagion.[68] It therefore required meticulous disinfection in all its different written or printed forms, whether as letters, parcels, books or journals. In the fumigation mail room, information could be sifted and recorded, and even censored if so required. Certainly, the expurgation of mail was one principle means for gathering intelligence on individuals or groups. In the British protectorate of the Ionian Islands, correspondence passing through quarantine was 'opened, and copied, translations [from Greek] or sometimes summaries were sent to London',[69] leading to the arrest of anti-British activists. A similar filtering expurgation of letters was conducted in the other British-controlled lazaretto in Malta, from where extensive mail – despatched from India and Egypt to Britain and Europe – passed to be fumigated. Here, the expurgation of letters and printed literature was a normal affair, with the superintendent of quarantine being also the head of intelligence at one time.[70] While the fumigation of paper – being 'susceptible matter' – was done to prevent the spread of contagious diseases, letters and printed matter were expurgated against the divulgation of ideas considered ostensibly 'contagious' and threatening, to the moral, political and social order of the receiving country.

For these reasons, the disinfection of postal correspondence was given utmost attention. Picked up with a lance-like cane stick in the Dalmatian lazarettos,[71] or a pair of long tongs in other quarantines, letters and packs were delivered by the guardians to the *stanza profumata* – or 'mail chambers' – and dropped onto a set of trays for their 'purification' to begin in earnest. From that point onwards, the procedure was taken over by the *fumigatore* – also known as *profumatore* – who picked up these letters with a pair of pincers and slit each one of them with a small chisel, making two to four cuts from one side to another.[72] This was done in such a way as to leave letters undamaged, yet perforated enough to enable sulphuric fumes – emanating from a mix of sulphuric acid, manganese and common salt poured on burning straw – to completely penetrate them.[73] All such letters were placed in the upper tray of the 'purifying oven', or in larger 'fumigation chambers', which were hermetically sealed compartments in the wall, to optimise disinfection.[74]

Although given little importance in the historical literature, the mail fumigation room was a vital part of the lazaretto complex, due to its filtering and expurgation of mail containing opinions/ideas considered threatening to society. In so doing, these procedures facilitated the gathering of intelligence for the state. Corroborated by the contagious theory, as a means to protect society from disease, the slitting and purification of paper mail continued to be practised until the early twentieth century with the official exclusion of all mail from disinfection by the Paris Convention of 1903.[75]

The lazaretto as archive: the production of scientific knowledge

The filtering and expurgation of letters and printed literature directs our attention to the lazaretto as also being a centre for the archiving of information and the production of medical-sanitary knowledge. All known movement and activities within these sites were detailed in registers and deposited in the quarantine archive, with at least one copy passed on to the public health authorities. Lazaretto registers therefore came to be filled with data on the number of passengers, their health and social status, gender, 'port of origin',[76] and the date of arrival and exit from quarantine. Taken in its wider context, the massive accumulation of knowledge from the principal lazarettos in southern Europe proved indispensable for each state's management of its territorial borders, and for the planning and implementing of sanitary policies and biopolitical strategies of social control. Besides, it also contributed to further scientific, medical-sanitary debates.

Widely circulated in print, quarantine-sourced information – in the form of raw data, case studies and detailed accounts – actually came to be used as fundamental evidence corroborating the main arguments found in the debate between the microbial-contagionists and the miasmatic-environmentalists. This is evident in the extensive volumes of official reports, medical literature,[77] and the minutes of the International Sanitary Conferences (from 1851) which led to the first international sanitary conventions – and the standardisation of quarantine procedures. Simultaneously, the various streams of information deriving from the different lazarettos were also used in engrossing global sanitary-medical archives located in the European metropoles. They were also consulted for the construction of regional, imperial and global-wide geoepidemiological cartography.[78]

Certainly, most data of a medical-sanitary nature were gathered first-hand by physicians themselves, which they based on their routine health inspection, clinical observations and questioning of quarantine passengers. The regulations obliged them to write reports clearly and to hand them straight away to the head of establishment[79] who was legally responsible for their care and archiving – and to have them ready for inspection.[80] Apart from these medical-sanitary records, other registers compiled by the director/superintendent himself contained lists and details concerning all arrivals and departures of sail and steam ships, their bills of health, the numbers and health status of passengers and crew, the quantity and quality of the cargo, any dues paid, as well as the dates and method used for the expurgation of merchandise by category.[81] Quarantine registers in their entirety, therefore, make empirically evident the multifunctionality of the lazaretto as a border-filter. Such edifices could be observed operating as a prophylactic against the inward spread of disease, but also as detention centres, collectors of quarantine dues, sanitary and social-behavioural laboratories, intelligence-gathering offices and knowledge-generating archives.

Expurgators: ritual performers, bodies observed

The expurgator – also known as the fumigator or purificator[82] – is ubiquitous in the extensive corpus of nineteenth-century scientific, medical-sanitary literature dealing with quarantine, where his role was mainly regarded as the focus of scientific inquiry. In comparison, the health guardians, who were present throughout the premises[83], attentive 'never to lose sight of the traveller'[84], were mentioned much more profusely in most travellers' accounts.[85] One important reason for the scientific interest in the expurgator was his disinfection practices, with all the risks they entailed. These also gained him respect in the lazaretto and beyond. The unique silk or canvas apparel – consisting of a jacket and long trousers with a hood which covered the head, a pair of gloves attached to the sleeves, and large boots[86] – which the expurgator wore to conduct disinfection tasks further enhanced the awe surrounding his person.

In truth, the ritualistic performance against contagion – usually associated with evil – in such close proximity to incoming bodies, animals and objects considered susceptible to infection distinguished the expurgators' job from that of other sanitary personnel. Their routine disinfection tasks – be they ventilation, fumigation, immersion or other methods – caused them to be regarded as the ones who really and courageously 'expose themselves to every possible risk'. This is what the renowned physician and superintendent of quarantine establishments in Britain, Gibraltar and Malta, Dr William Pym (1772–1861) declared in front of the select committee of the House of Commons on Quarantine in 1836.[87] Indeed, the very nearness to bodies and things 'susceptible to contagion', enticed medical-sanitary inquiry to focus specifically on the expurgator's body. This was partly achieved through the clinical observation and constant monitoring of the expurgator's state of health during and after disinfection practices. In view of the risk involved and the skills required in such purification procedures, an expurgator was actually selected for the job by the sanitary authorities, who took into consideration their previous experience as well as their 'moral character', sense of duty, and personal medical history.[88]

A crew of expurgators – whose numbers varied according to the quantity of passengers and the volume of merchandise landed,[89] – were always on the spot, including on Sundays and all religious feast days.[90] A list of those on duty and of the purification procedures they were conducting was issued each time a vessel unloaded,[91] thus keeping them accountable. They were also the first to climb aboard to perform 'complete and proper disinfection' of suspect ships, or others with a foul bill of health. During such times they were accompanied by a physician who was in charge of ensuring that the 'expurgation process was done exhaustively and to the letter of the regulations'.[92] Back on solid lazaretto ground, they proceeded to disinfect all luggage and personal belongings, in addition to seeing to the expurgation of all landed passengers as a group.[93]

Other expurgators were always in attendance at the cargo divisions, namely in the warehouses, yards, courtyards and sheds. It was here that all the merchandise being unloaded from the same ship was to be kept apart and prepared for disinfection. Stockpiles, bales or boxes of 'susceptible matter' were carefully separated according to an official list which classified all material ranging from 'non-susceptible' to 'highly-susceptible'.[94] The ventilation of any 'susceptible material' such as cotton or wool, unloaded from a ship with a clean bill of health, and with no cases of disease on board, would begin straight away. Expurgators would open the bales at one end and cautiously 'push[ed] their arms in so far as they can [...] for the express purpose of ascertaining whether there is infection'.[95] This same method was repeated by opening another end of the bale and 'pushing [their] arm in as deep as [they] can'. Dr Pym noted that while in England 'they use their hands; at Venice and Marseilles [they usually employ] iron hooks'. In all cases, such material was left out in the open, so that it would be 'exposed to air as much as possible'.[96]

Airing procedures were followed by fumigation, which was repeated many times as necessary – especially on a shipment with a foul bill of health. Taking extra care to keep all goods unloaded separately from those of other ships,[97] expurgators would begin the fumigation process 'calmly and carefully'.[98] While conducting disinfection, they were monitored for any symptoms of contagion by doctors on site.[99] Paradoxically, at this point, the body of the expurgator himself became an object of scientific-medical observation, and the source of experimental inquiry.[100] Detailed representations of expurgators' disinfection activities and corresponding health condition were copiously referred to or narrated to illustrate the veracity or otherwise of theses and theories in favour of or against quarantine, within the wider and lasting debate between the contagionists and the miasmatic-environmentalists.[101] On the one hand, supporting themselves with information gathered from these same quarantine sites, the miasmatic-environmentalists propounded the argument that there 'was no instance of *expurgatori* themselves in the lazarettos, exposed to all "susceptible and contagious goods", having ever contracted disease.'[102] Others of the same persuasion, such as public health essayist Thomas Hancock, pointed to the bodies of 'the expurgators of goods from infected cities'. They argued that if contagion was really spread by material things and bodies, then 'one should expect to hear something of annual sacrifices made to the public good in this hazardous occupation [but] none of the expurgators of goods have ever taken the plague'.[103] On the other hand, contagionists pointed out a few cases of expurgators who did actually die by contracting disease, intimating that this happened due to negligence during disinfection or because of infringements of quarantine rules.[104] While these few recorded cases proved the theory of the transmission of disease by contact according to the contagionists, they also strengthened their firm belief that lazarettos still provided the most tangible protection known against the intrusion and spread of contagious disease.

Conclusion

This study has shown that although quarantines were historically set up and legitimised by the contagionist theory of disease, the prevention practices operating within – such as the keeping of strict hygiene and the meticulous disinfection of separate rooms, persons and things – made the lazaretto a site where both contagionist and miasmatic-environmentalist ideas permeated and overlapped in daily practice.[105] The fact that both these sanitary-medical schools could point towards evidence gathered and archived from these lazarettos to corroborate their contrasting theories on aetiology and prophylaxis of disease further confirms this argument.

In truth, this contagionist versus miasmatic debate also reveals the extent to which lazarettos were used as sites of contestation, as much as of scientific inquiry, in which contexts the expurgators themselves became objects of scientific inquiry. Expurgation was considered a most vital procedure in the entire quarantine process, to the effect that all other practices and activities revolved around the disinfection of bodies, animals and merchandise as well as the purification of letters and printed literature. Certainly, as this chapter has made evident, the disinfection of mail led to the reading, annotation and censorship of correspondence, books and journals which expressed and divulgated ideas and opinions considered 'contagious' and therefore detrimental to the social, political and moral order of the receiving country. Therefore, while critically using Agamben's idea of apparatus to explore the lazarettos' function to constrain, regulate and govern the movement and influx of persons and goods on the sea border, this chapter has also brought out the quarantine's deeper and more complex levels of filtering and expurgation. Hence, taking all the procedures conducted in the sequential phases of selection, segregation and disinfection as part of the whole process of quarantine, the lazaretto comes to be presented as a truly multifunctional site. Its operation served as a crossover between detention/identification centre, infective hospital, asylum, sanitary and social behavioural laboratory, postal office, state-intelligence centre and archive which processed, produced and divulgated medical-sanitary knowledge.

Another important observation made in this chapter, and which requires further exploration, is that the duration, intensity and treatments imposed in quarantine on different groups of passengers were not only based on sanitary–medical criteria, but were imbricated with considerations of social class, power status, religious and ethnic factors. This resulted in the creation of an internal social divide within the quarantine precincts, which in turn reflected the social hierarchy and power structures of the receiving country.

One other conclusion drawn here is that these border-filtering operations also depended on the maintenance of strict internal discipline and order, as articulated in the very similar regulations of all these southern European lazarettos. By analysing these regulations in some detail, this study has further revealed their common underlying moral undertone. In much the same way as they were required to disinfect their bodies and personal belongings from contagious diseases, passengers were also expected to purify themselves through moral expurgation. Such had always been the case, since time immemorial, with cross-border rituals.

Notes

1 G. Deleuze and F. Guattari, 'Treaties on nomadology – the war machine', in *A Thousand Plateaus: Capitalism and Schizoprenia* (London; New York: Continuum Publishing, 2004).
2 D. Palermo, 'Introduzione, "Epidemie, Sanita" e controllo dei Confini', *Storia Urbana*, 147, Anno XXXVIII (April–June, 2015), 5–8; *l'Epidemia dei Messina del 1743* (Palermo: Epos, 1984); see also *Le Leggi Amministrattive del Regno Delle Due Sicilie Pe' Dominj al di qua e al di la del Faro – Opera [a cura di Francesco Dias]* (Napoli: Tipog. Classici Italiani, 1843).
3 T. Kurki, 'Borders from the cultural point of view: an introduction to writing borders', *Culture Unbound. Journal of Current Cultural Research*, 6 (2014), 1055–70.
4 See for instance: A. Bashford (ed.), *Quarantine: Local and Global Histories* (London: Palgrave Macmillan, 2016); J. Chircop and F. J. Martinez (eds), *Mediterranean Quarantines, 1750–1914: Space, Identity and Power* (Manchester: Manchester University Press, 2018); K. Maglen, *The English System: Immigration and the Making of a Port Sanitary Zone* (Manchester; New York: Palgrave Macmillan, 2014).
5 G. Agamben, *'What is Apparatus?' And Other Essays* (California: Stanford University Press, 2009), p. 14.
6 Ibid., p. 19.
7 *Repertorio Amministrattivo ossia Collezione di Leggi, Decreti, Reali Rescritti, Ministeriali di Massima Regolamenti Ed Instruzioni Sull Amministrazione Civile Del Regno Delle Due Sicilie (Compilato dal barone Pompilio Petitti (Quarta Edizione))*, Napoli, Dallo Stabilimento Del Tramater, 1846, vol. 2; *Raccolta Delle Leggi Ed Ordinanze*

Dell'Anno 1830 per la Dalmazia, Zara, Tip. Luigi Battara, 1831; *Raccolta delle Leggi e Disposizioni di pubblica amministrazione nello Stato Pontificio*, Roma, Stamperia R.C.A., 1834–1849.
8 G. Bussolin, *Delle Istituzioni di Sanita' marittima nel bacino Mediterraneo* (Trieste: L. Hermanstorfer, 1881); W. Heather, *The New Mediterranean Pilot. Containing Two Hundred and Twenty-Four Accurate Plans of the Principal Harbours, Bays, and Islands in the Mediterranean Sea* (London: W. Heather, 1810); J. Howard, *An Account of the Principal Lazarettos in Europe, with Various Papers Relative to the Plague and Additional Remarks on the Present State of Prisons in Great Britain and Ireland* (London: Johnson, Dilly & Cadell, 1791).
9 M. Harrison, *Contagion: How Commerce Has Spread Disease* (New Haven, CT: Yale University Press, 2012).
10 Bussolin, *Delle Istituzioni*, p. 220.
11 P. Baldwin, *Contagion and the State in Europe, 1830–1930* (Cambridge: Cambridge University Press, 2005), p. 201; J. Chircop, 'Quarantine, sanitization, colonialism and the construction of the "contagious Arab" in the Mediterranean, 1830s–1900', in Chircop and Martinez (eds), *Mediterranean Quarantines*, p. 204.
12 Q. Bonastra, 'Los Origines del Lazareto Pabellonario. La Arquitectura Cuarantenaria en El Cambio del Seicientos al Ochocientos', *Asclepio. Revista de Historia de la Medicina y de la Ciencia*, 60:1 (2008) 237–66; Bussolin, *Delle istituzioni*, see plates, *passim*.
13 Baldwin, *Contagion and the State*, p. 211.
14 M. Foucault, *Discipline and Punish. The Birth of the Prison* (London: Penguin Books, 1991), pp. 143–4.
15 T. Spencer Wells, 'Original communication: on the practical results of quarantine', *Medical Journal*, 15:2 (September 1854), 831–4, at 831.
16 J. Davy, *Notes and Observations on the Ionian Islands and Malta: With some Remarks on Constantinople and Turkey, and on the System of Quarantine* vol. 2 (London: Smith Elds., Co., 1842), p. 325.
17 Bussolin, *Delle Istituzioni*, p. 273; G. Galea, 'The quarantine service and the lazaretto of Malta', *Melita Historica*, 4 (1966), 18–45, at 24; P. Cassar, 'A tour of the lazaretto buildings', *Melita Historica*, 4 (1987), 369–80.
18 *Raccolta Delle Leggi*, Art. 192, 376; *Repertorio Amministrattivo*, Art. 193, 376.
19 *Raccolta Delle Leggi*, Art. 169, 408; Art. 192–3, 376.
20 Ibid., Art. 156, 403–4.
21 Ibid., Art. 211, 423; Art. 212, 427.
22 Ibid., Art. 169, 408.
23 Ibid., Art. 168, 406.

24 *Repertorio Amministrattivo*, Art. 193, 376.
25 *Raccolta Delle Leggi*, Art. 186, 46; Bussolin, *Delle Istituzioni*, p. 221.
26 Ibid., Art. 186, 416.
27 Ibid., Art. 188, 420.
28 W. Beamont, *A Diary of a Journey to the East in the Autumn of 1854* vol. 1 (London: Longman, Brown & Green, 1856), pp. 44–5.
29 *Raccolta Delle Leggi*, Art. 193/8, 376.
30 Ibid., Art. 169, 408; *Repertorio Amministrattivo*, Art. 211–15, 379–80.
31 Howard, *An Account of the Principal Lazarettos*.
32 Howard, *An Account of the Principal Lazarettos*, p. 23; J. Howard, *A Handbook for Travellers in the Ionian Islands, Greece, Turkey, Asia Minor, and Constantinople* (London: John Murray, 1845), p. 20.
33 E. Giffard, *A Short Visit to the Ionian Islands, Athens and the Morea* (London: John Murray, 1837), p. 383; Walter Scott, *The Man Behind the Books. Biography, Journals, Letters, Memoirs & Autobiographical Essays of the Author* (n.p.: Musaicum Books, 2017); Lord Byron, *The Works of Lord Byron* vol.17, G. G. Byron, T. Moore and John Wright (eds) (London: John Murray, 1833), p. 239.
34 *Repertorio Amministrattivo*, Art. 210, 379.
35 Ibid., Art. 184, 373; Bussolin, *Delle Institutioni*, p. 221.
36 *Repertorio Amministrattivo*, Art. 7, 341–2; J. D. Tully, *The History of Plague as it Has Lately Appeared in the Islands of Malta, Gozo, Corfu, Cephalonia &c. Detailing Important Facts* (London: Longman & Brown, 1821), p. 226.
37 Ibid., pp. 226–7.
38 Chircop, 'Quarantine, sanitisation, colonialism', pp. 199–231.
39 *Repertorio Amministrattivo*, Art. 11, 343.
40 S. Bevan, *Sand and Canvas. A Narrative of Adventures in Egypt with a Sojourn Among the Artists of Rome* (London: C. Gilpin, 1849), pp. 160–1.
41 Howard, *A Handbook for Travellers in the Ionian Islands*, p. 30
42 Ibid., pp. 16–17.
43 Galea, 'The quarantine service', at 187.
44 G. Viscount Valentia, *Voyages and Travels to India, Ceylon, the Red Sea, Abyssinia and Egypt in the Years 1802, 1803, 1804, 1805 and 1806* vol. 3 (London: William Miller, 1809), p. 483; G. Darby Griffith, *A Journey Across the Desert from Ceylon to Marseilles* vol. 2 (London: H. Colburn, 1845), p. 77.
45 Giffard, *A Short Visit*, p. 383.
46 Howard, *An Account of the Principal Lazarettos*, p. 23.
47 Howard, *A Handbook for Travellers in the Ionian Islands*, p. 23.

48 Scott, *The Man Behind the Books*; Bevan, *Sand and Canvas*, p. 161.
49 For the 'parlatorio zone' and for crafts serving a similar purpose in the Ionian Islands see C. Tsiamis, E. Thalassinou, E. Poulakou-Rebelakou and A. Hatzakis, 'Quarantine and British "protection" of the Ionian Islands, 1815–64', in Chircop and Martinez, *Mediterranean Quarantine*, p. 270; Bussolin, *Delle Istituzioni*, p. 271.
50 A. Slade, *Turkey, Greece and Malta* vol. 1 (London: Saunders & Outley, 1837), p. 130.
51 See K. Lehari, 'Purification of Landscapes', in *Koht ja Paik: Place and Location. Studies in Environmental Aesthetics and Semiotics V* (2006), 109–18, www.eki.ee/km/place/koht_5.htm (accessed: 25 April 2018); Kurki, 'Borders from the cultural point of view', 1055–9.
52 Bussolin, *Delle Istituzioni*, p. 201.
53 *Raccolta Delle Leggi*, Art. 157, 404.
54 Bussolin, *Delle Istituzioni*, p. 272.
55 Galea, 'The quarantine service', at 18–45.
56 Beamont, *Diary of a Journal*, p. 51; C. Terry, *Scenes and Thoughts in Foreign Lands* (London: William Pickering, 1848), p. 97.
57 Bussolin, *Delle Istituzioni*, p. 227.
58 F. Strong, *Greece as a Kingdom or a Statistical Description of that Country* (London: Longman, Brown, Green & Longman, 1842), p. 41; D. Dakin, *British Intelligence of Events in Greece 1824–1827: A Documentary Collection*, (Athens: s.n., 1959), p. 41.
59 Strong, *Greece as a Kingdom*, pp. 41–2.
60 Howard, *A Handbook for Travellers in the Ionian Islands*, pp. 24–5.
61 *Repertorio Amministrattivo*, Art. 193/3, 374.
62 *Raccolta delle Leggi*, Art. 151, 403.
63 Ibid., Art. 156/57, 404.
64 *Raccolta delle Leggi e Disposizioni [Stato Pontificio]*, Art. 33, 104.
65 Tully, *The History of Plague*, p. 228.
66 *Raccolta Delle Leggi*, Art. 143, 400; Art. 145; Bussolin, *Delle Istituzioni*, pp. 218–19.
67 Davy, *Notes and Observations*, p. 342.
68 *Repertorio Amministrattivo*, Art. 10, 343.
69 Dakin, *British Intelligence*, p. 20.
70 W. Hardman, *History of Malta During the French and British Occupations 1798–1815* (London: Longman, Green & Co., 1909), p. 495.
71 *Raccolta Delle Leggi*, Art. 210, 423.
72 Bussolin, *Delle Instituzioni*, pp. 343–4; *Raccolta Delle Leggi*, Art. 155, 404.
73 Galea, 'The quarantine service', at 29.
74 Ibid., at 32.

75 Chapt. II, Sect. 2, Art. 16, *International Sanitary Convention – Paris, 3 December 1903*, (London: H.M. Stationery Office, 1907).
76 Chircop, 'Quarantine, sanitization, colonialism', p. 200.
77 Davy, *Notes and Observations*, pp. 325, 254–364. From the large volume of literature in English based on records from the lazarettos see Charles Maclean M.D., *Observations on Quarantine: Being the Substance of a Lecture Delivered at the Liverpool Lyceum by Charles Maclean M.D.* (Liverpool: Liverpool Mediterranean Association, 1824), pp. 23–30; T. Hancock, *Research into the Laws and Phenomena of Pestilence including a Medical Sketch and Review of the Plague* (London: William Phillips, 1821), pp. 232–6 and *passim*. On the inconsistencies found in the quarantine procedures in the Mediterranean lazarettos, see A. B. Granville, *A Letter to the Right Hon. W. Huskisson by A. B. Granville* (London, 1825), pp. 8–10, 16–17 and Davy, *Notes and Observations*, pp. 347–8.
78 Chircop, 'Quarantine, sanitization, colonialism', pp. 204, 214–215.
79 *Raccolta Delle Leggi*, Art. 164, 406; *Repertorio Amministrativo*, Art. 205, 377–8.
80 *Repertorio Amminstrattivo*, Art. 183,191.
81 *Raccolta Delle Leggi*, Art. 181–5, 414–15; *Repertorio Amministrattivo*, Art. 190–1, 374–5.
82 Found in most texts as *fumigatori* or *purificatori*, or *sborratori* (as in the Ionian Islands).
83 Viscount Valentia, *Voyages and Travels*, p. 483.
84 Slade, *Turkey, Greece and Malta*, p. 130.
85 Ibid.; also Scott, *The Man Behind the Books*.
86 Galea, 'The quarantine service', at 19–20.
87 Dr Pym in evidence, *Select Committee, House of Commons*, 26 March 1836, *Selection of Reports and Papers of the House of Commons*, vol. 35 (Medical), 1836, 58–9.
88 Ibid., 235.
89 Pym in evidence, *Selection of Reports*, 58.
90 *Raccolta Delle Leggi*, Art. 153, 403.
91 Ibid., Art. 182, 414.
92 Tully, *The History of Plague*, p. 235.
93 Bussolin, *Delle Istituzioni*, pp. 218–19.
94 *Raccolta Delle Leggi*, Art. 145, 400.
95 Mr John Green in evidence, *Selection of Reports*, 1836, 40.
96 Pym in evidence, *Selection of Reports*, 57; *Raccolta Delle Leggi*, Art. 145, 400.
97 *Raccolta Delle Leggi*, Art. 140, 400; Tully, *The History of Plague*, pp. 228–9.

98 Tully, *The History of Plague*, pp. 231, 235.
 99 *Raccolta Delle Leggi*, Art. 164, 400.
100 Maclean, *Observations on Quarantine*, pp. 25–8. Hancock, *Research into the Laws*, pp. 232–5; Tully, *The History of Plague*, p. 235.
101 On the expurgator being used as an example in both arguments see Maclean, *Observations on Quarantine*, pp. 20–5.
102 Tully, *The History of Plague*, p. 342; Mr C. Grant, 'Quarantine Bill' – *Hansard* (30 March 1825), vol. 12, cc.1316; also M. Gavin, *Quarantine and the Plague: Being a Summary of the Report on the Subjects Recently Addressed to the Royal Academy of Medicine in France*, (London: Samuel Highley, 1846).
103 Hancock, *Research into the Laws*, pp. 232–3; J. Read, 'An appeal to the medical profession on the unity of the improved patent syring', *The London Medical Physical Journal*, 53(1825), 363.
104 A. B. Granville, *A Letter to the Right Hon. W. Huskisson*, 8.
105 See C. Hamlin, *Cholera: The Biography* (Oxford: Oxford University Press, 2009) and Baldwin, *Contagion and the State*, pp. 1–36, who argue against the long-prevailing historical dualist view that miasmatism versus contagionism dominated sanitary practice in Europe.

6

Sealing borders and containing prisoners: from free movement of migrants to containment in concentration camps

Paul Weindling

Onward and outward migration: from multi-ethnic to ethnically homogeneous states

In the wake of the First World War came a transformation of international relief for famine and epidemics. Before 1914, there had been free movement of peoples to escape starvation, disease and anti-semitic pogroms, as millions left distress in eastern Europe for a life in the New World, or to the East End of London. From the German–Russian border to the ports of Bremen and Hamburg, there was an elaborate system of border disinfection stations, sluicing through migrants with showers and fumigation of baggage, 'sealed' through trains from border to port, and before embarkation for the transatlantic crossing – quarantine to prevent typhoid on board.[1] The culmination was the vast human processing and medical inspection system of Ellis Island, instituted in 1893.[2] While the US port inspectors aimed to weed out carriers of infection, the system was essentially permissive, designed to admit the large numbers of migrants who had travelled from what was then Russia across Germany and then across the Atlantic. American port inspectors supervised the transit arrangements on the European side to make sure regulations were rigorously enforced.[3] While there was some charitable assistance, the mass migration predated a system of visas and migration quotas. The purchase of a ticket from the shipping company HAPAG Lloyd meant a series of sanitary procedures: entry into a migration system with border sanitary controls at medical hygiene stations on the German–Russian border, an approved transit route bypassing Berlin and on to one of Germany's western ports before crossing in steerage. The one concern on the United States side was importation of infections. This was similarly the case with the mass migration of Italians from 1890.[4] Ironically, the erection of welfare states would come to pose a barrier to those fleeing persecution and famine. This chapter explores the transition in migrant processing from mass migration to the Holocaust and the containment procedures in concentration and extermination camps; instead of making sure that migrants were free from pathogens, the Nazi procedures meant the migrants effectively became pathogens to be eradicated. Many aspects remain insufficiently appreciated such as barriers to migrants claiming welfare, medical controls in the 1930s, and the extent to which the Germans exploited prisoners for medical research, turning people into reservoirs of pathogens.

By the late nineteenth century, systems of medical controls on migrants had become essentially permissive; they were designed to screen and sanitise the passage of persons and goods, while filtering out infectious disease carriers from transmigrant persons and their possessions. Screening concerned cleansing of those carrying an infection and the identification of asymptomatic carriers, notably for typhoid ('typhus' in German). Measures involved showering and general cleansing with the need to sift out carriers of infectious parasites. A major target was body lice which harboured typhus (i.e. Fleckfieber or spotted fever) rickettsiae: a transmission pattern discovered by the Pasteurian microbiologist Charles Nicolle at Tunis in North Africa around 1909.[5] Such systems involved periodic segregation, cleansing regimes and the use of pesticides for clothing and possessions. The sanitary controls for the passage to the United States from eastern and southern Europe were a remarkably effective system, enabling millions to migrate in a permissive era of free movement of populations. A disinfection station was part of a railway junction. A chain of disinfection and quarantine stations provided sanitary showers and delousing on the borders of the Russian Empire with Germany and Austria–Hungary, and sealed trains transported migrants to ports. Then quarantine prior to embarkation was imposed at port cities such as Bremen and Hamburg with the aim of preventing outbreaks of illness at sea.[6] The system culminated in the reception and sorting centre of the vast human processing plant at Ellis Island. The systems were regimented, and although certain infections, notably trachoma, could mean exclusion, the procedures were, in principle, benign. However, these effective systems need to be set against what Markel and Stern see as the American propensity to blame outsiders for importing disease.[7]

Soldiers on all sides during the First World War underwent rigorous delousing. Lousiness became a chronic problem. Lice infested the seams of uniforms and the folds of personal possessions, and required scrupulous attention to personal hygiene. The Germans experimented with many sorts of delousing chemicals and other methods ranging from steam and hot air to toxic chemicals. By 1917 they had developed hydrocyanic acid as a pesticide for cleansing personal effects, clothes and baggage. In the wake of the First World War the United States imposed strict immigration quotas. Although social provision was late to come to the United States with Roosevelt's New Deal, the immigration quotas were motivated by concern to defend the ethnic homogeneity of the white elite with primacy accorded to British, Dutch, German and Scandinavian ancestry. Psychological screening was also imposed at Ellis Island to screen-out so-called 'idiots' and 'imbeciles'. Ethnic concerns thus fuelled anti-immigration restrictions, marking the decline of Ellis Island as a migrant processing centre, as the flood of migrants before 1914 became a mere trickle during the 1920s.

There was an equivalent change in Europe after the First World War when there was a profound shift from outward migration to elimination of the sources of disease and famine, and the prioritising of welfare systems. The context was a new system of borders, between fiercely nationalist and antagonistic states based on national self-determination. The focus was no longer outward migration but the containment of populations. Major relief operations took place to eradicate disease and famine at the focus of distress. Systems of quarantine and sanitary control changed in purpose; before 1914 the borders were porous and permissive but by 1918 the systems of border controls had become restrictive and designed to contain potential migrants, who were faced with immigration quotas and visas. What happened was a vast restructuring of international relief measures which changed from sanitary screening of migrants to sealing them in behind the borders of the new interwar state system based on national self-determination. The shift from imperial power blocs to the post-Versailles system of states based on national self-determination meant the imposition of additional borders and migration quotas, which came with severe emigration and immigration restrictions. As welfare state benefits increased, so did barriers to access. In effect, the modern system of welfare states meant ever more elaborate borders, and often this meant medical controls, vaccination certificates, health examinations and a raft of other immigration quota requirements.

The 1920s saw fundamental changes, with the transition to the system of post-imperial national self-determination. States developed social insurance, industrial health and welfare systems. As welfare benefits increased in scope, efforts increased to control and restrict inward migration so as to prevent the arrival of alien claimants. Consequently, sanitary controls became designed to exclude displaced populations after the First World War. Although ineffective against the 'Spanish flu', they were in force during the Russian famine years of 1918–1924 with delousing stations at railway junctions in order to prevent the feared epidemic of typhus. Major agencies such as the American Relief Administration provided food and sanitary assistance at the point of need. Smaller but more targeted organisations such as the Save the Children Fund (founded on 15 April 1919 in London) and Hoover's American Relief Administration were permitted by the Bolsheviks to work at points of distress, such as in the Volga region. The political paradox of an anti-communist United States assisting Bolshevik Russia is only explicable through shared priorities of containment of populations. The afflicted were meant to remain in place behind an 'iron curtain' of sanitary defences. The new League of Nations sent epidemic commissioners into central and eastern Europe and developed a sanitary zone stretching from the Baltic to the Black Sea with delousing stations at railway junctions. In 1919 the International Commission of the Red Cross mounted a sanitary expedition to a rapidly shrinking western Ukraine.

The new system was meant to be one of assistance and medical relief measures, to relieve distress as the vulnerable were supposed to stay in place. Relief in situ meant borders remained inviolable. This was, in effect, a modern system of disaster relief relying on externally organised relief teams in order to prevent outward migration. This system formed the origins of modern disaster relief procedures where containment in the epicentre of famine and/or epidemics is prioritised over free movement and fleeing the area of distress. Deception and ingenuity were necessary to pass constraining frontiers. Beyond this, new organisations such as the Rockefeller Foundation believed that destabilising epidemic disease could be eradicated by international relief teams. The Rockefeller Foundation kitted out each successor state with a monumental hygiene institute in the hope of reinforcing sanitary systems. The League of Nations, itself drawing on Rockefeller Foundation funding, boosted preventive medical systems as opposed to assisting the distressed.

The other way sanitary controls functioned was to facilitate the colossal population exchange, which was agreed in 1923 between Greece and the new Turkish Republic.[8] The population exchanges arose from the idea of national self-determination in territorially defined states. A state in the post-Versailles system was to be, as far as possible, culturally and ethnically homogeneous. The transition occurred from a world order dominated by imperial powers which had multi-ethnic patchworks. The post-Versailles system was one of national self-determination with nation states, each having a national welfare system with new and ever more elaborate systems of social insurance. It also meant a new international disaster relief system designed to deliver aid to the place of crisis rather than allow at-risk populations to freely migrate. The old imperial states, such as Austria–Hungary and the Ottoman Empire, had been ethnically mixed, albeit with the elite playing off different groups against each other. A border was administrative and fiscal. In the new interwar system, a border involved measures to exclude 'aliens'. Minorities – notably Jews (some stateless as in interwar Vienna) and migrant Roma – found themselves in vulnerable positions, lacking rights and subject to deportation. Ironically, the proliferation of post-imperial states based on national self-determination meant that many residents lost a claim to nationality where they resided, and instead received nationality on the basis of where they were born.

Policed borders went with rigorous measures to exclude those with mental and physical disabilities, along with visible infections, notably the eye infection trachoma. The list of contagious diseases justifying exclusion became ever longer. Soon mental illness and disabilities also became grounds for exclusion. Immigration quotas and visas, along with exit restrictions from the fledgling Soviet

Union stemmed the flow of refugees and migration. The Polish lawyer Raphael Lemkin presciently noted during the 1930s that ethnic minorities in states based on principles of national self-determination were vulnerable to persecution and state-sanctioned violence to the point of mass destruction. He saw that containment of vulnerable ethnic minorities could lead to barbarity and destruction.[9]

Persecution and containment under National Socialism

The rise of National Socialism imposed a new tension on the interwar system of migration quotas and restrictive controls. At-risk and persecuted people were no longer free to migrate. The persecuted became impoverished as they were dismissed from their jobs and excluded from welfare systems. The international state system could not adjust from regimes of containment to rescue. The system of immigration quotas and visas posed immensely difficult barriers to Jews seeking refuge from Nazism from 1933 to 1941 when the United States entered the war. The Nuremberg Laws of 1935 defined citizenship as based on racial purity. It meant that Jews and racial undesirables lost civic rights and social and professional status, losing also the freedom to cross frontiers. Nazi Germany rounded up and evicted its 17,000 Polish Jews from 27 October 1938, but Poland was unwilling to receive them (effectively cancelling their citizenship), leaving them stranded in hastily constructed refugee camps on the border at Zbaszyri/Zbąszyń. Romania similarly banned its Jewish citizens from returning, indeed stripping them of their civil rights (gained only in 1919) and access to the state welfare system to which they had contributed. Returning Jews from Germany (and its former Austrian territory) were held in vermin-infested prisons on the frontier, and then forced to return to Nazi Germany. The social deprivation of populations under persecution meant that the risks of malnutrition and infection increased. What the persecuted needed was at the very least a place of safety and temporary refuge, whereas the international systems were designed to keep afflicted populations in place, albeit sustained by external aid.

Even when allowed to migrate, medical certification was imposed as a condition for travel. The UK Movement for the Care of Children from Germany imposed, from February 1939, a requirement for medical certificates for children arriving from the estimated 10,000 Kindertransportees, coming from Berlin, Hamburg, Prague, Vienna, and the Jewish children stranded on the frontier with Poland, eventually able to come through the port of Gdynia. The basis for this was a commitment made by the British Jewish community that each refugee would be guaranteed that they would not be a burden on state/public welfare. A guarantee of 50 pounds had to be paid by a member of the public for each refugee admitted. Realising the urgency of the situation, a collective guarantee was issued by the Board of Deputies of British Jews to allow the immigration of concentration camp inmates, and Kitchener Camp was provided as a reception centre for those liberated.[10]

It was not an open door for children, even those fortunate enough to have a guarantor. Each child had to have a certificate to state they were not suffering from mental illness, physical disability or an infection. If suffering from an infection the child was not allowed to depart, although they might be eligible for a later place on transport, albeit the transport was, in retrospect, (and even at the time by those understanding the inevitability of war) subject to a finite time window. Mentally or physically handicapped children, including sight and hearing impaired, were unacceptable to the British-based hospitality committee. Asthma or bed-wetting also meant exclusion, even though the psychological stress on the children under Nazi occupation was intense. Here, the idea was that – as for immigration to Palestine – intelligent, physically strong and healthy children and juveniles should be prioritised. Families were forced to leave infirm or mentally incapacitated relatives behind. These unfortunate people were in the front line for deportation and systematic killing. 'Transport to the East' and 'disinfection' became euphemisms for killing so that the children left stranded at the outbreak of war in September 1939 were, by October 1939, on trains for resettlement in Polish towns under German occupation.[11]

The fact that a visa and financial guarantees were difficult for the physically and mentally disabled to obtain posed an immense impediment to migration. It meant that families had to leave their dependants behind – whether sick children or the elderly; a Jewish child with a disability had to be placed in a German institution; and a caring daughter might even return to Germany to look after an infirm parent. Nazi authorities cut welfare subsidies, overstraining

Jewish communities with immense burdens of welfare support.[12] This imposed huge burdens on the persecuted communities, as they assumed the tasks of dispensing meals and welfare subsidies to their excluded and persecuted members. In the circumstances, outward migration was a solution to the excessive financial strains on communities as well as offering life-saving sanctuary from the threat of concentration camps. Emigration was contingent on a 'flight tax' so migration meant that any individual could become impoverished. The United States stuck rigidly to restrictive quotas and challenged generous offers of guarantees. Further pressure came when the Nazi authorities centralised malnourished and impoverished Jews in overcrowded accommodation. The risks of infections massively increased. Despite valiant efforts of ghetto sanitary authorities, those deported to overcrowded and under-provisioned ghettoes only exceptionally escaped destruction.[13]

Initially, the concentration camp was designed primarily to contain political opponents of the Nazis, but also included vagrants and so-called 'asocials' who were generally Sinti or Roma. After the orgy of violence and destruction of Kristallnacht/the Night of Broken Glass, there were massive round-ups of Jews. At this stage the concentration camps had a reputation for appalling brutality which resulted in sporadic deaths due to severe beatings and brutality. It was, however, still possible to be extricated for immediate migration for a fortunate few. By the time war broke out in September 1939, 'stateless' Jews were rounded up in Vienna, and – after German anthropologists had taken the opportunity to take face masks and samples of hair – were sent to Buchenwald concentration camp.[14] The idea that rounded-up prisoners could be exploited for research was then transposed to concentration camps. This was a sign that stateless Jews could be deported to a concentration camp, ghetto or, from 1941, an extermination camp. Increasingly, the Nazi concentration camp came to represent the inverse of an open migration system; the sealed borders, and the designation of population groups as 'surplus' and 'pathogenic' meant that hygiene provided rationales and technologies for destruction. 'Resettlement in the East' was a genocidal fiction when all that awaited was a severely overcrowded and underprovided ghetto, a gas van, or, from 1941, a carbon monoxide or Zyklon gas chamber with a fake shower, or a firing squad in an isolated wood in Ukraine, Belarus or in one of

Sealing borders and containing prisoners 163

the German-occupied Baltic states. Originally benign disinfection procedures to ensure disease-free migration and accepted as routine by migrants became a part of the Nazi machinery of mass murder and genocide. The permissive hygienic controls of showers and disinfection devised in the 1880s found their opposites in the Nazi fake 'disinfection' procedures to kill human 'vermin'.

'Transport to the East' and 'disinfection'

Nazi extermination involved the inverse of the hitherto benign disinfection procedures in that over a million displaced and persecuted Jews were killed with the delousing agent Zyklon B (based on the pesticide hydrocyanic acid, developed from 1917) at Auschwitz. What had been a system designed to facilitate free movement of populations seeking to escape poverty and persecution became a procedure of systematised genocide. The delousing agent used for clothing and personal possessions was turned against the displaced persons by herding them into gas chambers disguised with fake shower heads. Thus Auschwitz – as an endpoint – was the inverse of the human processing centre of Ellis Island. The procedures of persecution were permeated by the routines of quarantine with the capacious poison gas chamber designed to process and kill batches of several hundred people at a single functioning (whereas carbon monoxide used first to kill psychiatric patients and then in the extermination camps of Treblinka, Sobibor and Belcec could kill around 80–100 people, Zyklon could kill ten times as many). The deception of the gas chamber exploited the expectation of displaced populations that they would be subject to disinfection of their possessions, showers and quarantine. The conditioning of multitudes to hygienic procedures ended in their killing. For a select few – retained for forced labour – delousing was a rite of passage for entry into Auschwitz Birkenau. It involved the dehumanising removal of hair from a prisoner's head, and caustic disinfectants. The tattoo of a camp number – uniquely for Jews in Auschwitz – transformed the person into a dehumanised numerical value. The procedure was humiliating and depersonalising. The containment in a concentration camp was the antithesis of free migration in search of a new identity in terms of sustaining work and instead was meant to be destructive of identity in systems designed to work the prisoners to death; the euphemistic inscription 'Arbeit macht frei' ('work sets you free') was indicative of the camp aims. As Primo Levi's writings show, personal identity was in jeopardy and physical survival was a strong motivator.[15]

The Nazi onslaught against Poland resulted in expulsion of Polish Jews from the annexed territory of the Warthegau, and consequent overcrowding of refugees in Warsaw. By December 1939 the Germans were alarmed by the epidemic typhus, triggered by their own aggression. Military pathologists were concerned about the threat to German troops, and that ultimately Fleckfieber would sweep through a non-immune Germany. The hazard of the vast Nazi schemes of population displacement of 'Heim ins Reich' ('Back to the Reich') of scattered German populations in the east and south resulted in screening of the physical and mental health of 'repatriated' Germans. Within this system of displacement and destruction, prisoners were subjected to a variety of classifications involving different levels of treatment. The Jewish prisoner was the lowest in the hierarchy of systematised abuse. Ideologically Jews were identified with a virus or bacteria. Typhus (louse-borne Fleckfieber) was identified as a 'Judenfieber', or Jewish disease; the carrier or infected person became the cause (although person-to-person infection could not occur), and the person as a pathogenic menace had to be destroyed. The outbreaks were precipitated by the Nazi invasion of Poland which caused population displacements, overcrowding and breakdown of the sanitary infrastructure. The situation was worsened by immunological susceptibility of young people from a non-immune area. The Germans thus blamed Fleckfieber on the victims, when in fact the invasion and severely brutal repression were the cause. In terms of racial pathology, Jews constituted a racial threat to the German race, however these two entities were defined, as race was conceptualised in different ways. For the German race to thrive, the Nazi racial trope dictated that all those deemed threats to the German racial hereditary stream, meaning Jews as well as Roma and the physically defective, had to be destroyed in order to promote German racial health and fitness. This went with the idea that primitive 'racial vigour' had to be restored. Delousing was thus part of an epic and monumental struggle with every killing being justified as having positive value as a type of racial therapy.

Under 'Aktion Reinhardt' (the plan to exterminate Jewish Poles), transportation from ghettos to death camps and to Auschwitz involved crowding victims in insanitary cattle trucks in so-called 'special trains' with supposed 'resettlement in the East'. Cattle trucks were used on numerous occasions such as in the Romanian district of Jassy/Iași when overcrowded cattle trucks without water meant that only around 700 people survived of the 2,700 who were herded into one set of trucks in June 1941.[16] These trains were overcrowded and deliberately insanitary, and the Romanian case shows they were deliberately designed as instruments of death.

The 'universe' of concentration camps was highly complicated with continuous transfers of prisoners between camps, as well as prisoner selection, brutal and dangerous forced labour on a vast scale, clusters of murderous research, and finally death marches designed more to kill by exhaustion and summary execution than to reach any destination. Prisoners who were selected for forced labour had to be deloused and shaved on their admission to a camp. For reasons of security any camp was subject to a range of sanitary measures. The containment of the persecuted constituted a vast opportunity for forced labour. This is well exemplified by Josef Mengele who, from May 1943, was one of the camp doctors in charge of sanitation and epidemic control. On the arrivals platform or 'ramp' at Auschwitz, Mengele's additional duties involved screening new arrivals to fulfil quotas for forced labour or, for most, being herded into a gas chamber, and then being disposed of in a cremation oven as a hygienic procedure for corpses. In the course of his sanitary duties, Mengele conducted constant selections for fitness to work and to prevent infections. He similarly stood by as the 'Gypsy camp' was liquidated on 2 August 1944 with some men retained for labour or as medical research subjects.[17]

Opportunistic physicians saw the reservoirs of prisoners as a research opportunity. Instead of emigration to hoped-for safety, trains deposited prisoners in situations where their bodies (and rarely their expertise) could be exploited. From late May 1944, especially, Mengele selected twins and others of genetic interest, notably dwarfs. They served as raw material for Mengele's scientific interest in hereditary pathology. Roma from the 'Gypsy Family Camp' were also used by Mengele to develop his research agendas in anthropology and the 'racial pathology' of infectious disease, as can be seen with Noma, or necrotic fasciitis to which the Roma children were highly susceptible. According to surviving twins, Mengele would inject one of a pair of twins with infectious pathogens. On death, the prisoner pathologist Myklós Nyiszli and his team, from June 1944, in their improvised laboratory dissected the bodies of deceased persons of scientific interest who were often killed to order. On occasions the organs – notably different-coloured eyes – and blood samples were sent to the Kaiser Wilhelm Institute for Anthropology in Berlin.[18] The organs of the dead were subject to dispatch and were held in scientific collections. Leading German scientific institutes were deeply involved in the deadly research, commissioning the testing of drugs and vaccines, and harvesting organs such as brains and reproductive organs.

The SS had multiple agencies, notably the SS-Ahnenerbe, and the Hygiene Institute of the Waffen-SS, furthering hygienic research. Himmler believed that through murderous research procedures, the SS could attain superiority in medicine. These medical stations for bacteriological monitoring stood outside camp hierarchies of command, often with their own facilities. Some experiments were arranged and approved by Himmler, but arrangements for the experiments varied administratively and in terms of facilities. There was 'export' of research subjects, notably of Sinti and Roma, and Jewish children from Auschwitz.[19] Sinti and Roma males were retained after the brutal destruction of the camp, and sent to the concentration camp of Buchenwald. From there, some were sent on to Dachau for a seawater-drinking experiment in 1944 while others were dispatched to Natzweiler in Alsace for Fleckfieber and yellow fever research by the virologist Eugen Haagen. In 1944, twenty Jewish children (actually, one child, Simone, was not Jewish according to German racial laws) were selected by Mengele and exported from Auschwitz to Neuengamme for the research by Kurt Heissmeyer on the immunology of tuberculosis.[20] Eleven Jewish boys were sent from Auschwitz to Sachsenhausen for yellow fever research by the bacteriologist Arnold Dohmen of the Robert Koch Institute. The Jewish boys at Sachsenhausen were affectionately known to prisoners, so when an order came through for their destruction, the prison workers did not pass on the deadly order.[21] The twenty children sent to Neuengamme survived the experiment but were killed shortly before the end of the war.

From late 1941 the worsening threat of infectious insect-borne disease due to the 'Barbarossa' invasion of the Soviet Union resulted in large-scale infectious disease experiments in concentration camps. Claus Schilling's malaria research at Dachau from mid-February 1942 was directly facilitated by the SS with Himmler's specific authorisation. Himmler ordered the camp commandant to supply Schilling with thirty non-tubercular prisoners a month. Commandants generally regulated supply of prisoner research subjects.[22]

The Hygiene Institute of the Waffen-SS took a major role in epidemic prevention, vaccine testing and development, and experimental research on vaccines. Its head, Joachim Mrugowsky, had an interest in a holistic 'geo-medical' approach to infectious disease. This was reflected in departments for sanitary technology (under the conscientious sanitary expert Kurt Gerstein), geology, hydrology and chemistry.[23] Mrugowsky espoused the 'geo-medicine' of the Berlin university professor Heinz Zeiss.[24] It meant animosity from advocates of a strictly genetic approach, notably Fritz Lenz who had designed the SS marriage regulations. Another aspect was that services for medical tests of pathogenic agents stood outside the formal hierarchy of command. Staff stationed at the bacteriological laboratories in concentration camps were subject to command from Mrugowsky in Berlin.

This separate status is well exemplified at Auschwitz, where the bacteriological station was moved from the experimental Block 10 (although a laboratory still remained there) to Raisko, which was situated several kilometres from the main camp. This was where thousands of bacteriological tests for kitchen staff, prostitutes and even twins on orders signed by Mengele were regularly carried out. Apart from Buchenwald's Research Station for Typhus and Vaccine Research, and at Sachsenhausen, there were malaria stations at Kiev and Kherson for biological research and disinfection. There were also laboratories at Riga, Kothla-Jarwe in Estonia, Lemberg, Dnjepropetowsk, Trieste, Udine and Istria for routine screening and research. These amounted to a vast system of geoepidemiology in German-occupied east and south-east Europe. The Nazis sought to remedy their failing war economy by massive exploitation of forced labour.

The medical experiments offered a form of surrogate labour for thousands of prisoners. The children held for research by Mengele, and the women in Block 10, who were subjected to intrauterine chemical injections to sterilise them, performed by the gynaecologist Carl Clauberg, were vulnerable to severe exploitation. The experiments in concentration camps occurred in a variety of locations, ranging from the prisoners being simply subjected to an intervention like the removal of a testicle but immediately returned to the camp (as with the X-ray sterilisation victims of Horst Schumann), simply using existing camp clinics, as opposed to strictly sealed blocks. When an open location was used for tetanus operations, wounding legs of women prisoners at Ravensbrück, this resulted in protest, evasion and general disruption.[25]

Each set of experiments represented a distinctive contrast in terms of the origins of victims, arising from the ebb and flow of deportations, policies to be rid of Jews, or Roma, or the arrest of partisans and anti-Nazis. Mengele's twins were composed overwhelmingly of Hungarians, Slovaks and Czechs. The males selected for sterilisation had Polish and Greek origins. Sephardic Greek Jews were the largest group among those selected for the Jewish skeleton collection planned for the anatomical institute at Strasbourg, something explained by their Sephardic characteristics.[26] Auschwitz offered multiple contrasts in terms of the locations of experiments. The most extreme was Block 10 for several hundred Jewish women, where the windows were boarded up and the inmates could not under normal circumstances leave the block. However, X-ray sterilisation experiments, conducted by Horst Schumann in Auschwitz provided a contrast; victims tricked by the offer of a day off work were subjected to sterilisation and released back into the camp. Block 10 was sealed to prevent evasion. Ironically, this very separation assisted the inmates' survival, although their reproductive systems often were irreparably damaged and there was severe pain. The malaria experiments in Dachau with over a thousand victims were conducted in the camp infirmary. Prisoners when cured were released back into the camp. At Buchenwald the research blocks were sealed off from the rest of the camp and, again, on recovery the prisoners would be released back into the camp.

The Buchenwald sanitary compound

Containment and isolation – effectively quarantine – provided a complete contrast to earlier regimes of surveillance and onward migration. The Buchenwald Isolation Station was established in response to the mid-1941 epidemic panic in Germany, blamed on inward migration (overlooking that the German onslaught on the east was the cause). The medical authorities placed the blame on Russian forced labourers and prisoners of war importing infectious diseases, especially louse-borne typhus. Public health experts looked to vaccine manufacturers (notably to IG Farben). Given the uncertainties of how to combat the infectious rickettsia, and their body louse carriers, there was agreement on the need for testing different methods of vaccine production and strains of vaccine. Ideally, the public health authorities favoured a vaccine-based strategy of control for the German army. The disinfection procedures which previously were a passage to escape from persecution became a pathway to exploitation for the benefit of the German military and German racial resettlement.

Typhus research was conducted under SS supervision in a research compound established in Buchenwald. Fleckfieber experiments were large-scale and long-term from 1941/1942 until the end of the war and involved several hundred prisoner research subjects, and for malaria over a thousand prisoners were used. Onsite efforts commenced on 5 January 1942 with the allocation of Block 49 – a prisoner barracks located in the *Schutzhaftlager* – to the medical division for use as an isolation and research facility. The block's formal institution as the 'Typhus Isolation and Research Station' rapidly followed. By the end of January 1942, any pretence as to the station's function as a quarantine compound was discarded, and Block 49 was referred to in official correspondence simply as the Typhus Research Station. In March 1942 the experimental programme acquired nearby Block 44. On 19 April 1942, staff relocated to Block 46, which served as the primary experimental headquarters.[27] On 9 January 1943, the senior SS physician Karl Genzken authorised the redesignation of the Buchenwald programme as the Division for Fleckfieber and Virus Research of the Hygiene Institute of the Waffen-SS. The decision was a result of the programme's overall expansion to include vaccine development and manufacturing at Block 50. Manufacturing capabilities were intended to hasten and economise ongoing research as the majority of vaccines and sera were acquired from external scientific institutions and for-profit corporations.[28]

As the Buchenwald programme was expanded, similar measures were being undertaken across the Reich and its occupied territories, including the expansion of the Hygiene Institute at Auschwitz-Rajsko as well as the establishment or absorption of other programmes (for example, hygiene and medical zoology centres, bacteriological stations, manufacturing facilities) in Belarus, Crimea, Estonia, Georgia, Latvia, Russia and Ukraine.[29] Overall, the establishment, relocation and frequent expansion of the programme evidenced not only its growing mandate but also the constantly evolving character of the concentration camps and SS projects more broadly. Delousing was a routine procedure imposed to induce not just medical benefits but also a sense of stigma and shame.[30] Internment meant that prisoners became a static group, targeted for experimentation to produce a vaccine for the realisation of racial planning.

On 5 January 1942, the Isolation/Research Station's first day of operation, 'Preliminary Test A' was conducted using five prisoners. The experiments can be reconstructed from the retrospectively written 'diary', compiled by the prisoner-clerk Eugen Kogon and endorsed by the SS officer and bacteriologist in charge, Erwin Ding. According to Kogon there were twenty-four series' of experiments by December 1944 in this sealed-off research compound with anything from 4 to 145 people in a group of research subjects.[31] Despite the supervision and assistance of Eugen Gildemeister, Director of the Robert Koch Institute in Berlin, the test did not succeed in infecting any of the research subjects. 'Preliminary Test B' was commenced shortly thereafter on 10 January 1942 and succeeded in infecting five prisoners via the cruder method of introducing the pathogen into four cuts made into the deltoid muscle. Following an incubation period ranging from two to six days, the prisoners exhibited an increased count of white blood cells. The experiment was concluded on 20 January 1942 with the death of one subject. This method of infection, while subject to a not infrequent degree of variation, proved sufficient until the spring of 1943 when a lack of discernible infections among the experimental cohorts led Mrugowsky and Gildemeister to conclude that the 'Matelska' strain provided by the Robert Koch Institute was no longer virulent.[32] The third preliminary test, commencing on 11 April 1943, was notable as the first usage of the euphemistically designated 'passage persons', that is, prisoners infected and left untreated so as to maintain a viable strain for use in experiments. The term was especially ironic; delousing had previously been a gateway to migration, whereas now the prisoner was exploited as a sustaining passage for pathogens, in many cases costing them their lives.

The bulk of the clinical research programme at Blocks 49 and 46 comprised 'Typhus Vaccine Research Series I-IX', conducted from 6 January 1942 to 25 April 1944. The goal of this research was to evaluate various vaccines for their ability to induce immunity with an acceptable number of side effects. Series I took place between 6 January and 19 April 1942 and involved approximately 145 research subjects divided into four vaccine groups and a fifth control group. The thirty-one members of the first testing group were administered the Weigl type of vaccine (IA) produced by Hermann Eyer's Kraków division. The thirty-five prisoners consigned to the second testing group were immunised with a Cox vaccine (IB) manufactured by the RKI in partnership with the virologist Eugen Haagen, who in October 1941 had moved from the RKI to the Reichsuniversität Straßburg. The final two groups, composed of sixty-nine inmates, were inoculated with 'Behring Normal' (IC) and 'Behring Stark' (ID), respectively. These vaccines were developed by the Behringwerke Sero-Bacteriological Department at Marburg (Lahn). The final ten research subjects, as members of the control group, were not provided with any form of artificial immunity. Each of the prisoners included within the first four groups were administered three courses of varying doses at intervals of five to eight days. On 3 March 1942, they were infected with typhus via the laceration method developed in Preliminary Test B. Procedures were performed by Ding under the supervision of Gildemeister and Gerhard Rose (Consulting Hygienist, Luftwaffe Medical Service; Chief of the Division for Tropical Medicine at the Robert Koch Institute). Following an incubation period of seven to nine days, the infection presented with a heightened virulence in comparison with naturally acquired typhus.

German camp personnel feared the spread of infections imported into camp by louse strains, and of prisoner resistance. Blocks 46 and 49 had four wings, so that in each wing the various batches of prisoners could be isolated. The prisoner group of 140 people was deliberately separated into four groups, one in each wing, to prevent resistance. The blocks were isolated from the camp with a double row of barbed wire. Block 49 was designated the 'Isolierstation'. There were 'passage people', mainly Russians, as human cultivation reservoirs. About five people a month were exploited, making 120 for the period to March 1945.[33]

On 9 January 1943 the isolation station became a research station. Ding preferred not to have Jews as research subjects. Ideology combined with the view that eastern Jews had contracted typhus when young so had acquired immunity. Instead the 140 prisoner 'guinea pigs' were Poles, as well as Austrians and Germans. One memorable incident was when a potato salad appeared. The prisoners were delighted, but the next day became extremely sick. The salad had been dressed with typhoid bacteria as part of an experiment. Henryk Mikołajczak on entering the isolation block recollected: 'It was surrounded by barbed wire again, and windows painted white. You could not have contact with general population of the camp.' His vivid account of his experiences as a research subject show how the research station was in fact an entry to what was meant to be a fatal location.

Entry required strict hygienic controls:

> Two men in white uniform received us. They made us strip, delousing us, stripping clothes, quick shower, new uniform, then from there to the main hall, 30 beds on either side, tables in the middle. Peaceful, music was playing. I couldn't understand.

The paradise soon became a hellish location as the potato salad, which seemed like a benign German gift, was poisoned with typhoid bacilli. The interned prisoners became extremely sick to the point of death.

> Of the 60 people, how many got serum? I don't know, perhaps all perhaps few, depends on stage of the sickness. Who knows. I young. Maybe my heart strong . . . but out of 60 only 8 of us were leaving through the gate. That number is always on my mind. During the experiment every bowel movement they took samples [of] and sent it to laboratory in Berlin. I said to my friend, 'I hope they serve this to Adolf on a platter'.

On 9 January 1943 the Economic Administration of the SS provided resources for vaccine production in Buchenwald. Instead of situating production at Sachsenhausen, the SS bacteriologist, Ding, urged that the existing Buchenwald 'Station' become a fully fledged Department for Typhus and Virus Research. The Department began to test its own vaccine. This was produced by prisoner-researchers in Block 50 using the French rabbit lung technique for culturing rickettsiae. The agenda involved comparing four different types of vaccines, and a non-vaccinated 'control group'. The research problem was whether vaccines shortened the disease, attenuated it, or assisted recovery.

A total of 688 prisoners can be identified by name as research subjects, of whom 116 died.[34] The prisoners were selected by the camp administration. Ding sent a request on 26 May 1943 that Jews, Poles and Russians be excluded.[35] When a newly consigned prisoner, Fritz Kleinmann, was found to be Jewish, he was rapidly evicted from the experiment block, avoiding a dangerous experiment.[36] The prisoner-clerk Eugen Kogon's involvement in the political resistance in the camp meant a preference for using prisoners identified as criminals by a green triangle.[37] On some occasions prisoners designated for execution received a new prisoner number. By nationality they were mainly German, Austrian and Polish research subjects. Only a small number were Jewish. 'Russians' (a loose and derogatory term) were 'passage persons' (used to maintain the rickettsial cultures) then injected to test the efficacy of vaccines. For the most part the experiments involved testing of typhus vaccines. For the unvaccinated and passage persons, there was a high degree of mortality. Prisoner assistants supported strategies of sabotage and evasion.

Overall, the immense German scientific effort produced only marginal results. DDT was far more effective but was better operationalised by the Allies than the Germans. This can be seen in the sanitary catastrophe of Bergen-Belsen concentration camp. Here ever larger numbers of prisoners were herded, and typhus raged. Handed over to the British military by the retreating Germans but without due notification of the raging epidemic, the epidemic was brought under control by sluicing prisoners through a 'human laundry' where they were dusted with DDT. Whereas the Germans (largely) clung to regimented delousing, the Allies found DDT to be flexible in averting sanitary disasters.

Final reckoning

In conclusion, the Buchenwald isolation and experimental station represented containment of imprisoned victims as opposed to being able to flee Nazi terror through any border. The camp vaccine research station was a sealed-off compound within a concentration camp where all sorts of prisoners were channelled. Rather than porosity, the rationale was to contain, infect and exploit; rather than hygienic prevention of infection, the system was one of deliberately infecting the contained prisoners. Ostensibly, the rationale was the discovery of a preventive method to contain typhus. In fact, the procedures resulted in approximately a sixth of the research subjects being killed. Containment represented the final stage in a system of migration which became paralysed under wartime conditions. The result was that the death and deprivation wrought by the Nazis meant that the concentration camps became sanitary disasters. This callous medical neglect is well illustrated by the epidemic catastrophe of Bergen-Belsen.[38] Typhus similarly raged in the final months at Buchenwald, as the camp became an overcrowded destination for death marches from other locations. Containment and disease eradication represented sanitary tragedies with inhumane exploitation and ultimately failure to produce a wholly effective vaccine.

The termination of outward migration from Nazi Germany meant that the concentration camp and associated exploitation turned migratory procedures into methods of extermination and, beyond this, of exploitation for medical research. The bodies of the killed were to serve the interests of the racial elite in terms of sustaining the war economy, military fitness and racial settlement. The survivors of Bergen-Belsen were themselves subject to selection procedures, based largely on fitness for physical labour.[39] In post-World War II Europe, welfare states compounded by the iron curtain meant that the interwar era of intolerance to refugees improved. After a decade of slow assimilation of displaced persons (the elderly and disabled remained stateless) the era of free but regulated migration of the 1890s was never to return.

Notes

1 Paul Weindling, *Epidemics and Genocide in Eastern Europe* (Oxford: Oxford University Press, 2000), pp. 56–7.
2 Amy L. Fairchild, *Science at the Borders: Immigrant Medical Inspection and the Shaping of the Modern Industrial Labor Force* (Baltimore, MD: Johns Hopkins University Press, 2003).

3 Weindling, *Epidemics*.
4 Howard Markel and Alexandra Minna Stern, 'The foreignness of germs: the persistent association of immigrants and disease in American society', *Milbank Quarterly*, 80:4 (December 2002) 757–88.
5 Kim Pelis, *Charles Nicolle, Pasteur's Imperial Missionary: Typhus and Tunisia* (Rochester, NY: Rochester Studies in Medical History, 2006).
6 Weindling, *Epidemics*.
7 Markel and Stern, 'Foreignness of germs'. Howard Markel, '"The eyes have it": trachoma, the perception of disease, the United States public health service, and the American Jewish immigrant experience, 1897–1924, *Bulletin of the History of Medicine*, 74 (2000) 525–60.
8 Renée Hirschon, *Crossing the Aegean: An Appraisal of the 1923 Compulsory Population Exchange between Greece and Turkey* (New York: Berghahn Books, 2003).
9 Irvin-Erickson Douglas, *Raphaël Lemkin and the Concept of Genocide* (Philadelphia: University of Pennsylvania Press, 2017). John Cooper, *Raphael Lemkin and the Struggle for the Genocide Convention* (Basingstoke: Palgrave Macmillan, 2008). Samantha Power, *A Problem from Hell: America and the Age of Genocide* (New York: Basic Books, 2002). Philippe Sands, *East West Street: On the Origins of 'Genocide' and 'Crimes Against Humanity'* (New York: Alfred A. Knopf, 2016).
10 Claire Ungerson, *Four Thousand Lives: The Rescue of German Jewish Men to Britain in 1939* (Cheltenham: The History Press, 2019).
11 Paul Weindling, 'The Kindertransport from Vienna. The children who came and those left behind', *Jewish Historical Studies: Transactions of the Jewish Historical Society of England*, 51 (2019), 16–32.
12 Wolf Gruner, *Öffentliche Wohlfahrt und Judenverfolgung. Wechselwirkungen lokaler und zentraler Politik im NS-Staat (1933–1942)* (Munich: Oldenbourg Verlag, 2002).
13 On ghetto health see Miriam Offer, *White Coats Inside the Ghetto: Jewish Medicine in Poland During the Holocaust* (Jerusalem: Yad Vashem Publications, 2019).
14 Volkhard Knigge and Jürgen Seifert (eds), *Vom Antlitz zur Maske. Wien – Weimar – Buchenwald 1939. / Gezeichneter Ort. Goetheblicke auf Weimar und Thüringen* (Weimar: Gedenkstätte Buchenwald, 1999). Gershon Evan, *Winds of Life. The Destinies of a Young Viennese Jew 1938 to 1958* (Riverside, CA: Ariadne Press, 2000).
15 Primo Levi, *Se questo è un uomo* (Torino: De Silva, 1947) translated (1959).
16 Radu Ioanid, 'The Holocaust in Romania: The Iasi Pogrom of June 1941', *Contemporary European History*, 2 (1993), 119–48.

17 Paul Weindling, 'Mengele at Auschwitz: reconstructing the twins', in Suzanne Bardgett, Christine Schmidt and Dan Stone (eds), *Beyond Camps and Forced Labour* (London: Palgrave Macmillan (in press)).
18 Miklós Nyiszli, *I was Dr Mengele's Assistant* (Oswiecim: Frap Books, 2010), pp. 45–8.
19 Paul Weindling, *Victims and Survivors of Nazi Human Experiments: Science and Suffering in the Holocaust* (London: Bloomsbury, 2014).
20 Günther Schwarberg, *The Murders at Bullenhuser Damm. The SS Doctor and the Children* (Bloomington, IN: Indiana University Press, 1984).
21 Astrid Ley and Günter Morsch, *Medical Care and Crime* (Berlin: Metropol, 2007), pp. 370–7.
22 Eugene Ost, 'Die Malaria-Versuchstation im Konzentrationslager Dachau', *Dachauer Hefte*, 4 (1988) 174–89
23 Saul Friedländer, *Kurt Gerstein ou l'ambiguïté du bien* (Paris: Castermann, 1967).
24 Paul Weindling (ed.), *Fleckfieberforschung im Nationalsozialismus. Joachim Mrugowskys Fleckfieber-Abhandlung und seine Tätigkeit als Hygieniker der Waffen-SS* (forthcoming).
25 Weindling, *Victims and Survivors*.
26 Hans-Joachim Lang, *Die Namen der Nummern: wie es gelang, die 86 Opfer eines NS-Verbrechens zu identifizieren* (Hamburg: Hoffmann und Campe, 2004).
27 Archiv der Humboldt Universität Berlin, Personalakt Mrugowsky Zusammenfassender Bericht über Fleckfieberimpfstoffversuche im K.L. Buchenwald nd, f. 125–8.
28 Weindling, *Epidemics*, pp. 324–8, 334–7, 343, 348, 356–7.
29 Weindling, *Epidemics*, 339–45.
30 Eva Hallama, '"Wir waren irgendwie zu Anderen geworden, als hätte man uns ausgetauscht." Medizinische Musterungen, Scham und Verdinglichung im Kontext der NS-Zwangsarbeit', in Daniela Angetter, Birgit Nemec, Herbert Posch, Christiane Druml and Paul Weindling (eds) *Strukturen und Netzwerke: Medizin und Wissenschaft in Wien 1848–1955*, (Vienna: Böhlau, 2018).
31 Eugen Kogon, *Der SS-Staat. Das System der deutschen Konzentrationslager* (Munich: Karl Alber, 1946), translation as *The Theory and Practice of Hell* (New York: Farrar, Straus and Cudahy, 1950), p. 148.
32 Annette Hinz-Wessels, *Das Robert Koch-Institut im Nationalsozialismus* (Berlin: Kulturverlag KADMOS, 2008).
33 Bundesarchiv Berlin, Zusammenfassender Bericht über Fleckfieberimpfstoffversuche im K.L. Buchenwald.

34 For the latest evaluation see Paul Weindling (ed.), *Fleckfieberforschung im Nationalsozialismus. Joachim Mrugowskys Fleckfieber-Abhandlung und seine Tätigkeit als Hygieniker der Waffen-SS* (in press).
35 USHMM RG14.050M Pt III p. 302 to Schutzhaftlagerführer 26 May 1943.
36 Weindling, *Victims and Survivors*, p. 98.
37 Kogon, *Der SS-Staat*.
38 Paul Weindling, '"Belsenitis" liberating Belsen, its hospitals, and selection for re-emigration, 1945–1948', *Science in Context*, 19:3 (2006), 401–18. (Special issue on Medical Borders: Historical, Political and Cultural Analyses).
39 Weindling, '"Belsenitis"'.

7

Locating disease: on the coexistence of diverse concepts of territory and the spread of disease[1]

Sarah Green

One of my most impressive family stories concerned the World War II adventures of my maternal grandfather, Robert Pulvertaft. After qualifying as a doctor, he served as a British medical officer in Egypt in 1942, where he was faced with many soldiers who were dying from infections that developed in their wounds, rather than from the wounds themselves. Major Pulvertaft was aware that a new potential treatment for bacterial infections, extracted from *penicillium* mould, was now available (penicillin).[2] He received a few doses from London, but they were nowhere near enough, so he made a crude version of penicillin himself, and used it to treat his patients.

Recently, I learned that this story was actually true.[3] Major Pulvertaft commanded a hospital in Cairo in 1942 and, while there, he made batches of crude penicillin. He published the results of experimental treatments with penicillin in *The Lancet* in 1943.[4] He also actively ignored Allied policy that knowledge of how to make penicillin should be kept secret; in line with H. W. Florey, who is credited with demonstrating that penicillin had some remarkable antibacterial properties, Pulvertaft was against patenting and happy to instruct anyone who asked him how to make it.[5]

Major Pulvertaft's experiments with home-made penicillin, used directly on live patients, sounds both illegal and unethical by today's standards. But this was 1942, it was in the middle of a world war, and my grandfather knew that he had both science and a large colonial power (the British Empire) on his side. In those days, treatments for diseases and infections were part of immensely strong discursive, medical and legal structures; the knowledge (science) upon which the treatments were based was unquestionable.[6] In that Cairo hospital, Major Pulvertaft, a doctor and officer in the British military, was the authority who could make life and death decisions with impunity.

It was a similar unquestionable authority that allowed the medical researchers working within the German Nazi regime to conduct their deadly medical experiments on people, even if their ideals were diametrically opposed to Major Pulvertaft's. Paul Weindling has studied Nazi medical researchers' focus, in their medical experiments, on a presumed link between lice and typhus.[7] This research was based on the new science of bacteriology, as were the penicillin experiments. Weindling, among others, has noted that the point of all of these bacteriology-based projects was eradication: to destroy the bacteria that could cause illness or death in the living entity you are trying to protect. It was a chillingly short step for people who held eugenic views to conclude that some types of humans (classified according to the logic of eugenics) carried such a powerful danger of pathological infection for other humans that they should also be eradicated, just like the bacteria, microbes and parasites that cause disease.[8]

Major Pulvertaft was appalled by the medical experiments carried out by the Nazi regime; yet he would not have denied that the researchers working on the Nazi side were using the same science (bacteriology) as he himself was drawing upon in Egypt. Perhaps the main difference between the two was that while Major Pulvertaft was never quite sure about the wisdom of any of his treatments or experiments, the Nazi doctors seemed entirely certain of their practices. For my grandfather, certainty could only be achieved by having faith rather than knowledge, and in his view, faith had no place in the world of science.

The coexistence of contradictory political ideologies among people who nevertheless shared the same scientific knowledge is one key part of how different regimes have responded to the outbreak of infectious diseases over the centuries. When governments have to decide what to do about the threat of contagion, their political concerns and, in particular, their understanding of the relationship between territory and people, are bound to inform their decisions. Drawing on accounts of how different political regimes responded to outbreaks of infectious disease in the Mediterranean region in the past, I am going to focus on how different regimes understand the *spread* of the disease: its movement across space.

The rapid spread of COVID-19 during 2020 and the highly diverse political responses to it have demonstrated the importance of this point. Close the borders or not? Quarantine the population or not? The issue here is how people understand, organize and structure spatial relations and separations, as well as how they understand the disease in itself. Given that the spread of a disease involves movement across space, including the crossing of political borders, the way that location is understood and organized is important to how diverse peoples and regimes respond to the spread of disease. The question I deal with, then, is how diseases are located – in the Mediterranean region, in this case.

I mean 'location' in a literal spatial sense, in terms of where diseases are thought to reside in bodies and places, and how they spread from one body and place to another. And I also mean it in terms of how those locations are understood politically, epistemologically and morally. The discomfiting thought that both the Nazi doctors and Major Pulvertaft shared the same science, and that both benefitted from powerful and transnational forces that created deep spatial hierarchies (the British Empire on the one hand and the Nazi regime on the other), also points to the historical contingency of how science, politics and locations come together.

Here, I will draw on this simple point to explore how political constructions of territory have informed efforts to attempt to control the spread of disease across space. I will focus on historical attempts to control the spread of disease in the Mediterranean region, and the way that quarantine sometimes did, and sometimes did not, become involved in that effort.

Avian influenza and cross-locations

I will begin with Frédéric Keck's work on outbreaks of various types of avian influenzas (bird flu) in Asia. Keck argues that certain scientific accounts of disease can become involved in defining a hierarchical difference between spatial locations.[9] This is important, because attempts to control the spread of disease have historically often transgressed political borders. The transgression of such borders has usually been justified by the suggestion that the vectors of the disease do not respect political borders, so those charged with controlling the spread of disease also have to transgress them. As Bashford put it: 'Over and over again, the aspiration to promote health and prevent disease has resulted in pre-emptive activity beyond the border'.[10] In the same edited book, Zylberman presents a study of international health practices in the late nineteenth and early twentieth centuries in Europe, which outlines three ways in which attempts to control the spread of disease either pre-emptively crossed borders (especially by the French and the British into Ottoman territory), removed borders in order to create 'health zones', or created borders that had not previously existed by generating health cordons.[11] Zylberman argues that these practices sometimes reflected nation state border logic and at other times completely ignored that logic by violating the basic principles of nation state borders. Zylberman's findings suggest that, here, more than one logic of location is operating: the familiar nation state border logic, and an additional logic, what might be called a disease-vector locational logic, which was occasionally superimposed upon, or cross-cut the nation state logic. That kind of cross-cutting of border logics implies the coexistence of different ways to classify and subdivide the same space; and where these classifications involve the operations of power, that can have a significant effect.[12]

I suggest that such a situation existed in the Mediterranean area, both during the nineteenth century when various empires coexisted and were beginning to be replaced by states, and in the twentieth century, with the arrival of new transnational entities such as the European Union. I will be suggesting that historically the logic by which most of the empires managed their territories (which could loosely be called a logic of bordered territories)[13] coexisted with at least one other rather different logic: that of the Ottomans (which could loosely be called a logic of territories as route/road networks). Both were overwritten by (nation) state logic, which currently coexists with a newer, transnational, locating logic, which could be crudely called the logic of cross-border alliances, particularly as exercised by the European Union and other transnational entities such as the World Health Organization (WHO).

Locating sentinels

It is worth taking a closer look at the example of the disease-vector locational logic that Keck discussed before getting to the different logics of the political regimes in the Mediterranean. Keck noted that medical researchers studying different historical avian influenza events described Hong Kong, in which three strains of bird flu appeared before they were recorded anywhere else, as a 'sentinel', that is, the location of the early warning of the arrival of a potential new epidemic.[14] In military terminology, a sentinel is a soldier who stands at the perimeter of an encampment to act as an early warning of the presence of the enemy. The sentinel is often the first to be killed if an attack occurs; the death warns the others that they have to scramble and get ready to fight. In medical terms, a sentinel is a mechanism that communicates the existence of some danger to health. In this sense, the medical researchers defined Hong Kong as being located at the border between some postulated potential threat of epidemic disease, present in the bird population, and a healthy human population. Hong Kong's engagement with that potential threat could alert the rest of the world to its existence, as long as someone was there to read the signs (the medical researchers).

Keck's main interest was in the way the researchers set up the engagement between the threat and the sentinel, which he called a form of cynegetic power, a hunting/hunted relation between the sentinel and the virus-carrying birds.[15] This involved a process through which certain birds are re-described by the researchers as the vectors of a disease that, at a certain point, may cross a virtual border and reach humans. Much the same identification process has been described in 2020 in tracing the origins of COVID-19.

Keck's description of this process involves the definition of two kinds of location: a virtual map created by the scientists, who imagine the movement of the birds as part of an arc that allows the influenza virus to cross the borders of species (from birds to humans); and a specific geographical location – Hong Kong – that stands at the border between health and disease for humans and communicates to the medical researchers the presence of disease. For Keck, sentinels are always located at borders (in this case, between birds and humans in the geographical space of Hong Kong).

Locating disease 183

They engage with the relations between inside and outside, and communicate information about the presence of danger.[16]

Here, there are two hierarchically organized spatial logics that have been brought together. First, which is Keck's main focus, the bodily world of birds and the point at which infection which exists within that world transgresses the bird world boundary and enters the bodily world of humans. And second, the geographical location of Hong Kong, identified as the location from which the infection travelled and crossed other geographical boundaries. Spaces that had previously been separated were now being transgressed.

This has some similarities to the account that Weindling gives of Nazi medics' research on lice and their link to the spread of typhus, followed by intensive delousing programmes.[17] These programmes were particularly focused on the dangers that the Nazi scientists believed were coming from eastern Europe. As in Keck's study, there was a locational logic involved: a perceived spatial distinction between friend and foe. As many others have noted, this kind of spatial distinction is common in descriptions of the spread of disease.[18]

In that sense, a key element in common between Keck's and Weindling's studies is the way both sets of scientists perceived movement of the disease across both spatial and bodily borders. However, there is also a crucial difference. In the case of the Nazi researchers, racist beliefs combined with ultra-nationalist approaches towards territory implied that any crossing of these spatial and/or bodily boundaries was a transgression or invasion that was axiomatically harmful. In contrast, in the hunter/hunted (cynegetic) metaphor used by the bird flu scientists described by Keck, the hunters and hunted always coexist in the same place; the issue is how to manage that coexistence, how to prevent the hunted from killing the hunter. Indeed, there is a necessary relation between the hunter and hunted, as Willerslev has richly described in the case of the Yukaghir elk hunters.[19] That kind of spatial coexistence and mutual dependence is impossible within the racist nationalist rhetoric of the Nazis; within that logic, the borders should not be managed on the assumption of coexistence. On the contrary, the borders must remain as impermeable as possible. The avian influenza scientists' concept of Hong Kong as the sentinel and the Nazi scientists' notion of lice as parasites being carried by Jews from the east draw on two very different understandings of the connections and disconnections between places. In the latter case, coexistence is impossible.

Many researchers working on the history of disease have noted that something to do with the 'where' of infection and disease – that is, how its spatial location is understood both geographically and within bodies – has always been an important part of attempts to control disease and infection. Studies ranging from research on the theory of miasma to explain medieval plague (the idea that bad air spreads disease), to considerations of geopolitics and trade in the management of disease, and to various studies of the practice of quarantine, have all noted the importance of the presumed relations between places in the story.[20] The crucial additional point I want to add here, and that is implied in the work by researchers such as Weindling and Keck, is that these historically variable theories of the causes and treatment of disease might work differently in different parts of the world and at different times as a result of their engagement with different political ideologies of location.

With all of that in mind, the remainder of this chapter briefly explores how the coexistence of different logics of location have become entangled with attempts to control the spread of disease. Much of the literature and debates on attempts to manage and control disease across the Mediterranean region have focused on the direction from which the disease is thought to come (almost invariably from the east and sometimes from the south), and the direction into which it might spread (almost invariably towards the west and north).[21] At times, as in the case of Nazi German doctors' concern with typhus, the question has concerned human bodies as much as it has concerned whatever is thought to act as the vector of infection across space: animals, insects, vermin, parasites, bacteria, microbes, as well as miasmas and a distinctly Mary Douglas-inspired notion of 'general filth'.[22] At other times, the main concern has been the terrain from which pestilence arrives, with little concern for the human bodies that carry or suffer from the diseases that have been targeted for attempted control.

This difference is important, as it signals shifts in border policies across time and space. Alison Bashford suggests that it was not until the development of nationalism that medical control over human bodies began to be closely associated with state borders and their use in territorial control.[23] Introducing an edited book on the history of quarantine, she notes: 'quarantine was a key mechanism through which the authority and territoriality of modern nation-states was asserted and became meaningful'.[24] Although it was during an earlier European colonial period that concepts of race, eugenics and indigeneity developed – ideas which posited that human bodies can be biologically divided into different types, and that these types are rooted in their connections with certain geographical territories[25] – it was not until nationalist ideas developed that this logic was applied to specific bodies in political border management.

In short, the way in which human bodies and their relation to territories was understood changed over time, and even when ideas about race and eugenics began to circulate in Europe, these ideas were not necessarily instantly applied to all colonial regions, or not in the same ways. This means it cannot be assumed that distinctions between different types of bodies would always be a matter of concern in border management.

In that sense, earlier, pre-nationalist, quarantine practices around the Mediterranean region, which involved keeping people, as well as animals and goods, sequestered somewhere for long periods of time, were not motivated by a fear of the polluting character of foreigners' bodies. Rather, they were more concerned with fear of whatever those people, or their clothes, or their ships, or their goods or animals, or the air around them, may be carrying along with them. It was not until the late 1860s that surveillance of human bodies began in the Mediterranean region in earnest, indicating closer attention to, and control over, particular people's bodies, rather than human bodies in general.[26] And it is important to note that this surveillance of bodies has been informed by different ideas about human bodies at different moments. Sometimes, there has been a classification of bodies according to some racial profiling, in which certain bodies are assumed to be more likely to be diseased than others. In almost all such cases, the assumed geographic origins of different kinds of bodies has had a strong part to play in this profiling (Africa, Asia, Arab World, etc.). At other times, surveillance has been more an attempt to identify the presence or absence of a particular bacterium or virus, or focuses on some distinctive characteristic of particular individuals, irrespective of how their bodies might be classified in biological or geographic terms.

Here, it is important to recall that the history of the passport, which allows state authorities to identify particular individuals at borders, rather than simply check whether they are sick or whether they have a ticket or pass which allows them to cross, is a relatively recent development.[27] It is not simply that technical developments in surveillance, as a selective form of 'neoquarantinism', allows most people (and goods and animals) to avoid quarantine and go through borders unhindered; it is also that attention to individual persons and bodies at borders is relatively new. Amy Fairchild's detailed analysis of medical inspections for immigrants at the main borders of the United States between 1891 and the 1920s provides an excellent example of the variable way that different elements of these issues came together in the medical border inspections of that period. Fairchild shows that a complex amalgam of premises about disease (both physical and mental), race and class came together in the assembly-line health inspection system that was developed for examining migrant bodies for fitness to enter the United States.[28] Fairchild argues that the underlying logic of the whole system was an attempt to provide a healthy and able workforce for American industry[29], but that this logic coexisted with a persistent racial hierarchy that distinguished 'all Europeans from "coolies" (Chinese, Japanese, Koreans and 'Hindus'), Mexican "peons", and other Latin American immigrants'.[30] By the time this system was put in place, the significance of the territories from which these migrant bodies came was apparently self-evident: different regions of the world were placed in a hierarchy of generating more or less desirable bodies.

Two implications can be drawn from this variation in the connection between territories, human bodies and different attempts at the control over disease. First, it is only under certain political and historical conditions that human bodies, as such, have been differentiated from one another and have been the focus of attention in the management of the spread of disease. And second, at the same time, all forms of attempted control over the spread of disease – quarantine, fumigation, inspection and examination of people, animals, and goods, as well as surveillance – have *always* involved spatial management. Such measures have always been attempts to impose a certain kind of order in the relations and separations between here and somewhere else. The final section briefly outlines what kind of location logics might have been coexisting in the Mediterranean region during the (mostly late) Ottoman period, and how that was played out through the management of the spread of disease.

All roads lead through Istanbul

In the extensive literature on the management of the spread of disease across the Mediterranean region, most particularly plague and cholera, there are several key areas of discussion. These centre around geopolitics, the different forms of knowledge people had about the causes of disease, and other factors that might have affected responses towards the outbreak of disease, including religious pronouncements about the meaning of pestilence. In these detailed historical accounts, several key tropes emerge.

One of the most prominent is a scholarly critique against the frequent assertion in European countries from the late eighteenth century onwards that the Ottomans were 'fatalistic' about contagious disease because of their Islamic beliefs and/or general lack of understanding of the medical causes of disease. This self-evidently orientalist assertion was frequently accompanied by the conclusion that the Ottomans most often caused the spread of the most dangerous and deadly diseases across Europe, via both sea and land routes across the Mediterranean region. One subcategory of this rhetoric has been that the Hajj, the annual Muslim pilgrimage to Mecca, has been particularly effective at spreading contagious disease.[31] I will mention just three of the critiques against these orientalist assertions.

First, Birsen Bulmuş's study, *Plague, Quarantines and Geopolitics in the Ottoman Empire*[32] particularly focuses on Istanbul and the events leading up to, and leading on from, the year 1838. In that year, the Ottomans implemented a strict quarantine system that others (the British, French, Venetians, Genoans) had been using in a variety of forms during earlier outbreaks of plague and cholera. At the same time, a comprehensive free trade treaty was agreed between the Ottomans and the British, called the Treaty of Balta Liman. This was one of the most liberal treaties ever agreed between the Ottomans and any other power, and it allowed the British to flood the Ottoman markets with (for example) British cotton.

Bulmuş notes that almost as soon as the quarantine measures were imposed by the Ottoman Porte, British authorities became strongly involved in attempting to restrict and control these quarantine regulations, to ensure that British mercantilist interests were not harmed. Bulmuş argues that the vast majority of measures taken to try and control the spread of disease in the Mediterranean region was actually about business interests, and little to do with science, let alone any attempts to protect the health of people living along the trade routes. In her words, 'Quarantines were in fact mercantilist tools that protected and promoted internal economic development, and often flew in the face of free trade'.[33]

Peter Baldwin, my second example of this debate, argues in his lengthy study, *Contagion and the State in Europe, 1830–1930*[34] that things were not necessarily as straightforward as Bulmuş suggests. Britain had been very pro-quarantine in some periods and very anti-quarantine in others. For example, in 1865, when there was a major outbreak of cholera along a Mecca pilgrimage route, Britain agreed with other countries that while quarantine was 'no longer needed' in Europe (meaning the north Mediterranean), it was needed, they decided, 'in the Orient'.[35] Mecca, combined with the opening of the Suez Canal in 1869, had 'turned Mecca into an epidemiological turntable' in the views of the British at the time.[36]

The earlier period studied by Bulmuş (1838) was indeed one during which the British were against quarantine in the Ottoman territories, even though the Ottomans were in favour. During that period, Britain was viewed by other European countries and by others in the Mediterranean as a 'nation of shopkeepers' who did not care about the risks to the lives of Mediterranean people through the spread of disease, so long as British trade could continue unabated.[37] Slight, in a detailed study of the involvement of the British Empire in management of the Hajj, argues that this non-intervention approach changed after the 1865 outbreak of cholera among pilgrims, which led to considerably greater British involvement in attempts to manage and control the spread of disease to the Mediterranean through Hajj.[38] The development of steam ship travel and the opening of the Suez canal in the mid to late 1800s meant that people (and their diseases) could travel much faster than in previous years.

In any case, Baldwin notes that when it suited the British, they implemented the same quarantine rules as everyone else within their own territories in the Mediterranean region, even when they were anti-quarantine in general, in part because if they did not, they would not be accepted as trade partners with others, such as Marseilles, Istanbul and Genoa. As Baldwin points out, quarantine is something that requires agreements across territories, and so nobody can 'go it alone'.[39] Yet again later, in 1881, there was an international agreement to carry out surveillance for diseases in the Red Sea area, particularly focusing on the routes to Mecca. This was broken when the British occupied Egypt in 1882, and completely loosened the rules to allow unhindered shipping of British goods from India.[40] The British complained that the previous arrangements were an 'affront to liberty', but others argued, again, that the motivation was selfish business interests and that everybody else was going to get sick as a result. It was only in 1892 that the British were deprived of their monopoly of the Alexandria Council that regulated such matters, and new sanitary regulations were added.[41]

Baldwin's overall argument is that during the period between 1830 and 1930 that he focuses upon, states were developing new techniques of governance and experimenting with what these meant in terms of control over territories and populations. For that reason, it is not surprising that a variety of different approaches towards trying to control the spread of disease were carried out. Baldwin suggests that some of the first areas where governments tested out these new governing techniques involved efforts to control the spread of disease, both within their own territories and at their borders. He goes so far as to conclude that, 'It was not the nature of the disease which specified how it would be prevented and limited, but the kind of political regime under epidemic attack'.[42]

Many other studies have made a similar point about the impossibility of separating political and economic motivations from the efforts to control the spread of disease, and in the Mediterranean region, this has been a particularly marked argument.[43] That is not surprising, given the number of competing political and economic interests across that region. The Ottoman territories were almost entirely based in, or contiguously linked to, the Mediterranean region, and many others either had some stake in the region or had to pass through in order to move merchandise and other goods, as well as military and civilians, between disparate colonial territories. Among the most important of these political and economic powers were the British, the French (especially the port of Marseilles), the Venetians and the Genoese.

What all of the studies of the jostling between these powers show is that there was no consistency over time of efforts to control the spread of disease across the Mediterranean by different political regimes. It depended in part on the kinds of political relations with others that were held at the time; in part on trade and other financial or economic interests; in part on military interests; and in part on contemporary knowledge about the nature of the disease that was being confronted. None of these motivations seem to have ever existed in isolation of one another, so it is not possible to identify any single cause or motivation for tackling the threat of the spread of disease in a particular way.

Moreover, while some regimes developed techniques that others later adopted (for example, lazarettos were developed in Venice and later spread to other Mediterranean areas, and the structured procedure for quarantine, implemented by the Ottomans in the nineteenth century, was modelled on those developed in places such as Marseilles, Genoa and Venice), the idea that any regime was 'passive' in the face of serious outbreaks of fatal disease, has been thoroughly debunked by more recent scholarship. This is important, as it underlines Baldwin's point that any one political regime's attempts to control the spread of disease was always carried out in the company of other political regimes, even if each party acted more or less selfishly. The Ottomans were never unaware of the actions of their trading partners and political allies and foes, and they almost invariably took those into account in how they attempted to deal with the matter.

That brings me to the third study of contagious disease that I want to discuss, Nükhet Varlık's *Plague and Empire in the Early Modern Mediterranean World: The Ottoman Experience, 1347–1600*.[44] The book deals with the period leading up to the beginnings of the Ottoman Empire and its rapid expansion during the 'long sixteenth century' (1453, when Constantinople was conquered, to 1600). This is considerably earlier than the periods covered by Bulmuş or Baldwin, though she makes many of the same points about the lack of evidence to support the orientalist claims being made against the Ottomans by the European powers. In particular, she carries out a detailed study of the concept of Ottoman 'fatalism' in the face of contagious disease, which she traces back to European travel writing in the sixteenth and seventeenth centuries, that she calls a form of 'epidemiological orientalism'.[45] She demonstrates that not only did the Ottomans regularly take action to try to avoid contracting diseases when outbreaks occurred (especially in urban areas, and most particularly in Istanbul), but the accounts which suggested that they did not were systematically edited so that the belief matched what witnesses reported seeing.[46] She concludes that the 'trope of the fatalistic Turk ... came to figure as an important difference, one that helped differentiate "West" from "East"'.[47] This particular trope defined 'the East' as being inherently and thus timelessly 'plague-ridden' and 'the West' as 'plague-free' except when contagion came in from the east.

The element of Varlık's work that is most significant for my purposes is that she implies that the Ottomans understood the spatial aspects of their empire in a distinctly different way from the other colonial powers that had an interest in the Mediterranean region. This is linked to Varlık's analysis of the way episodes of plague occurred in Ottoman regions, which was different from other Mediterranean and European areas. Instead of sporadic outbreaks every so often as occurred in British territories, for example, the Ottoman Empire had constant outbreaks of plague. She argues that the disease travelled along the same routes as the traded goods, animals and people to create what she calls 'plague networks'.[48] This was the outcome, she suggests, of a very particular form of management of the Ottoman territories, which created certain kinds of interconnections between different parts of the empire, and in which Istanbul acted as the hub. Along with many others, she notes that the Ottomans had been seasonally mobile pastoralists before establishing their empire, and as such, they were peoples who travelled constantly, and their empire was built with that logic of mobility in mind. Lengthy studies of Ottoman economic and social history show that the Ottomans systematically developed an enormous network of trading roads and routes (often taking pride in strictly enforcing security along these routes). All kinds of international trade and commerce could travel along these routes, under a variety of controls by Ottoman authorities.[49]

Varlık suggests that particularly from the time the Ottomans conquered Constantinople in 1453 (thereafter also called Istanbul) and up to 1600, the Ottomans systematically interconnected previously separated networks of routes – roads, caravan routes, sea routes – and secured them. While the empire was expanding, the Ottomans particularly focused on taking over border areas. Whereas the British were travelling the globe and taking over far-flung chunks of the planet, which they were linking mostly through sea travel, the Ottomans were spreading out around the entire Mediterranean region and adjacent areas, closing the gaps between previously independently ruled areas, and thus creating links across networks of routes.

Varlık's argument is that this densely interconnected network created by the Ottoman approach towards developing and managing its empire, created a secure meshwork, to borrow a word from Ingold,[50] across which plague and later cholera could constantly travel. And since Istanbul was the hub of this dense network, it was also the city, she argues, that became the hub for infectious disease. This implies that, unlike the idea of Roman empire, in which the aim, as noted by Malkin, was that all roads should lead to the centre, to Rome,[51] in the case of Istanbul, it seems the aim was that all roads should lead *through* Istanbul, or at least be connected to a road or route that leads through it.

Note that this is quite different from Keck's concept of the sentinel. In that metaphor, there is a body–place vector across which an infection travels, and the sentinel is capable of warning of its presence. In Varlık's account of Istanbul and the Ottoman territories, the coexistence was much closer: everything and everyone travelled along the same routes, constantly.

Varlık's work implies that the Ottomans, despite developing in dramatically different ways across the centuries, consistently structured, managed and understood their territories in terms of routes and borders – roads, paths, seaways and crossing points. This confirms an argument I have also made in earlier work, that Ottoman territorial logic was distinct.[52] In particular, Varlık's study implies that Ottoman statecraft was guided by an underlying understanding of their territories as a network of routes, rather than blocks of land, as such. In contrast, most other political powers with an interest in the Mediterranean appear to have been guided in managing their colonial territories through an underlying understanding of them as bordered areas of land which are interconnected, both externally and internally, via routes. For example, the French approach towards managing their colonial territories was based on the idea of fixed lands that had specific characteristics (flora, fauna, peoples, etc.), that could be divided according to clear borders. The

Locating disease 193

implicit assumption of this model is that people mostly remain within each bordered area. This caused problems in the Chad Basin region, for example, where that model simply did not match most local people's practices.[53] In the Maghreb region of North Africa, a strongly pastoral area, the problem for the French colonial authorities was much the same.[54]

As I have already outlined, official Ottoman responses to the outbreak of disease over the centuries were as varied as the British, French or Genoan responses, for these were usually carried out with the other political powers in mind; yet the Ottomans were always, it appears, acting with the idea of a network of routes and roads in mind, rather than one of blocks of territories or the classification of different kinds of bodies according to their assumed eugenic/territorial characteristics, as was done by the Nazis. The network of routes logic of location that appears to have informed the Ottoman approach was not necessarily any less hierarchical than any of the others that were around at the time, but it did not create a fixed, bodily or material, connection between people and place that the eugenic and nationalist approaches towards territory that replaced it in the twentieth century.

Beyond sentinels

This brings me, finally, to the question of what might be happening in the contemporary moment in relation to location and disease, given moves towards defining disease in terms of biosecurity,[55] in which supra-state political entities such as the European Union and transnational organizations such as the World Health Organization (WHO) are increasingly important in attempts to manage the spread of disease. What can the approach suggested here, which focuses on how the space across which disease spreads is understood and defined, contribute towards understanding how the response to outbreaks of disease works in today's Mediterranean? I have three answers, which are all necessarily brief.

First, it is clear that most contemporary official responses are attempting to align more closely to the concept of location as network. This replaces the earlier approach of fixed territories that are interconnected via routes, and it comes a little closer to the former

Ottoman understanding of territory. Second, the nation state, which understands location as a fixed territory enclosed by a clear border, has not disappeared; it coexists with that more networked approach. This can be seen to be at work in the tensions between the WHO and a number of states' responses to the COVID-19 pandemic. And third, the concept of location as a virtual space has been introduced, or perhaps more accurately, re-introduced. In earlier centuries, people around the Mediterranean spoke of miasmas and evil spirit worlds through which disease would be visited upon mortal people. The more contemporary versions, one of which I discussed earlier drawing on Keck's work, in which there is a vector across which infection travels, appear to be more like abstractions than unseen places or bad substances in the air; but they are nevertheless increasingly acted upon as if they are there. This is particularly the case when scientific research redefines a place (Hong Kong) as a sentinel, the gate between one kind of diseased body-place (birds in the air) and another kind of diseased body-place (humans in Hong Kong). In accounts of attempts to prevent the spread of disease in the Mediterranean over the centuries, nobody has yet defined Istanbul as a sentinel. Instead, as Baldwin, Varlık, and many others have demonstrated, an orientalist logic was imposed on the Ottomans, most particularly from the mid-nineteenth century onwards, in which a clear separation was asserted between Ottoman peoples and territories, and places and peoples outside of that realm. Within that logic, Keck's cynegetic (hunter/hunted) metaphor, in which both hunter and hunted inevitably coexist in the same place, is replaced by a binary metaphor of absolute difference, in which the location of one must exclude the location of the other, and there can be no overlap between them. More recent historical studies of how things were organized in practice in the Mediterranean region demonstrate that even while racist and later nationalist spatial logics were developing, other logics coexisted and cross-cut them. Not only have orientalist accounts of 'fatalistic' Ottoman responses to contagious disease been shown to be highly inaccurate, this chapter has tried to demonstrate the importance of understanding both the engagement between different political, commercial and ideological interests in the region, and how different ways of understanding location informed diverse responses to the threat of the spread of disease. This might have something to teach us today about how to approach the idea of the spread of disease. It might require an acknowledgement of the coexistence of different understandings of location, which means that closing some kinds of borders is never going to be effective in closing all of them.

Notes

1 The research for this chapter has received funding from the European Research Council (ERC) under the European Union's Horizon 2020 research and innovation programme (grant agreement no 694482).
2 My grandfather both knew H. W. Florey, who worked on Fleming's original finding that some organic materials had anti-bacterial properties, and had read results of experiments Florey's team had carried out on penicillin in E. Chain, H. W. Florey, A. D. Gardner, N. G. Heatley, M. A. Jennings, J. Orr-Ewing and A. G. Sanders, 'Penicillin as a chemotherapeutic agent,' *The Lancet*, 236:6104 (1940).
3 H. V. Wyatt, 'Robert Pulvertaft's use of crude penicillin in Cairo,' *Medical History* 34:3 (1990); R. J. V. Pulvertaft, 'Local therapy of war wounds I: with penicillin,' *The Lancet*, 242:6264 (1943).
4 Pulvertaft, 'Local therapy of war wounds I', 339–48.
5 Wyatt, 'Robert Pulvertaft's use of crude penicillin, p. 324.
6 I. Harper, T. Kelly and A. Khanna (eds), *The Clinic and the Court: Law, Medicine and Anthropology* (Cambridge: Cambridge University Press, 2015); R. Richardson, *Death, Dissection and the Destitute* (Harmondsworth: Penguin, 1989); M. Foucault, *The Birth of the Clinic* (tr. Alan Sheridan) (London: Tavistock, 1986).
7 P. Weindling, *Epidemics and Genocide in Eastern Europe, 1890–1945* (Oxford; New York: Oxford University Press, 2000).
8 As Peter Baldwin noted, 'Bacteriology is routinely identified as a conservative doctrine that shifted the blame for disease from social conditions to microbes, requiring only limited statutory intervention' and the same kind of logic allowed a link to racism, through 'bacteriologically inspired imagery of interwar racialist thought and especially analogies drawn by Nazi ideology between pestilential microbes and Jews': P. Baldwin, *Contagion and the State in Europe, 1830–1930* (Cambridge: Cambridge University Press, 1999), p. 33.
9 F. Keck, 'From purgatory to sentinel: "forms/events" in the field of zoonoses.' *Cambridge Anthropology*, 32:1 (2014), 47–61; F. Keck, 'Sentinels for the environment. Birdwatchers in Taiwan and Hong Kong.' *China Perspectives*, 2 (2015), 41–50.

10 A. Bashford (ed.), *Medicine at the Border: Disease, Globalization, and Security, 1850 to the Present* (Basingstoke: Palgrave Macmillan, 2006), p. 2.
11 P. Zylberman, 'Civilizing the state: borders, weak states and international health in modern Europe', in Bashford, *Medicine at the Border*, pp. 21–40.
12 The idea of the coexistence of more than one way to define the relative value of a place (leading to several locations coexisting in the same place) is one that I am currently working on, along with a team of researchers, within a research project called *Crosslocations*. See www.helsinki.fi/en/researchgroups/crosslocations. A nascent version of it can be seen in S. Green, 'Making grey zones at the European peripheries,' in I. Harboe Knudsen and M. Demant Frederiksen (eds), *Ethnographies of Grey Zones in Eastern Europe: Relations, Borders and Invisibilities* (London; New York: Anthem Press, 2015). I have been working on the concept of relative location for quite a bit longer than that. See S. Green, 'Performing border in the Aegean: on relocating political, economic and social relations', *Journal of Cultural Economy*, 3:2 (2010), 261–78; S. Green, 'A sense of border,' in T. M. Wilson and H. Donnan (eds), *A Companion to Border Studies* (Oxford: Wiley-Blackwell, 2012), pp. 573–92; S. Green, 'Money frontiers: the relative location of euros, Turkish lira and gold sovereigns in the Aegean,' in P. Harvey, E. Casella, G. Evans, H. Knox, C. McLean, E. Silva, N. Thoburn and K. Woodward (eds), *Objects and Materials: A Routledge Companion* (Abingdon: Routledge, 2013), pp. 302–11.
13 On the historical development of this understanding of territory, see S. Elden, *The Birth of Territory* (Chicago: The University of Chicago Press, 2013).
14 Keck, 'From purgatory to sentinel, at 51.
15 Ibid., at 58.
16 Keck 'Sentinels for the environment, at 48.
17 Weindling, *Epidemics and Genocide*, pp. 200–3, 232.
18 Donna Haraway has studied issues of biological miscegenation and the way that transgression of bodily boundaries between species generates a sense of category transgression that deeply concerns many people: D. Haraway, 'Mice into wormholes: a comment on the nature of no nature,' in G. Lee Downey and Joseph Dumit (eds), *Cyborgs and Citadels: Anthropological Interventions in Emerging Sciences and Technologies* (Santa Fe, NM: School of American Research Press, 1997); D. Haraway, *Modest_Witness@Second_Millenium. Femaleman©_Meets_Oncomouse*™. *Feminism and Technoscience* (New York; London: Routledge, 1997). What I am focusing on here is the spatial transgression combined with the coexistence of diverse logics of connection and disconnection, not the transgression of identities implied in the language of miscegenation.

19 R. Willerslev, *Soul Hunters: Hunting, Animism, and Personhood among the Siberian Yukaghirs* [in English] (Berkeley, CA; London: University of California Press, 2007).
20 Notable examples include Baldwin, *Contagion and the State*; A. Bashford (ed.) *Quarantine: Local and Global Histories* (New York: Palgrave Macmillan, 2016); B. Bulmuş, *Plague, Quarantines and Geopolitics in the Ottoman Empire* (Edinburgh: Edinburgh University Press, 2012); N. Varlık, *Plague and Empire in the Early Modern Mediterranean World: The Ottoman Experience, 1347–1600* (Cambridge: Cambridge University Press, 2015); and T. Mitchell, *Rule of Experts: Egypt, Techno-Politics, Modernity* (Berkeley, CA; London: University of California Press, 2002): Chapter 1 – 'Can the mosquito speak?'
21 Some examples include Baldwin, *Contagion and the State*; A. Chase-Levenson, 'Early nineteenth-century Mediterranean quarantine as a European system' in Bashford, *Quarantine*; Varlık, *Plague and Empire*; Bulmuş, *Plague, Quarantines and Geopolitics*.
22 M. Douglas, *Purity and Danger: An Analysis of Concepts of Pollution and Taboo* (London: Routledge & Kegan Paul, 1976).
23 Bashford, *Medicine at the Border*, p. 14.
24 Bashford, *Quarantine*, p. 9.
25 L. Malkki, 'National geographic: the rooting of peoples and the territorialization of national identity among scholars and refugees', *Cultural Anthropology*, 7:1 (1992), 24–44; A. McClintock, *Imperial Leather: Race, Gender and Sexuality in the Colonial Contest* (New York; London: Routledge, 1994).
26 Baldwin, *Contagion and the State*, pp. 141–2.
27 J. Caplan, '"This or that particular person": protocols of identification in nineteenth-century Europe', in J. Caplan and J. C. Torpey (eds), *Documenting Individual Identity: The Development of State Practices in the Modern World* (Princeton, NJ; Chichester: Princeton University Press, 2001), pp. 49–66.
28 A. L. Fairchild, *Science at the Borders: Immigrant Medical Inspection and the Shaping of the Modern Industrial Labor Force* (Baltimore, MD: Johns Hopkins University Press, 2003).
29 Ibid., p. 253.
30 Ibid., p. 18.
31 John Slight's highly insightful book about the British Empire's involvement in the Hajj in the late nineteenth century argues that British direct management of the event was partly triggered by the outbreak of a major cholera epidemic among the pilgrims in 1865: J. P. Slight, *The British Empire and the Hajj, 1865–1956* (Cambridge, MA: Harvard University Press, 2015).

32 Bulmuş, *Plague, Quarantines and Geopolitics*.
33 Ibid., p. 98.
34 Baldwin, *Contagion and the State*.
35 Ibid., p. 229.
36 Ibid., p. 230.
37 Ibid., p. 208.
38 Slight, *The British Empire and the Hajj*. See also S. Mishra, *Pilgrimage, Politics, and Pestilence: The Haj from the Indian Subcontinent, 1860–1920* (Oxford: Oxford University Press, 2011).
39 Baldwin, *Contagion and the State*, p. 205.
40 Ibid., p. 207.
41 Ibid., p. 208.
42 Ibid., p. 13.
43 See, for example, Bulmuş, *Plague, Quarantines and Geopolitics*; Bashford, *Quarantine*; A. Smart and J. Smart, 'Biosecurity, quarantine and life across the border', in Wilson and Donnan, *A Companion to Border Studies*; M. I. Ticktin, *Casualties of Care: Immigration and the Politics of Humanitarianism in France* (Berkeley, CA; London: University of California Press, 2011); J. Booker, *Maritime Quarantine: The British Experience, c.1650–1900* (Aldershot: Ashgate, 2007).
44 N. Varlık, *Plague and Empire*.
45 Ibid., p. 71.
46 Ibid., p. 72–88.
47 Ibid., p. 88
48 Ibid., pp. 8–10.
49 H. Inalcik and D. Quataert (eds), *An Economic and Social History of the Ottoman Empire* (Cambridge: Cambridge University Press, 1997), pp. 195–217.
50 T. Ingold, *Lines: A Brief History* (London: Routledge, 2007).
51 I. Malkin, *A Small Greek World: Networks in the Ancient Mediterranean* (Oxford: Oxford University Press, 2011), p. 7.
52 S. F. Green, *Notes from the Balkans: Locating Marginality and Ambiguity on the Greek–Albanian Border* (Princeton, NJ: Princeton University Press, 2005).
53 J. L. Roitman, *Fiscal Disobedience: An Anthropology of Economic Regulation in Central Africa* (Princeton, NJ; Oxford: Princeton University Press, 2005).
54 F. Ben Slimane, 'Between empire and nation-state: the problem of borders in the Maghreb', in D. Bechev and K. Nicolaidis (eds), *Mediterranean Frontiers: Borders, Conflict and Memory in a Transnational World* (London: Tauris Academic Studies, 2010), pp. 35–55.
55 F. Keck, 'Feeding sentinels: Logics of care and biosecurity in farms and labs. *Biosocieties,* 10:2 (2015), 162–76.

8

Fear and panic at the borders: outbreak anxieties in the United States from the colonies to COVID-19

Amy Lauren Fairchild, Constance A. Nathanson and Cullen Conway

It is March 22, 2020. Text messages arrive by the hour telling us to stay home, to only buy the food we need, to report price gouging. The newspapers report a surge in gun buying for fear of public disorder. In Spain people fleeing the cities are turned back. In New York, we have 40% of the country's cases. Our governor speaks words of reassurance – we will overcome. We escape to the Poconos. The real and the surreal are indistinguishable.

Constance A. Nathanson

The air is heavy with heat in the southern port city of New Orleans. The mayor and his closest advisors consider the potential crisis behind closed doors. The city's long-time police commissioner, smug and contemptuous, dismisses as preposterous the idea of epidemic plague. Self-righteous and slightly overwrought, the Public Health Service officer pounds the table, warning, 'I've seen this disease work, and I'm telling you if it ever gets loose it can spread over the entire country! And the result will be more horrible than any of you can imagine!' There would be, as the title of this 1950s film noir spelled out, *Panic in the Streets*. And, of course, there would be not just local or national mayhem but global catastrophe if the health officer (Richard Widmark) and the police detective (Paul Douglas) – assigned both to help him and to keep him in check – don't find a murderer (a sinister Jack Palance) with pneumonic plague before he reaches the docks and escapes, like a rat, onto a vessel bound for international waters.

The dominant themes in this cinema of fear are the certainty of mass panic and the breakdown of social order in the wake of a breach of national boundaries.[1] Philip Wylie (1902–1971), a consultant for the Federal Defense Administration and popular science fiction writer whose novels included *Tomorrow*,[2] a 1954 account of nuclear holocaust,[3] set the tone. Wylie made the case that Cold War America had a bad case of the 'atomic jitters' and populations would most certainly panic in the aftermath of nuclear war. If the fact of war didn't do it, then the sight of the charred survivors, 'hideous and ambulatory', would rob those who remained of rational thought and behavior.[4] This forms the core assumption of both the aesthetics and, in that period, the politics of outbreak anxieties, in the face of events that mar, maim and kill, panic reigns.

A relatively new academic literature exploring collective fears and mass panic has surfaced since the era of global health and emerging infections.[5] These scholars argue that the pitch and intensity of panic discourse exponentially increased in the period after World War II, amplified by 'fear entrepreneurs' and by national leaders who came to see 'fear as foundational for national unity in the absence of confidence in more positive programs'.[6] Remarkably, historians of public health have not questioned collective social fear or panic. When disease panics are given extended historical treatment, those careful studies are located in a tight time period, preventing an analysis of change from one era to the next.[7] More often, considering the pressing and legitimate need to understand not just the past but the present, panic is treated as one of several 'universal truths about the enduring relationships between microbes and human beings'.[8]

Mass panics are challenging to define.[9] Most broadly, panic serves as the *attribution* of an amplified emotional state of deep fear or anxiety to individuals or groups in response to an unfolding, anticipated or even fabricated event. As an attribution, panic might have very little connection to either what populations genuinely felt or events that can be verified. Panic might be labelled rational or irrational. Panic might be attributed to populations or officials. It might be attributed to measures meant to stop the spread of disease just as easily as it might be used to attack a failure to intervene. Above all, panic serves as a mode of dramatic framing, meant to manage or even manipulate events as much as to describe them.[10]

Sander Gilman argues that collective fear of disease is always tied to the possibility of an unfettered, catastrophic spread of deadly infections.[11] Collective fears related to disease are thus often focused on borders as disease travels from one place to another place. But as the literature on moral panics makes clear (and as those of us living through the coronavirus pandemic in the spring of 2020 are reminded every day) borders of concern are not necessarily geographic. Boundaries of race and ethnicity, between natives and strangers, even whether you wear a mask are deployed to separate 'us' from the threatening 'other'. Fear and disease invoke what Lamont and Molnar call 'symbolic' and 'social' boundaries. The former assign cultural meaning to groups, the latter translate those meanings into patterns of unequal access to resources and power.[12]

Understanding the social meaning and political work of fear and panic requires not simply locating events in particular times and places but identifying major shifts over time. What disease events has panic framed? What does panic look like? That is, how is it manifested? What borders is it attached to? What groups? To what end? What political work does panic do? And finally, what does panic mean in different contexts? In other words, does theoretical or conceptual thinking about panic connect to social experiences and understandings? By asking these questions over the course of more than a century, we can determine what, if anything, has changed from one era to the next. We map broad changes in both theoretical and social understandings and experiences of fear and panic using four distinct periods that historians of international history and public health have employed to study the rise of public health institutions and the shifting politics of public health: (1) the quarantine era (before germ theory), dating from the colonial period to roughly the 1880s in the United States; (2) the bacteriological era (after germ theory), dating from the 1880s to World War II; (3) the era of international health (from the end of World War II through the AIDS epidemic); and (4) the current era of globalization, defined by the emergence of new structures and networks beginning in the 1980s, which we turn to by way of conclusion.[13]

While panic might always be considered disruptive, it began as a concept that was not necessarily irrational and, indeed, had some salutary effects in the era of quarantine, which we call the era of 'flight'. The borders of concern in this era were primarily geographic, primarily internal. In the bacteriological era, both fear and panic were framed as base and therefore dangerous emotions. A 'fright' became a threat both to institutional and personal health. Both symbolic and social borders were at stake; new institutions were drawing boundaries between the variously imagined 'us' and 'them' in the name of population health. During the Cold War, panic and fear were newly contested. In this era of 'fight' over meaning and the uses and abuses of fear and panic, both attached to discussions about the limits of the state, at issue were the social boundaries around power and how its exercise could limit resources and freedoms. In the global era the threat of emerging infections has brought national geographic borders back into the ambit of fear.

The quarantine era: flight

In September 1888, the Postmaster in Cairo, Illinois, dispatched a telegram to the Post Office Department in Washington, DC. He warned, the 'country below is in the hands of a howling mob'.[14] Yellow fever terror radiated from the Deep South. It was one of many unwanted visits from Yellow Jack in the years after the Civil War – a plague causing painful, gruesome death whose cause was unknown, but popularly connected to the exchange of infected bedding and clothing. Locales not yet touched by disease often went into lockdown. In the absence of permanent public health officials or institutions, coalitions of citizens and elected officials living in uninfected areas sometimes took up arms to impose 'shot gun' quarantines to fend off outsiders. In Jackson, Mississippi, residents ripped up railroad tracks leading into the city in 1897.[15] 'Indignation is at fever heat here', stated a news account, 'and the people say that if necessary to compel observation of their reasonable quarantine regulations they will burn every bridge between here and Vicksburg'.[16] Notably, the targets of such reactionary 'shot gun' quarantines were typically middle- and upper-class citizens with the resources to attempt to flee. In Jackson, Mississippi, the governor was barred from entering 'his own capital', as 'the public officers had no respect of persons in enforcing the rule'.[17] Significantly, the events most often labelled panics were focused within the US borders, not at the nation's borders.

Scholars, citizens and elected officials did not consider panic to be inherently irrational during the nineteenth century, particularly before the existence of enduring public health institutions; dangerous and threatening, yes, but not a collective state in which people lost all reason.[18] Flight itself was chaotic and disruptive, but the social imagery of panic – not only an attribution made by newspaper accounts but also personal diaries describing epidemics – in a nation inexorably expanding its North American empire into a seemingly boundless frontier with the prospect of a safe place to retreat[19] was never tarred as a kind of atavistic reaction. Flight was, in fact, recommended by no less an authority than the eighteenth century physician and politician Benjamin Rush (1746–1813): 'There is but one preventative [for yellow fever] that is certain, and that is "to fly from it."'[20] Outbreak panics were deemed protective, helping to ensure the removal of kindling that might fuel an epidemic fire.[21] 'Fancied security' was, in the face of a 'scare', the far more dangerous state of mind.[22]

Communal fears did, however, give rise to a quest for structures to manage disease and disorder.[23] Cholera – another common cause for panic – was directly linked to the creation of the first permanent municipal Board of Health in New York City in 1866, a date and an institution that Charles Rosenberg describes as being singularly important in the history of public health. In the 1870–71 annual report, New York City's health officials noted that in New Orleans the absence of a basic organizational structure led to the city pointedly ignoring cases of yellow fever for fear of stirring a panic it lacked the resources to control.[24] Yellow fever often led to calls for a national quarantine law. Without it, *The Atlanta Constitution* argued in 1899, 'there will be no alleviating the evils of panic, and no end to the system of shotgun quarantine,'[25] which involved one state turning against another.[26] Panic provoked collective hand-wringing – not because destructive behavior had no rhyme or reason, but because of the absence of structures to effectively manage outbreaks within the nation's borders.

The bacteriological era: fright

Permanent health structures along with changing scientific understandings of disease altered language, and panic began to do different work. In the early bacteriological period, attributions of panic took on pejorative connotations in the wake of mounting concerns about immigration, industrialization and crowding in cities, particularly tenement districts in the later decades of the nineteenth century. But by the time of the influenza pandemic, as the New York City Department of Health began to extend its scope and influence with the dual aims of disease and panic control, health officials and clinicians framed panic as an internal process destructive to individual health rather than as a reasonable response to the threat of disease.

Early bacteriology and the immigrant threat at the US borders

Collective anxieties were increasingly focused on threats from beyond the national borders. Just as immigration from China was restricted, immigration from southern and eastern European countries began to soar, and political efforts to extend restrictions to these 'new' immigrant groups – viewed as dirty, illiterate, uncivilized and thus destined for poverty and disease – were given voice.[27] Like the Chinese, southern and eastern European immigrants represented a threat to democracy and the social order. They were also widely viewed, sometimes quite literally, as vectors of contagious disease.[28]

In the late nineteenth century, French physician and anthropologist Gustave Le Bon (1841–1931) proposed the kernel of what became labelled 'contagion theory': primal emotions were transmitted through the crowd, which developed a kind of 'collective mind' capable of *irrational* action. It was a theory that mirrored not only European social history, but also social history in America, where 'milling masses' arrived in a seeming flood.[29] Importantly, while American commentators objected to Le Bon's notion that any and all individuals, regardless of social position,[30] were just as susceptible to the influence of the crowd as those of 'a low measure of understanding',[31] reviewers embraced Le Bon's 'pertinence to current events'.[32] Particularly compelling was the notion that an effort to 'differentiate the crowds of different nationalities' was a valuable exercise for 'the practical politician'.[33] And so the Frenchman, Le Bon, was appropriated to the American work of symbolic boundary construction along ethnic lines.

Nationalists deployed the language of panic to tar the new immigrants. Panic in the face of disease was to be expected of the 'frenzied' Italians of New Orleans or the 'illiterate' immigrants in New York's East Side, but not of 'respectable and cultivated citizens' who knew better.[34] The poor were the 'dazed people' who both created the cauldron of contagion[35] and reacted in unreasoning ways in its face. The implications of germ theory for the panic narrative went beyond the targeting of immigrants, however. Health departments made real progress against the threat of contagious diseases. William Sedgwick, one of the nation's leading scientists and educators, summed up the scientific triumph of the bacteriological age: 'Before 1880 we knew nothing; after 1890 we knew it all; it was a glorious ten years.'[36]

The implications of germ theory for the panic narrative were complex, contradictory and went well beyond the targeting of immigrants. From the perspective of America's elites, the 'triumphs' of bacteriology and attendant mastery of nature promised freedom from unreasoning terror of the unknown.[37] Fear was a kind of prehistoric emotion characterizing the ignorant poor. It was also a source of human suffering, therefore something to be conquered. Yet for the public, the popularization of germ theory led, counterintuitively, to increased fears by vastly multiplying the sources of contagion.[38] 'Americans' mental map of potentially dangerous forms of intercourse with the outside world,' argues Nancy Tomes, 'expanded dramatically' from the 1890s onward.[39]

On the one hand, then, there was vituperative, anti-immigrant rhetoric based on the belief that the ignorant masses spread not only disease but panic. On the other hand, there was genuine public health confidence that 'so many things have been done for the protection of the health of mankind that fear is being driven further and further into the background'.[40] The great expansion of the public health authority after 1900 – quarantine, surveillance, vaccination, fumigation, school inspections – was built at one and the same time on fear of disease and the growing imperative to control it and on increases in public confidence in the lessons of the laboratory.[41]

As the nation began to increasingly fortify its borders against the immigrant onslaught and health departments vastly expanded the scope and visibility of disease control measures, panic became a slur to tar those at the margins of society. Panic was reframed as a kind of 'state of exception,' a departure from the 'normal' quotidian confrontations with disease, debility and death.[42] In 1920, just a year before the United States began to tightly restrict immigration from southern and eastern Europe, William McDougall (1871–1938), a psychologist with eclectic interests,[43] characterized panic not simply as intense fear, but a state in which the individual 'experiences that horrible emotion in full force and is irresistibly impelled to save himself by flight'. Panic had been transformed from Rush's reasonable response to the threat of contagious disease to 'the crowd in dissolution' comparable to 'a flock of sheep'.[44] Disease anxieties multiplied during this period, but well-reasoned fears were effectively marshalled to advance public health authority. Panic as something distinct from sober, middle-class fears became inextricably linked to judgments about class and the capacity for self-governance.

Influenza, the conquest of mass panic, and the rise of mass worry

The 1918 flu pandemic, which claimed the lives of some 50 million worldwide and 550,000 in the United States, represented perhaps the greatest test of the state's ability to control not only disease but panic.[45] Historians have argued that while there was a surge of panic that accompanied the devastating and swiftly moving 1918 influenza outbreak, it prevailed only for 'a brief period'.[46] There were scattered reports of specific incidents of overt chaos that recalled the old flight response. In Colorado, for example, a hundred miners were reported to be 'stampeding' toward a town free from disease. A 'battle between armed guards' and the 'panic-stricken miners [seemed] imminent'. Yet (the account continued), this incident was 'the nearest approach to panic that has yet been reported.'[47]

Disease crises and a perceived need for panic management ushered in a new era of building up public health institutions. There were three notable years when the New York City Health Department (NYCHD) substantially increased its institutional capacity, 1891 (when the United States mandated the medical inspection of immigrants at the nation's ports), 1910–11 and 1918 (the year of the Spanish flu). In the 1870s, the department had eight to nine executive officers, ten sanitary inspectors, and a vaccination corps. By 1919, the NYCHD had more than 200 bureaus, subdivisions and activities. The report for that year singled out the new Division of Epidemiology for celebration; in previous years, it had done little beyond 'the routine supervision of typhoid fever, epidemic cerebro-spinal meningitis, and poliomyelitis'.[48] Newly expanded, it now 'developed plans and methods which had for their aim the immediate detection in any part of the city of an undue prevalence of any one of the communicable diseases'.[49] NYCHD extended its reach through systematic surveys that threw 'light upon ... how to deal most intensively with' a host of new conditions.[50] The city health department boasted a kind of radar to detect and respond not only to disease but also attendant fear and panic.

Even if there was broad contemporary and historical agreement that the mass panic of the old yellow fever variety was successfully contained through the swift and sweeping action of health officials, there was, in fact, widespread talk of panic throughout the influenza pandemic. And although threats from outside US borders had, for several decades, been the subject of a kind of paranoid national debate,[51] containment efforts in this instance were focused *within* rather than *at* the US borders. The NYCHD, for example, took steps in 1918 to prevent a panic that might have prematurely closed the schools, targeting its activities like a laser: daily school nurse inspections – in which children were examined and teachers lectured – and home nursing visits to absent children to identify cases.[52] On school grounds, health department nurses engaged in 'continuous observation of school buildings and playgrounds, with particular reference to cleanliness, ventilation, and other sanitary and hygienic measures'.[53] Officials believed outbreak anxieties were triggered by overreaching 'social distancing' measures such as school closures, church closures and staggered business hours as well as the absence of 'sharp and decisive action'.[54] For New York City, the schools were the barometer. The health department paid careful attention to crowding in the school and redirected school nurses to the supervision of sick children with an eye to making informed decisions about closure. When it came to controlling panic, the department was self-congratulatory. 'These procedures result in a feeling of security in schools and an almost immediate abatement of the hysteria which had led many parents to keep children at home.'[55]

In a context in which panic was the terrain of the ignorant masses and the public was, on the whole, supportive of state efforts to contain the spread of disease, the language of panic also turned inward.[56] Panic was increasingly framed as an internal individual event: 'every little ache or pain that may be harmless in itself' might cause a person to 'give himself over to dismal imaginations', concluded one clinician. The 'mind fears [disease], becomes receptive to it, invites it'. In contrast 'the mind that stolidly refuses to entertain the thought of disease, that rejects it, that repels panicky conditions, is far better prepared to ward off disease'. Health officials thus cheerfully coached the public to maintain 'a fearless and hopeful attitude of mind'.[57]

These historical transformations in experience and popular discourse anticipated critical changes in the theoretical assessments of panic. In the context of the Great Depression, where fear was once again projected on a national scale as the ultimate liability, management of social fright took on new importance. In the late 1930s Stanford University sociologist Richard Tracy LaPiere (1929–1965) set forth the most extended treatment of social panic to date. His work had scientific roots in psychoanalytic theory and political roots in the New Deal era, which saw a remarkable expansion of the federal government as the solution to 'fear itself'. The core of LaPiere's ideas, which held sway into the 1960s, was that people would not panic so long as there was no void in leadership. In a moment of crisis, to be sure, individuals would immediately react by temporarily turning inward and touching base with deeply rooted, atavistic self-interests. But they could be quickly drawn back by 'regimental leadership'. With proper guidance, the group would ultimately *fall in line* rather than *fall apart*.[58] Panic was not a result of rationality being hijacked by hysteria, but of the state's failure to maintain the confidence of populations in its authority and ability to act.[59]

The international era: fight

The history of panic and fear has been, in the international era, a tale of mounting anxiety tied to the threat of nuclear war, biowarfare and pandemic threats. As in previous periods, it is a history of panic-backed institution-building. This history of anxious eyes trained *at* the borders is critical, and we explore it through the lenses of nuclear and biological warfare directly below. Yet the threat at the national borders is only half of the story. In testing the limits of fear as a political tool, the potential and limits of the state in exercising power were paramount. The most fundamental questions were how can and should the state protect its land borders, but additionally what are the limits of state action? What bounds should be placed on state power?

Biowarfare and the uses and abuses of panic

In the post-war years, the United States joined other nations and new international organizations in focusing on the importance of policing borders when it came to the international spread of disease.[60] The United Nations,[61] the US Public Health Service, the short-lived US Mutual Security Agency,[62] but also private corporations, professional societies, non-governmental organizations and academic health centers[63] promoted an international surveillance network that established the borders of nation states as essential to the control of disease during a period of time in which European borders were being re-established. Mainly through propaganda films, these organizations not only sought to establish their expertise, but also demonstrate how, in the international era, borders were porous.

But the prospect of nuclear and biowarfare threatened both health and national borders in new and sometimes surprising ways. New agencies – the US Civil Defence Administration and the US CDC (centers for disease control and prevention) – were created to control panic in the event of a Soviet nuclear or biological attack. This new administrative order was sustained by older panic theories that had concluded nuclear and, in particular, biological warfare would send the nation spinning into raving chaos.[64] In addition to control *of* borders, control *within* the borders following an attack was key. Here we focus on control within the US border and on attendant concerns that the state in its zeal to protect the population might transgress the lines of what makes a liberal society.

Val Peterson (1903–1983), President Eisenhower's first Administrator of the Federal Civil Defense Administration (FCDA) created in 1951, was concerned that mass panic might 'produce a chain reaction more deeply destructive than any explosive known ... Mass panic – not the A bomb – may be the easiest way to win a battle, the cheapest way to win a war.'[65] Peterson, in a widely circulated 1953 article in *Colliers*, harked back to nineteenth-century images by describing a scenario in which bombs decimated Manhattan: 'Those who did succeed in fleeing the island would pour into adjacent areas to become a hungry pillaging mob – disrupting disaster relief, overwhelming local police and spreading panic in a widening arc.'[66]

While much of the subsequent work of the FCDA focused on preventing the panics they believed would attend a nuclear holocaust,[67] the specter of biowarfare, argued some emergency planners, was more terrifying to the public. Participants at a meeting called by the Secretary of Defense on 7 April 1949 explained that the covert nature of biological warfare – a 'clandestine weapon par excellence' – made it particularly panic-provoking. Attackers could deny having used biowarfare (BW). Just as easily they could *pretend* to have used such weapons, inspiring widespread chaos in the face of otherwise mundane seasonal outbreaks. Most critically, the committee concluded, 'people are afraid of disease in peace and war, whereas they have to fear conventional weapons only in time of war. Therefore, BW is a weapon which has the potentiality of eradicating psychologically the difference between peace and war,'[68] thereby threatening a symbolic border, the line between war and peace, as opposed to a territorial border.

The committee's rationale drew implicitly on social psychological perspectives articulated in the mid-1940s. Kurt Riezler (1882–1955) was a German diplomat and philosopher opposed to the Nazi regime who immigrated to the United States before the outbreak of World War II. Riezler argued that social fears, that is, fears widely held by individuals, fell along a spectrum from fear of the known (which made potential disorder manageable) to fear of the unknown (which suggested potential catastrophe since a government's ability to respond was uncertain). In the case of novel fears, 'the shock' of the unknown 'shatters our scheme of order,'[69] wrote Riezler, potentially leading to the breakdown of behavioral norms. Fear could spread like a contagion, but it was better understood as a yardstick for measuring the strength of democratic systems; if panic took hold, it was, in fact, 'the democratic procedure' that had failed, not human rationality. Thus, Riezler aligned with LaPiere in pointing to 'a common scheme or order' as the antidote to panic.[70]

Given this understanding, what was needed to combat the terror of biowarfare was an institution to demystify, and manage, the unknown. Dr Alexander Langmuir (1910–1993) would emerge as the most influential of the federal officials concerned with biowarfare.

Before coming to the CDC, Langmuir had consulted with the Armed Forces Epidemiological Board and served on the Commission on Respiratory Diseases at Fort Bragg. As a faculty member in epidemiology at Johns Hopkins University, he became involved in biological warfare through the Department of Defense's Committee on Biological Warfare, first as a member and later as the committee's chair.[71] When Langmuir arrived at the CDC in 1949 as Chief Epidemiologist, he recognized that the seemingly remote threat of biowarfare – the threat at the borders – was dwarfed by the day-to-day concerns of 'natural' epidemics: the threats within the borders. Yet the need for national border protection gave him an unparalleled opportunity for funding and expansion of the CDC.

By the spring of 1951, Langmuir later recalled, the Korean war 'was six months old and had been going badly'. The Chinese were mounting 'a massive propaganda campaign claiming with no justification whatsoever that the USA had used biological warfare. The 'emotional tension'[72] – indeed, 'emotional hysteria'[73] – about biological warfare 'was unbelievable and worse the higher one reached into the establishment.'[74] In an effort to capitalize on these mounting anxieties, Langmuir 'submitted a detailed plan and a budget and published a plain unvarnished statement of the potentialities of biowarfare and sneaked it through military intelligence.'[75] The CDC's famed Epidemic Intelligence Service was created using military funds.

Langmuir proceeded to make the case both in the public health literature and in the popular media that pathogens could be aerosolized over cities, that water or food could be contaminated, and that strategic buildings could be sabotaged in order 'to incapacitate key individuals and industries or create hysteria and undermine public morale.'[76] In a television episode entitled 'What you should know about biological warfare' that aired on 3 April 1951, as part of *The Johns Hopkins Science Review*, Langmuir demonstrated the ease with which a rogue actor might successfully aerosolize a pathogen with dry ice using a simple household blender, as well as the simplicity of contaminating public drinking water with a simple pipette filled with dye.[77] FCDA booklets and propaganda films advanced these themes. A consummate public health entrepreneur and fully conscious of his own ambitions, Langmuir later described a pattern that has long shaped the politics of public health in the United States and elsewhere: 'each emergency led to increased budgets, increased recruiting, and absorbed career officials'.[78]

The rise of totalitarian regimes that led to World War II and the threat of nuclear war that succeeded it led to intense intellectual and political engagement with the experience of fear and panic. Whether fear was a legitimate tool in the arsenal of politics to scare people into acting 'for their own good' or a blunt instrument more likely to have consequences worse than the disease was debated by public intellectuals such as Hannah Arendt (1906–75), Stefan Possony (1913–95), Harry Emerson Fosdick (1878–1969), Judith Shklar (1928–92) and Robert Oppenheimer (1904–67).[79] The consensus of these scholars was a broad rejection of fear-inspired policy. During the same period, a generation of historians who began to write 'history from below' – Eric Hobsbawm, George Rude and E. P. Thompson – rescued the crowd from its status as little more than mindless, feral mob.[80] Crowds, classes, masses – all had specific objectives in their collective behavior. Group agitation could no longer be characterized as the inchoate rumblings of the 'rabble'. Sociologists followed suit. Civil rights and student movements led social movement theorists to see collectivities as organized actors, legitimate stakeholders. Fear and panic, then, lost legitimacy as political tools and those earlier perceived as in its grip were restored as rational social actors.

Chronic disease, epidemics and containment within

This, then, was the backdrop when public health began to confront the problem of chronic disease – the scourge of smoking, in particular – on the home front in the 1950s. A landmark 1953 study by Irving Janis and Seymour Feshbach concluded that the use of fear to motivate behavior change had inevitably backfired.[81] Fear-based appeals were particularly liable to foment 'maladaptive responses', including tuning out the message, minimizing the risks, or even engaging in self-destructive behavior (people might smoke more to cope with the stress of viewing scary anti-smoking images). Chronic anxiety was viewed as one of the consequences of Cold War rhetoric in the era of 'nerves'.[82] Given the ways in which the 'stresses of modern life' were already said to increase the epidemiological risks of heart disease, stroke and cancer,[83] the prescription was less, not more, fear. As a consequence, from the 1950s through to the 1970s, the widely accepted academic wisdom was that fear-based appeals did not work to change behavior.[84]

Public health initially combatted the rise of chronic disease for a population weary of the 'propaganda of fear' with information:[85] cold hard facts were trumpeted as both an antidote to panic and a powerful behavior-change lever in the new crusade against cancer.[86] For example, 1950s efforts to counter the threat of tobacco were primarily numerical in a decidedly 'statistical era'.[87] Numbers were objective and neutral, conveying the imprimatur of science. Public health, like clinical medicine, seized on a language of odds and probabilities to establish its authority.[88] Media reports on smoking in the mid-1950s were peppered with risk assessments with no precedent in prior public discussions of disease: 'The odds of a nonsmoker dying of cancer in the next 12 months are 10,000 to 1. They shorten to 300 to 1 in the case of a heavy smoker'; 'The two-pack-a-day smoker multiplies his chances of lung cancer 52 times.'[89] The assumption was that conveying this kind of statistical information would help the smoker 'decide whether smoking is worth the possible risk of cancer' and – informed by sound science – make the obviously superior, logical choice. Yet another strand of thinking about fear suggested that this emotionless approach was bound for failure. Following more than a decade of attempting to get Americans to take biological warfare seriously, Dr Alexander Langmuir described his chief problem in the Cold War panic drama as an astonishing 'level of disbelief'.[90]

Beginning in the late 1960s, public service announcements sponsored by voluntary associations such as the American Cancer Society and American Lung Association shifted, becoming highly emotional and playing on fears related to damage to children, family and friends, and, finally, self.[91] 'The fact that something is dangerous is not enough to keep people from doing it,' concluded a scientist who had contributed to the first Surgeon General's report on smoking and cancer.[92] By the 1980s, public health counter-ads began to rely on fear appeals when it came to the most important cause of both cancer and coronary heart disease: smoking.[93] And popular disquiet about advertising and manipulation began to mount.[94] The line to police was the social one separating the legitimate use of fear to persuade in a way that allowed true individual judgment from the use of fear to manipulate with hyperbolic or untruthful misrepresentation that made authentic judgment impossible.

Philosophers who weighed the threat of chronic diseases were not uniformly hostile to fear. This was noteworthy given widespread scepticism about the Cold War political manipulation of panic and fear that had emerged by the 1960s, the new health consensus that fear always backfired, and, significantly, the ascendency of autonomy as the pre-eminent value in ethical analyses of the clinical relationship in the years after the Nuremberg Trials and their revelations about research abuses involving gross violations of respect for human dignity.

From 1982 to 1987, figures central to the intellectual and philosophical foundations of bioethics – Dan Wikler, Ruth Macklin, Tom Beauchamp, Gerald Dworkin and Ruth Faden – scrutinized the differences between informing, educating and manipulating. When information alone, communicated in the neutral language of science, was insufficient to convey the seriousness of a threat, a good scare could enhance autonomy.[95] The philosopher Robert Goodin, an ardent champion of forceful public health measures, argued that people might be able to repeat the 'facts' without truly understanding risk 'in their guts'.[96] Such superficial understanding could not really count as knowing.[97] Most provocatively, leading bioethicist Ruth Faden argued in 1987 that fear did, in fact, take advantage of anxiety, pain, suffering and other states of mind known to compromise rationality. Such manipulation violated the principle of autonomy.[98] But, she reasoned, 'merely because violations [of autonomy] are involved ... it does not necessarily follow that the [fear-based] campaigns [to change public health behaviors] are morally unacceptable.'[99] Fear was potentially fair game depending on the severity of the health threat.

Since World War II, then, fear has been at the root of both remarkable national institution-building and policy-making. The manipulation of fear was not limited to the state. In the context of chronic diseases, stirring collective fears was central to the development of a powerful anti-tobacco movement and the reshaping of social norms. Fearmongering, as a result, again became a target of public concern. The CDC was accused of stirring mass fears to get more money and staff. In the instance of civil society, while the anti-tobacco organizations largely avoided the charge of fearmongering, that would change as fear tactics were extended to AIDS and obesity in the era of global health.[100]

Conclusion: the global era and reflections on COVID-19

Deterritorialization defines the global era. Global capital is not bounded by national borders. Neither is cultural experience nor, of course, is disease. The sociologist Anthony Giddens explains that in the context of modernity social life is 'disembedded' from social systems. That is, experiences are 'lift[ed] out' of social relations from local contexts of interaction and are 'restructure[ed] across indefinite spans of time-space.'[101] On the one hand, with globalization as a backdrop, borders matter less because 'worldwide social relations ... link distant localities in such a way that local happenings are shaped by events occurring many miles away and vice versa.'[102] The international public health approach to cross-national disease control, fuelled by emerging infections, shifted to stopping infections at the source rather than at increasingly porous national borders.[103] On the other hand, borders defined by geography take on new symbolic weight in a period marked by new movements of disease, goods and people, particularly economic and political refugees and asylum seekers.

The old Cold War threat of an attack within US borders was realized on 11 September 2001. Panic was, as historians have argued, instrumental in framing subsequent events.[104] SARS, H1N1, Ebola and Zika subsequently suggested a world teetering on the threshold of pandemic disaster. In the context of the 2014–2015 Ebola crisis, for example, panic over a handful of US cases led to unwarranted policy solutions that many argued exacerbated the outbreaks on the ground in West African nations. Leading science pundits argue that we aren't panicking enough when it comes to pandemic disease.[105] Signalling that there is no end to potential infectious panics, the World Health Organization adopted the term 'Disease X' to designate the next pandemic.

This chapter was originally drafted in 2018, well before what would become the global pandemic of COVID-19 that struck first in China in the waning months of 2019. In a chapter on 'fear and panic at the borders', this pandemic cannot be ignored. Our reflections are inevitably premature (it is late April) and inevitably tentative. They are largely limited to the United States. We are struck, nevertheless, first, by how closely the present moment inscribes the history of the past and, second, by the profound difference made by instant global electronic communication.

In some ways, we (in the United States) are in the middle of the nineteenth century. We are all about borders. President Trump's first response, at the end of January 2020, was to close the national border to flights from China. He went on to congratulate himself and do nothing for over a month. Neither facts nor fear nor sober leadership were in his lexicon. He not only failed to deploy the powerful public health institutions built over the past century and a half, he hobbled them, leaving individual states to cope as they would, instituting 'social distancing' or not, as they saw fit, competing among themselves for critical medical supplies, and even closing internal borders on their own initiative to 'refugees' fleeing the epidemic from other states. Trump publicly labelled COVID-19 the 'China virus' targeting anyone with a 'Chinese' appearance for public shaming and opprobrium. All our borders, geographic, symbolic, social, political and personal have been brought into the ambit of fear.

'Institutions reveal much about themselves when under stress or in crisis, when they face the unexpected as well as the routine.'[106] What the COVID-19 crisis has so far revealed about the United States as it is today is profound institutional fragmentation, the absence of organized state capacity for coordination of (often) competing public health institutions, and an institutional vulnerability to politicization of the most trivial to the most consequential dimensions of public health (and all other) policy decisions. These are not novel observations. They have been frequently noted but never perhaps so starkly and never with the potential consequences for social chaos and economic devastation that they carry in the time of COVID-19. But they underscore a point that is novel in our history of thinking about disease and panic. Some legitimate alarm during a period of uncertainty can facilitate public deliberation and sound decision-making. It can spur the public to listen more closely to official public health communications and to support necessary public health investments.

Whether they refer to national or internal borders, debates about disease prevention and control inevitably raise symbolic questions regarding who belongs and political questions about the role of the state and its limits, questions that have been paramount since the Cold War. As we have seen here, panic never entirely sheds older meanings or work. Nancy Tomes wrote of disease that the 'memories of one generation are handed on and reinterpreted by the next'.[107]

The same holds true for fear and panic. But this history underscores that we must also interrogate and historicize the attributions and uses of collective fears and panic. Communal panic is not a transhistorical idea. There have been shifts in the meaning of fear and panic, in the locus of concern (that is, the boundaries at stake, either geographic, symbolic, social or political), and the role these attributions play in building institutions and justifying policy.

Notes

1 *Panic in the Streets* is only one example of a much larger genre, including *Night of the Living Dead* (1968), *The Killer that Stalked New York* (1950), Stephen King's *The Stand* (1978), *Outbreak* (1985) and *Contagion* (2011), Hollywood's *Panic in the Year Zero* from 1962, as well as the fictional and informational nuclear survival films of the Federal Civil Defense Administration from the 1950s.
2 Philip Wylie, *Tomorrow!* (New York: Rinehart, 1954).
3 See R. Glossop, *The Orphan of Space: A Tale of Downfall* (London: G. MacDonald & Company Limited, 1926) for the first use of the term.
4 P. Wylie, 'Panic, psychology, and the bomb', *Bulletin of the Atomic Scientists*, 10 (1954), 37–40, 63.
5 T. Brown, M. Cueto and E. Fee, 'The World Health Organization and the transition from "international" to "global" public health', *American Journal of Public Health*, 96:1 (January 2006), 62–72; N. Tomes, *The Gospel of Germs: Men, Women, and the Microbe in American Life* (Cambridge, MA: Harvard University Press, 1998), p. xi; J. Bourke, *Fear: A Cultural History* (Emeryville, CA: Shoemaker and Hoard, 2005), p. ix; B. Glassner, *The Culture of Fear: Why Americans Are Afraid of the Wrong Things* (New York: Basic Books, 1999); F. Furedi, 'The market in fear', *Spiked* (September 2005).
6 P. Stearns, *American Fear: The Causes and Consequences of High Anxiety* (New York: Routledge, 2006), p. 477; R. Corey, *Fear: The History of a Political Idea* (New York: Oxford University Press, 2004); C. R. Sunstein, *Laws of Fear: Beyond the Precautionary Principle* (Cambridge UK; New York: Cambridge University Press, 2005).
7 Humphreys, 'No safe place'; C. Rosenberg, *The Cholera Years: The United States in 1832, 1849, and 1866* (Chicago: University of Chicago Press, 1962, 1987).
8 H. Markel, *When Germs Travel: Six Major Epidemics That Have Invaded American and the Fears They Have Unleashed* (New York: Vintage Books, 2004), p. 12.

9 Ibid., pp. 114–16, p. 126.
10 V. Turner, *Dramas, Fields, and Metaphors: Symbolic Action in Human Society* (Ithaca, NY: Cornell University Press, 1974). See also D. A. Stone, 'Causal stories and the formation of political agendas', *Political Science Quarterly* (Summer 1989), 281–300. See also Bourke, *Fear*, pp. 124–6 and Markel, *When Germs Travel*, p. 7.
11 S. Gilman, 'Moral panics and pandemics', *The Lancet*, 375:9729 (2010), 1866–7.
12 M. Lamont and V. Molnar, 'The study of boundaries in the social sciences', *Annual Review of Sociology*, 28 (2002), 167–95.
13 Brown, Cueto and Fee, 'The World Health Organization and the transition'; A.-E. Birn, 'The stages of international (global) health: histories of success or successes of history?', *Global Public Health*, 4:1 (2009), 50–68. We have adapted their periodization for this analysis focused on the United States. Whereas Brown, Cueto and Fee see the first major era as that of tropical medicine, they are primarily concerned with world health paradigms. Because we are focusing on the United States, we break this into two periods: before and after germ theory.
14 'The mail service is demoralized', *The Atlanta Constitution* (25 September 1888), p. 1.
15 'Railroad track destroyed', *Chicago Daily Tribune* (19 September 1897), p. 3.
16 Ibid.
17 'Gov. M'Laurin barred out', *Chicago Daily Tribune* (19 September 1897), p. 3.
18 A. L. Fairchild and D. M. Johns, 'Don't panic! The "excited and terrified" public mind from yellow fever to bioterrorism', in R. Peckham (ed.), *Panic: Disease, Crisis, Empire* (Hong Kong: University of Hong Kong Press, 2015), pp. 155–80.
19 A. L. Fairchild, *Science at the Borders: Immigrant Medical Inspection and the Shaping of the Industrial Labor Force* (Baltimore, MD: The Johns Hopkins University Press, 2003). E. K. Abel, '"Only the best class of immigration": public health policy toward Mexican and Filipinos in Los Angeles, 1910–1940', *American Journal of Public Health*, 94:6 (June 2004), 932–9.
20 Rush in a 1793 letter to his wife, quoted in Tomes, *The Gospel of Germs*, p. 51.
21 M. Carey, *A Short Account of the Malignant Fever Lately Prevalent in Philadelphia* (Philadelphia, PA: Gale Ecco, 1794), pp. 54–5, 58, 95–6.
22 'The cholera scare', *The Jewish Messenger* (17 November 1865), p. 145.
23 Humphries, 'No safe place'; Rosenberg, *The Cholera Years*.

24 *Annual Report of the Department of Health of the City of New York 1870–71*, p. 383.
25 'Wanted – a national quarantine law', *The Atlanta Constitution* (17 October 1899), p. 6.
26 'Over quarantine two states clash', *San Francisco Chronicle* (2 August 1905), p. 5.
27 A. M. Kraut, *Silent Travelers: Germs, Genes, and the 'Immigrant Menace'* (Baltimore, MD: Johns Hopkins University Press, 1994); Markel, *Quarantine!*; Abel, 'Only the best class'.
28 Fairchild, *Science at the Borders*.
29 A. Trachtenberg, *The Incorporation of America: Culture and Society in the Gilded Age* (New York: Hill and Wang, 1982).
30 G. Le Bon, 'How civilization makes barbarians', *Chicago Daily Tribune* (8 June 1908), p. G5.
31 'The people as chaos', *New York Tribune* (6 September 1896), p. B2.
32 'A very solemn warning', *New York Times* (1 June 1910), p. 8.
33 'Among the new books', *Chicago Daily Tribune* (21 April 1897), p. 7.
34 'Threat to burn a fever hospital', *New York Times* (3 September 1905), p. 1; 'A senseless protest', *New York Tribune* (30 August 1916), p. 8. See also 'Paralysis hysteria', *New York Times* (16 July 1916), p. E2.
35 Home economist Mabel Kittredge, describing the immigrant poor in America, quoted in Tomes, *The Gospel of Germs*, p. 190.
36 Quoted in E. Fee, 'History and development of public health', in F. Douglas Scutchfield and C. W. Keck (eds), *Principles of Public Health Practice* Second edition (Clifton Park, NY: Delmar Learning, 2003), p. 17.
37 *Annual Report of the Department of Health of the City of New York for the Years 1910–1011* (New York, 1912), 12; Tomes, *The Gospel of Germs*; Stearns, *American Fear*, p. 478. G. T. W. Patrick, *The Psychology of Relaxation* (Boston, MA: Houghton Mifflin Co. 1916). G. T. W. Patrick, 'The new optimism', *Popular Science Monthly*, 82 (May 1913), L492–503, quoted in Stearns, *American Fear*, p. 478.
38 Tomes, *The Gospel of Germs*, pp. 158, 110–11, 165.
39 Ibid., p. 92.
40 'Bubonic plague invades England once more, but causes no panic', *New York Tribune* (20 November 1910).
41 Tomes, *The Gospel of Germs*, pp. 92, 186.
42 G. Agamben, *State of Exception: A Brief History of the State of Exception* (Chicago; London: The University of Chicago Press, 2005).
43 E. Asprem, 'A nice arrangement of heterodoxies: William McDougall and the professionalization of psychical research', *Journal of the History of the Behavioral Sciences*, 46:2 (2010), 123–43.

44 R. E. Park and E. W. Burgess, *Introduction to the Science of Sociology* (Chicago, IL: University of Chicago Press, 1922), p. 876.
45 A. Minna Stern and H. Markel, 'Influenza pandemic', in M. Crowley (ed.) *From Birth to Death and Bench to Clinic: The Hastings Center Bioethics Briefing Book for Journalists, Policymakers, and Campaigns* (Garrison, NY: The Hastings Center, 2002), p. 89.
46 A. M. Stern, M. S. Cetron and H. Markel, 'The 1918–1919 influenza pandemic in the United States: lessons learned and challenges exposed', *Public Health Reports*, 125:3 (2010), 6–8.
47 '100 miners flee from influenza', *Rocky Mountain News* (22 October 1918), www.influenzaarchive.org (accessed: 1 June 2013).
48 *Annual Report of the Department of Health of the City of New York 1919*, p. 56.
49 Ibid., p. 56.
50 Ibid.
51 Fairchild, *Science at the Borders*.
52 *Annual Report of the Department of Health of the City of New York 1919*, p. 156.
53 Ibid., p. 157.
54 'The cholera scare', *The American Hebrew* (21 November 1884), 18; Fairchild and Johns, 'Don't panic!'; Tomes, *The Gospel of Germs*, p. 91.
55 *Annual Report of the Department of Health of the City of New York 1919*, p. 157.
56 J. Orr, *Panic Diaries. A Genealogy of Panic Disorder* (Durham, NC: Duke University Press, 2006).
57 Dr W. T. Howard, Assistant Commissioner of Health, 'The truth about influenza', *The Municipal Journal* (18 October 1918); 'Deplores epidemic fear', *St Paul Pioneer Press* (9 October 1918), www.influenzaarchive.org (accessed: 1 June 2013).
58 R. T. LaPiere, *Collective Behavior* (New York: McGraw-Hill, 1938), p. 441. See also S. Freud, *Group Psychology and Analysis of the Ego* (London: Hogarth, 1922), p. 46; D. P. Schultz, 'Panic in organized collectivities', *Journal of Social Psychology*, 63 (1964), 353–9.
59 There were, of course, exceptions to this broad theoretical shift: H. Cantril, *The Invasion from Mars* (Princeton, NJ: Princeton University Press, 1982, first published in 1940 and republished in 1966). See also E. L. Quarantelli, 'The sociology of panic', in N. J. Smelser and P. B. Balte (eds.), *International Encyclopedia for the Social and Behavioral Sciences*, 4 (2001).
60 K. Ostherr, *Cinematic Prophylaxis: Globalization and Contagion in the Discourse of World Health* (Durham, NC: Duke University Press, 2005).

61 The United Nations Film Board, *The Eternal Fight* (1948).
62 The Mutual Security Agency, *A Monthly Review from Europe* 1:3 (1952).
63 The Westinghouse Corporation, The University of Pittsburgh, the American Medical Association, and the US Public Health Service, *The Silent Invader* (1957).
64 P. Boyer, *By the Bomb's Early Light: American Thought and Culture at the Dawn of the Atomic Age* (Chapel Hill; London: University of North Carolina Press, 1994 [1985]).
65 V. Peterson, 'Panic: the ultimate weapon?' *Colliers Weekly* (21 August 1953), pp. 99–109.
66 Ibid., p. 101.
67 D. P. Schultz, 'Theories of panic behaviour: a review', *Journal of Sociology Psychology* (June 1963), 31.
68 Minutes of the First Meeting of the Sub-Committee on the Public Relations Aspects of Biological Warfare of the Secretary of Defense's Ad Hoc Committee on Biological Warfare, Held at 4.30 p.m. 7 April 1949, Room 5159, New State Department Building, Washington, DC pp. 3–4. RB 59 General Records of the Department of State, Office of the Secretary, Special Assistant to Secretary of State for Atomic Energy & Outer Space, General Records Relating to Atomic Energy Matters, 1948–1963; Box 60, ARC ID 2517138, A1 Entry 3008-A; Folder: 9B Secretary of Defense's Ad Hoc Committee on Biological Warfare, 1949, Minutes of Subcommittee Meeting. Declassified NND 50551. See also C. Perrow, *Normal Accidents: Living with High Risk Technologies* (New York: Basic Books, 1984).
69 K. Riezler, 'The social psychology of fear', *American Journal of Sociology*, 49:6 (May 1944), 492.
70 Reizler, 'Social psychology of fear', at 498. See also A. Mintz, 'Nonadaptive group behavior', in E. Maccoby, T. M. Newcomb and E. L. Hartley (eds), *Readings in Social Psychology* (New York: Holt, 1958), p. 575.
71 E. Fee and T. M. Brown, 'Preemptive biopreparedness: can we learn anything from history?' *American Journal of Public Health*, 91:5 (2001), 721–6.
72 Handwritten talk c. 1978, Alexander D. Langmuir Papers, Alan Mason Chesney Medical Archives of The Johns Hopkins Medical Institutions, Box #1, Folder 'JHV Honorary Degree 1978'.
73 Handwritten lecture notes, 12 March 1971, Alexander D. Langmuir Papers, Alan Mason Chesney Medical Archives of The Johns Hopkins Medical Institutions, Box #5, Folder 'Lecture Notes, Miscellaneous History CDC'.

74 Handwritten talk c. 1978, Alexander D. Langmuir Papers, Alan Mason Chesney Medical Archives of The Johns Hopkins Medical Institutions, Box #1, Folder 'JHV Honorary Degree 1978'.
75 Ibid.
76 A. D. Langmuir, 'The potentialities of biological warfare against man – an epidemiological appraisal', *Public Health Reports*, 66:13 (1951), 387–99, at 388.
77 'What you should know about biological warfare', *The Johns Hopkins Science Review*, WAAM, Baltimore, MD, 3 April 1951.
78 Handwritten notes, Alexander D. Langmuir Papers, Alan Mason Chesney Medical Archives of The Johns Hopkins Medical Institutions, Box 5, Folder 'Lecture Notes. Miscellaneous EIS History CDC'.
79 H. Arendt, *Totalitarianism: Part Three of the Origins of Totalitarianism* (Boston, MA: Houghton Mifflin Harcourt, 1968), p. 153; Boyer, *Bomb's Early Light*, p. 72.; E. L. Quarantelli, 'The nature and conditions of panic', *The American Journal of Sociology*, 60:3 (November 1954), 270, 272; N. R. Johnson, 'Panic and the breakdown of social order: popular myth, social theory, empirical evidence', *Sociological Focus*, 20:3 (August 1987),172; H. Arendt, *Eichmann in Jerusalem: A Report on the Banality of Evil* (London: Penguin Classics, 1963); J. N. Shklar, *Legalism: An Essay on Law, Morals, and Politics* (Cambridge: Harvard University Press, 1964); S. Benhabib, 'Judith Nisse Shklar: biographical memoirs', *Proceedings of the American Philosophical Society*, 148:4 (December 2005), 531; J. Shklar, 'The liberalism of fear', in N. L. Rosenblum (ed.), *Liberalism and Moral Life* (Cambridge: Harvard University Press, 1989).
80 E. Hobsbawm and T. Ranger (eds), *The Invention of Tradition* (New York: Cambridge University Press, 1953); G. Rude, *The Crowd in the French Revolution* (London: Oxford University Press, 1959); E. P. Thompson, *The Making of the English Working Class* (London: Victor Gollancz Ltd, 1963).
81 E. C. Green and K. Witte, 'Can fear arousal in public health campaigns contribute to the decline of HIV prevalence?' *Journal of Health Communication*, 11:3 (2006), 245–9.
82 '"Scare" hits sales of cigarette firms', *The Christian Science Monitor* (12 March 1955), p. 7.
83 H. Marks, *The Progress of Experiment: Science and Therapeutic Reform in the United States, 1900–1990* (Cambridge: Cambridge University Press, 1997).
84 Green and Witte, 'Fear arousal'.
85 'The "scare" campaigns to raise medical funds', *The Baltimore Sun* (23 April 1950), p. 12.

86 J. E. Hague, 'Epidemic of fear spreads faster than polio', *The Washington Post* (13 August 1950), p. B3; 'Can fear outfight fact on fluoridation?' *The Hartford Courant* (26 July 1956), p. 14; N. Haseltine, 'Reason replaces fright in fight against cancer', *The Washington Post* (12 April 1953).

87 H. Marks, *The Progress of Experiment: Science and Therapeutic Reform in the United States, 1900–1990* (Cambridge: Cambridge University Press, 1997).

88 Green and Witte, 'Fear arousal'.

89 'The "scare" campaigns'; Hague, 'Epidemic of fear'; 'Can fear outfight fact'; Haseltine, 'Reason replaces fright'.

90 Memorandum from Langmuir to Robert Smith, 31 January 1961. Alexander D. Langmuir Papers, Alan Mason Chesney Medical Archives of The Johns Hopkins Medical Institutions, Box 2, Folder '1951 BW'. Langmuir would lament the public apathy over the possibility of biowarfare till the end of his days.

91 A. L. Fairchild, R. Bayer, S. H. Green, J. Colgrove, E. Kilgore, M. Sweeney and J. K. Varma, 'The two faces of fear: a history of hard-hitting public health campaigns against tobacco and AIDS', *American Journal of Public Health*, 108:9 (2018).

92 United States Surgeon General. *Smoking and Health: Report of the Advisory Committee of the Surgeon General of the Public Health Service* (Washington, DC: US Department of Health, Education and Welfare Public Health Service, 1964).

93 A. L. Fairchild, R. Bayer and J. Colgrove, 'Risky business: the history and politics of fear-based campaigns in New York City', *Health Affairs*, 34:5 (2015), 844–51; R. Bayer and A. L. Fairchild, 'Means, ends, and the ethics of fear-based public health campaigns', *Journal of Medical Ethics*, 42:6 (2016), 391–6; A. L. Fairchild and R. Bayer, 'Public health with a punch: fear, stigma, and hard-hitting media campaigns', in B. Major, J. F. Dovidio and B. G. Link (eds), *Oxford Handbook of Stigma, Discrimination, and Health* (New York: Oxford University Press, 2018), pp. 429–38.

94 W. Gaylin, 'Behavior control: from the brain to the mind', *The Hastings Center Report*, 39:3 (May–June 2009), 13.

95 Fairchild and Bayer, 'Public health with a punch'.

96 R. Goodin, *No Smoking: The Ethical Issues* (Chicago, IL: University of Chicago Press, 1989), pp. 30–1.

97 Fairchild et al., 'Two faces of fear'.

98 Ibid.

99 Cited in Fairchild and Bayer, 'Public health with a punch'.

100 Fairchild et al., 'Two faces of fear'.

101 A. Giddens, *The Consequences of Modernity* (Cambridge: Polity Press, 1990), pp. 16, 21, 64.
102 Ibid.
103 A. Merianos and M. Peiris, 'International Health Regulations (2005)', *The Lancet*, 366 (8 October 2005), 1249–51; D. P. Fiedler and L. O. Gostin, 'The new international health regulations: an historic development for international law and public health', *Journal of Law, Medicine & Ethics* (Spring 2006), 85–93; J. Youde, 'Mediating risk through the international health regulations and bio-political surveillance', *Political Studies*, 59 (2011), 813–30.
104 D. Rosner and G. Markowitz, *Are We Ready? Public Health Since 9/11* (Berkeley, CA: University of California Press, 2006).
105 L. Garrett, 'You are not nearly scared enough about Ebola', *Foreign Policy* (15 August 2014); M. T. Osterholm, 'What we're afraid to say about Ebola', *New York Times* (11 September 2015).
106 M. Burawoy, 'The extended case method', *Sociological Theory*, 16:1 (1998), 4–33.
107 Tomes, *The Gospel of Germs*, p. xv.

Part III

Selection

9

'Suspect' screening: the limits of Britain's medicalised borders, 1962–1981

Roberta Bivins

Like their peers across western Europe, Australia and the Americas, large segments of the British public and a significant proportion of Britain's medical establishment have enthusiastically promoted medical screening (and de facto medical selection) of would-be migrants since World War II. Politically, such medicalised controls have been relatively uncontroversial both domestically and internationally, and across Europe have arguably provided 'objective' scientific cover for efforts in fact directed towards controlling the entry of migrants from specific ethnic groups and countries of origin. Targeted groups were, above all, those who were 'racialised': that is, those to whom the receiving nation ascribed homogenising racial identities predicated (implicitly or explicitly) on phenotypical or biological as well as cultural and behavioural differences.[1] However, despite widespread enthusiasm for medical selection of migrants in Britain, the implementation of genuinely restrictive or exclusionary health controls on migration proved challenging.

Immigration policy in Britain was shaped by a number of distinctive geopolitical and cultural constraints after World War II. At least initially, these delivered migration policies favouring relative generosity towards postcolonial migrants, not least to avoid the appearance of racism. Large-scale migration to Britain in this period began in the context of post-war reconstruction. The consequent labour shortages militated strongly against restrictive border controls. Simultaneously, despite the lingering after-effects of a devastating war, Britain envisioned itself as a 'tolerant nation with liberal traditions', mother to a multiracial empire and Commonwealth.[2] For a considerable period, the interplay between these factors, operating in the wider context of the Cold War, played a powerful ideological role in the UK. Significant changes in medical knowledge, ethics and practices across this period also shaped the art of the (medically) possible at the border. Finally, and uniquely, from 5 July 1948, the UK operated a comprehensive national health service, funded almost entirely from general taxation, and (at least initially) free at the point of need. Crucially, legal migrants to the UK, like all other residents, were entitled to use the health services immediately upon arrival, irrespective of whether they had yet contributed to the system through income, business or property taxes.

To explore the implications of these interwoven factors for the British use of medical tools in the management of migration, this chapter will focus on the emergence, extension and effects of medicalised immigration control for migrants originating from the UK's 'New Commonwealth'. Common across migrant-receiving nations since the nineteenth century, medicalised controls hinge on the application of medical expert claims, knowledge and technologies to evaluate migrant bodies and groups for both inclusionary and exclusionary purposes. Britain's new regime developed between 1962, when the first Commonwealth Immigrants Act [CIA62] stripped British subjects from the colonies and Commonwealth of their automatic right of abode in the UK, and 1981, when a new British Nationality Act [BNA81] finally defined an exclusive British citizenship rooted in *jus sanguis* (and available to others only in accordance with an exacting suite of new conditions) and invested such citizens alone with an automatic right of abode.[3] Although rhetorically race-neutral, in practice this legislation and the medicalised controls instituted under its remit affirmed the racialisation of migrants coming to Britain from its former colonies, defining them by their physical differences in skin colour and 'exotic' practices of embodiment, rather than by their shared status and experiences as imperial British subjects.

Across this period, the imposition of new medical surveillance and controls generated three separate medicalised zones to be traversed by would-be migrants to the UK. They were spatially and culturally distinct from the largely coincident border spaces and processes that enforced the array of non-biomedical regulations and processes through which migrants were controlled and restricted. Here, I will refer to these medicalised sites of migration control – distinct physical spaces at which migrants were subject to a scopic medical regime – as Britain's 'medical borders'.

Migrants to the UK first encountered an external medical border: exported medicalised inspections in their countries of origin, initially for work-voucher holders and later for their dependants. The second followed Britain's geographical border, where migrants' right to entry was again rendered contingent upon 'health checks' and medical scrutiny. The third, and perhaps most idiosyncratic was internal, located at migrants' 'port of arrival' – their eventual destination in the UK. Here, migrants were obliged to meet any medical conditions set at the port of entry, but also urged and in some cases pressured to comply with the ever-changing requirements of 'hygienic citizenship' in their dwellings and practices of embodiment. In particular, they were exhorted to place themselves under medical surveillance through registration with a family doctor, while other forms of medical surveillance were imposed through environmental health regulations enforced by Medical Officers of Health.[4] Sold as a 'health measure' intended to protect host communities and migrants alike, this internal border relied heavily on Britain's National Health Service (NHS).

Who were these migrants? They included professional, skilled and unskilled workers and their dependants, principally from Britain's former African, Caribbean and South Asian colonies. Students and visitors (defined as individuals staying for less than six months) from the Commonwealth increasingly fell into the surveillance remit of UK immigration law, but rarely experienced restrictive medical controls in this period and will not be considered here. Migrants from Ireland were exempt from control, but until Britain joined the European Economic Community in 1973, all other nationals were categorised and legally regulated as 'aliens'.

Like most voluntary migrants, New Commonwealth migrants to the UK were generally young and healthy. Most primary migrants were unaccompanied men; the Caribbean also sent substantial numbers of unaccompanied women, with smaller numbers arriving from other destinations. Secondary migrants ranged in age from the very young to the very old: spouses, affianced partners, dependent children and elderly parents all had varying degrees of entitlement to join settled adults in the UK. Nonetheless, repeated epidemiological surveys and other forms of medical surveillance from the 1950s–1970s identified only two significant health 'burdens' presented by New Commonwealth migrants; they experienced higher rates of tuberculosis and venereal disease than local UK populations.[5] Popular myth and moral panics also implicated the migrants as vectors of leprosy and intestinal parasites, and as victims of mental disorder, but these claims were not supported by convincing evidence, and were regularly dismissed by ministry officials and medical specialists.[6]

Before turning to the specific details of the UK's medical borders, this chapter will examine the legislation that gradually enabled medical control. Having established the legal powers which underpinned medical controls on the movements of British subjects, I will turn to questions of practice: what do we know about what actually happened at Britain's medical borders at home and abroad? Finally, it will explore the reasons why Britain's two domestic medical borders remained highly porous in the face of wider trends towards the implementation of strict medical regimes of immigration control and exclusion.

The legal foundations of medical control in Britain

Associations between immigrants and infection are deeply rooted and persistent in British culture, becoming florid in the nineteenth century, when epidemics of cholera and typhus were linked to Irish newcomers.[7] However, unlike many of its settler colonies and the United States of America, the United Kingdom neither legally restricted the migration of specific racialised groups nor implemented ongoing migrant medical inspection between the 1870s and 1900. Even long-established regimes of port sanitary inspection and quarantine for ships arriving from known infected ports faced opposition for their incompatibility with both the economics of empire and 'British liberal principles'. Worse, they were condemned as ineffective.[8] Only with the 1905 Aliens Act was the free movement of groups of people travelling from non-infected ports restricted by law and made subject to medical clearance. In this instance, the targets of the legislation were east European Jews fleeing pogroms; they were perceived and presented by anti-immigrationists as threatening the nation on both economic and racial grounds, rhetorical claims that would reappear prominently in the post-war era. Medical justifications for exclusionary controls, however, seemed to offer 'more honourable' grounds for exclusion than either lucre or prejudice.[9]

The 1905 Aliens Act finally gave British officialdom the power to regulate and restrict the entry of 'alien' immigrants (but not migrating

British subjects) at Britain's ports. It enabled immigration officers to exclude or expel 'undesirable' aliens for crime, dependency, disease, or once landed, 'living under insanitary conditions'.[10] The Act notably also placed the burden of proving that they were not aliens on the immigrants themselves.[11] It did not define 'alien', though it did explicitly exempt those born in the UK of British subject fathers from exclusion on economic grounds.[12] The 1905 Act was followed by a succession of wartime and interwar acts and orders intended to control 'enemy aliens', including the notorious 1920 Order which included an array of medical controls on 'alien' entrants to the UK.[13] However, British subjects from across the multiracial empire remained exempt from any form of legal restriction on migration until after World War II.

As Hansen and others have argued, the persistence into the post-war period of Britain's 'Open Door' for Commonwealth migrants reflected British political, financial and affective investments that were unevenly distributed across her subject populations.[14] Australians, New Zealanders, Canadians and the white settler populations of East and South Africa were, like the Irish, regarded as 'kith and kin' with whom economic and cultural ties were to be maintained at all costs. In contrast, the 'coloured' populations of Britain's tropical colonies and New Commonwealth figured in popular discourse as 'aliens' despite their shared status as British subjects.

Throughout the post-war and Cold War periods, officials at the Home and Colonial Offices were at pains to correct this confusion publicly, whatever their private views. Moreover, the 1948 British Nationality Act [BNA48] appeared to reinforce and codify inclusive notions of a shared and stable imperial citizenship. Yet beneath the surface, Whitehall's civil servants and their political masters in Westminster responded to increasing rates of migration from the New Commonwealth to Britain with a mixture of anxiety and hostility. These inchoate tensions surfaced regularly in parliamentary debate. Some, like Henry Hopkinson, Minister of State for the Colonial Affairs, were determined to maintain Britain's standing as the racially tolerant and liberal 'mother' to a multiracial Commonwealth.[15] Others in Parliament believed that only racially targeted immigration restriction would prevent violent popular racism from taking hold in Britain itself.[16]

Successive post-war governments charged their civil servants with uncovering the impacts of racialised migration, either to justify

Britain's 'Open Door', or to generate a race-neutral rationale for closing it. They completed a series of investigations between the 1948 arrival of the *Empire Windrush* and her 802 Caribbean passengers, and the 1961 introduction of the Commonwealth Immigrants Bill.[17] But these studies uncovered little evidence of any significant problems which could be laid at the migrants' doors. Housing was certainly in short supply but as newcomers, few migrants met local criteria for receiving public housing, public outcry notwithstanding. In the full-employment labour market, migrants were rarely unemployed for long, and they committed fewer crimes proportionately than their British-born peers. Nor did they significantly burden the new National Health Service. Medical experts even suggested that their higher rates of tuberculosis and venereal disease were due to exposure in the UK.[18] At the same time, the newcomers provided, from the outset, a significant proportion of the NHS workforce, as they did for other key public services. Beyond the politically unpalatable suggestion that their mere visibility triggered racism, civil servants found no specific grounds to exclude the new racialised migrant groups.

In 1961, restrictive legislation was nevertheless introduced for Parliamentary debate. Controversial and highly contested, the Bill that would become CIA62 passed through Parliament in the shadow of an outbreak of smallpox inadvertently carried to the UK by migrants from Pakistan desperate to 'beat the ban' they expected to follow. In part, as a result of this coincidence, the Act for the first time introduced the specific power to medically inspect and if necessary exclude British subjects not of UK origin at the border. Moreover, medical inspectors were explicitly entitled to demand 'any test or examination required' in order to satisfy themselves of health of an intended migrant.[19] This power was intended specifically to enable radiographic screening for tuberculosis at Britain's borders.

The 1962 Act was repeatedly renewed in the 1960s, and then supplanted by more restrictive laws. In 1965, the milestone White Paper on Commonwealth Immigration advocated extending Britain's medicalised border outwards to migrants' countries of origin, where its costs could be imposed on the migrants themselves. As we will see, while it was long-established practice in the United States and in some European nations, implementing offshore medical inspections proved challenging for Britain.[20] In part, Britain was hampered by the complicated geopolitical position I have mentioned above; in part, by the continuing legal complexities generated by the migrants' status as British subjects. Medical underdevelopment in migrants' nations of origin – underdevelopment which many attributed to British imperial neglect – also played a role in undermining medical selection and screening. So too did the existence of the NHS; experts, politicians and members of the public alike understood that the service depended heavily on migrant labour and, through its voracious demand for professional staff, actively contributed to a damaging clinical brain drain from the global South to the global North. Nonetheless, by 1968, most primary migrants were medically screened abroad.

The 1968 Commonwealth Immigrants Act [CIA68] extended medical controls from Britain's ports and airports into the British interior, mandating that any Commonwealth migrant whose entry was subject to control could also be required as a condition of admission to report to local health authorities for further surveillance and screening after entering the UK, in the 'interests of public health'.[21] The wives and young children of settled Commonwealth migrants remained exempt from exclusion or inspection under this Act, but could be landed subject to such medical conditions. And in 1969, the Immigration Appeals Act smuggled in a new requirement that the dependants of primary migrants gain Entry Certificates before coming to the UK. For all but the closest family members, this entailed medical examination. As this chapter will discuss below, in practice, entry certification served as a vehicle for medicalising the certification of 'entitlement' even for these protected groups.

Only two years later, the 1971 Immigrants Act codified the existing administrative imposition of mandatory radiographic examination in country of origin for all primary migrants, their dependants over the age of 18, and dependent elderly parents; and mandated port medical inspection of primary migrants' dependants, though not their exclusion on health grounds. British law still could not reasonably require medical examinations before departure for immigrating spouses and underage children, since they were entitled to entry irrespective of their health status, but both groups were encouraged to invest in such examinations even though any certificates of health they received abroad bore no legal weight at

Britain's borders, and would not necessarily exempt them from further medical inspection.

Acts in 1981, 1988, 1996, 1999, 2002 and 2004 further restricted immigration and – importantly – responded to the new legal right to freedom of movement enjoyed from 1973–2020 by Europeans as part of the UK's membership in the European Community and, later, European Union. In addition, all primary legislation around entry to the UK was repeatedly reshaped and tightened administratively through changes to the 'Instructions for Immigration Officers' and official guidance to entry clearance officers in Britain's diplomatic outposts abroad. Pressure to re-task medical interventions at Britain's external and geographical borders – officially instituted as health protections for the British public – to serve the wider agenda of drastically reducing inward flows of migration remained intense across this period. Only in 2005, however, did additional pre-departure medical restrictions enter into UK law rather than regulatory guidance.

Controlling subjects, creating medical borders: health checks and commonwealth migrants 1962–1967

The medical powers to control inward migration of British subjects enacted by CIA62, though not uncontested, were among the least controversial in the measure. I have argued elsewhere that legislators may have found it difficult to protest against these powers at a moment when the UK was experiencing a deadly imported outbreak of smallpox.[22] Certainly bureaucrats and medical civil servants within the Ministry of Health, though themselves ambivalent about the need for and efficacy of border medical inspections for non-epidemic disease, were unable to resist their inclusion. CIA62 incontrovertibly granted border agents the power to screen British subjects not only for epidemic conditions already covered by the International Sanitary Regulations, but also for endemic illnesses such as tuberculosis and sexually transmissible diseases. Moreover, from 1962, British law explicitly empowered the exclusion on health grounds of work-voucher holders, both in their countries of origin and at Britain's ports and airports.

Before, during and after the debates that framed the passage of the 1962 Act, popular opinion and professional arguments in favour of such exclusionary screening repeatedly mobilised claims about Britain's welfare state, and especially the National Health Service. As the Ministry's civil servants observed, 'uninformed public prejudice' against the migrants often cited the supposed 'demands they placed on the Health Services'.[23] Nonetheless, in practice, Britain's geographical border remained comparatively free from medicalised controls during this period.

Instead, Britain idiosyncratically internalised its medical border and surveillance of migrants under what became known as the 'port of arrival' system.[24] Structurally and functionally, the 'port of arrival' system was a medical border envisioned strictly as a health control, rather than a barrier to transnational movement. Operated by local public health authorities and encompassing environmental health surveillance as well as clinical screening, it relied explicitly on the existence and accessibility of the NHS. Only this system of universal health care, delivered free at the point of need, and the dense network of general and specialist medical providers it entailed, made the deferral of border medical inspections both economically efficient and, at least potentially, epidemiologically effective. And because all landed migrants were instantly eligible for NHS services, radiographic examination costs were massively reduced by using existing systems and equipment, while the Ministry of Health and its successors could argue that receiving communities would be protected from imported illness as long as immigrants were swiftly 'integrated' into the NHS safety net.

But what actually happened at these borders immediately after controls were instituted? Border zones are notoriously sites of multiple and contested agency. Individual migrants and officials; governments in both sending and receiving nations; advocacy groups (whether for or against migration); transnational ethnic communities; state, media and corporate interests; competing expert constituencies; non-human physical entities such as diseases; and the technologies of movement, communication and control, all operate as agents in border spaces. The freedom with which actors in each of the categories can express their agency in and through 'border performances' is constrained by factors including shifting and historically contingent hierarchies of power, relative visibility, and technical intransigence.[25]

Suspicious practices: enacting control at the geographical medical border

In seeking to understand border health controls, legal mandates and policy advice are of limited value, particularly since most national systems vest individual immigration officers with substantial freedom in exercising their powers. Neither official guidance nor political exigency can successfully constrain the actions of the personnel on the spot, often deeply suspicious of particular migrant groups on both racial and epidemiological grounds.[26] Furthermore, even UK government ministries consistently struggled to ascertain reliable information about practices at the nation's ports and airports, to say nothing of the UK's internal medical border where both primary and secondary migrants were intended to experience close medical surveillance and supervision.[27]

Moreover, while historians and others have mapped the visibility and persistence of medical discourses asserting 'the foreignness of germs' and the need for their expert medical control, in the postwar British context, medical expertise did not translate directly or readily into power.[28] Port and Airport Medical Officers had only advisory powers, while the Ministry of Health and its successors were politically weak departments. Britain's Ministry of Health had neither sought nor much desired the power specifically to deploy radiographic screening at the border, yet once enabled by CIA62, came under increasing public pressure to do so. Their preparations reflect this ambivalence. Universal medical screening of all migrants at the border was impossible, given cramped port spaces, scanty facilities, inadequate funding, staff shortages across the health services, and rising numbers of migrants. Much time was therefore spent seeking sensible epidemiological grounds for screening selection while ensuring that the targeted groups would include at least some non-racialised groups.[29] While the Ministry feared accusations of 'disingenuousness' if it did not reinforce the medical border, the legislation was fundamentally impractical.[30] Ministry staff were hampered, too, by resistance from other, stronger departments across Whitehall, which had no desire to see medical controls infringe on their own powers; deplete their budgets; contribute to their workloads; or add to existing tensions surrounding the decision to restrict the free movement of British subjects.[31]

After CIA62, the Ministry of Health and its border agents were enduringly caught between the public and (non-expert) medical appetite for exclusionary medical inspections and the pragmatic and political forces weighted against such inspection. Public and professional opinion routinely accused the Health Minister of 'neglecting his duty' to prevent importations of disease by immigrants.[32] Yet instituting universal high-tech screening at all UK ports and airports, as George Godber, Britain's formidable Chief Medical Officer from 1960 to 1973, noted would be 'extravagant in the use of plant and staff' when Britain's medical fabric desperately required renewal and modernisation.[33] Expending valuable resources to stop the occasional importation of an already endemic and treatable disease was both economic and epidemiological madness.[34] But such arguments carried little weight with the public or the medical profession, determined to protect both the gains they had made against endemic tuberculosis and the always impecunious NHS.

In fact, Britain's normal regime of tuberculosis screening and control was so successfully reducing domestic rates of infection that TB wards and sanatoria were closing or being returned to hospitals for other uses. Consequently, the Ministry much preferred approaches that would use border controls only to supplement what were clearly effective standard public health measures.[35] Ironically, while popular opinion frothed against a hypothetical immigrant 'burden' on the NHS, it was the Health Service's success that most powerfully rationalised inaction at the geographical border. With the advent of chemotherapies, it was increasingly cheap to treat TB via the NHS but prohibitively expensive to exclude it.

Implementation costs were not the only deterrent to the institution of a thoroughly medicalised, radiographic port regime. The Home Office raised 'grave difficulties of both principle and practice'.[36] It rejected any proposals to improve the accuracy of screening if they would retard Immigration Officers' decision-making or involve passengers leaving the port. As they presciently admitted, any such delays invited 'legal challenge' by 'aggrieved' individuals.[37] As the volume of informally referred immigrants rose, local NHS hospitals also 'jibbed'. Such referrals incurred costs and interrupted the provision of regular services.[38] Blocked from accessing appropriate diagnostic aids, port medical officers were frustrated, and this also worried the Ministry of Health: 'denied access to X-ray facilities … they may start to refuse entry to suspects who may subsequently be shown in their own countries not to have T.B.' This would, the Ministry hinted, result in 'awkward' conversations for the Home and Commonwealth offices.[39]

However, even when it was available, more and better equipment did not necessarily offer a solution. By 1964, when an 'experimental' X-ray scheme at London (later Heathrow) Airport was fully operational, it was clear even to non-medical observers that the system was straining at the seams under ever-increasing volumes of passengers from epidemiologically 'suspect' regions.[40] Operating under extreme pressure, even with the latest technology, port medical inspections could never provide the impenetrable shield against imported disease envisioned either by the public or by the British Medical Association.[41]

Expecting, experiencing and contesting control: Britain's domestic medical borders, 1965–1968

Daily practices at Britain's medical borders in the 1960s and early 1970s are largely opaque; however, clues can be found in a series of contentious individual cases as they criss-crossed Whitehall, circulating between the Home Office and Ministry of Health. Clustered between the influential 1965 White Paper on 'Immigration from the Commonwealth' and CIA68, these cases reveal the complex nexus of competing forces which shaped day-to-day practices of medical inspection before and at the UK border. Here I will explore two in detail; together, they challenge both contemporary claims that these particular medical borders could protect British bodies, and abiding presumptions that medicalised borders in general were, are, or can be epidemiologically effective or politically neutral.

The first case, that of a Pakistani man, M.A., reveals the extent to which procedures at the geographical medical border deviated from (admittedly fluid) immigration policy and presumed professional norms.[42] It also demonstrates that medical evidence, prized as definitive by non-medical authorities, was often far from conclusive or neutral. M.A. sought to enter Britain as a work-voucher holder in May 1965. As a primary migrant, he was referred to the airport

Medical Inspector, inspected visually, tentatively certified as suffering from primary syphilis, and sent to a local NHS hospital for further examination. On his return to the airport, the Chief Immigration Officer refused M.A. entry on medical grounds and returned him to Pakistan. He had been detained nearly five hours longer than the primary legislation allowed.

Had M.A. been removed from the country in under twenty-four hours, or had he simply accepted the decision, this Report of Refusal would have remained as apparent evidence of the effective and correct application of CIA62's medical provisions.[43] But those extra hours meant that immigration officials were required to inform the Pakistan High Commission (its UK embassy) of M.A.'s detention, exposing the weak clinical case, and prompting M.A.'s UK-based brother, S.A., to contest it through a solicitor.

In particular, they questioned the 'alleged medical grounds' for M.A.'s deportation: M.A., they reported, had been medically examined on his return to Pakistan, and diagnosed with 'a mosquito bite'.[44] Their challenge promoted consternation in the Home Office and eventually, consultation with the Ministry of Health. Beneath an unruffled surface, the Ministry of Health moved from initial certainty of its Medical Inspector's diagnosis through to anxious confidence – 'I could not find details … but it *seems* that he had syphilis confirmed by investigations'[45] – to a flat internal rejection of the 'rather flimsy' grounds for refusal.[46] Yet medical officialdom remained committed to the refusal itself. Right or wrong, border medical assessments were upheld, to 'preserve the right to examine' at the geographical border.[47]

In part, the Ministry's internal debate about the validity of M.A.'s refusal reflected a perennial weakness of medicalised borders: the pace of medical change. In this case, definitive diagnosis was hindered by rapidly changing standards of medical proof, as an increasing number of competing diagnostic procedures and tests emerged. Crucially, whether for TB or VD, none could swiftly exclude infection. As one Ministry of Health official grumbled in the M.A. case, 'if medical clearance of this sort is required, immigrants must be kept available … for adequate tests to be performed'.[48] Yet the primary legislation itself derailed any such detailed examinations of incoming migrants, even if, as in M.A's case, scarce NHS resources were expended on screening.

If medical screening to exclude venereal disease was too slow for border procedures, conclusive screening to exclude tuberculosis there was nearly impossible. Here, concerns about the expertise and honesty of medical certifiers abroad were concatenated by heated UK debates about the rate and origins of TB among migrants, what constituted 'cured' tuberculosis, and the level of 'threat' posed even by clearly infected migrants to the wider community.[49] Cases centred around tuberculosis, including the one explored below, also demonstrate the efforts of migrants and their allies to limit or control their exposure to the vagaries of the medical border; and emerging tensions between the Ministry of Health and Home Office about the operation and especially the desired *outcomes* of the medical border.

By 1966, would-be immigrant M.L.C. from Hong Kong was clearly aware of the unpredictable system that would determine his fate at the British border. In his village, migration to the UK was common and first-hand information about the UK system of medical control was widely shared. Eager to take charge of his future, M.L.C. wrote to a British Member of Parliament, Hong Kong-born Jeremy Bray, seeking reassurance that his cured tuberculosis would not precipitate a medical refusal. He was 'desperate' to migrate, refusal would be 'disastrous', and he feared the uncertainty of the UK's medical border.[50] Such fears did not, as some in the Ministry of Health had hoped, have a 'deterrent effect' on this migrant.[51] Rather, they prompted determined efforts to navigate the system. Sadly for M.L.C., Bray could do nothing; the Home Office jealously preserved its Immigration Officers' rights to demand border medical inspections, even of migrants certified abroad as healthy.[52]

It is notable, of course, that the Immigration Officer was the decision-maker. Immigration officers were not medically qualified or trained to spot signs of ill health. Thus only suspicion, rather than clinical expertise, could inform their decisions to send migrants for medical exams. As would become ever more evident, border medical examinations did not operate as the 'health checks' initially envisioned – clinical measures intended to protect the nation from disease and the NHS from expense. Instead, they were already becoming a biomedical addition to the Home Office's surveillance machinery.[53]

While the Home Office clearly regarded racialised migrants and their foreign doctors as inherently suspect, the Ministry of Health had other, equally intractable, concerns. Tuberculosis was complicated, and the diagnostic tools available to border officers were inadequate. As one medical officer explained, certifying a patient as TB-free really required radiological surveillance over a period of months.[54] Clearly, this was not obtainable at the border, nor was it a reasonable standard of proof to expect of voucher holders and their dependants coming from nations without advanced medical infrastructure. Under such conditions, and given wider suspicions of medical expertise abroad, he argued that overseas certificates, capturing only a single clinical datum, offered 'very little assurance … at a port of entry.'[55]

It is also worth noting that the experimental X-ray scheme which threw up these complicated TB cases was explicitly instituted to identify and quantify, rather than to exclude tuberculosis cases.[56] Only the most clear-cut cases of active infection were to be refused. Otherwise, all were to be landed while the films were sent to a specialist for assessment. Any cases of TB later identified would be notified to the Medical Officer of Health in the migrant's 'port of arrival', where migrants could be assessed and treated as normal via the NHS.[57] In fact, from the point of view of the Ministry of Health, the principal public health benefit of port radiographic screening was its potential to improve medical surveillance at the internal border: 'what really matters is to get the immigrant and their families … involved with the health service as soon as possible after arrival.'[58] Yet clearly, only months after it was initiated, the scheme was already morphing from a fact-finding to an exclusionary apparatus.

Of course, these cases challenge rhetorical claims that the medical exclusion of otherwise eligible British subjects was intended solely to protect the public from 'the categories [of immigrants] we know to be dangerous to public health'.[59] None of the Ministry's medical experts argued that M.L.C. or M.A. were 'dangerous' to others. Instead they referred to signs of *possible* ill health that might require costly NHS treatment. Officials at the Ministry of Health were well-aware that no regime of medical inspection at the border could guarantee the exclusion of diseases such as tuberculosis or syphilis. Meanwhile for the Home Office, medical opinions and evidence were merely tools with which to defend contested immigration refusals.

Medicalised but not healthy: UK border controls 1969–1981

From the late 1960s through the 1970s, pressure mounted on those agencies charged with controlling entry at Britain's borders. Growing evidence of popular racism, combined with ever louder calls for effective immigration controls, prompted new measures intended to further restrict immigration from the New Commonwealth. On the heels of the 1965 White Paper on Immigration's equation between healthy 'race relations' in Britain and tightly restricted immigration came growing panic that the processes of 'Africanisation' and emerging anti-Asian sentiments in the newly independent nations of British East Africa would spark uncontrollable mass migration of affected populations to the United Kingdom.[60] The disgraceful result was CIA68, specifically designed to remove the right of Kenyan Asians to enter Britain, while protecting the rights of white colonial populations by privileging those with a 'qualifying connection' with the British Isles.[61] The Act was followed by new guidance for Immigration Officers, forcefully encouraging all dependants seeking to enter the UK to gain an entry certificate before leaving their countries of origin. It mandated that those seeking settlement do so. The 1969 Appeals Act made entry certificates mandatory for all Commonwealth migrants; moreover, only certificate holders acquired the right to appeal granted by the new legislation.[62] Entry certification required both identity and health checks; as we will see, these two processes were almost immediately conflated in practice.

The 1971 Immigration Act further tightened restrictions on migration from the New Commonwealth and put them on the same footing as aliens. The Act was structured to virtually end the primary migration for work of all non-Europeans without professional qualifications. It provided the basis of UK immigration policy and practice until BNA81 amended it. Even after 1971, the spouses of resident primary migrants and their children up to age 18 remained legally exempt from exclusion on health grounds. However, since they could be admitted subject to medical conditions enforceable at Britain's internal medical border, the new instructions for UK Immigration Officers recommended that all dependants be referred for medical inspection on entry.[63] In practice, medical inspection regimes at both domestic levels were far from comprehensive, vitiating the protective powers expected of the 'health checks' by legislators and the public. However, their inability to protect public health from the (scant) risks presented by inward migration did not affect their exclusionary function, particularly as medical examination expanded at the external border.

For a decade after 1971, immigration law remained relatively stable. During this period, practices at all three of Britain's medical borders – internal, geographical and external – came under increasing scrutiny from a variety of angles. Abroad, chronic understaffing and ever tightening 'guidance' for entry clearance officers in migrant-sending nations rapidly led to embarrassing 'queues' of would-be migrants and increasingly exclusionary practices, both medical and administrative. In Britain, anxieties about compliance with Race Relations laws, a continuing shortfall in funding for migrant integration programmes (including public health), and growing activism among and around established ethnic communities combined to produce great variability in the operations of the 'port of arrival' system. Yet at the UK's geographical border, medical procedures apparently remained static and largely invisible until, as will be discussed below, they were exposed in 1979 under the glare of media attention.

So did these shifts substantially intensify the medicalisation of Britain's borders? Yes and no. After 1968–69, many more would-be migrants were subjected to medical screening, particularly through the entry certification process.[64] As DHSS files repeatedly reported, from a health perspective, such medical examinations varied in quality and detail and offered numerous opportunities for error and subversion.[65] Instead, it was an unintended consequence of the expanded entry certificate regime that would prove the most impactful, by bringing 'entitled' dependants under biomedical surveillance not to assess their health, but to test claims about their identity and entitlements.

Examined for exclusion: undermining 'entitlement' at the medical borders

As Henry Yellowlees, CMO from 1973 to 1984, would later complain of Britain's medicalised borders, 'The kind of medical examination applying ... is determined ... not so much by health criteria but more by the individual's immigration category.'[66] For example, from the late 1960s, entry clearance officers in some New Commonwealth nations – particularly Pakistan and Bangladesh where state record keeping was notoriously scanty – routinely used radiography to check the ages of dependants where the documentary evidence was deemed insufficient or unreliable. Costs for such examinations and the associated expense of travelling to often distant medical facilities added another barrier to migration for many.[67]

Clearly, then, the effort by UK authorities to create a medical border abroad increased the cost and decreased the freedom even of entitled dependants to migrate. The medicalisation of Britain's external border, like the medicalisation of its domestic borders, was officially enacted to prevent the importation of disease and reduce domestic fears of infection that were seen as one factor in the growth of racism. However, it was *used* to enable the collection of biological data not about health status, but about identity. Rather than an aid to the inclusion and integration of legal migrants, it became a tool to enable their exclusion.

The fact that these medicalised controls received relatively little critical attention from state bodies investigating Britain's new immigration procedures reveals the continued persuasive power of medical claims to produce authoritative and objective knowledge about human bodies. In the late 1960s and 1970s, members of the Select Committee on Race Relations were tasked with assessing whether Britain's border practices complied with UK Race Relations legislation. They toured British High Commissions around the world, as well as UK ports and airports, seeking evidence and questioning the civil servants charged with managing migration. While Committee members routinely scrutinised the operation of the external medical border, the thrust of their questions was in general to test its rigour and efficacy in preventing disease importation, rather than its fairness. As the tenor of interviews with DHSS International Health Division staff makes clear, the Committee itself leaned strongly towards tightening medical controls on dependants, and applying them abroad, 'as other countries do'.[68] Even the testimony of the Joint Council for the Welfare of Immigrants [JCWI], highly critical of the new entry certification process and the actual and apparent racism that informed the 1968 and 1969 Acts, offered little criticism of the health checks themselves. In the eyes of the JCWI, they were an insignificant barrier in comparison with the many other hurdles placed between Commonwealth dependent migrants and their legal entry to and residence in Britain (including the operations of the internal medical border, described by JCWI as the 'harassment of immigrant households by the public health authorities').[69]

At the UK geographical border itself, the 1968, 1969 and 1971 extensions of the medical remit produced far less change, and little satisfaction for those intent on eliminating the importation of tuberculosis or other ill health. In fact, the new measures and instructions increased the challenges faced by medical border agents. With Commonwealth spouses, fiancé/es and minor children newly eligible for medical inspection, and widespread mistrust of health certificates issued in Pakistan, India, Nigeria and Cyprus, Port Medical Inspectors were empowered and eager to screen a growing number of entrants. But beyond Heathrow, they were unable to do so routinely, given the constraints that operated against off-site screening. Moreover, while secondary family-reunification migrants could now be medically screened, they still could not be refused entry and settlement on health grounds. Frustrated Medical Inspectors could only pass details of illness uncovered at the port of entry to the often overburdened health authorities at migrants' destinations. These addresses were notoriously insufficient, transient and erroneous, rendering contact tracing and medical follow-up all but impossible. In 1968, of the 42,124 advice notes alerting local medical officers to the arrival of new migrants, only 24,501 were successfully visited.[70] In the same year, of the 537,405 Commonwealth persons arriving at British ports and airports, 53,327 were medically examined, but only 59 were refused on medical grounds.[71]

By 1970, as the new rules bedded in, the DHSS could report that virtually all entitled dependants entering the UK through Heathrow – at this time approximately 90 per cent of such migrants – were 'medically examined'. However, only some 9 per cent were X-rayed. Detailing the procedures he observed at Heathrow, unchanged even a decade later, Britain's Deputy Chief Medical Officer, Dr N. John Evans expressed the long-held DHSS view: 'These arrangements fall very short of an effective *health* screen. They are more of a token than a real safeguard.'[72] Yet despite the limitations – of time, personnel and technology – that hampered effective health examinations, border agents commissioned some tests which offered no protection to the public; at least some passengers were transferred to a local NHS hospital to receive 'bone X-rays for age assessment'.[73] In other words, far from offering protection by border health screening, NHS resources being were appropriated for medicalised identity surveillance.

Disputes at the frontier: medical controls and the Yellowlees Report

In 1979, Heathrow's medical border was suddenly exposed to public view by an international scandal. It was triggered by reporter Melanie Philips of the left-leaning *Guardian* newspaper. Philips reported that some female migrants – almost all of South Asian heritage, arriving as entitled fiancées, wives or even daughters – were subjected to 'virginity testing' at Heathrow Airport.[74] This involved genital examinations described by affected women themselves as an exercise in humiliation. Girls and women had their pubic hair shaved and were internally examined, often by male medical staff 'chaperoned' by male interpreters, for evidence of prior sexual intercourse or childbirth, or to assess their age.[75]

Rendered visible by an unusual combination of journalistic scrutiny, direct testimony, and Parliamentary inquiry, Heathrow's medical controls demonstrated the paradox of Britain's invasive and yet porous 'health' border; medical procedures which were manifestly unfit for their supposed public health purposes were instead harnessed by the Home Office to serve an exclusionary agenda. The legal powers, time and equipment granted to the port medical inspectorate were clearly inadequate to halt a (hypothetical) 'wave' of contagion from entering the country in the bodies of 'entitled' secondary migrants. Yet, as Evan Smith and Marinella Marmo have documented, their scope was (just) sufficient to enable unsavoury and unsound medical practices including both 'virginity testing' and radiographic 'age assessments' of would-be child migrants.[76]

By comparing Home Office and DHSS responses to the scandal, a key shift becomes clear. The UK's tripartite medicalised border was neither the universal exclusionary 'health check' long sought in vain by medical professionals, nor the looser form of border surveillance and risk-based contact tracing deemed practical and achievable by the Ministry of Health and its successors. Instead, physical and radiographic examinations at the geographical border were used selectively to support efforts to exclude otherwise 'entitled' racialised migrants for failing to meet biologised criteria such as age limits, or (for women) presumed cultural expectations about sexual behaviour.[77] These facts were known at Whitehall; the ensuing scandal simply exposed them to a much wider public.

Controversially, the DHSS report responding to the 'virginity testing' crisis – known popularly as the *Yellowlees Report* – forcefully recommended the comprehensive exclusionary screening of all migrants in countries of origin. Only such controls, applied to existing 'entitled' as well as new primary migrants, could truly protect Britain's medical border and 'the health and financial interests of those already in the UK.'[78] Yellowlees acknowledged that a retroactive 'health bar' on the dependants of settled migrants might be criticised as 'morally undesirable or politically injudicious', but he was only prepared to offer deferred entry – post-treatment – to such entitled migrants.

It is in Home Office responses to the *Yellowlees Report* that the final set of tensions which explain the abiding porousness of the UK's medical borders become clear. As Smith and Marmo have shown, the Home Office was deeply committed to, and deeply unapologetic for operating a *racially* discriminatory immigration system. As one official asserted in an internal memo, 'Migration is essentially a racial matter and the only basis on which the periodic migrations to which all peoples are subject can be regulated, is by numbers according to race.'[79] However, neither Home Office civil servants nor its Minister, Willie Whitelaw, had any intention of accepting Yellowlees' calls for a *medically* discriminatory border. Yellowlees expressed his view that all medical procedures should be applied only to serve the domestic disease prevention agenda and to preserve NHS resources. This was certainly the established popular understanding of the checks, and the rationale for their inclusion in successive Immigration Acts. However, this was far from the Home Office view. In fact, they were furious that he had used the pretext offered by the scandal to air the Department's long-silenced frustrations with existing health controls.[80] Internally the Home Office admitted that, from their perspective, the examinations in question 'are not concerned with the health of the person examined … they are directed to producing answers to what are non-medical questions.'[81] As in the past, the Home Office sought putatively objective and irrefutable medical evidence to constrict migrants' rights and withstand their legal appeals.

The DHSS had long resented providing such leverage.[82] As they had since the 1960s, the medical professionals in the DHSS resisted politicisation of their remit, irrespective of their views on 'race' or migrants' rights. Political colonisation of medical expertise undermined the Department's ability to act in accordance with their own professional commitments to what they saw as 'objective' medical evidence. As Dr N. John Evans – whose drafting of the 1980 *Yellowlees Report* offered few signs of liberality – insisted: 'the racial or ethnic characteristics of a migrant ... are not a medical matter, still less a medical problem'. 'Health controls', he emphasised, 'are not a surreptitious way of discriminating for or against particular classes of immigrants and must not be allowed to become so'.[83] Yet, of course, questions of immigrant health were deeply political, particularly as the racist and anti-immigrant British National Front had recently attacked migrants by deploying explicitly medical claims and anecdotes.[84]

Fear that publication of the *Yellowlees Report* would have 'disastrous' effects on race relations in the UK triggered a dazzling display of institutional cognitive dissonance at the Home Office. Bureaucrats who urgently sought medical evidence to exclude racialised family reunification migrants nonetheless dismissed Yellowlees' focus on disease (and cost) prevention as 'much too narrow' and – in light of international considerations – as 'selfishness of a high order'.[85] Condemning the Report, the Home Office ironically reverted to the enduring discourse of the UK's humanitarian and ethical responsibilities to its Commonwealth.[86] In particular, the Home Office leveraged both the success of the NHS and its dependence on migrant professionals to excuse border practices which impeded the free movement of entitled but unwanted migrants, but could not prevent the importation of disease. Contrasting the UK's advanced health services with service provision in migrants' countries of origin, the Home Office correctly (if disingenuously) contended that admitting Commonwealth medical migrants while enforcing health barriers against their co-nationals constituted: 'consigning to greater disadvantage those who are disadvantaged already' while 'weakening further the[ir] health services'.[87]

Despite the active efforts of Home Office immigration officers at the geographical border, and Foreign and Commonwealth entry clearance officers at its external equivalent to medicalise disputes about access to the UK, they feared the effects of 'the medical factor' introduced by the DHSS.[88] As a result, the *Yellowlees Report* was never formally published. Its recommendations for the mandatory medical examination of all dependants at origin, and for the deferred entry or outright exclusion of those judged to be unwell found no place in BNA81. Not until 2005 would such an approach be instituted in law.

Conclusions

Only after World War II did the UK gradually begin to erect medical borders analogous to those long established in its former colonies and dominions, and by the USA. Despite popular and professional enthusiasm for strong health controls, a range of factors worked against their implementation. As a former imperial power, Britain's legal powers to close the 'open door' offered to its far-flung subjects were initially limited. Moreover, labour shortages, economic and cultural ties, national commitments to economic and social liberalism, and a desire to maintain Britain's international influence all initially militated for relatively open borders. Medically, too, instituting effective health controls seemed both impractical and uneconomic. The migrants posed little threat of disease, border screening was costly, and the availability of the NHS allayed experts' concerns about transmission of 'imported' disease to local communities, if not about cost to the health services. Moreover, continued support for family reunification on humanitarian grounds also meant that, by the late 1960s, the bulk of migrants were the wives and young children of men already established in the UK, who could not be excluded on health grounds, making investment in border health controls largely pointless.

These factors did not prevent a gradual medicalisation of Britain's borders. The effects of this process were most visible at the UK's externalised borders in Commonwealth migrants' countries of origin. Here, biomedical processes initially intended to assess the health and productive capacity of labour voucher applicants were relatively quickly extended in the search for robust evidence justifying the exclusion of otherwise entitled secondary migrants. Internally, the ability to apply medical conditions to the admission of entitled migrants had more variable effects, depending on their locations and the levels of commitment, funding and cultural sensitivity offered to the 'port of arrival' system by local health authorities. At the UK's geographical border – its ports and airports – however, medicalisation proved partial, perfunctory, controversial when exposed to public scrutiny, and ultimately ineffective. Practical and political constraints consistently outweighed health concerns and, between 1962 and 1981, medical refusals at the border were rare, even when public anxieties about immigrant health were highest.

So how was the shift to mandatory health screening in 'high risk' nations – so long the goal of the UK's health authorities – eventually enabled? After the Cold War, political sensitivity to global (but not national) 'race relations' declined, and the Commonwealth was devalued as vehicle for political influence. A series of 'asylum crises' in the late twentieth century refashioned migration as 'uncontrolled' and 'uncontrollable', in the process, revisiting and revivifying narratives of migrants as burdens on a threatened NHS. Resulting legislation placed more migrants into 'controlled' categories, rendering them available for medical sanction and at least temporary exclusion. The expansion of the European Union similarly expanded what were perceived as 'uncontrollable' economic migrants. At the same time, British authorities gained increased confidence in the reliability and sensitivity of medical testing abroad, as medical expertise in migrant-sending nations developed and could be co-opted. Finally, with the virtual disappearance of TB from Britain's ethnic majority population, a medical consensus emerged that the condition was 'imported', and thus could be excluded. The ability to outsource screening to international agencies, and to impose the costs of that service on migrants themselves made such exclusion economically appealing. In the end, tensions between 'traditions of tolerance' and 'deep-seated prejudices' both at the borders and in the NHS created opportunities for migrant health screening, but also limited its exclusionary effects and rendered it 'suspect'.

Notes

1 H. Gans, 'Racialization and racialization research', *Ethnic and Racial Studies* (2016) DOI: 10.1080/01419870.2017.1238497; K. Murji and J. Solomos (eds), 'Introduction: racialization in theory and practice', in *Racialization: Studies in Theory and Practice* (Oxford: Oxford University Press, 2004), pp. 1–28.
2 W. Webster, 'The empire comes home: commonwealth migration to Britain', in A. Thompson (ed.), *Britain's Experience of Empire in the Twentieth Century* (Oxford: Oxford University Press, 2012), pp. 122–60.
3 The term 'subject' is an important one in the UK context, where an exclusive national citizenship emerged slowly. Until 1948, all persons born within the British Empire were classified not as 'citizens' but as 'subjects' of the British crown. Unlike 'citizenship' in which citizens both acquire and can claim *reciprocal* rights through their membership in a given community, the privileges of 'subjecthood' are unilaterally granted by the monarch, against whom claims cannot be made. Only through the 1948 British Nationality Act did Parliament grant individuals born within the empire a 'citizenship' linked to their British subjecthood, and it too was tied to the Commonwealth. 'British citizenship' was defined only in 1981. See R. Hansen, *Citizenship and Immigration in Post-War Britain: The Institutional Origins of a Multicultural Nation* (Oxford: Oxford University Press, 2000), especially pp. 35–45.
4 On the 'port of arrival' system see J. Welshman, 'Compulsion, localism, and pragmatism: the micro-politics of tuberculosis screening in the United Kingdom, 1950–1965', *Social History of Medicine*, 19:2 (2006), 295–312; R. Bivins, *Contagious Communities: Medicine, Migration, and the NHS in Post-War Britain* (Oxford: Oxford University Press, 2015), pp. 168–266. On hygienic citizenship, see W. Anderson, *Colonial Pathologies: American Tropical Medicine, Race, and Hygiene in the Philippines* (Durham, NC: Duke University Press, 2006), pp. 180–207; A. Bashford, *Imperial Hygiene: A Critical History of Colonialism, Nationalism, and Public Health* (Basingstoke: Palgrave Macmillan, 2003), pp. 79–80.
5 Later, female migrants would also be criticised for their fertility.
6 See, for example, The National Archives, London [TNA], MH58/671, MH148/30.
7 C. Cox, H. Marland and S. York, 'Itineraries and experiences of insanity: Irish migration and the management of mental illness in nineteenth-century Lancashire', in C. Cox and H. Marland (eds), *Migration, Health and Ethnicity in the Modern World* (Basingstoke: Palgrave Macmillan, 2013), pp. 36–60 at pp. 38–40.

8 K. Maglen, '"The first line of defence": British quarantine and the port sanitary authorities in the nineteenth century', *Social History of Medicine*, 15:3 (2002), 413–28 at 413.

9 K. E. Collins, *Be Well! Jewish Health and Welfare in Glasgow, 1860–1914* (East Lothian: Tuckwell Press, 2001), pp. 97–112, quoted in K. Maglen, 'Importing trachoma: The introduction into Britain of American ideas of an "immigrant disease," 1892–1906', *Immigrants & Minorities*, 23:1 (2005), 80–99; J. Pellew, 'The Home Office and the Aliens Act 1905', *Historical Journal*, 32:2 (1989), 369–85.

10 Aliens Act 1905, p. 5 at www.legislation.gov.uk/ukpga/1905/13/pdfs/ukpga_19050013_en.pdf (accessed: 1 December 2017).

11 Aliens Act 1905, p. 7.

12 Aliens Act 1905, p. 4.

13 B. Taylor, 'Immigration, statecraft and public health: the 1920 Aliens Order, medical examinations and the limitations of the state in England', *Social History of Medicine*, 29:3 (2016), 512–33.

14 Hansen, *Citizenship and Immigration*; R. Karatani, *Defining British Citizenship: Empire, Commonwealth, and Modern Britain* (London: Routledge, 2003), pp. 153–4; J. Tomlinson, 'The Empire in economic thinking', in Thompson, *Britain's Experience of Empire*, pp. 211–50.

15 H. Hopkinson, 'Colonial immigrants' *Hansard*, Commons Deb 05 November 1954 vol. 532. cols 821–32 at 827–8.

16 See, for example, J. Hynd, 'Colonial immigrants', *Hansard*, Commons Deb 05 November 1954 vol. 532. cols 821–32 at 822–3.

17 See Hansen, *Citizenship and Immigration*; Bivins, *Contagious Communities*.

18 See E. Hess and N. MacDonald, 'Pulmonary tuberculosis in Irish immigrants and in Londoners: comparison of hospital patients', *Lancet* (17 July 1954), 132–6; N. Macdonald, 'West Indian settlers responsibility of Great Britain', *The Times* (12 November 1954), p. 9.

19 *Commonwealth Immigrants Act 1962* (London: HMSO, 1962), pp. 3, 15.

20 S. Topp, 'Medical selection in the recruitment of migrant workers ("Gastarbeiter")' in I. Ilkılıç, H. Ertin, R. Brömer and H. Zeeb (eds), *Health, Culture and the Human Body. Epidemiology, Ethics and History of Medicine. Perspectives from Turkey and Central Europe* (Istanbul: Betim Center Press, 2014), pp. 19–38.

21 *Commonwealth Immigrants Act* 1968, p. 2.

22 Bivins, *Contagious Communities*, pp. 115–67.

23 TNA, MH55/2276, Minutes, 'The medical examination of immigrants' Meeting between Ministry of Health and Association of Municipal Corporations, 11 December 1957.

24 J. Welshman, 'Tuberculosis and ethnicity in England and Wales, 1950–70', *Sociology of Health & Illness*, 22:6 (2000), 858–82.

25 T. M. Wilson and H. Donnan (eds), *A Companion to Border Studies* (Hoboken: John Wiley & Sons, Incorporated, 2012), and especially D. B. Coplan, 'Border show business and performing states', in Wilson and Donnan, *Companion to Border Studies*, pp. 507–21.
26 J. A. Gilboy, 'Deciding who gets in: decisionmaking by immigration inspectors', *Law Society Review*, 25:3 (1991), 571–600; TNA, MH148/27, G. Godber to R. Smith, 8 April 1963; 'Port Medical Inspection', 6 February 1963.
27 TNA, MH148/32, H. N. Roffey to Benjamin, 17 December 1965.
28 See H. Markel and A. M. Stern, 'The foreignness of germs: the persistent association of immigrants and disease in American society', *The Milbank Quarterly*, 80:4 (2002), 757–88.
29 See Bivins, *Contagious Communities*, pp. 177–8.
30 TNA, MH55/2632, B. D. Fraser to E. Powell, 14 March 1962.
31 See TNA, MH148/27–MH148/31; MH55/2632–MH55/2634; MH55/2277.
32 TNA, MH148/29, H. N. Roffey to Hill (Ministry of Aviation), 15 November 1963.
33 TNA, MH55/2632, G. Godber to B. D. Fraser, 7 February 1962.
34 TNA, MH55/2632, B. D. Fraser to E. Powell, 14 March 1962.
35 TNA, MH55/2632, B. D. Fraser to E. Powell, 14 March 1962.
36 TNA, MH148/28, K. B. Paice to H. N. Roffey, 26 August 1963.
37 TNA, MH148/28, R. Wood to H. N. Roffey, 16 August 1963.
38 TNA, MH148/28, H. N. Roffey to Pater, 12 September 1963.
39 TNA, MH148/28, Lord Newton to E. Powell, 19 September 1963.
40 TNA, MH148/29, Memo, E. M. Atter to H. N. Roffey, 19 May 1964.
41 See 'BMA seek health check on immigrants before entry', *The Times* (3 December 1965), p. 7.
42 The case files include the full names of their subjects; here, I use initials to protect the identities of the individual migrants.
43 House of Commons. *Eleventh Report from the Estimates Committee, Together with Part of the Minutes of the Evidence Taken Before Sub-Committee C and Appendices, Session 1962–62. The Home Office* (London: HMSO, 1963). 'Minutes of Evidence Taken Before Sub-Committee C of the Estimates Committee', pp. 61–3.
44 TNA, MH148/37, Howe & W. to Immigration Officers, 9 July 1965.
45 TNA, MH148/37, T. J. B Geffen to Roden and E. Atter, 4 January 1966.
46 TNA, MH148/37, Burbidge to Roden, 12 January 1966.
47 Geffen to Roden and Atter.
48 TNA, MH148/37, A. T. Roden to Geffen, 12 January 1966.
49 See Bivins, *Contagious Communities*, pp. 21–61, 168–226.
50 TNA, MH148/37, [M. L. C.] to J. Bray, 17 February 1966.

51 TNA, MH55/2634, H. N. Roffey to Wood, 27 June 1963.
52 See extended correspondence on file TNA, MH148/37.
53 TNA, MH148/37, Home Office to J. Bray, 26 May 1966.
54 TNA, MH148/37, A. J. Eley to H. N. Roffey, 23 May 1966.
55 TNA, MH148/37, A. J. Eley to H. N. Roffey
56 TNA, MH148/28, Pater to Godber, 20 September 1963.
57 TNA, MH148/28, 'Medical Examination of Immigrants'.
58 TNA, MH148/28, Memo to Pater, 30 September 1963.
59 TNA, MH148/27, C. R. O. Jones, 'Medical Examination of Immigrants', 1 January 1963.
60 For detailed analysis of these shifts, see Hansen, *Citizenship and Immigration*, pp. 153–243; Karatani, *Defining British Citizenship*, pp. 145–80; E. Smith and M. Marmo, *Race, Gender and the Body in British Immigration Control: Subject to Examination* (Basingstoke: Palgrave Macmillan, 2014), pp. 22–74.
61 A 'qualifying connection' (later 'patriality') was defined as having either personally or through parental or grandparental descent been born, adopted, registered or naturalised in the United Kingdom. Karatani, *Defining British Citizenship*, pp. 158, 162.
62 Home Department, 'Commonwealth Immigrants Acts 1962 and 1968 Instructions to Immigration Officers May 1969' (London: HMSO, 1969).
63 Home Department, 'Commonwealth Immigrants Bill 1968 Instructions to Immigration Officers March 1968' (London: HMSO, 1968), p. 3.
64 TNA, HO418/33, Henry Yellowlees, *The Medical Examination of Immigrants* [hereafter *Yellowlees Report*], 22 April 1980, p. 2.
65 See for example, TNA, MH154/1510, J. R. Reid, 'Tuberculosis and Immigrants: Draft Paper for the Home Office', 29 April 1976.
66 *Yellowlees Report*, p. 3.
67 This issue was repeatedly if inconclusively canvassed by parliamentary inquiries.
68 *Select Committee on Race Relations and Immigration* [henceforth *SCRRI*], *Session 1969–70. Control of Commonwealth Immigration. Volume I. Evidence and Appendices* (London: HMSO, 1970), p. 391.
69 *SCRRI*, *Session 1969–70* Vol. 1, pp. 329–79, at 333–4. See also the testimonies offered in A. Wilson, *Finding a Voice: Asian Women in Britain* (London: Virago Press, 1978).
70 *SCRRI*, *Session 1969–70* Vol. 1, p. 382.
71 *SCRRI*, *Session 1969–70* Vol. 1, p. 384.
72 *Yellowlees Report*, pp. 23–4. Emphasis added.
73 *Yellowlees Report*, p. 20.
74 M. Philips, 'Virginity tests on immigrants at Heathrow', *Guardian* (1 February 1979), p. 1.

75 Wilson, *Finding a Voice*, pp. 74–6; see also Smith and Marmo, *Race, Gender and the Body*, pp. 75–101.
76 Smith and Marmo, *Race, Gender and the Body*, pp. 75–101.
77 Smith and Marmo, *Race, Gender and the Body*, pp. 75–134, 149–74. For a flavour of public and professional concern, see J. Galloway, 'Immigration and the M.O.H. – A retrospect', *Public Health*, 86 (1972), 83–8; 'Tuberculosis retreats – slowly', *Lancet*, 303:7866 (1 June 1974), 1087–8; 'Migrants admitted with TB', *Daily Telegraph*, 8 September 1976.
78 *Yellowlees Report*, p. 30.
79 TNA, HO418/30, J. D. Semken to Nursaw, 18 June 1979, quoted in Smith and Marmo, *Race, Gender and the Body*, p. 112.
80 As documented in Bivins, *Contagious Communities*, pp. 62–109, 111–226.
81 TNA, HO418/33, G. I. de Deny to P. J. Woodfield, 17 July 1980.
82 See TNA, MH154/1510, 'Health Control Arrangements', 1976.
83 *Yellowlees Report*, p. 31.
84 See copies of BNF materials on TNA, HO418/33.
85 TNA, HO418/33, P. J. Woodfield to J. F. Halliday, 26 June 1980; and G. I. de Denny, 'Medical Examinations' 16 May 1980.
86 J. F. Halliday, 'Note of a Meeting Held on 22 July 1980', 23 July 1980.
87 TNA, HO418/33, G. I. de Denny, 'Medical Examinations', 16 May 1980.
88 TNA, HO418/33, 'Medical Examinations'.

10

A question of hygiene or nationality? Exclusion and non-Jewish labour migrants, refugees and asylum seekers in Israel, 2006–2017

Robin A. Harper and Hani Zubida[1]

Introduction

A core sovereign action of states is determining who is a member and who is not. Establishing physical, political, social, economic and cultural borders demarcates insiders who belong and outsiders who do not. Particularly in the modern state, presence is an insufficient marker of membership. Zionist ethos establishing Israel imagined a site for the ingathering of the exiles, a place for Jews to reside and preside over their own state in self-determination. This conjures notions of Israeli Jews as a monolithic group; they are not, Israeli Jews are fragmented by class, race, religiosity and ethnicity. All of these cleavages are important. An argument could be made that any of these divisions is 'the' dominant source of division between Jews. However, ethnic cleavage is a core fissure generating a power imbalance between the founders of the state and later arrivals, compelled to accept the extant power structures. For 150 years, since European Jews (Ashkenazi[2]) first called for settlement of a Jewish state in Palestine, they have maintained leadership of the pre-state and now seventy-plus years of Israel.

Zionism remains the primary philosophy holding Israeli society together. Since Israel's Declaration of Independence and establishment as a state in 1947, the state's political borders have remained undetermined in international law, but internal social borders between insiders and outsiders have been erected. Many people throughout Israel's history remain hidden or suppressed from the dominant national story, like Jews from across the Middle East,

Africa, Asia and, of course, Arabs.[3] Their search for a place in the state territory has been coloured by state and societal efforts towards exclusion, political and social suppression and displacement, all achieved under the guise of protecting the host society from disease, uncleanliness and unhygienic practices.

Over the last two decades (since 2000), 70,000 refugees/asylum seekers have fled from Sudan, South Sudan, Eritrea and Ethiopia to Israel. These arrivals, along with a spectrum of 'temporary' labour migrants (TLM), are affixed to the periphery of the Israeli state and society. The Israeli reception and political discourse concerning these new arrivals is reminiscent of the 'cold welcome' offered to Mizrachi[4] Jewish refugees in the 1950s and the treatment of Arabs who remained after the founding of the state. The current discourse shares with that period the exclusionary practices and policies, negative framing and disparaging views. The similarity is not complete, as the possibility of eventual inclusion of refugees and asylum seekers today is more complicated. No question, Mizrachi and Arabs still experience stigma and disparate treatment in Israel. However, due to both the Mizrachi's political citizenship and nationality rights through Jewishness, and the Arabs' claims to land, Mizrachi and Arabs can negotiate the political, social and economic arenas in ways not available to these recent arrivals. In this chapter, we examine how the exclusion of these outlying groups follows a long-standing rejection of 'others' from mainstream Israeli society and state institutions through a discourse of cleanliness and hygiene juxtaposed with perceptions about hierarchies of culture, national identity and belonging.

On the surface, hygiene and cleanliness appear as objective, irrefutable concepts. Science can prove uncleanliness. Epidemiologists apply scientific criteria to distinguish between dirty and clean, mapping illness and curbing contagion through separating the infected from the healthy. Yet social norms of behaviour and practice, even in hygiene and cleanliness, are less simple. Norms are self-referential, meaning that what one group does or permits is categorized as 'normal' while what others do or permit is deemed 'aberrant'. As Edelman[5] observes, this category formation is dependent on history and culture and so is not a value-neutral event. Sometimes politics shapes categories, reflecting and shaping specific meanings at points in time or space and affecting policy.[6] The continuous loop of that assigns placement within categories and uses those categories to inform policy decisions which then shape categories. Edelman reminds us that 'categories are especially powerful as shapers of political beliefs ... when they appear to be natural, self-evident, or simple description rather than devised'.[7] By grouping people into mutually exclusive siloed categories, we separate them and attribute features and qualities of being. We then rank the categories and imbue values. Sometimes, category composition morphs as we attribute one group's characteristics to others, including new people and/or excluding some previous members. As a result of this seemingly benign categorization, we then are able to allow ourselves to treat similar groups or individuals differently.

The discourse of hygiene and cleanliness is a classic mode for classifying, categorizing and justifying exclusion of people. Dirty or diseased people must be separated to protect and preserve the whole. This means that through categorization people may be treated differently. Hygiene and cleanliness have long been used in different contexts to shape discourse and resulting policies of exclusion. In colonial Australia, Bashford posits that lines of hygiene practices generated borders of rule, marking, separating and reinforcing social hierarchy.[8] Similarly, in early twentieth-century Los Angeles, Molina argues that perceptions of cleanliness shaped the immigrant incorporation trajectory, framing some people as too unclean and disease-ridden to be considered as potential citizens.[9] Thus, they were relegated to misery and exclusion. Hygiene practices delineated clean and healthy acceptable compatriots and those too unclean to be polity members. Those marginalized from civic life due to supposed unhygienic practices could rationally be prevented from full citizenship.[10] Protecting the whole from infection by some has been extended from physical illness, uncleanliness and hygiene to controlling socially unacceptable behaviour from spreading.[11] The study of *orientalism*, where 'the West' conjures a subaltern, exotic, backward, dangerous 'East' in order to subjugate and control it, reveals how discourses of difference can be mobilized in the name of power between East and West.[12] Such social application invokes a normative and hierarchic differentiation between the civilized and the uncivilized.

We will show that the contemporary discourse about diseased and unclean refugees/asylum seekers follows an endemic Israeli societal politics of pollution. Ashkenazi Jews used this discourse to marginalize Mizrachi Jews and Arabs in the pre-state and early days of Israel and is now similarly applied to refugees and asylum seekers. Multiple groups in Israeli society employ a discourse of pollution and purity for different reasons, all with the aim of solidifying an extant social hierarchy that transitions desirable others into the polity and excluding undesirable others. We will engage mainstream and social media discourses as part of our analysis.

The Israeli case

Unlike many other states, until the early 2000s, Israel never experienced large-scale, unwanted or irregular immigration (such as visa overstayers, unauthorized border-crossers, or those without proper residency papers or work authorization). Israeli migration policy – with virtually no exceptions – permits only those who fall under the Law of Return (all Jews and their immediate relatives) to Israeli territory and citizenry (per modified Law of Return, 1970). In the late 1980s Israel recruited non-Jewish, non-Arab migrant contract workers, due to an internal pressing need for agricultural, construction, industrial and domestic workers. However, the state considered them then (and now) as 'temporary' residents without any possibility for permanent tenure.[13] This remained as an uneasy but relatively stable status quo for about three decades.

At the turn of the twenty-first century, immigration control policy shifted when migrants from north-eastern Africa traversed Israel's southern border with Egypt. They claimed to be asylum seekers or refugees. In official and public Israeli discourse, they are referred to as 'Mistanenim' (Hebrew for 'infiltrators'), reflecting their categorization as undesirable outsiders who have illegally broached national territory.[14] According to official state data, between 2006 and 2011 approximately 55,000 refugees/asylum seekers entered Israel from various crossing points. Some were deported and some remained in Israel. Two-thirds came from Eritrea, another 25 per cent came from Sudan and the remainder hailed mostly from across Africa. (See Tables 10.1 and 10.2 for refugee and asylum-seeking status and countries of origin).

Their residency patterns morphed quickly. In 2010 most of the asylum seekers and refugees resided in two places: Israel's largest

Table 10.1 Number of refugees/asylum seekers entering Israel in recent years

Year	Up to the end of 2006	2007	2008	2009	2010	2011	2012	2013	2014	2015	2016	Total entered	Total in Israel currently
Numbers of refugees/asylum seekers	2,706	4,995	8,707	5,186	14,616	17,268	10,431	117	42	230	33	64,318	40,274

Source: Foreigners data in Israel, The authority of population and immigration (PIBA), February 2017, p. 4. Table A.1 (Hebrew) www.gov.il/BlobFolder/reports/foreigners_in_israel_data_2016/he/foreigners_in_Israel_data_2016.pdf (accessed: June 2019)

Table 10.2 Refugees and asylum seekers in Israel by country of origin

	Country of origin				
	Sudan	Eritrea	Rest of African countries	Rest of the world	Total
Number of refugees and asylum seekers	8,002	29,014	2,754	504	40,274[1]
Per cent	20%	72%	7%	1%	100%

[1] Between 2014 and 2016 according to PIBA 3,246 refugees and asylum seekers left Israel willingly. (Original text in Hebrew)

Source: Foreigners data in Israel, PIBA, February 2017, p. 5. Table A.3 (original text in Hebrew) www.gov.il/BlobFolder/reports/foreigners_in_israel_data_2016/he/foreigners_in_Israel_data_2016.pdf (accessed: June 2019)

city, Tel Aviv, and Israel's southernmost city, Eilat, with tiny concentrations elsewhere. By 2012, the population had spread across the country. Currently (2020), about 25,000 reside in Tel Aviv and 5,000–10,000 reside in Eilat. The remainder are dispersed among twenty municipalities including Jerusalem, Netanya, Rishon Le-Zion, Ashdod and others.[15]

Israel's official stance towards non-Jewish immigrants is clear: permanent immigration accommodation for non-Jewish immigrants and their children is undesirable.[16] This policy stems from the rationale for the Israeli state as defined in its Declaration of Independence as the site for the 'ingathering of the (Jewish) exiles' and as a Jewish and democratic state.[17] The state permitted TLM starting in the 1980s ostensibly only because of crushing labour shortages. Like labour migrants around the world, their labour was welcomed but they were not wanted as permanent members of society. Migrants' arrivals and tenures in Israel have been roller-coaster rides of toleration – even welcome – offset by intermittent, arbitrary mass deportations. In contrast, the asylum seekers and refugees have always been rejected. Their arrival was unforeseen and their presence deemed undesirable by state authorities and the general public. The arrival of the refugees and asylum seekers opened a new discourse. First, they were neither considered part of the labour force nor recognized as 'refugees'; they were considered illegal border-crossers by both the state and the general public.[18] The term 'Mistanenim' or 'infiltrators' is not new with respect to unwanted populations. Following the 1948 war establishing Israel when Palestinians were banished from Israel, many tried to return to their homes. The state of Israel marshalled its forces to prevent their return. These people were called 'Mistanenim'. In 1954, the Knesset (the Israeli parliament) legislated the Anti-Infiltration Law to stop recurrent attempts of Palestinians to return to their homes and villages. Twice in the last decade the Knesset attempted to amend this law and it apply to the refugees.[19] The first amendment, 30A, referred to the state's ability to detain African 'Mistanenim' for three years without trial to encourage voluntary repatriation; in September 2013 the Israeli Supreme Court rejected its lawfulness. The government was not deterred. In December 2013, the Knesset legislated a 'softer' amendment stipulating a six-month detention without trial. The Supreme Court reviewed the proposal and in August 2017 granted the 'voluntary departures' policy which disallowed unlimited detention of asylum seekers and refugees and set the bar at sixty days of detention, even if a refugee refused voluntary repatriation.[20] The landmark decision permitted voluntary departure to third countries with questionable human rights records – even states not previously traversed by migrants, if the migrant agreed to voluntary deportation. Israel rejects pleas for adjudication of claims for asylum seeker/refugee status, arguing international law and state sovereignty. The state points to the 2005 Asylum Protection Directive asserting that asylum seekers should seek refuge in the first safe country they enter. Thus, they should not be treated as asylum seekers in Israel, but have their cases adjudicated in a 'safe third country', such as Egypt or any other country they traversed on their travel journey. Since Israel denies their claims for refugee status and asserts that the migrants have breached the Israeli borders without official entry, they are deemed to be illegally present and should be deported. However, state institutions have not performed mass deportations mainly due to local and international public opinion. The state invokes 'voluntary departures' as standing policy and, as can be seen from Table 10.2, the policy has been (at least partially) implemented. Lacking a more comprehensive policy, Israel engages in ad hoc solutions such as long-term confinement in now infamous detention sites, Saharonim ('incarceration') and Holot ('holding'),

A *question of hygiene or nationality?* 263

located in the Negev desert far removed from any residential neighbourhoods and 'voluntary' departures. To date, Israel refuses to implement any policies that could create claims for permanency such as issuing work permits or visas.

The Israeli discourse of cleanliness and hygiene

Zionists envisioned establishing a European-style Jewish state located in what was first Ottoman and then British-controlled Mandatory Palestine.[21] Early settlers came from Europe at the end of the nineteenth and beginning of the twentieth centuries. Their numbers jumped precipitously as Jews escaped the Holocaust or resettled thereafter. Zionists imagined their new state populated with Ashkenazi immigrants and their descendants. Their first challenge was the mass arrival of Mizrachi Jews in the late 1940s and 1950s. Once Israel declared independence in 1948, Arab countries erupted in anti-Jewish actions, expelling almost one million Jews from across the Middle East, most of whom resettled in Israel.[22] Zionist leaders perceived these newcomers as an unforeseen (if distasteful) necessity, bolstering the state's population. However, the refugees brought foreign ideas and cultures and potential threats to the vision of the Israeli 'Sabra' and its European hegemony. This will require some explanation. 'Sabra' or 'Tsabar' is the Hebrew name of the thick-skinned thorny Opunita cactus that grows in the unforgiving desert and bears a soft and sweet fruit and became the nickname for the 'new Jew' who was born in Israel. Like the cactus, the Israeli 'new Jew' is said to be tough on the outside but sweet on the inside. The term was associated predominantly with Israeli-born Ashkenazi Jews but not Mizrachi Jews.[23] Why? The new Jew, the Israeli, was a product of the land of Israel imbued with the best of European culture (and none of its bad traits) and was not of Middle Eastern or Asian or African culture which were deemed inferior to European culture (even by those who were forced out of Europe or survived the Holocaust). Thus, the presence of Mizrachim questioned 'the unmarked norm of "Ashkenaziness"',[24] offering alternatives to the dominant narrative of who was or could be Israeli. Lacking exposure to European thought, music, art, style of cooking, manners, dress, etc., Mizrachim were considered backward and uncivilized.

Ironically, most of the east European Jews, who composed Israeli Zionist elites, lacked these urbane sensibilities as well. That said, the Mizrachim appeared markedly different in their mannerisms, modes of prayer and dress. Their distinctiveness was unwanted and the Ashkenazi proffered no warm reception. Public discourse largely ignored commenting on their social practices but described them as disease-ridden, unclean and socially undesirable. A contemporary report in 1949 from journalist Arye Gelblum: 'Most of them have serious eye, skin and sexual diseases, without mentioning robberies and thefts. Chronic laziness and hatred for work, there is nothing safe about this asocial element'.[25] Descriptions of newcomers as dirty, diseased, sexually or socially deviant became the norm. This projection of social and physical disease onto outgroups is not unique.[26] As Davidovitch and Shvarts observe, 'The "marking" of the immigrant as an Other by veteran populations – as a source of disease, crime, and social ills that contaminates local societies – is a recurrent theme in various host countries and at various time periods'.[27]

Discursive marking of otherness transpires at initial contact. When 'new' Jewish (pre-state) immigrants came from Eastern Europe to Palestine[28] and first encountered Jews from Arab countries they referred to them as 'Sefardim' (Spanish in Hebrew), recalling the name of Jews from the Iberian peninsula, the 'Spanish' part of the Ottoman Empire. Later, they were renamed 'Mizrachim' ('easterners' in Hebrew).[29] Aziza Khazzoom[30] argued that this renaming resulted in order to rectify a historic social inferiority of eastern European Jews. In Europe, they were called 'Ostjuden' (eastern Jews in German) – a derogatory term used by western Europeans to denigrate eastern European Jews. Khazzoom argues that by calling the Mizrachim 'eastern Jews', the formerly eastern European Jews could 'elevate' themselves vis-à-vis the Mizrachim and in the process become lauded 'westerners'. Further, the renaming solidified the Arabness of the Mizrachim, bringing undesirable, Middle Eastern Arab culture, behaviours and practices to the western-style state of Israel. Following Said,[31] this closure represents a fundamental hierarchic struggle of the west to hegemonize the east. The west was clean, civilized and modern, and thus could mobilize attempts to civilize the dirty, diseased, uncivilized east. Since the Mizrachi emanated from the (deemed inferior) Arab world, they, too, were dirty and backward.

A question of hygiene or nationality? 265

The public discourse centred on hygiene and then shifted to a discourse of modernity.[32] Hygiene and cleanliness became proxies for culture and were used to disenfranchise and marginalize the Mizrachim to the social and cultural periphery of the new state.[33] The Mizrachim were perceived as inseparable from their Arab origins. The Mizrachi presence was a reminder that Israel was not Europe's southernmost border but geographically in the Middle East thus challenging the Eurocentric Zionist imagination.

The Mizrachi–Ashkenazi rift represents yet another facet of the Arab–Jewish cleavage. In quotidian Israeli culture, negative behaviours are associated with Arabness. For example, the popular term for performing a bad job is 'avoda aravit' (Arab labour) and for a bad smelling thing is 'aravi masriach' (stinking/smelly Arab.) Still today, such negative connotations appear in hygiene and cleanliness discourses about Palestinians to marginalize them. Smooha suggests that these concepts were intended to create cleavage from the Middle East and cement Israel to the west and present Jews as civilized and European.[34] The macro-argument positions the west versus the east. Arabs are perceived as an undifferentiated homogeneous collective, suffering from permissiveness, dirtiness, sexism and ignorance. By delineating Arabs and Jews from Arab lands as dirty, smelly and stupid, and their work as inferior and poor quality, disparate treatment could be justified.[35] Thus, Ashkenazi Jews positioned themselves as hygienic, progressive and bearers of elite cultural capital.[36] The connection between hygiene and civilization, modernity and westernness became the core argument in justifying the colonial regime and its acculturation practices.[37] This social division remains today. It serves as the basis for ethnic cleavage within the Jewish-Israeli society: Mizrachim–Ashkenazim. The disparate treatment presents itself through reduced access to public resources such as education, and governmental and private sector employment.[38]

Current discourse-framing about refugees

The pattern of the discourse about the dirtiness, disease-ridden, unintelligence of asylum seekers shares many similarities with the discourses aimed at local Arabs, Mizrachi Jews (and later migrating Ethiopian Jews and TLM, who are beyond the scope of this inquiry).

Of course, like most discursive moments, this discourse does not match perfectly. The refugees/asylum seekers have no historic claims to residency as they are neither Jewish nor were present at the founding of the Israeli state. Thus, they have limited claims to belonging. However, there is a similar pattern; the descendants of the Mizrachi Jews were poorly absorbed and excluded from the dominant Israeli society which rationalized their exclusion by complaints of hygiene, deviant practices and cultural incompatibility. Ironically, the Mizrachi have become the main proponents of the same hierarchic unhygienic and social deviant discourse now used against the refugees and asylum seekers. Politicians and others invoke this hygiene discourse to justify marginalization and demonization of refugees and asylum seekers to shore political support, as they once did to the Mizrachim, appealing to Ashkenazi sensibilities and, à la Khazzoom, the Mizrachi's newly found hierarchic reversal. The discourse concerning asylum seekers has morphed quickly from expressions of disgust over unhealthiness and diseasedness to a biologically racist and confrontational discourse. The refugees and asylum seekers are considered by the general public and the state as not merely backward (and thus still capable of reform) but ill-suited to life in the modern state because of their alleged inherent biologically diseased nature and thus, incapable of change or worthy of sharing residency space.

Cleanliness and hygiene

Many people now get their information or interact with policy through social media; media stories matter. Both professional journalists and social media outlets publish hosts of pictures of the unhygienic practices of refugees or asylum seekers, for example defecating in socially unacceptable places, disposing of garbage anywhere, maintaining poor sanitary living conditions, and lying in the parks at all hours (especially in south Tel Aviv). These images set the tone for xenophobic comments and practices. For example, in a Facebook group for future mothers, 'Mama-Zone', discussions developed about not wanting to be in the same post-partum room with Sudanese refugees – one under the heading: 'Is there a separation or can one ask to be admitted in a room without Sudanese or Eritrean women?' This is similar to other posts requesting room assignments away from Arab or Bedouin women because of different hygiene and

A question of hygiene or nationality? 267

cultural practices. A different post queried: 'Can I ask for a room without any Arab or Bedouin women that have different hygiene habits and different culture?' (see Table 10.3 in the Appendix). Many publicly lambasted these mothers, while others voiced support.

There are increasing complaints about fear of contracting communicable diseases through contact with 'unhygienic' or 'diseased' refugees. Israeli hospitals reported that although a few Jews make requests for separate rooms from Arab or Bedouin women, hospitals receive many requests demanding rooms separate from refugees and asylum seekers. The number of requests for different rooms has ballooned since ten staff members in Ichilov hospital were infected with tuberculosis, reportedly after Eritrean women gave birth in the hospital (see Table 10.3 – 1). Collocation complaints occur in resorts as well. In the tourist city of Eilat, an arriving hotel guest noticed dark-skinned people in the lobby and shouted that she refused to lodge there 'I do not want the dirty black Sudanese here' (Table 10.3 – 2). Despite the fact that the 'black people' were not Sudanese (but Ethiopian Jewish Israelis), the framing of blackness as dirty and unwanted remains.

Diseases

Outgroups are frequently described as diseased.[39] When the Mizrachim first arrived in Israel they were described as dirty and unhygienic. In the 1950s and 1960s, they were accused of ringworm infestation.[40] The state ordered their children to receive X-ray treatment to cure the skin lesions. Israel initially denied subjecting the children to this treatment, but eventually admitted it and legislated compensation for those subjected.[41] More recently, refugees and asylum seekers have been accused of reintroducing tuberculosis, a disease that was thought to be virtually eradicated in Israel. The media widely reported the spread of tuberculosis among hospital workers in Tel Aviv's Ichilov hospital and among prison guards in the Holot detention centre where the refugees and asylum seekers were housed (Table 10.3 – 3 and 4). Ichilov hospital conducted an internal investigation (which was eventually publicly leaked) about the increase in contagious diseases thought to be from the 'infiltrators from Africa' (Table 10.3 – 5). Interestingly, the report differentiated between the 'infiltrators' and the TLM from Africa, that is, between diseased *bad* migrants and healthy *good* migrants. Soon after, reports of refugees contracting measles and rubella multiplied. The government health bureau ordered measles vaccinations for refugees under the age of six months (Table 10.3 – 6). Thereafter, there was an outburst of the poliomyelitis virus (polio). Epidemiologists traced the polio back to Egypt and the refugees/asylum seekers although there were other sources. Public health officers issued normal directives for best practices for public health (hand washing) to decrease the probability of transmitting or being infected with the virus. Ironically, no one mentioned that these were not the first outbreaks in recent history. In 1988 there was an outbreak. However, then there were no refugees in Israel and thus it did not fit the framing of the story as 'refugees bring disease' (Table 10.3 – 7).

These outbreaks could have been handled discreetly by the Israeli national health bureau as normal control of an epidemic. Rather, it became a public debate that focused not on how to control disease but how to control the 'dirty' and 'disease-ridden' migrants, fuelling the anti-infiltrators' discourse. The discourse framed the issue on two related directions. First, since many refugees work behind the scenes in the service industry, especially the food industry, for instance as dishwashers and cleaners, they were blamed for bringing disease and harming the Israeli economy. After an outbreak of a communicable disease, Dr Rafi Karasso MD, a well-known television personality, said on an Israeli morning show that people should be careful about contact with refugees because they carried diseases that had previously been virtually eradicated. He tried to distinguish people from their social conditions, noting that refugees and asylum seekers are 'gentle and kind people' and that 'they maintain sanitation, but the problem is that they stay 20–30 people in small apartments and as a result these apartments become a breeding bed for diseases'. He warned that the diseases could be fatal and that people needed to be very careful about contact with refugee workers in restaurants, hospitals and hotels. Although he prefaced his remarks with kind words, the presentation resulted in panic, further deepening the framing of the refugees as unhygienic, disease-ridden and dangerous to Israel (Table 10.3 – 8).

Fear of disease led to xenophobic actions in schools too. As refugee and asylum seekers sought to enrol their children in school, local Israeli parents objected, arguing that refugee children would contaminate Israeli children with diseases (Table 10.3 – 9). Others feared that accepting any refugee children would alter the school's

A question of hygiene or nationality?

demographic make-up and thus destroy the quality and reputation of the school. One parent stated:

> ... at first we have one or two infiltrator's children in the school; now they want to add more and finally they will take over the entire school, not in our school! ... [T]hey say we are racists and primitive. Let them say whatever they want. Does anyone know what her health condition is? Is she vaccinated? We worry that they will take over our school; they already took over Rogozin and ha'Yarden (two schools in Tel Aviv with high numbers of non-Jewish/non-Arab pupils, mostly children of temporary labour migrants). No Israeli children are left there. We have nothing to lose. (See Table 10.3 – 10)

School registration became a contentious political issue. Prime Minister Benjamin Netanyahu spoke against opening a school for the 'infiltrators' children (Table 10.3 – 11). Tel Aviv Mayor, Ron Huldai, countered that Netanyahu's policy was part of the problem and that the Prime Minister should stay out of municipal decisions (Table 10.3 – 12). The mayor's attempt to resolve the issue was met with a local community backlash. In Tel Aviv, residents circulated a pamphlet rejecting the refugees:

> Warning!!! Our neighbourhood is the next target of occupation ... do not rent apartments to infiltrators ... Dear residents, wake up!! The children of infiltrators are in our schools. The value of apartments has fallen drastically. Our backyards and staircases have become public urinals. Residents are fleeing the neighbourhood. They are not under medical supervision and as a result we are in danger of contamination by third world diseases – tuberculosis, whooping cough ...[42]

Crime, violence and diseases

Allegations of contagious diseases and unhygienic practices became conflated with other social ills, namely, crime and violence, developing into the most salient part of the discourse. Media reports at first described refugees and asylum seekers as dirty and disease-ridden, but later, as sexually violent and criminal, drug addicted, and carriers of sexually transmitted diseases, especially HIV/AIDS.

The public discourse that linked refugees and asylum seekers with disease, sexual offences, drug abuse, criminality and violence, proved particularly hard to disentangle.[43] The migrants were

Figure 10.1 Local pamphlet

subjected to a well-known trajectory of dehumanization, stigmatization and, eventually, isolation.[44] The media presented refugees and asylum seekers as socially aberrant, with culturally undesirable practices. Over time, migrants appeared almost stripped of human characteristics. They were portrayed as fonts of social destruction. Thereafter, migrants were stripped of institutional support and then isolated. Examining the titles of articles about life among the refugees in Tel Aviv, the discourse about migrants is framed by terms such as violent, dangerous and hopeless: 'Jungle teeming with violence, drugs and theft: a dire journey in south Tel Aviv' (Table 10.3 – 19). 'South Tel Aviv at the brink of explosion: "it is scary to walk through here at night"' (Table 10.3 – 20). 'Between violent street fights at night and a housing project that spurs hope' (Table 10.3 – 21); 'Hundreds and thousands of infiltrators will bring AIDS and drugs' (Table 10.3 – 22). As Davidovitch and Shvarts note, this pattern is not unique to Israel or contemporary history.[45] What is especially intriguing is the revisiting of modes of discourse about Mizrachim has now been revived to describe refugees and asylum seekers.

To be fair, this reporting is not knee-jerk xenophobic hyperbole. The neighbourhoods where refugees reside are low-income and suffer from relatively poor living conditions, drug addiction and violence. Lacking work and contact with non-affected people in similar circumstances, and facing increasing exclusion, many refugees and asylum seekers experience downward mobility, engage in substance

A question of hygiene or nationality? 271

abuse and perpetrate violence. Reports of sexual violence appear frequently: the rape of an 83-year-old woman by an Eritrean in south Tel Aviv (Table 10.3 – 14); a street camera documenting the sexual assault of women in the middle of the street in broad daylight (Table 10.3 – 15); a group of three Eritreans raping a 15-year-old girl and assaulting her boyfriend (Table 10.3 – 16, 17 and 18). These events, coupled with xenophobic hysteria, generate an irresistible framing of refugees as socially undesirable, violent, crime-ridden, sexually deviant infiltrators who plague Israeli society.

This discourse became more prevalent, capturing the attention of the public and politicians, among them the political leader of the Mizrachi ultra-orthodox religious party, Shas, and the former Minister of Interior, Eli Yishai, who maintained administrative jurisdiction over the issue of refugees and asylum seekers. The hotspot was geographically concentrated in south Tel Aviv – an area predominantly inhabited by low socio-economic stratum Mizrachi Jews, many of whom were homeowners, small-business people or working class and, serendipitously for Yishai, supporters of Shas. Yishai adopted the hygiene–criminality discourse, making it the official state rhetoric. He stated 'the infiltrators arrive in Israel without work, they commit sex and property offences – the way to treat this problem is to build a fence, incarcerate those who are here, and in time return them to their home countries' (Table 10.3 – 23). He stressed the security threats against Israeli citizens by the 'infiltrators': 'all migrant labourers and infiltrators should be in prison or detention centres – and from there back to their home country. Those who are defined as refugees will be able to stay; however, only a limited number. We cannot forsake the security of the citizens of Israel' (Table 10.3 – 24). After two violent acts in early 2013 – the murder of an elderly woman and the rape of another elderly woman by Eritrean asylum seekers – Yishai disseminated an official letter to the national media, ordering municipalities to tighten the enforcement of infiltrators' businesses, assuring that businesses would not operate without licenses and/or valid work visas. He argued that because of the refugees and asylum seekers, local Israelis had lost security in their communities. He demanded that public officials take the problem seriously, taunting the interior security minister, Yitzhak Aharonovitch, to spend the night in south Tel Aviv to observe personally the insecurity of the local residents (Table 10.3 – 23 and 24). The stigmatized and dehumanized refugees, through the discourse of disease-infestation, addiction, sexual violence and property offenders, compelled the political solution for Yishai's followers: refugees should be removed from the general population and quarantined in a detention facility (Table 10.3 – 25).

The rhetorical connection between the refugees/asylum seekers and dirtiness, illness, and criminality was clear. However, interestingly, the government's own data did not support (or refute) these contentions. Although this population grew threefold between 2009 and 2013, the official governmental report stated that: '... due to the limitation of the data, police and national immigration authorities, it cannot be asserted that the number of crimes committed by this population exceeds its proportion in the population ... '.[46] Nevertheless, the framing of them as 'disease-infested criminal substance abusers' became a significant trope to refer to refugees and asylum seekers.

Anti-democratic and anti-Zionist

State institutions maintain that the refugees and asylum seekers threaten both the Jewish and democratic nature of Israel.[47] Framing their presence as an existential threat to Israel weaves together arguments about borders and national security, international law, national identity, national sovereignty, and, overall, democracy:

1. Border security: if Israel's sovereignty is imperilled by insecure borders. As refugees traversed the border without official admission, they should be expelled.
2. International law: although international law allows sovereign states to determine refugee/asylum status, if migrants traverse a safe third country, then the migrants are not entitled to a determination hearing. Since these migrants traversed Egypt before coming to Israel, they had to return to Egypt for status determination (Table 10.3 – 28).
3. Demographic survival: Israel is a state only for Jewish refugees (and by the Law of Return, two generations of their non-Jewish immediate relatives). Non-Jewish refugees are not – and cannot – become Jewish[48] therefore, they cannot be welcomed as refugees. State officials assert that their arrival poses a demographic threat to the existence of the state of Israel as a Jewish state.[49]

Yet, Israel has historically made exceptions for non-Jewish refugees such as Vietnamese boat people, members of the South Lebanese Army who assisted Israel in the 1980s war with Lebanon, and Bosnians fleeing 'ethnic cleansing'.[50]
4. Quality of life – crime scourge hyperbole: politicians accuse migrants of threatening community life by perpetrating illegal activity in Israel and duping local NGOs into believing fabricated claims of persecution, asserting that the NGOs and the 'infiltrators' must be stopped or parts of the state will crumble (Table 10.3 – 26).
5. Zionist imagination imperilled: the refugees' presence is an existential threat to the Zionist dream for the state of Israel. (This is a stretch as the government, itself, reports that there are around 42,000 refugees and asylum seekers (Table 10.3 – 27). Their numbers are declining due to 'self-deportation' efforts.[51] However, the refugees/asylum seekers have been incapable of manufacturing a rights discourse establishing attachment or belonging to Israel and so cannot challenge these concerns. Symbolism trumps reality in popular and official discourses.

The 'counter-framing'

Israelis' opinion about refugees and asylum seekers remains mixed. Attempts by NGOs, left-leaning intellectuals and social activists to create a counter-discourse has been highly contentious. Local civil rights NGOs[52] (for example, Hotline for Refugees and Migrants) assist vulnerable individuals (particularly those in detention) to uphold legal rights, promote impact litigation and wage policy initiatives, and mobilize public outreach to achieve broad-based, systematic recognition of human rights for migrants.[53] A host of organizations have similar agendas, while catering to different groups and goals, for example: Worker's Hotline; Physicians for Human Rights; ARDC African Refugee Development Center and The Garden Library, and the Community Education Center.[54] These NGOs promote a civil rights discourse that has been attacked as anti-Zionist and anti-Israeli by both state officials and the public. The government invoked legislation to limit financial donations to NGOs to curtail their power. Despite massive mobilization, the

NGOs failed to stop the legislation.[55] Overall, the NGOs' impact on the public debate about refugees is limited. It is unclear whether this is the result of the discourse framing of hygiene, diseases, and crime associated with the refugees or if this is part of the normal politics in the Israeli society, with NGOs having a negligible impact.

Second, physicians and intellectuals have tried to counter the populist discourse. Over time, they have founded local affiliates of aid organizations for non-Israelis and the underprivileged, for example: Physicians for Human Rights – Israel[56], the Hebrew Immigrant Aid Society (HIAS),[57] and the Israeli Refugee Rights Clinic.[58] Moreover, they have attempted to bring rationality to public discourse, for example an editorial by Katvan and Dochanin[59] in Ha'aretz (Israel's newspaper of record) stating that linking public health hazard arguments and achievement of political goals is dangerous. As most people tend to obey health-care decrees, using public health arguments for political causes may undermine public trust in the government, unleashing public health crises and eventually a discounting of government determinations of who belongs, based on medical considerations. Finally, they argue, after asserting that Zionist organizations picked only the physically fittest Mizrachim to enter Palestine, that the state and the Israeli public are facing a similar contemporary scenario, cherry-picking who may be admitted and preventing absorption of refugees into Israeli society by using public health endangerment arguments (Table 10.3 – 29). Many similar editorials have been published by NGOs attempting to change public opinion and the institutional discourse. Yet, the public discourse remains fixedly anti-immigrant/refugee/asylum seeker.

Sometimes, progressive organizers have botched efforts to be helpful. To create a welcoming environment, volunteers called 'Lewinski Soup' organized a soup kitchen and clothing closet in a public park frequented by refugees (Table 10.3 – 30). They attracted public ire, as the free food drew crowds, exacerbating tensions between area residents who feared danger to their children playing in the park. Their good works came under further fire when 'Lewinski Soup' started a different initiative 'Lewinski Jam' for people to play music together in Lewinski Park (Table 10.3 – 31). Many rebuked the refugees and asylum seekers dancing with volunteers as patronizing and inappropriate. A rift expanded between out-of-neighbourhood Lewinski Soup volunteers and local, generally lower-income south

Tel Aviv residents who felt besieged by refugees/asylum seekers and projects to help them while the residents' own social problems were ignored. Reacting to the residents' displeasure, a member of Lewinski Soup, Yigal Shtaim, unleashed a racist and misogynistic screed attacking the (mostly Mizrachi) residents.[60] One news article[61] castigated volunteers from the affluent (northern and central) parts of Tel Aviv for helping refugees and asylum seekers at the expense of the local Mizrachi Jews in southern Tel Aviv. The article galvanized fomenting discord between the two groups and effectively ended the Lewinski Park initiatives. Although this volunteering venture had the potential to change the discourse and build a partnership between residents and refugees, it did not, mainly because it collided with the multiple extant cleavages in Israeli society: Ashkenazi–Mizrachi, rich–poor, north–south. Hence, attempts by media outlets and cooperation efforts between locals and refugees/asylum seekers to create a different discourse failed. Since then, attempts to reframe the discourse have become more infrequent and less significant.

Concluding remarks

The refugees/asylum seekers/infiltrators discourse poses distinct challenges that are different from previous attempts to incorporate Mizrachi, Arabs or Ethiopians into Israeli society. The refugees maintain no legal, social, cultural, or ethnic claim of belonging to the Israeli – Jewish or Arab – collective. Therefore, their otherness cannot be elided in the same way that it could for Mizrachi (and Ethiopians, and to some extent, Arabs). Conversely, given their current size and composition, they pose no real meaningful demographic risk to the Jewish socio-demographic dominance or even to the burgeoning Arab population in Israel. However, the symbolic issues shaping the discourse may be more difficult to counter than concrete ones. Since Israel understands itself as a place where Jews will find refuge/home, what does it mean to include non-Jews as refugees as well? (Of course, Israel has a historic record of admitting a few non-Jewish refugees when politically expedient to do so.)[62] Race may be an important issue, but, as in most states, it has a particular shape embedded in the national context. In Israel, Jewishness/non-Jewishness is a subtext. Until the arrival of Ethiopian

Jews in the mid-1980s, Israel was virtually racially homogeneous, and predominantly white. These new migrants changed the racial composition of Israel. When Mizrachi Jews came to Israel, they were known as 'black', as they were generally phenotypically darker than their Ashkenazi compatriots. Once the Ethiopians Jews came and assumed the label 'blacks', Mizrachi were generally no longer referred to as 'black'. The refugees and asylum seekers have now been subsumed into the category of 'black', reigniting questions about the Jewishness of Ethiopian-origin Jews. The addition of black African people to Israeli society has not made it more accepting; on the contrary, Israeli society has become increasingly racist and less tolerant of racial difference.[63]

Refugees and asylum seekers suffer from multiple social handicaps in the new environment: first, they are non-Jewish in a Jewish state; second, they are black in a predominantly white society; and finally, some of them are Muslims, which instantly places them with the subaltern Arab-other. Public discourse does not engage these issues, but rather subsumes the topic into one of 'objectivity' through the seemingly scientific category of hygiene. The migrants are thus reframed as unclean and their culture as degenerate, leading to unclean lives of criminality, sex offences and disease. In the extreme, Bandura[64] warns that discursive dehumanization allows for the rationalization of disparate treatment, even immoral and inhumane behaviour. We have presented the refugees/asylum seekers cleanliness/hygiene discourse in Israel. This is not a new way to frame undesirable groups in the Israeli sociopolitical arena: the Arabs and Mizrachim examples are a precedent for such practices in Israel. Although we have not delved into labour migrants' or the Ethiopian Jews' experiences, they have suffered similar patterns of negative treatment: tropes of uncleanliness, then disease, then socially corrupting influences, and then exclusion.[65] Our analysis has examined various (latent) racial, national, cultural and socio-economic aspects (looking beyond the ethno-religious/Arab and Muslim one which is always a critical part of the Israeli story) that were implemented to dehumanize the members of this group. Racist discourses have been used with respect to the Mizrachi and Ethiopian-Jews in Israeli history. What remains different is that Mizrachi and Ethiopian-Jews had a connecting thread to the collective – Jewishness – while the refugees and asylum seekers do not share any aspect of this religious, social, historical, ideological connection. The ideas of foreignness, unhygienic behaviour and disease-ridden bodies were easily accepted with respect to the refugees and asylum seekers by the general population because of a history that primed this idea. The discourse effectively dehumanized refugees and asylum seekers in Israel and allowed for separation, imprisonment and deportation in an attempt to exclude them from Israeli society and keep Israel as a Jewish-dominant state, the ostensible political goal. As the discourse shifted from cleanliness and hygiene to socially aberrant, socially undesirable behaviour, such as sex offences, violence, criminality, drug use and HIV/AIDS, framings were more easily accepted because of the 'otherness' of the refugees/asylum seekers, lack of contact and previous framing as diseased, unhygienic and unhealthy. Further, the anticipation of a quick departure, meant that there was no need to incorporate refugees into Israeli society, as they were not expected to remain. Although criminality was part of the anti-Mizrachi and Ethiopian-Jews discourse, it did not command the core of the discourse, as the media and general public understood that however different Mizrachi and Ethiopian-origin Jews were, they would remain in Israel permanently and, therefore, necessitated integration. The message for these Jews was 'if you adopt our ostensibly western mode of life, it will be easier for you to integrate'.[66] To a limited extent, this approach is mimicked for the Palestinian Citizens of Israel who are kept on the periphery of Israeli society but tolerated because of their adoption of Hebrew as a language and, in the case of Druze and some others, participation in Israel's military or police forces. In contrast, the discourse about refugees and asylum seekers reifies their presence as illegal *infiltrators*, breaching the state and nation. Given the fact that Israel maintains no permanent internationally recognized borders, this breach of assumed Israeli border space takes on a heightened, if only symbolic, sensibility. The rapid transformation of the discourse from unclean to criminally violent diseased bodies polluting the purity of the nation has exacerbated tensions between newcomers and long-standing residents. The severity of the discourse compels exclusion as a mode of security. For the Mizrachi and others, the adoption of local hygiene and health practices, approaches and behaviours as well as adopting local attitudes towards cleanliness opened paths of assimilation into Israeli society. Here, it appears that it is not possible to 'cleanse the infiltration' and therefore allow for eventual assimilation into Israeli society.

Appendix

Table 10.3 Appendix: Framing table

Framing table		
Framing	Link	
Framing I cleanliness and hygiene diseases	1.	Fucse Elinore. (2013, March 19). Mothers: we do not want to be in the same room with infiltrators. *Mako*. www.tbk.co.il/article/2691385
	2.	Shani Rami. (2012, June 02). Suspicion: A woman shouted in a hotel 'Filthy Sudanese' about Ethiopian Jews. *Walla*. http://news.walla.co.il/item/2538148
	3.	Even Yoav. (2012, August 22). Outbreak of tuberculosis in Ichilov: an attempt to prevent additional contagion. *Mako*. Retrieved from www.mako.co.il/news-israel/health/Article-60c1e6c3b5e4931017.htm
	4.	Ashkenazi Avi. (2008, March 06). Refugees infected five prison guards with tuberculosis. *NRG*. www.nrg.co.il/online/1/ART1/706/103.html
	5.	Reznik Ran. (2012, February 23). Ichilov Hospital Internal Report states: a significant jump in contagious diseases among infiltrators from Africa. *Israel Hayom*. www.israelhayom.co.il/site/newsletter_article.php?id=15235
	6.	Cohen Shimon. (2012, May 09). Outbreak of measles among infiltrators in Tel Aviv. *Channel 7*. Retrieved from www.inn.co.il/News/News.aspx/237709
	7.	Even Dan. (2013, June 07). Outbreak of polio: the Health Department will locate children who were not vaccinated. *Ha'aretz*. www.haaretz.co.il/news/health/1.2048804
	8.	Karaso Rafi Professor (Medical Doctor). (2012, May 27) *Seniro* Doctors warn the population of diseases among migrant labourers and refugees/Interviewers: *Orly Vilnai and Guy Meroz*. Morning Show Channel 10 Israel, Israel. www.youtube.com/watch?v=Z0B0GXxkhZE

Table 10.3 (continued)

Framing table		
Framing	Link	
	9.	Liss Tony. (2012, September 13). Parents protested against integration of refugee children: they will transmit diseases. *MyNet*. www.mynet.co.il/articles/0,7340,L-4280947,00.html
	10.	Shlomo-Melamed Merav. (2015, September 03). Kiryat Shalom Tel Aviv: Parents against Eritrean school students. *MyNet*. www.mynet.co.il/articles/0,7340,L-4696918,00.html
	11.	Azuly Moran, Eitai Blumental and Omri Efraim. (2016, August 31). The Prime Minister against Bennet: not to turn school in South Tel Aviv into a 'learning institution for infiltrators'. *Ynet*. www.ynet.co.il/arrticles/0,7340,L-4848723,00.html
	12.	Lis Yehonatan and Lee Yaron. (2016, August 31). Netanyahu: Against school for foreigner children in Tel Aviv; Huldai: The Prime Minster is part of the problem. *Ha'aretz*. www.haaretz.co.il/news/education/1.3055107
	13.	Shlomo-Melamed Merav. (2015, September 10). Kiryat Shalom Tel Aviv: Parents handed out flyers against foreigners. *MyNet* www.mynet.co.il/articles/0,7340,L-4699633,00.html
Framing II Sex offenders	14.	Walla editorial staff. (2012, December 31). Rape of an elderly woman ends a year full of violence in South Tel Aviv. *Walla*. http//news.walla.co.il/item/2602108
	15.	Ashkenazi Avi. (2015, March 26). Documentation: sexually assaulted woman in Tel Aviv, while passers-by turn a blind eye. *Walla*. http://news.walla.co.il/item/2840896
	16.	Ashkenazi Avi. (2012, May 17). Foreigners suspected of rape and robbery of a woman in South Tel Aviv on Independence Day were arrested. *NRG*. www.nrg.co.il/online/1/ART2/369/138.html
	17.	Ashkenazi Avi. (2012, May 29). Suspicion of another rape attempt in South Tel Aviv: an Eritrean youngster arrested. *NRG*. www.nrg.co.il/online/1/ART2/372/373.html
	18.	Kobobitz Yaniv. (2012, May 17). Suspicion: Eritreans raped a 15- year-old minor in South Tel Aviv. *Ha'aretz*. www.haaretz.co.il/news/law/1.1710228

(Continued)

Table 10.3 (continued)

Framing table

Framing	Link
AIDS and drugs	19. Smoocha Shachar. (2013, January 12). A jungle swarming in violence, drugs and theft: a dire journey in South Tel Aviv. *Globes*. www.globes.co.il/news/article.aspx?did=1000812991
	20. Even Yoav and Brahano Teganya. (2012, May 17). South Tel Aviv at the brink of explosion: 'It is scary to walk here at night". *Mako*. www.mako.co.il/news-israel/education/Article-f4e-d879e24c5731018.htm
	21. Smoocha Schahar. (2014, June 05). Between violent street fights at night and a housing project that spurs hope. *Globes*. www.globes.co.il/news/article.aspx?did=1000943463
	22. Ynet Editorial Staff. (2009, October 31). Interior Minister Eli Yishai: hundreds and thousands of infiltrators will bring AIDS and drugs. *Ynet*. www.ynet.co.il/articles/0,7340,L-3798115,00.html
violence and security	23. Shlezinger Yehuda and Avi Cohen. (2013, January 02). Eli Yishai intensifies his struggle over the infiltrators. *Yisrael Hayom*. www.israelhayom.co.il/site/newsletter_article.php?id=25299&newsletter=02.01.2013
	24. Channel 2 News Room. (2012, May 16). Eli Yishai attacks the infiltrators: 'sex offenders – all of them to prison'. *Mako*. www.mako.co.il/news-military/politics/Article-67b2d25321453731018.htm
	25. Ha'aretz Editorial Staff. (2012, May 16). Eli Yishai: put all migrant labourers and refugees in prisons or detention facilities. *Ha'aretz*. www.haaretz.co.il/news/education/1.1709119

Table 10.3 (continued)

Framing table

Framing	Link
Framing III anti-democratic destroying the Jewish state and the Zionist dream – demographic balance	26. Shai Doron. (2014, January 05). MK Eli Yishai on the infiltrators mega demonstration: 'put them in prison and get them out of Israel'. *Nana10*. http://news.nana10.co.il/Article/?ArticleID=1028927 27. Yerushalmi Shalom. (2012, June 01). Eli Yishai in special interview: 'It's us or them'. *NRG*. www.nrg.co.il/online/1/ART2/373/346.html 28. Wolf Pinchas and Tal Shalev. (2012, June 05). Yishai established a Special Task Force: 'There will be no infiltrators here'. *Walla*. http://news.walla.co.il/item/2539082
Framing IV the 'counter-framing'	29. Katvan Eyal PhD. and Prof. Yoel Dochanin. (2011, September 18). Do refugees endanger our health? *Ha'aretz*. www.haaretz.co.il/news/health/1.1476398 30. Lewinski Soup: www.facebook.com/soup4lewinski/ 31. Lewinski Jam: www.facebook.com/jam4lewinski/

Notes

1. Authors are listed alphabetically.
2. Ashkenazi/Ashkenazim (Hebrew) are European and North American Jews and their descendants.
3. A. Zeltzer-Zubida and H. Zubida, 'Patterns of immigration and absorption', in M. G. Brad and D. Nachmias (eds), *Israel Studies: An Anthology*, (Jewish Virtual Library, 2012) www.jewishvirtuallibrary.org/israel-studies-an-anthology-immigration-in-israel
4. Mizrachi/Mizrachim are Asian and African Jews and their descendants.
5. M. J. Edelman, *From Art to Politics: How Artistic Creations Shape Political Conceptions* (Chicago, IL: University of Chicago Press, 1995).
6. Edelman, *From Art to Politics*; D. Stone, *Policy Paradox: The Art of Political Decision Making* Third edition (New York: W. W. Norton & Company, 2011); D. Yanow, *Constructing 'Race' and 'Ethnicity' in America: Category-making in Public Policy and Administration* (New York: Routledge, 2015).
7. Edelman, *From Art to Politics*, p. 129.
8. A. Bashford, *Imperial Hygiene: A Critical History of Colonialism, Nationalism and Public Health* (New York: Palgrave Macmillan, 2004).
9. N. Molina, *Fit to Be Citizens? Public Health and Race in Los Angeles, 1879–1939* (Berkeley, CA: University of California Press, 2006).
10. F. Wilson, 'Indian citizenship and the discourse of hygiene/disease in nineteenth-century Peru', *Bulletin of Latin American Research*, 23:2 (2004), 165–80, DOI:10.1111/j.1470-9856.2004.00102.x
11. D. Hirsh, *'We Are Here to Bring the West': Hygiene Education and Culture Building in the Jewish Society of Mandate Palestine* (Hebrew) (Sede Boqer: Israel, The Ben-Gurion Research Institute Ben-Gurion University in the Negev, 2014).
12. E. W. Said, *Orientalism* (New York: Random House, 1979).
13. R. A. Harper and H. Zubida, 'In or out – migrant workers in Israel: boundaries of Israeli citizenship', *In-Spire Journal of Law, Politics and Societies*, 5:1 (2010), 1–23.
14. We recognize the official term but use the terms 'asylum seekers' and 'refugees.'
15. G. Natan, 'The geographical scattering of refugees and asylum seekers in Israel', Retrieved from Jerusalem (Research Paper: the Knesset Research Centre) www.knesset.gov.il/mmm/data/pdf/m03052.pdf (February, 2019).
16. R. A. Harper and H. Zubida, 'In or out'; H. Zubida, L. Lavi, R. A. Harper, O. Nakash and A. Shoshani, 'Home and away – hybrid perspective on identity formation in 1.5 and second generation adolescent

immigrants in Israel', *Glocalism. Journal of Culture, Politics and Innovation* 1(2013), DOI:10.12893/gjcpi.2013.1.6

17 The Jewish People's Council 1948; Basic law: Israel – the nation state of the Jewish people, 19 July 2018; https://knesset.gov.il/laws/special/eng/BasicLawNationState.pdf (accessed: June 2019).

18 H. Yaron, N. Hashimshony-Yaffe and J. Campbell, '"Infiltrators" or refugees? An analysis of Israel's policy towards African asylum-seekers', *International Migration*, 51:4 (2013), 144–57; Y. Paz, 'Ordered disorder: African asylum seekers in Israel and discursive challenges to an emerging refugee regime', *New Issues in Refugee Research*, (Geneva, Switzerland: Policy Development and Evaluation Service, United Nations High Commissioner for Refugees, 2011).

19 Full text of 2017 amendments to the anti-infiltration law (Hebrew): http://main.knesset.gov.il/Activity/Legislation/Laws/Pages/LawBill.aspx?t=lawsuggestionssearch&lawitemid=2006021 (accessed: June 2019). Original law 1954 (Hebrew): www.google.co.il/url?sa=t&rct=j&q=&esrc=s&source=web&cd=5&cad=rja&uact=8&ved=0ahUKEwjg6IuexprXAhWBLhoKHeWsC_AQFghBMAQ&url=http%3A%2F%2Fwww.justice.gov.il%2Funits%2Fmishmoret%2Fmaindocs%2Fimmigration-1954.doc&usg=AOvVaw2i6POlR9nM4p4g0FpLAzLf (accessed: June 2019).

20 See I. Lior, 'African asylum seekers can be deported to countries like Rwanda and Uganda, Israel's top court rules' *Haaretz* (29 August 2017), www.haaretz.com/israel-news/1.809406 (accessed: June 2019).

21 A. Dowty, *The Jewish State: A Century Later* (Berkeley, CA; Los Angeles; London: University of California Press, 1998). The book discusses Herzl's 'state of Jews' and Ahad Ha'am's 'state with Jewish principles'.

22 Zeltzer-Zubida and Zubida, 'Patterns of immigration'; Y. Shenhav, *The Arab Jews: A Postcolonial Reading of Nationalism, Religion and Ethnicity* (Stanford, CA: Stanford University Press, 2006).

23 See: O. Almog, *The Sabra: The Creation of the New Jew* (Berkeley, CA: University of California Press, 2000).

24 E. Shohat, 'The invention of the Mizrahim', *Journal of Palestine Studies*, 29:1 (1999), 5–20, DOI:10.2307/2676427

25 As cited in E. Shohat, 'Sephardim in Israel: Zionism from the standpoint of its Jewish victims', *Social Text*, 19/20 (1988), 1–35, DOI:10.2307/466176

26 On Australia, see A. Bashford, *Imperial Hygiene*; on the USA at the turn of the twentieth century see N. Molina, *Fit to Be Citizens*.

27 N. Davidovitch and S. Shvarts, 'Health and hegemony: preventive medicine, immigrants and the Israeli melting pot', *Israel Studies*, 9:2 (2004), 150–79, at 150. DOI:10.1353/is.2004.0024
28 Zeltzer-Zubida and Zubida, 'Patterns of immigration'.
29 S. Smooha in 'Mizrahim and Ashkenazim in Israel' at the Schusterman Centre for Israel Studies at Brandeis University symposium, Friday 15 June 2012 quipped that it was a political fight to be called 'Mizrachim' and thus assert their Middle Eastern origins, rather than be collapsed into the Ibero-centric and therefore still European context contained in the name 'Sephardim' (lecture notes).
30 A. Khazzoom, *Shifting Ethnic Boundaries and Inequality in Israel, or: How the Polish Peddler Became a German Intellectual* (Stanford, CA: Stanford University Press, 2008).
31 Said, *Orientalism*.
32 D. Hirsch, 'Zionist eugenics, mixed marriage, and the creation of a "new Jewish type"', *Journal of the Royal Anthropological Institute*, 15:3 (2009), 592–609; S. J. Frantzman, '"They will take the country from us": labor Zionism, the origins and legacy of the "other" in Israeli mass media, and hegemonic narratives', *Digest of Middle East Studies*, 23:1 (2014), 156–89.
33 Shohat, 'The invention of the Mizrahim'; S. Smooha, 'The mass immigrations to Israel: a comparison of the failure of the Mizrahi immigrants of the 1950s with the success of the Russian immigrants of the 1990s', *The Journal of Israeli History*, 27:1 (2008), 1–27, DOI: 10.1080/13531040801902708; Hirsch, 'Zionist eugenics'; Frantzman, 'They will take the country'.
34 Smooha, 'The mass immigrations'.
35 Hirsch, 'Zionist eugenics'.
36 Frantzman, 'They will take the country'.
37 D. Arnold, *Colonizing the Body: State Medicine and Epidemic Disease in Nineteenth-Century India* (Berkeley, CA: University of California Press, 1993); M. Harrison, *Public Health in British India: Anglo-Indian Preventive Medicine 1859–1914* (Cambridge, UK: Cambridge University Press, 1994); Y. Conforti, 'East and west in Jewish nationalism: conflicting types in the Zionist vision?' *Nations and Nationalism*, 16:2 (2010), pp. 201–19.
38 Shenhav, *The Arab Jews*; Y. Shenhav and Y. Yonah (eds), *Racism in Israel* (Jerusalem: Van Leer Kerusalem Institute/Hakibbutz Hameuchad Publishing House, 2008 [Hebrew]); Shohat, 'The invention of the Mizrahim'.
39 A. Bandura, 'Moral disengagement in the perpetration of inhumanities', *Personality and Social Psychology Review*, 3:3 (1999), 193–209, DOI: 10.1207/s15327957pspr0303_3
40 N. Davidovitch and M. Avital, 'Public health, racial tensions, and body politic: mass ringworm irradiation in Israel, 1949–1960', *The Journal of Law, Medicine & Ethics*, 36:3 (2008), 522–9.

41 R. Morgenstern, 'New immigrants were treated with x-ray during the 1950s, the state will compensate', *The Attorney* http://p-il.co.il/article-f27ca9738bdcc31006 (accessed: June 2019) (Hebrew – Translation by Hani Zubida).
42 See Table 10.3 – 13.
43 Y. H. Duman, 'Infiltrators go home! Explaining xenophobic mobilization against asylum seekers in Israel', *Journal of International Migration and Integration*, 16:4 (2015), 1231–54; B. Kalir, 'The Jewish state of anxiety: between moral obligation and fearism in the treatment of African asylum seekers in Israel', *Journal of Ethnic and Migration Studies*, 41:4 (2015), 580–98, DOI:10.1080/1369183X.2014.960819
44 Bandura, 'Moral disengagement'; Molina, *Fit to Be Citizens*; Bashford, *Imperial Hygiene*.
45 Davidovitch and Shvarts, 'Health and hegemony'.
46 N. Moshe and S. Sofer (approved by Dr Shirly Avrahami, Head of the research and information center). 'Reported criminal activity of foreigners and infiltrators in Israel, 2009–2013'. (2014) Retrieved from Jerusalem: www.knesset.gov.il/mmm/data/pdf/m03432.pdf
47 Kalir, 'The Jewish state of anxiety'.
48 Although not impossible, conversion is difficult to do and is treated as an undesirable for those unrelated to Jews in Israel.
49 Kalir, 'The Jewish state of anxiety'.
50 R. A. Harper and H. Zubida, 'One of us? Reaction formation and inclusion as a strategy in the ethnic state', *Social Identities*, 21:2 (2015), 149–68, http://dx.doi.org/10.1080/13504630.2015.1018155
51 L. Ilan, 'Three years of Holot facility: the state managed to overpower the asylum-seekers', *Ha'aretz*, www.haaretz.co.il/news/education/.premium-1.3149830 (Hebrew) (Translation by Hani Zubida) (accessed: June 2018).
52 Full disclosure: Hani Zubida, one of authors, is a member of the governing council and an active member in an NGO's CEC, Arteam (http://thegardenlibrary.org/).
53 More on the Hotline for Refugees and Migrants: http://hotline.org.il/en/main/
54 Other NGOs: Worker's Hotline: www.kavlaoved.org.il/en; Physicians for Human Rights: www.phr.org.il/en/; ARDC African Refugee Development Center: www.ardc-israel.org/; The Garden Library and the Community Education Center: http://thegardenlibrary.org/about-us/. For a complete list of Israeli NGOs see: www.frlan.org/node/263.
55 Kalir, 'The Jewish state of anxiety'; T. Shalev, '"Enhancing Transparency": NGO's Law was approved in Second and Third Vote in the Knesset', *Walla*, 12 July 2016. http://news.walla.co.il/item/2977932 (Hebrew) (Translation by Hani Zubida) (accessed: June 2019).

56 Physicians for Human Rights: www.phr.org.il/en/about/.
57 HIAS in Israel: www.hias.org/hias-israel
58 Refugee Rights Clinic at Tel Aviv University: https://en-law.tau.ac.il/clinics/Refugee_Rights
59 E. Katvan and Prof. Y. Dochanin, 'Do refugees endanger our health?', *Ha'aretz*. 18 September 2011: www.haaretz.co.il/news/health/1.1476398 (Hebrew) (Translation by Hani Zubida) (accessed: December 2018). Dr Katvan is a law professor at the College of Law and Business Israel and Prof. Dochanin is the Chief of the Center of Patient Safety at Hadassah Ein Karem hospital in Jerusalem.
60 K. Sefingold, 'Tel Aviv: a struggle against Yigal Shtaim founder of "Lewinski Soup"', *MyNet* (22 April 2013): www.mynet.co.il/articles/0,7340,L-4370417,00.html (in Hebrew, translation by Hani Zubida) (accessed: December 2018). Located at https://hanizu.files.wordpress.com/2013/04/d79bd7aad791d794-d799d792d790d79c-d7a9d7a-ad799d799d79d-19-4-13.pdf.
61 Ibid.
62 Harper and Zubida, 'One of us?'.
63 U. Ben Eliezer, 'Becoming a black Jew: cultural racism and anti-racism in contemporary Israel', *Social Identities*, 10:2 (2004), 245–66, DOI: 10.1080/1350463042000227371; Shenhav and Yonah, *Racism in Israel*.
64 Bandura, 'Moral disengagement'.
65 Hirsh, *'We Are Here to Bring the West'*.
66 Regardless of the fact that the Ashkenazi Israelis were not necessarily perceived as part of the west by westerners or were part of its culture; Khazzoom, *Shifting Ethnic Boundaries*.

11

Medicalised borders and racism in the era of humanitarianism

Sevasti Trubeta

In October 2014, only a few months after the identification of the disease that had recently broken out in Africa as being Ebola, the German populist newspaper *Bild* carried these headlines: '100,000 have been stranded this year in Lampedusa. Are the refugees bringing Ebola to Europe?'[1] In the subheadings we read: 'Lampedusa. Circa 1500 Deaths. Ebola rages in West Africa! Yet, the Virus throws Europe into panic as well. Are the boat refugees bringing the plague through the Mediterranean area to us?' And, it went on: 'The pictures are alarming: Men in protective clothing, security gloves and pantaloons, masked for protection from illnesses, plagues. Beside them, crowded together, several hundred people, emaciated, weakened. They *escaped* from Africa to Europe [emphasis in original]. But also, fear is coming with them.' The message of the threat *ante portas* was effectively conveyed by the pictures which associated Ebola diseased persons in Africa with border-crossers: human crowds at the borders to Europe whose misery might have evoked pity, but the fact that they had *escaped* from Africa rendered them potentially dangerous, given that they had slipped through all controls – especially disease control during the Ebola outbreak. The medical face masks and the full-body protective uniforms the border guards were wearing made real the alleged threat coming with the 'boat refugees', yet simultaneously also indicated Europe's beneficence.

Even if these protective measures were justified at the time by the outbreak of Ebola, it was not the first instance of reports with such content circulating in the European press; nor was the appearance of border guards in protective clothing and face masks at the European maritime or continental borders an isolated incident. Rather, media reports and protective measures had been quite common long before the outbreak of Ebola, even during and after the so-called 'summer of solidarity' in 2015. In her book (in German) *A Gestural Story of the Border: How Liberalism at the Border Reaches its Limits*, Francesca Falk[2] shows Italian border agents wearing medical face masks during three periods of immigration into Italy: the exodus of the Albanian population in 1991; the arrival of Albanians in Italy subsequent to what was called the 'pyramid crisis' or civil war in Albania in 1997, and later, the arrival of refugees and migrants from Africa to Italy in the twenty-first century. Diachronically, protective face masks (including the 'plague masks') have always been 'potent symbols of existential risk', the medical anthropologist Christos Lynteris argues.[3] During the SARS crisis in Hong Kong, protective masks were not only a measure of individual protection but first and foremost an act of solidarity with the community. But even so, it culminated in the rise of what Peter Baehr has termed 'the mask culture'.[4] With respect to the current COVID-19 outbreak, scholars juxtapose the different premises behind wearing face masks in 'East Asia' and in western countries; in the former, they say, 'by protecting others, you are protecting yourself', whereas in the latter the premise is 'by protecting yourself, you are protecting others'.[5] Moreover, in European countries the mandatory wearing of face masks is controversial even among doctors; for example, the representative of the NHS doctors in Germany stated in the press that it is merely a matter of 'symbolic politics'.[6] In the refugee camps, on the other hand, the face mask is a minimal prophylactic medium, but camp residents must often fight for receiving its benefit. Refugee advocacy organisations alert that camps have become sites of mass quarantine or/and their residents are hardly protected.[7] In the German city Suhl, after the detection of a positive case of COVID-19 among the residents, the refugee camp became a classical quarantine. When the residents protested against their isolation and the lack of tests, the police responded with a repressive operation (which reminds one of the scenario in José Saramago's novel *Blindness*) while wearing full-body protective uniforms and using water cannons.[8] Such actions suggest that camps, similar to maritime and continental borders, are considered as places at which the threat exists in high density although invisible in the bodies of those who cross the borders.

The concern at the heart of this chapter is to explore the kind of relations that such protective measures as face masks and full-body uniforms communicate when they are worn by those receiving refugees and migrants at the European borders. The focus of this study is in the period during and after the summer of 2015, and prior to the outbreak of the Coronavirus crisis. I chose this period because what was called the 'welcome culture' had shaped a framework of political correctness that conformed with humanitarianism and anti-racism. Moreover, the observations I made during my ethnographic research[9] revealed that there was no unified implementation of such protective measures by those engaged in humanitarian and/or surveillance operations at the borders. Rather, there were different attitudes among the guardians of the borders themselves, as well as between border guards and solidarity agents. There are a lot of emblematic examples: the press reports on the first official deportation action from Greece to Turkey (4 April 2016) after the EU–Turkey migration deal had been signed, and the Frontex staff accompanying the deported people in the ferry boat from Lesvos to Dikili, wearing protective masks, with the striking exception of one Frontex individual.[10] During my fieldwork in Greece (2016), I visited several ad hoc and newly established camps for refugees and made the observation that it was predominantly military personnel who wore protective face masks and sometimes also sterile gloves. In an ad hoc camp in the harbour area of Thessaloniki (May 2016), only one person among the security staff and civil personnel was wearing gloves and a face mask. The harbour personnel and a policewoman told me in an informal conversation that there was no reason actually: 'the people are not diseased', however, 'everybody is free to take individual action'. The director of the epidemiological department at the hospital of Lesvos told me the following story (interview May 2016): when he advised the marine guards to wear gloves on rescue missions, they objected, saying that the last thing they thought about when they were 'dragging a grandmother or a kid out from the sea' was putting on sterile gloves. As a counter-example, he told me about a street cleaner working in the port area of the island's capital (Mytilini): 'wearing a white full-body uniform, he looked like an astronaut [laughing]; I demanded that the communal office speak seriously with him … You know, his appearance could give the wrong impression.'

Strikingly contradictory attitudes were present between the border guards and the civic and transnational solidarity agents (rescuers and volunteers generally) at the borders of different European countries. In summer 2015, media reports carried images of border surveillance staff at the German–Austrian border-crossing points (2015) wearing face masks and gloves in contrast to volunteers who provided the new arrivals with food and water. But the most excessive protective measures as well as the most demonstrative contradictions appeared in the Mediterranean area. As a rule, border guards wear full-body protective uniforms when receiving refugees and migrants arriving from Africa, in contrast to the transnational solidarity agents who are engaged in rescue operations in the Mediterranean and do not take such measures.

What elicits such contradictory attitudes among those working 'on the front lines' of the so-called refugee crisis? To what extent do prejudices play a part in such attitudes? How do health experts estimate the probability of spreading infectious disease through the arrival of refugees and migrants?

In the course of the increasing arrivals (in the last five years) of refugees to Europe, public debates in the European countries have revealed concerns about a possible spread of infectious diseases in Europe. I have shown elsewhere[11] that, as a reaction to this rising mood, international and transnational health organisations, EU-research services, and independent public health scholars have attempted to eliminate prejudices against the new arrivals as alleged carriers of infectious diseases. Immediately after the increase of refugee arrivals to the EU (in summer 2015), WHO, UNHCR and UNICEF (2015)[12] published a common document where, among other things, they emphasised the good health of the refugees, migrants and asylum seekers arriving in Europe. Subsequent reports and scholarly studies argue along the same vein. For example, the WHO states in a report from 2018: 'There are indications that there is a very low risk of transmitting communicable diseases from the refugee and migrant population to the host populations in the WHO European Region.'[13] In the same report, the WHO points to the great complexity of issues related to the health of refugees and migrants and suggests that 'it is often difficult to generalize research findings to wider refugee and migrant populations in a country, in a region, or globally, and this should be kept in mind when considering information on the health status of refugees and migrants in the WHO European Region.'[14] Scholars point out the hardship refugees and migrants experience during the flight as important factors which can affect their health, but they 'cannot be systematically associated with the introduction of infectious pathogens in host countries'.[15] The UCL–Lancet Commission on Migration and Health has come to similar conclusions[16] and further identifies the challenge for European societies as lying in the dual task of providing refugees and immigrants with appropriate health care and, at the same time, avoiding any nurturing of xenophobic prejudices among the local population. The UCL–Lancet Commission notes that prejudices and xenophobic sentiments in the population did not first emerge with the current arrivals of refugees: 'Suspicion against migrants as carriers of disease is probably the most pervasive and powerful myth related to migration and health throughout history.'[17]

These debates on prejudice against refugees and migrants cast a new light on the observations which were the point of departure for this study and further specify my main concern, which is to explore the relations that are communicated through protective measures such as the wearing of face masks and full-body uniforms by those in direct contact with refugees and migrants at the borders. Are such measures indications of xenophobic attitudes? And do they represent the reactivation of long-standing racialised prejudices against migrants as dangerous carriers of infectious diseases? In dealing with these questions I revisit current scholarly debates about the external borders of the EU as racial borders and social scientific studies about race, racialisation and racism, and more specifically about the uses of the disease argument in racialising migrants and refugees. What features could racialisation, or even racist attitudes, have in the cases explored in my study, given that humanitarianism is integrated into border regimes? Is the humanitarian provision of care to the refugees and border-crossers incompatible with racism? With regard to the latter questions the analysis builds upon the current scholarly debates on the ambivalence inherent in humanitarianism in relation to humanitarian operations at the borders; 'the paradoxes of humanitarian rhetoric' in the words of Giuseppe Campesi.[18] These derive from diverse factors, including the involvement of a large range of actors (including EU and state actors, and transnational solidarity agents) and the fact that at the European borders, security regimes appear to be interwoven with humanitarianism.[19]

In this chapter I argue that at the bottom of these prejudices there is a racism that absolutises the biomedical perception of disease and writes the narrative of migratory biographies in terms of pathogenic germs transmitted from one generation to another.

On bordering, disease prevention, race and racism

The interconnections between bordering processes, disease prevention and racism have been mostly examined by scholars with respect to the uses of the disease argument in public health policies in order to reinforce prejudices in racist representations of immigrants. A significant examination of the triptych 'borders–disease–racism' is provided by Natalia Molina in her studies about Mexican immigrants to the USA from the nineteenth century onwards.[20] Molina illustrates how US public health services initiated and implemented cleaning rituals at the borders that racialised Mexican immigrants. The racist attitudes were manifested in the ways in which, at the beginning of the twentieth century, Mexican immigrants to the USA were depicted as '[t]he type of people who are bringing typhus and other diseases into California from Mexico'.[21] In such representations '[d]isease, or just the threat of it, marked Mexicans as foreign, just as much as phenotype, native language, accent, or clothing'.[22] In a similar way, the health screening of the newcomers to Ellis Island had a deeply racialised character, and not just because racial–anthropological measurements were part and parcel of the examinations. Alison Bateman-House and Amy Fairchild have demonstrated that with respect to these examinations 'the demand for labor conformed to racial ideology. Influenced by scientific racism, the medical examination procedures differed for European, Latin American and Asian immigrants.'[23]

Certainly, there are fundamental differences between the abovementioned racialised medical controls and discourses and the engagement of medicine in preventing the spread of disease at the European borders in the context of my study. A crucial difference lies in the present ambivalent character of the borders to present sites where human mobility is controlled, and simultaneously humanitarian aid is provided to the arriving immigrants and refugees. A further difference is related to the recognition that nowadays anti-racism occupies a central position in the mainstream public and political discourses of western countries. These circumstances have had a modifying impact upon the idea (or the semantics) of race and its significance in shaping societal relations. The idea that we live in a 'post-racial' era which is marked by 'a supposed decline in the significance of race' occupies centre stage in current scholarly debates, albeit prompting controversies.[24] Opponents of this view, such as the historian Natalia Molina and the sociologist Eduardo Bonilla-Silva, argue that the silence about race does not mean its disappearance. On the contrary, in the supposed 'colour-blind racism' in the United States, white supremacy continues to exist, hidden but effective.[25] The conviction that 'racialism' has not ceased to be operative in social worlds despite the decrease, or even the absence, of the normative term of race leads scholars to suggest the 'absent-presence' of race with respect to Europe as well.[26]

Certainly, the significance of 'race' in the US-American and European contexts are quite different from each other. In the former, race is incorporated into administration and, in an ambivalent way, acts as a signifier of both racist policies and the emancipation and struggle for justice. In the European context, on the other hand, 'race tends to be a shadowy and slippery object',[27] not least because of its association with the Nazi era and the Holocaust, as David Theo Goldberg notes. In his noteworthy studies on race, Goldberg suggests that at the heart of the 'post-racial' society rests the vanishing of racial criticism from mainstream public discourses. As regards the European context, this seems to happen once the Holocaust has been established in the public discourse as 'the referent point for race',[28] upstaging other forms of racism, with these being first and foremost those associated with colonialism. This has the consequence that 'Europe's colonial history and legacy dissipate if not disappear'.[29] Goldberg comes to the conclusion that in current European societies, racism is thought to be an exceptional phenomenon associated primarily with right-wing, neo-Nazi groups or, in France, with adherents of the Front National.

In the years following Goldberg's publication (2006), Europe has experienced a resurgence of right-wing populist movements, political parties and governments. As a reaction to these developments, diverse programmes for anti-racist political education have been initiated by civil society agents, national and EU institutions. In Germany, for example, anti-racism is increasingly becoming a component of educational programmes as a reaction to the rising influence of the populist right-wing and neo-Nazi groups. Counteracting these developments (most recently including anti-Muslim racism) anti-racist groundwork has emerged as a focal point of educational projects such as 'School without Racism – School with Courage'. But, for all the recent sociopolitical changes, Goldberg's observation remains topical in Germany as in other European countries, because mainstream anti-racist work still places emphasis on the extreme right wing, whereas racist attitudes, latent but efficient in the mainstream society, remain largely discounted. The matter continues to be an 'exceptional racism', as Goldberg terms it: one that 'reinforces the status quo of exonerated, guiltless institutional forms and responsible individuals and more silently and invisibly structuring European societies at large.'[30] In contrast to the Holocaust which 'transpired on European soil, [and which] continues to traumatize political dialogue and debate in Europe', colonialism 'is considered to have taken place elsewhere, outside of Europe, and so is thought to be the history properly speaking not of Europe'.[31]

The silence about colonialism in mainstream anti-racism discourses and the general public leads to the imaginary displacement of colonial racism to a place outside European territory, beyond its geographical borders and political boundaries. However, recent occurrences at the external European borders have given rise to criticism that may relativise this paradigm. The criticism of current policies at the Mediterranean borders has become a visible trend among scholars who indicate that the spectre of past colonialism is currently hauntingly at play at the European borders.[32] This is the case especially in the Mediterranean region where border-crossers from the former colonies, from Africa and countries of the global South, are subjected to racial and security regimes. Moreover, the vast numbers of deaths at the maritime borders and the inaction of surveillance institutions to prevent new deaths indicates how little weight is given to the lives of these border-crossers. The 'deadly European border regime' exemplifies, as Nicholas De Genova puts it, that the European borders 'must be understood as *racial* borders'. The fact that 'targets of these diverse tactics of bordering are overwhelmingly Black and Brown people immediately confronts us with a cruel fact of (post)coloniality'.[33] From the point of view of the postcolonialism scholar Miguel Mellino, racism is at play in the managing of the humanitarian crisis. He describes it as 'humanitarian racism', meaning a racism 'that ... is fully complementary with institutional racism, or with the racism that emanates from the current European neoliberal dispositive of citizenship.'[34] At the heart of this racism rests a hierarchisation in the granting of citizenship, in consequence of which refugees and migrants are denied the right to citizenship and to asylum.

What features shape this kind of racial border if one considers the absence of a normative term of race and the establishment of anti-racism as a mainstream ideology? In their pioneering works Pierre-André Taguieff, Étienne Balibar and Immanuel Maurice Wallerstein[35] have persuasively argued that racism needs neither a normative term of race nor a normative concept of racial hierarchy to underpin its arguments. Much less does it need a direct reference to biology. But, what remains effective in the racial issue is biologisation: even though the existence of biologically determined races (or the race concept at all) is explicitly denied or simply omitted, biology is used (and abused) in shaping social relations and hierarchies among groups of people.[36] This is exactly the case discussed here; even though the importance of the biological concept of race has been decreasing in the public and political discourses, the significance of biology in imagining and materialising world hierarchies has not been abolished. On the contrary, biology continues to be operative in racialising population groups. The deciding moment for the creation of racialised groups comes with the *interpretation* of biological traits, as Adam Hochman puts it, even though 'human biological diversity is not understood *as racial*'.[37] In view of the shifts in the significance of both race as well as biology, Robert Miles' sociological concept of racialisation gains topicality. Being a critic of the analytical usefulness of race, Miles suggests turning the focus towards social relations that are understood as racial relations. He suggests racialisation, rather than race, as an analytical concept and he understands it as 'a dialectical process of signification. Ascribing a real or alleged biological characteristic with meaning to define the Other necessarily entails defining self by the same criterion.'[38] Miles has conceptualised racialisation as a term that 'refers to a process of categorisation, a representational process of defining an Other (usually, but not exclusively) somatically'.[39]

Indeed, biology remains a crucial signifier in underpinning social relations and ascribing otherness to certain populations who are being treated as unequal. With respect to the management of human mobility, this is exemplified quite clearly in biometric identification technology and the integration of DNA tests in the procedures for the family reunification of migrants and refugees.[40]

Returning to the issue of preventing the transmission of disease by border-crossers, the question arises as to how far the differences and inequality that come to the fore in the use of biology are based on racial logic, or produce such a logic? How does it work currently, given that in Europe anti-racism and humanitarianism shape the contours of political correctness and this is incompatible with discourses regarding inferiority of the refugees and migrants?

In the following section I will argue that in the treatment and representation of refugees and immigrants as potential vectors of infectious diseases there are codified global inequalities and a racial logic that draws on the current ambivalence of humanitarian aid and securitisation which is inherent to border regimes.

The racial logic in the interface of humanitarian aid and health security

The arrival of rescued migrants and refugees in Mediterranean ports is communicated to the broad public through diverse pathways, which include the mainstream media, alternative social media, and documentaries by transnational agents who are engaged in rescue operations. In the impressive documentary film 'Eldorado' (Markus Imhoof, 2018), the camera records details about the reception of rescued border-crossers by border guardians in Italy. The film contains a density of virtual details which visualise the ambivalent treatment of the rescued persons, i.e. the provision of humanitarian aid, bodily control for signs of disease, and biometric registration for security reasons. While disembarking from the rescuing ships, vulnerable individuals (children, pregnant women and extremely weak people) are collected first. The others are visually inspected en masse for possible infectious diseases. The procedure for this screening takes on the character of a border ritual of cleaning, very similar to those described by John Chircop in this volume or by Ronald Bayer and Amy Fairchild with respect to intimidating procedures of bodily control of immigrants who entered the United States from the end of the nineteenth century up to 1930s.[41] Border personnel wearing protective uniforms and avoiding any physical contact with the rescued people, visually inspect the newcomers whose first step in EU territory leads to their biometric registration. Later, they receive a digital bracelet – regardless of whether they are children or the elderly. The process is humiliating, their individual dignity and bodily integrity are violated. Nevertheless, the reception of rescued immigrants and refugees is a humanitarian action and as such 'morally untouchable'.[42] The statement the International Organisation for Migration made (following a visit of its Director General to a camp on Lampedusa) regarding the provision of 'humanitarian assistance for many exhausted migrants who arrive after perilous journeys on unseaworthy vessels'[43] is certainly not wrong, but neither is it the whole truth; the missing aspect is that humanitarian assistance goes hand in hand with security policies. The ambivalent coexistence of contradictory operations of surveillance and care of migrants and refugees has been described as the 'the birth of the humanitarian border' with respect to the Mediterranean,[44] or more generally as a 'tension between humanity and security, between compassion and repression'.[45] The ambivalence of humanitarian and security operations in bordering processes is much discussed in scholarly studies. However, the medical screening and its significance in the creation of what has been critically termed a 'racial border' is a less addressed aspect, if even attended to at all.

The physical inspection of those who have just crossed the borders points out the coalition between the politics of security and global health which shapes the regimes of biosecurity and health security; in other words, these are the '"efforts to "secure health"' as Stephen J. Collier and Andrew Lakoff put it.[46] The threat to global health is considered to arise from infectious diseases, among other sources. Critical scholarship has provided a great deal of remarkable analysis as to how security interacts with health and how they appear interwoven in the institutional frames of the regimes of security and global health. Two fundamental aspects of their connections are: biological warfare that uses pathogenic germs as weapons; and diseases which were long ago eradicated in the global North, but still remain endemic in the global South and threaten to re-emerge in the global North as a consequence of migration.[47] With respect to the latter, scholars in the social sciences remark that the matter is not the 're-emergence' of these diseases, but rather their 'rediscovery' as soon as they are thought to pose a threat for the broader societies of the global North.[48] The WHO warns of this threat in one of its recent reports: 'Tropical and parasitic infections that are not normally seen in Europe may enter the Region via refugees, migrants and travellers originating from or visiting areas of higher endemicity'.[49]

The representation of refugees and migrants as a biological threat for the European countries has its effect owing to an essentialisation of health disparities which in fact are contingent on the unequal distribution of welfare at a global level. Moreover, in the logic of security, the metaphorical signification of disease as a biological threat emerging from the global South (from 'elsewhere') mediates between biological warfare and migration and comes to represent migrants and refugees as dangerous vectors of a biological threat for the wealthy world. Such representations employ warfare terminology.[50] The connection to security comes about as soon as refugees and immigrants are perceived in a dual characteristic: as invaders, in that they evade border controls and penetrate the territorial area of the western countries, and as potential carriers of infectious diseases. Through them the invisible threat of diseases travels and transgresses borders imperceptibly. In his book *Anthrax: Bioterror as Phantasm*, Philipp Sarasin suggests that 'illegal immigration and bioterrorism appear *on the same level* as interchangeable forms of the same threat for the national body'.[51] According to Sarasin, in the logic of security, 'illegal immigrants' and 'bioterrorists' are subsumed under the same pattern of an invasion of microbes, and thus they should be 'combatted' according to the same 'standardised methods of a political–military epidemiology and anti-terror warfare'. But what is particularly remarkable in Sarasin's approach is not the similarities he points to (and they are underscored by several other scholars), but more so the *difference* he sees existing between the representations of 'illegal migrants' and 'bioterrorists'; unlike bioterrorists (who are deemed to damage western countries deliberately and maliciously), 'illegal migrants' cause harm unwittingly.[52]

Sarasin's suggestion about the different paths (though with similar effects) through which 'illegal immigrants' and 'bioterrorists' are thought to threaten the public health of their host countries leads to my next argument: the harm refugees and (undocumented) migrants are deemed to cause is unintentional, but also inevitable because the reasons are inherent in their bare biological existence. This is because the risk of disease becomes naturalised and ascribed to their origins, but their origins are perceived in biological terms of descent. In what follows I will argue that this association acts as the connecting link between disease and the racial/racist representation of migrants and refugees.

Exotic disease as heredity

When viewed from the perspective of the global North, the endemicity of such diseases in the global South renders the diseases 'exotic' in terms of being located in (and 'belonging' to) distant places. The exoticisation of disease (as exoticisation generally works) is everything but value-neutral. The distance ascribed to the exotic places is not defined primarily in geographical terms, but rather in terms of civilisational disparities between the more and less developed parts of the world. It is a process of 'othering' in that the idea of the 'exotic' charges the distant places – and their inhabitants – with not merely difference but backwardness. 'There' continues to harbour what now belongs to the past of the developed world. The achievements of modern medicine act as a signifier of these civilisational disparities. The diseases at issue are considered 'exotic' in terms of having disappeared in wealthy countries a long time ago, owing to modern medicine, but still remaining endemic in the underdeveloped part of the world, that is, in countries afflicted with weak public health infrastructures and reliant upon humanitarian medicine. But even while residing 'there', exotic diseases still pose a threat for the wealthy countries due to both the mobility that interconnects and networks the different parts of the world, as well as the porosity of the borders which abolishes the safe distance between the global North and the global South. This is the explicit message conveyed in the text of the senior editor of biomedical sciences at Encyclopaedia Britannica in the online edition of Britannica:

> 6 Exotic Diseases That Could Come to a Town Near You. A virus from Africa that emerges in Italy, a parasite restricted to Latin America that emerges in Europe and Japan – infectious diseases that were once confined to distinct regions of the world are showing up in unexpected places. If the exotic invaders on this list haven't appeared yet in a town near you, they may do so soon, courtesy of increased human travel and climate change – two factors thought to play a major role in the spread of infectious agents and the animals that carry them.[53]

The high degree of menace of such diseases is owing to the invisibility of the pathogenic germs which are responsible for the transmission of the disease. Invisibility renders the germs potentially omnipresent and transmittable by individuals who are asymptomatic. The damaging effects may come to the fore after a long time, even in the following generations of the affected individuals. Drawing on the metaphorical signification of disease and the logic of biological warfare, the invisibility of pathogenic germs renders all immigrants and refugees suspect carriers of disease merely due to people's origins (or the origins of their ancestors) in countries in which 'exotic' diseases are endemic. Even though the pathogenic germs reside imperceptibly in their bodies, the migratory biography of individuals can at any time betray their possible existence and thus present the *risk* of transmission of the disease. In the vein of these associations, owing to the invisibility and longevity of the disease germs, the immigrants are deemed to incorporate a permanent threat for the western world. The medical lawyer, and teacher at the City University of New York (and well-known for her conservative views), Madeleine Pelner Cosman (1937–2006), asserts in an article published in the Journal of American Physicians and Surgeons that the porosity of the borders allows the invasion of 'illegal aliens' into the USA who threaten the achievements of American medicine and the welfare state. Her concern is 'the Seen and the Unseen'. 'The influx of illegal aliens has serious hidden medical consequences. We judge reality primarily by what we see. But what we do not see can be more dangerous, more expensive, and more deadly than what is seen.'[54] Using the 'illegals' as a point of departure, Pelner Cosman generalises her views to encompass all immigrants from less-developed countries, suggesting that all of them potentially harbour pathogenic germs from their origins. The invisibility of the lethal pathogenic germs is counteracted by the visible or verifiable migratory background. This association becomes possible as soon as the narrative of heredity is written in terms of pathogenic germs that are allegedly harboured in the bodies of immigrants and can be transmitted to their offspring. The endemicity of the disease in a place and the origins of the migrants or refugees in the same place (the distant global South) exchange their significations. The exchangeability of their semantics becomes possible through the intermediating role of heredity. And, as heredity is usually thought to operate in naturalising and racist discourses, the determining hereditary features continue to exist latently and can come to the fore after time, in subsequent generations. According to the same pattern, the latent but lethal germs of a disease can break out even after several generations. In effect, refugees and migrants pose a potential biological threat for the wealthy countries which host them regardless of whether they are undocumented migrants, or assimilated and naturalised, or even second or third generation immigrants. They cannot change this since they cannot – nobody can – change their own heredity.

This kind of association between disease and genealogies of migrants and refugees draws upon colonial sanitary imagery of the world racial order. But the subject of the imagery is now rediscovered in the wealthy world and represented without using any racial terminology. Indeed, racial vocabulary is absent in such discourses in whose logic disease acts as a natural condition. Out of the societal context, disease appears to be determined by biological factors, embedded in their nature. It becomes naturalised and operates similarly to 'naturalised culture' in 'new racism': *'culture can also function like a nature, and it can in particular function as a way of locking individuals and groups a priori into a genealogy, into a determination that is immutable and intangible in origin'*.[55]

Concluding thoughts: uses of disease in the groundwork of racism

In a world notable for the continuous rolling back of the limits to scientific, technological and cultural manipulation, racism proclaims that certain blemishes of a certain category of people cannot be removed or rectified – that they remain beyond the boundaries of reforming practices, and will do so forever. (Zygmunt Bauman)[56]

At the beginning of this chapter, the focus was directed towards the arrival of migrants and refugees at the European borders, especially the maritime ones, and their bodily inspections for infectious diseases. I have argued that these practices have not been and are indeed not accompanied by any racial rhetoric or association of disease and race. Moreover, they take place under the banner of humanitarian aid and, indeed, anti-racism shapes the politically correct frames in European migration and refugee policies. At the same time, it cannot be denied that the border-crossers and rescued individuals are treated as neither patients nor ordinary citizens who freely dispose of decision-making power about their health treatment. Rather, their treatment corresponds to the multiple roles ascribed to them in the context of the current border regimes; they become subject to security regimes as soon as they transgress the borders (when unauthorised), they become subject to humanitarian aid and medical inspection because of their origins from developing countries (or, so-called crisis regions) and also due to the hardship of the flight.

These correlations become particularly obvious in the Mediterranean border. In its role as an external EU border, the Mediterranean represents a transit area from the global South to the global North and as such it is governed by the logic of securitisation. Once refugees and migrants from the global South cross the external EU borders, they also transgress lines of civilisation whose benchmark is based upon (among other factors) the achievement of western medicine and health security. The idea that they can cause harm to European societies because they potentially harbour pathogens of 'exotic' diseases in their bodies, is clearly communicated by exaggerated preventive measures such as the white full-body protective uniforms that prevent any physical contact between border guardians and the migrants and refugees. That this measure is exaggerated is revealed clearly in the reports by health experts who deconstruct such views. It is also indicated by the contradictory attitudes among those who are engaged with the refugees and migrants. This border performance appears even more exaggerated when one considers the scepticism of The UCL–Lancet Commission on Migration and Health on how to provide health care to refugees without feeding stigmatisation. The Lancet Commission remarks that even though the (tuberculosis) screening could be beneficial for the individuals, 'screening is often stigmatising and can spur xenophobic media messages'.[57]

In view of these reflections, the wearing of protective face masks and full-body protective uniforms to avoid physical contact with the refugees and border-crossers appears to be a manifestation of the 'phantasmagoria of supremacy' as Hinrich Fink-Eitel has depicted the western supremacy over the 'wild strangers',[58] which also calls to the mind what Balibar suggests is resting at the core of the new racism: 'the harmfulness of abolishing frontiers, the incompatibility of life styles and traditions.'[59] In the case explored in my studies the 'incompatibility' refers not to the culture (what is at the heart of the culturalist new racism), but rather to biological health conditions. Zygmunt Bauman has shown that the representation of the 'other' as harmful is a diachronic feature of racism but the semantics of harmfulness are adjustable to current relations: 'the choice of the semantic field in which "harmfulness" of the resented Other is theorized is presumably dictated by the current focus of social relevance, conflicts and divisions'.[60] In the use of the disease argument, the harm that migrants and refugees are thought to cause to wealthy countries is owing to their poor health due to either the hardship of the flight or their origins in countries where certain diseases are endemic. The bottom line is that it makes no difference what the reason is, what remains is the ascribed harmfulness. The line that divides their deserving pity as vulnerable individuals from their causing harmfulness is thin. The distinction blurs, so that these representations do not represent different stages of imagining the refugees and immigrants, but rather appear intertwined and feed each other. But what is more, the association of refugees and migrants with diseases endemic in their countries of origin (or the global South generally) charges them with a descent into the backward parts of humanity. In these places the achievements of western medicine (a meaningful signifier of civilisation) are 'imported' mostly in the form of humanitarian aid. Once the endemicity of disease in a place is translated into endemicity of the pathogens in the bodies of the inhabitants, the risk of disease appears to be ascribed to the collective heredity. I have argued that this translation of endemicity is at the bottom of the ascribed harmfulness to the migrants and refugees; as soon as their harmfulness is ascribed to their biology, it appears to be deliberate, but fatal.

This prejudice against migrants and refugees is not a novelty but perceptible in different periods of modern history, in that it very usually appears interwoven with racial rhetoric or even racial scientific theory. In the current context, however, this prejudice operates without making use of any racial terminology. And still, heredity comes to act as a vehicle for transmitting migratory genealogies by means of which refugees and immigrants seem to epitomise humanity's past in a way that threatens the wealthy world. For all absence of racial rhetoric, this kind of interconnection of pathogenicity and heredity corresponds to what Zygmunt Bauman has termed 'a "secondary" or (rationalized) racism' in which '[t]he repelling Other is represented as ill-willed or "objectively" harmful – in either case threatening to the well-being of the resenting group'.[61]

The 'secondary racism' that uses the argument of disease raises an alarm of possible biological menace which the refugees and migrants from the 'backward' part of the world can cause to the wealthy societies. In an analogy to the cultural racism of the postcolonial era, which absolutised cultural difference, this kind of racism absolutises the biomedical perception of disease. It writes the narrative of migration in terms of pathogenic germs that are inherent in the bodies of the migrants and, like hereditary features, can be transmitted from one generation to another.

Notes

1 '100.000 Strandeten Dieses Jahr auf Lampedusa. Bringen die Flüchtlinge Ebola nach Europa?', *Bild* (28 August 2014): www.bild.de/news/ausland/ebola/afrika-fluechtlinge-europa-angst-37399786.bild.html (accessed: 26 May 2020).
2 F. Falk, *Eine gestische Geschichte der Grenze: Wie der Liberalismus an der Grenze an seine Grenzen kommt* (Paderborn: Fink, 2011).
3 C. Lynteris, 'Plague masks: the visual emergence of anti-epidemic personal protection equipment', *Medical Anthropology*, 37:6 (2018), 442–57, DOI: 10.1080/01459740.2017.1423072.
4 P. Baehr, 'City under siege: authoritarian toleration, mask culture, and the SARS crisis in Hong Kong', in S. Harris and R. Keil (eds), *Networked Disease: Emerging Infections in the Global City* (Oxford: Wiley-Blackwell, 2008).
5 E. Schüttpelz and U. van Loyen, 'Die Überwindung der Maskenphobie', *Merkur* (6 April 2020), www.merkur-zeitschrift.de/2020/04/06/die-ueberwindung-der-maskenphobie/ (accessed: 26 May 2020).

6 'Chef der Kassenärzte hält Maskenpflicht für "reine Symbolpolitik"', *Die Welt* (30 March 2020), www.welt.de/vermischtes/live206505337/ Coronavirus-live-Kassenaerzte-Chef-Maskenpflicht-reine-Symbolpolitik.html (accessed: 3 May 2020).
7 M. Lavelle, 'Growing calls to evacuate Greek refugee camps amid virus threat', (19 March 2020), www.aljazeera.com/indepth/features/growing-calls-evacuate-greek-refugee-camps-virus-threat-200319163512654.html (accessed: 26 May 2020).
8 'Polizeieinsatz gegen Geflüchtete in Suhl', *TAZ* (18 March 2020), https://taz.de/Polizeieinsatz-gegen-Gefluechtete-in-Suhl/!5668971/ (accessed: 26 May 2020).
9 These observations are based on my ethnographic fieldwork (2015–2016) in Dunkerque (France), the Aegean island Lesvos, the Greek northern region (Idomeni, Kilkis, Thessaloniki, Oraiokastro, Diavata, Lagadikia) and Berlin, and also on systematic research of the press and the social media.
10 E. Cossé, '"My brother is being deported today" Iranian asylum seeker's case shows flaws of EU-Turkey deal', *Human Rights Watch* (28 April 2017), www.hrw.org/news/2017/04/28/my-brother-being-deported-today (accessed: 26 May 2020).
11 S. Trubeta, 'Vaccination and the refugee camp: exercising the free choice of vaccination from an abject position in Germany and Greece', *Journal of Ethnic and Migration Studies* (2018), DOI: 10.1080/1369183X.2018.1501269.
12 WHO-UNHCR-UNICEF, 'Joint technical guidance: general principles of vaccination of refugees, asylum-seekers and migrants in the WHO European region' (23 November 2015), www.euro.who.int/en/health-topics/communicable-diseases/poliomyelitis/news/news/2015/11/who,-unicef-and-unhcr-call-for-equitable-access-to-vaccines-for-refugees-and-migrants/who-unhcr-unicef-joint-technical-guidance-general-principles-of-vaccination-of-refugees,-asylum-seekers-and-migrants-in-the-who-european-region
13 WHO 'Report on the health of refugees and migrants in the WHO European region. No public health without refugee and migrant health', 2018, p. ix., https://apps.who.int/iris/bitstream/handle/10665/311347/9789289053846-eng.pdf?sequence=1&isAllowed=y.
14 Ibid., p. 23.
15 F. Castelli and G. Sulis, 'Migration and infectious diseases', *Clinical Microbiology and Infection*, 23 (2017), 283–9; see also A. Z. Kortas, J. Polenz, J. von Hayek, S. Rüdiger, W. Rottbauer, U. Storr and T. Wibmer, 'Screening for infectious diseases among asylum seekers newly arrived in Germany in 2015: a systematic single-centre analysis', *Public Health*, 153 (December 2017), 1–8, https://doi.org/10.1016/j.puhe.2017.07.011;

E. Isenring, J. Fehr, N. Gültekin and P. Schlagenhauf, 'Infectious disease profiles of Syrian and Eritrean migrants presenting in Europe: a systematic review', *Travel Medicine and Infectious Disease*, 25 (2018) 65–76, https://doi.org/10.1016/j.tmaid.2018.04.014.

16 The Lancet Commission, 'The UCL–*Lancet* Commission on Migration and Health: the health of a world on the move', *Lancet,* 392 (2018), 2606–54 (Published online 5 December 2018), http://dx.doi.org/10.1016/S0140-6736(18)32114-7.

17 Ibid.

18 G. Campesi, 'Frontex, the Euro-Mediterranean border and the paradoxes of humanitarian rhetoric', *South East European Journal of Political Science (SEEJPS)*, 2:3 (2014), 126–34.

19 M. Stierl, 'A fleet of Mediterranean border humanitarians', *Antipode* (2017), 1–21, DOI: 10.1111/anti.12320; W. Walters, 'Foucault and frontiers: notes on the birth of the humanitarian border', in U. Bröckling, S. Krasmann and T. Lemke (eds), *Governmentality Current Issues and Future Challenges* (New York: Routledge, 2011), 138–64.

20 N. Molina, *Fit to Be Citizens? Public Health and Race in Los Angeles, 1879–1939* (Berkeley, CA: University of California Press, 2006).

21 N. Molina, 'Borders, laborers, and racialized medicalization: Mexican immigration and US public health practices in the 20th century', *American Journal of Public Health*, 101 (2011), 1024–31, at 1024, DOI: 10.2105/AJPH.2010.300056.

22 Ibid.

23 A. Bateman-House and A. Fairchild, 'Medical examination of immigrants at Ellis Island', *Virtual Mentor American Medical Association Journal of Ethics*, 10:4 (2008), 235–41, at 238.

24 N. Brooke and M. Samura, 'Social geographies of race: connecting race and space', *Ethnic and Racial Studies*, 34:11 (2011), 1933–52, DOI: 10.1080/01419870.2011.559262, at 1934.

25 E. Bonilla-Silva, *Racism without Racists, Color-Blind Racism and the Persistence of Racial Inequality in America* Third edition (Lanham, MD: Rowman & Littlefield, 2010); N. Molina, *How Race is Made in America: Immigration, Citizenship, and the Historical Power of Racial Scripts* (Berkeley, CA.: University of California Press, 2014).

26 A. M'charek, K. Schramm and D. Skinner, 'Topologies of race: doing territory, population and identity in Europe', *Science, Technology, & Human Values*, 39:4 (2014), 468–87.

27 A. M'charek, K. Schramm and D. Skinner, 'Technologies of belonging: the absent presence of race in Europe', *Science, Technology & Human Values*, Special Issue: Technologies of Belonging, 39:4 (2014), 459–67, at 462.

28 D. T. Goldberg, 'Racial Europeanization', *Ethnic and Racial Studies*, 29:2 (2006), 331–64, at 336, DOI: 10.1080/01419870500465611.
29 Ibid.
30 Ibid.
31 Ibid., at 336.
32 D. Bigo, 'Death in the Mediterranean Sea: the results of the three fields of action of European Union border controls', in Y. Jansen, R. Celikates and J. de Bloois (eds) *The Irregularization of Migration in Contemporary Europe* (London: Rowman & Littlefield, 2015), pp. 55–70. C. De Cesari, 'Memory as border work: the 2008 Italy–Libya Friendship Treaty and the reassembling of Fortress Europe', in O. Demetriou and R. Dimova (eds), *The Political Materialities of Borders. New Theoretical Directions* (Manchester: Manchester University Press, 2019), pp. 36–55; N. De Genova, 'The "migrant crisis" as racial crisis: do black lives matter in Europe?' *Ethnic and Racial Studies*, 41:10 (2018), 1765–82.
33 N. De Genova, 'Europe's racial borders', in *Monitor Global Intelligence of Racism*, January 2018, http://monitoracism.eu/europes-racial-borders/.
34 M. Mellino, 'Crisis of humanism, critique of humanitarian reason. A conversation with Miguel Mellino' (From the Spanish by Kelly Mulvaney), *Transversal*, 01 (2016), https://transversal.at/blog/Crisis-of-humanism-critique-of-humanitarian-reason.
35 P.-A. Taguieff, *The Force of Prejudice: On Racism and its Doubles* (Minneapolis, MN: University of Minnesota Press, 2001 [1988]); É. Balibar and I. M. Wallerstein, *Race, Nation, Class Ambiguous Identities* (London: Verso, 1991).
36 Biologisation takes central stage in my previous work: S. Trubeta, *Physical Anthropology, Race and Eugenics in Greece (1880s–1970s)* (Leiden; Boston: Brill Academic Publishers [Balkan Studies Library], 2013).
37 A. Hochman, 'Replacing race: interactive constructionism about racialized groups', *Ergo, An Open Access Journal of Philosophy*, 4:3 (2017), at 80, http://dx.doi.org/10.3998/ergo.12405314.0004.003.
38 R. Miles, *Racism* (London: Routledge, 1989), p. 75; see R. Barot and J. Bird, 'Racialization: the genealogy and critique of a concept', *Ethnic and Racial Studies*, 24:4 (July 2001), 601–18.
39 Miles, *Racism*, p. 75.
40 M. Ticktin, *Casualties of Care: Immigration and the Politics of Humanitarianism in France* (Berkeley; Los Angeles, CA: University of California Press, 2011), p. 193; I. Van der Ploeg, 'Written on the body: biometrics and identity', *Computers and Society*, 29:1 (1999), 37–44; S. Scheel, *Autonomy of Migration? Appropriating Mobility within*

Biometric Border Regimes (New York: Routledge, 2019); T. Heinemann, H. Ilpo, T. Lemke, U. Naue and M. Weiss, *Suspect Families. DNA Analysis, Family Reunification and Immigration Policies* (Farnham: Ashgate, 2015); T. Heinemann and T. Lemke, 'Biological citizenship reconsidered: the use of DNA analysis by immigration authorities in Germany', *Science, Technology and Human Values*, 39:4 (2014), 488–510.

41 R. Bayer and A. Fairchild, 'The limits of privacy: surveillance and the control of disease', *Health Care Analysis* 10 (2002), 19–35; see also M. Gandy, 'Zones of indistinction: bio-political contestations in the urban arena', *Cultural Geographies*, 13 (2006), 497–516.

42 D. Fassin, *Humanitarian Reason: A Moral History of the Present* (Berkeley, CA: University of California Press, 2011), p. 244.

43 IOM UN Migration 06/28/07 Director General Visits Reception Facility on Island of Lampedusa, www.iom.int/news/director-general-visits-reception-facility-island-lampedusa (accessed: 17 May 2020).

44 W. Walters, 'Foucault and frontiers: notes on the birth of the humanitarian border', in U. Bröckling, S. Krasmann and T. Lemke (eds), *Governmentality Current Issues and Future Challenges* (New York: Routledge, 2011), pp. 138–64, at p. 145; see also Campesi, 'Frontex'.

45 Fassin, *Humanitarian Reason*, p. 135. See also D. Fassin, 'Humanitarianism: a nongovernmental government', in M. Feher (ed.), *Nongovernmental Politics* (New York: Zone Books, 2007), pp. 149–60.

46 S. J. Collier and A. Lakoff, 'The problem of securing health', in A. Lakoff and S. J. Collier (eds), *Biosecurity Interventions Global Health and Security in Question* (New York: Columbia University Press, 2008), pp. 120–46, at p. 8.

47 According to Elbe, security reports of the early 1990s pointed to more than twenty such diseases. S. Elbe, *Security and Global Health. Towards the Medicalisation of Insecurity* (Cambridge: Polity, 2010).

48 E. Koch, 'Disease as security threat. Critical reflections on the global TB emergency', in Lakoff and Collier, *Biosecurity Interventions*, p. 124; see also M. Gandy and A. Zuml (eds), *Return of the White Plague: Global Poverty and the 'New' Tuberculosis* (New York: Verso, 2003), especially Introduction, pp. 7–14.

49 WHO, 'Report on the health of refugees', p. x.

50 See some representative works: Gandy and Zumla, *The Return of the White Plague*; D. L. Heyman, 'Evolving infectious disease threats to national and global security', in L. C. Chen, J. Leaning and V. Narasimhan (eds), *Global Health Challenges for Human Security* (Cambridge, MA: Harvard University Press, 2004) especially p. 106; Lakoff and Collier, *Biosecurity Interventions*.

51 P. Sarasin, *Anthrax: Bioterror as Phantasa* (Frankfurt am Main: Suhrkamp, 2004), p. 176 (my translation). See also R. Keil and H. Ali, 'Multiculturalism, racism and infectious disease in the global city: the experience of the 2003 SARS outbreak in Toronto', *TOPIA: Canadian Journal of Cultural Studies*, 16 (2006), 23–49.
52 Sarasin, *Anthrax*.
53 K. Rogers, '6 exotic diseases that could come to a town near you', www.britannica.com/list/6-exotic-diseases-that-could-come-to-a-town-near-you (accessed: 1 May 2020).
54 M. Pelner Cosman, 'Illegal aliens and American medicine', *Journal of American Physicians and Surgeons*, 10:1 (2005), 6–10, at 6.
55 E. Balibar, 'Is there a "neo-racism"?' in Balibar and Wallerstein, *Race, Nation, Class*, pp. 17–28, at p. 22.
56 Z. Bauman, 'Modernity, racism, extermination', in L. Back and J. Solomos (eds), *Theories of Race and Racism: A Reader* (London; New York: Routledge, 2000), pp. 212–28, at p. 215.
57 *The Lancet Commission*.
58 H. Fink-Eitel, *Die Philosophie und die Wilden. Über die Bedeutung des Fremden für die europäische Geistesgeschichte* (Hamburg: Junius, 1994), p. 101.
59 Balibar, 'Is there a "neo-racism"', p. 21.
60 Bauman, 'Modernity, racism, extermination', p. 214.
61 Ibid., p. 213–14.

Index

Ackerknecht, E. (1906–1988) 61
Adrianople 47, 81, 87
Adriatic Sea 17, 35, 70n.2, 105, 120, 131
Africa, African 15, 185, 229, 257, 259, 261–3, 267, 275–6, 278, 282n.4, 287–8, 290, 294, 300
  East Africa 241
  North Africa 11
  South Africa 80, 137, 156, 193, 231
  West Africa 215, 287
'Africanisation' 242
Agamben, G. (1942–) 1, 9, 17, 130, 148
AIDS 201, 214, 269, 270, 277, 280
airing 39–40, 47, 60, 142, 146
airports 233, 235–9, 244–5, 250
Albania 34, 60, 288
Anatolia 34
  see also Asia, Asian, Asia Minor
Ancona 64–5
animals 5, 18, 33, 39, 41, 48, 56, 59–60, 83, 84, 130, 140–2, 145, 148, 184, 185–6, 191, 300
  see also epizootics
anti-Asian sentiments 242
anticontagionism 9–10, 40, 46, 60–2, 69, 73n.37, 93
anti-immigrant attitudes 157, 205, 230, 248, 274

anti-racism 16, 289, 293–6, 302
Arab world, Arabs 15, 138, 150n.11, 185, 257, 259, 263–7, 275–6
architecture of lazarettos and quarantines 8, 39–40, 43, 131–5
Ashkenazi 256, 258, 263, 265, 282
Asia, Asian 15, 92, 180, 185, 242, 257, 263, 282n.4, 292
  Asia Minor 89
  'East Asia' 288
  South Asia(n) 229, 246
  see also Anatolia
asylum seekers 8, 15, 215, 290, 305n.12, 305n.15
  in Israel 256–262 *passim*, 265–77 *passim*, 282n.14, 282n.15, 283n.18, 283n.20, 285n.43, 285n.51
  see also refugees
Auschwitz 19, 163, 165, 166, 167, 168, 170
Austria/Austrian Empire 60, 62, 82, 85, 109–13, 115, 120, 160
  Austrian Littoral/Coastlands 38, 58, 63, 71n.14, 111, 120
Austria-Hungary/Austro-Hungarian Empire 103, 105–6, 156, 159
  see also Austria/Austrian Empire; Cisleithania; Habsburg Empire/Monarchy

Index

bacteriological age/era 13, 201, 203, 205
bacteriology 2, 11, 62, 75n.61, 94, 166–7, 170–1, 179, 195n.8, 201–5,
Baldwin, P. (1956–) 10–11, 61, 65, 75n.61, 94, 100, 119, 132, 188–90, 194, 195n.8
Balibar, É. (1942–) 7, 12, 295, 303
Balkans 11, 80–1, 89
Baltic states 163
  see also Estonia; Latvia
Banat 36, 38, 52n.48, 54n.66, 82, 84
bandits 84, 92
Bashford, A. 5, 80, 181, 184, 258
Bauman, Z. (1925–2017) 301, 303–4, 309n.56
beggars 68, 107
Belarus 20, 162, 170
Berlin 2, 7, 81–2, 156, 161, 166–7, 170, 172
Bessarabia 85
Bila Krynytsia (village in Bukovina, now Ukraine) *see* Fontina alba
bills of health *see* health certificates
biological warfare *see* biowarfare
biometrics 6, 296–7
biopolitics 1, 144
biosecurity 6, 13, 193, 198n.43, 198n.54, 297, 308n.46
bioterrorism 6, 218n.18, 298
biowarfare 14, 208–11, 213, 298, 300
Black Death *see* plague
Black Sea 81–2, 88–9, 91, 106, 158
bodies 9, 17, 40, 48, 132, 140, 145–9, 165–6, 174, 180, 184–6, 193
  British 244, 246
  diseased 10, 132, 288, 300, 301–4
  migrant 228, 238, 277
Bohemia 82, 105
border/borders 8, 130, 132, 136, 149n.3, 152n.51, 180–6 *passim*, 189, 191–2, 195, 227–8, 232, 237, 241, 248, 277, 287
border-crossers 7, 8, 16–17, 21, 34–5, 41, 43, 45–6, 69, 75n.72, 259, 262, 287, 291, 294, 296, 302–3
  Austrian–Italian 57
  Austrian–Russian 82–3, 120
  civilisational 83
  continental 288
  European (EU) 289, 291–2, 294, 302
  filtering operations 7, 15, 17–18, 20–1, 129–49 *passim*, 156
  geographical 229, 234–5, 237, 239, 243, 245, 247, 249, 250, 294
  German–Austrian 290
  German–Russian 7, 155
  Greek–Ottoman 92
  Habsburg–Ottoman 31, 33, 35–6, 38, 43, 82–3
  health 246
  health controls 236, 249
  humanitarian border 297, 306n.19, 308n.48
  maritime borders 16, 294
  medical 228–30, 234–6, 238, 240, 242–5, 247, 249–50
  medical border inspections 186, 234–5, 238–9, 243, 246, 287
  medicalised 7–8, 12–13, 16, 18, 21, 31, 227, 232
  Mediterranean 294, 302
  performances 235, 302
  political 180–1, 185, 256
  porosity of 129, 174, 299–300
  purification 9, 18, 38–9, 40–1, 44–7, 52n.37, 140
  racial borders 291, 294–5, 297, 307n.33
  regimes 294, 296, 302, 308n.40

rituals 9, 16, 18, 79, 94, 129–31, 140, 149, 292, 297
screening 236, 249
sea borders 131–2 *passim*, 148
shutdown of 1–2, 6
social 256
spatial and bodily 183
surveillance 246, 290
territorial 129, 135, 144
border studies 2, 100
Bosnia (and Herzegovina) 34, 67, 82, 108, 109, 114, 273
Brașov (town in Romania) 42, 87
Bremen 155, 156
Britain *see* United Kingdom (UK)
Brody 81–2, 84
Budapest 104
  see also Pest
Bukovina 82, 84, 100, 103–6, 109–13, 115–22
Bulgaria 34, 68, 81, 88

Cairo 179, 195
camps 6, 18, 21
  forced labour 20
  Nazi concentration and extermination 17, 19, 20, 156, 161–74
  refugee 160–1, 288–9, 297, 305n.7, 305n.11
  see also encampment
cancer 212–13
cargo 59, 137, 141–2, 145–6
Carniola 63, 74n.57
Carpathian Mountains 35, 81
Centers for Disease Control and Prevention (CDC) 209, 211, 214
centre–periphery relations 101–3, 119
Charles VI (1685–1740), Holy Roman Emperor 37, 59

Chase-Levenson, A. (1985–) 8, 9, 17, 80
Chenot, A. (1722–1789) 42, 44, 47, 52n.50
children 14, 115–16, 119, 121, 158, 160–1, 166–7, 207, 213, 229, 233, 242, 245, 249, 261, 267–9, 274, 278–9, 296–7
China 204, 215–16
cholera 9, 10, 11, 56–70, 74n.50, 74n.57, 75n.61, 78, 79, 87, 89, 91, 92, 93, 105–12 *passim*, 114–15, 120, 121, 187, 188, 192, 197n.31, 203, 230
  pandemics 10, 79, 87, 92, 93
chronic diseases 212–14
Cisleithania 104–5, 111–12, 114
citizenship 160, 257, 258, 282n.10, 295, 306n.25
  biological 308n.40
  British 228, 251n.3, 252n.14–254n.61 *passim*
  hygienic 229, 251n.4
  imperial 231
civilisation 85, 101, 265, 302–3
civilisational disparities 299
civilised – uncivilised 15, 77n.89, 83–4, 204, 258, 263–5, 299
civil rights 1, 160, 212, 273
civil society 8, 132, 214, 294
Climăuți (village in Bukovina, now in Romania) *see* Klimoutz
Cold War 200, 202, 212–15, 231, 250
colonialism 4, 293–5
colonial regimes 17, 178, 185, 189, 191–3, 201, 231, 242, 258, 265, 301
Commonwealth 16, 227, 228–34 *passim*, 229, 242, 244, 245, 248–50, 251n.2, 252n.14
  British acts and bills on immigration 228, 232–3,

238, 252n.19, 252n.21,
    254n.62, 254n.63, 254n.68
  citizenship and 251n.3
  migrants 229, 231, 233, 234, 242,
    245, 248–9
  multiracial 231
communicable diseases *see*
  infectious diseases
Constantinople 43, 83, 86, 89–90,
  93, 190, 191
  see also Istanbul
contagion 2, 36, 46, 61, 86, 120–2,
  140, 142, 145–7, 179, 191, 205,
  210, 246, 257
contagionism 9, 46, 60–2, 73n.37,
  73n.39, 75n.65, 92, 100, 131,
  134, 144, 147–8, 154n.105, 204
  contingent 69, 73n.37
contagion theory 40–1, 204
contagious diseases *see* infectious
  diseases
containment 2–3, 7–8, 16, 19, 21,
  33, 46, 56, 59, 156–60 *passim*,
  163, 165, 168, 173–4, 207
cordon sanitaire *see* sanitary cordon
coronavirus 1–2, 201, 289
COVID-19 pandemic 1–20 *passim*,
  31, 180, 182, 194, 215–17, 288
  see also pandemics
crime, criminality 15, 173, 231–2,
  264, 269, 271–4,
Croatia 35–6, 38, 74n.57, 82, 84, 86,
  105, 108
Czernowitz/Chernivtsi 84, 105, 117,
  118

Dalmatia 100, 103–5, 108–14,
  119–122, 131, 142–3
Danube River 47–8, 80–8, 92–3,
  96n.30, 106
  Russian quarantine at the Sulina
    estuary 87, 93

Danubian Principalities 38, 46–7,
  79–80, 82–3, 85, 87–8
  see also Moldavia; Wallachia
dehumanisation 163, 270–1, 276–7
delousing 156–8, 163–4, 170, 173, 183
detention 2, 8–9, 17, 21, 53n.54, 64,
  69, 80
  British migration and 239
  Israel migration and 262, 267,
    271–3 *passim*, 280
  lazarettos and 132, 137–8, 145, 148
Ding, E. (1912–1945) 170–3
diphtheria 107, 112
dirty, dirtiness 15, 44, 59, 204, 257–8,
  264–5, 267–9, 271–2, 276–7
disaster relief 19, 155–9, 210
  see also humanitarianism
disease eradication 174
disease prevention 7–8, 10–11, 20,
  57, 64, 80, 100, 111, 159, 216,
  247–8, 292
  see also prevention
disease transmission 9, 11, 42,
  59–62, 68–9, 78, 129, 147, 156,
  249, 296, 300
disease vectors 181–2, 184, 192,
  194, 204, 230, 296, 298
disinfectants 9, 110
disinfection 8, 9, 11, 18, 27n.52, 60,
  65, 75n.61, 94, 108, 114, 120,
  121, 132, 140, 155, 161–9 *passim*
  in lazarettos 140–3, 145–8
  steam 110–11, 120
  see also lazarettos, expurgators in
displaced persons 14, 158, 163, 174
DNA tests 296, 308
Dresden 106
Dubrovnik 10, 108
  see also Ragusa

Ebola 215, 287–8, 304
Edirne *see* Adrianople

Egypt 34, 64, 80, 89, 137, 143, 178–9, 189, 259, 262, 268, 272
elites 92, 103, 205, 264
  see also upper classes
Ellis Island 12, 19, 155, 157, 163, 292, 306
emigrants 64, 107
  see also immigrants; migrants
encampment 16–120, 182
endemic state, endemicity 57, 83, 88, 137, 234, 237, 298–301, 303
England 43, 146
  see also United Kingdom (UK)
epidemic diseases 1, 6, 9, 11, 31, 33, 42, 46, 47, 56–7, 61–3, 65, 68–70, 73n.39, 76n.77, 78–9, 81, 83, 85, 88–9, 91–4, 96n.30, 102, 106–7, 111, 114, 115, 117, 119, 121, 123n.13, 129, 155, 158, 167, 203, 211–12, 216, 230, 234, 268
epidemic prevention 63, 93, 100–3, 105–6, 108–11, 113, 115, 117, 119–20, 123n.13, 167
  see also prevention
epidemiology 130, 206, 211, 298
  see also geoepidemiology
Epirus 34, 92
epizootics 82, 85
  see also animals
Eritrea 15, 257, 259, 261, 266–7, 271, 279
Estonia 167, 170
  see also Baltic states
Ethiopia 257, 265, 267, 275–8
eugenics 14, 179, 185, 193, 307
  Zionist 284
Europe 3–20 passim, 46, 48, 57, 60, 67–8, 76n.74, 79–80, 87, 89, 91–3, 100–1, 106, 137–8, 143, 157, 174, 181, 185–8, 190–1, 204, 209, 227, 232, 263–5, 287–96, 298, 300, 302
  central 10, 80, 84, 86–7, 89, 112, 158
  continent 3
  eastern 11–12, 80, 155–6, 158, 167, 183, 206, 264
  south-east 10, 32–3, 35, 37, 42, 46, 48, 78–9, 87, 89, 92, 156, 167
  southern 129, 131, 136, 144, 149, 156, 206
  western 10, 13, 78, 83–4, 87, 227
European Community 234
European Economic Community 229
European Union (EU) 2, 13, 181, 193, 195, 234, 250, 290, 291, 292, 294, 297, 302, 305, 307
EU–Turkey migration deal 289–90
Evans, N. J. (1933–2018) 245, 248
exclusion 3, 7, 13–14 passim, 15, 19, 21, 157, 159, 161, 227–8, 230–1, 233–5, 237, 241–4, 246–7, 249–50, 257–8, 266, 270, 276–7
'exotic' diseases 299–300, 302

face masks 287–291 passim, 303
  culture 288, 304n.4
  plague 288, 304n.3
Faden, R. (1949–) 214
Fântâna Albă (village in Bukovina, now Ukraine) see Fontina alba
fear 13, 33, 35–6, 41, 65–70 passim, 75n.71, 79–80, 118, 140, 185, 199–203, 205–8, 210, 212–17 passim, 244, 267–9, 274, 287
  see also panic
filth, filthy 184, 278
First World War see World War I

Index

Fiume *see* Rijeka
Florey, H. W. (1898–1968) 178, 195
flu pandemic *see* influenza pandemic (1918–1919)
Fontina alba (village in Bukovina, now Ukraine) 115–19
forced labour 163, 165, 167, 169
Foucault, M. (1926–1984) 4–5, 9, 33, 132
Fracastoro, G. (1476/8–1553) 40
France 62, 100
free movement of people 19, 155–6, 159, 163, 230, 236, 248
Frontex, 289, 306, 308
fumigation 9, 40, 60, 64–5, 86, 94, 140–3, 145, 147, 155, 186, 205

Galen (129–c.200/c.216) 40
Galicia 81, 84, 105, 110, 111, 115, 117, 118
Gdynia 161
Genoa 187, 188, 190, 193
genocide 21, 163
 see also Holocaust
geoepidemiology 10, 100–1, 119, 122, 132, 144, 167
 see also epidemiology
geopolitics 87, 93, 184, 187, 227, 233
Germany 13, 14, 83, 86, 100, 155–6, 288, 294
 see also Nazi Germany
germs 16, 59–60, 68, 73n.41, 236, 292, 298, 300–1, 304
 see also pathogens
germ theory 11, 14, 94, 201, 205
ghettoes 18, 19, 20, 162, 165
Giddens, A. (1938–) 215
Gildemeister, E. (1878–1945) 170–1
global health 6, 17, 200, 214, 297
globalisation 4, 12, 201, 215

global north 6, 16, 233, 298–9, 302
global south 16, 233, 294, 298–9, 301–3
Godber, G. (1908–2009) 237, 253, 254
goods 8–9, 20, 33, 39–41, 44–5, 48, 56, 58–60, 69–70, 72n.22, 79, 94, 100, 106, 108–9, 120, 134, 142, 147–8, 156, 185–6, 189, 191, 215
Goracuchi, A. (1807–1887) 62
Great War *see* World War I
Greece 40, 80, 90–3, 159, 289
Guterres, A. (1949–), Secretary General of the UN 6
'Gypsies' 84, 165
 see also Roma; Sinti and Roma

Haagen, E. (1898–1972) 166, 171
Habsburg Empire/Monarchy 10–11, 31–48 *passim*, 57, 79, 80, 82–3, 88, 93, 107, 110–12, 123n.13, 124n.33
 see also Austria/Austrian Empire; Austria-Hungary/Austro-Hungarian Empire; Cisleithania
Habsburg Military Border 32–8, 41–2, 45–8, 50n.18, 50n.20, 52n.49
Hajj 138, 187, 197n.31
 see also Muslim pilgrims
Hajjis 137–8
 see also Muslim pilgrims
Hamburg 155, 156, 161
hand washing 135, 268
health certificates 13, 41, 58–9, 62, 67, 90–1, 118, 137, 142, 145–7, 158, 160–1, 233, 241–5
health inspection 58, 70, 75n.61, 144, 186

health policies 3, 4, 6, 13–14, 101, 103, 106, 111, 292
heart disease 212–13
heredity 299–304 *passim*
  collective 303
  exotic disease and 299
  narrative of 301
Himmler, H. (1900–45) 166–7
Hobbes, T. (1588–1679) 34
Holocaust 14, 156, 263, 293, 294
  see also genocide
Hong Kong 182, 183, 194, 195, 218, 240, 288, 304
Hopkinson, H. L. (1902–1996) 231
humanitarian aid 293, 296, 302–3
humanitarian assistance 297
humanitarian crisis 295
humanitarianism 8, 14, 25n.24, 198n.43, 287, 289, 296, 307n.40, 308n.45
  ambivalences of 291, 296–7 *passim*
  association of racialisation and 16
  border regimes and 291
  medical 8
  security regimes and 292
  see also disaster relief
humanitarian medicine 299
human mobility 2–4, 6, 12, 16, 19, 34, 68, 191, 293, 296, 299
human processing 19, 155, 157, 163
human rights 262, 273
  Human Rights Watch 305n.10
  Physicians for Human Rights (Israel) 273–4, 285n.54, 285n.56
Hungary 35, 84, 121
  see also Austria-Hungary/ Austro-Hungarian Empire
hygiene 4, 14, 15, 18, 20, 61, 63, 67, 68, 135, 148, 155, 157, 159, 162, 170, 257–8, 263, 265–7, 271, 274, 276–8

immigrants 3, 6, 13, 15–17, 21, 64, 68, 186, 204–6, 232, 235, 237, 240–1, 244–5, 248, 250, 258, 261, 264, 274, 291–3, 296–301, 303–4
  labour 13
  see also emigrants; migrants
immigration quotas 155, 157–60, 162
immunisation, immunity 112, 115, 171–2
inclusion 3, 7, 15, 21, 228, 244, 247, 257
  see also integration
incubation period/time 11, 42, 94, 170, 171
infection 14, 37, 41–2, 46, 56, 59, 61, 64, 66–7, 69, 72n.22, 86, 100, 103, 113, 115–16, 118, 121, 145–6, 155
infectious diseases 6, 13, 32, 36, 56–7, 60–3, 68–70, 103, 105, 107, 110–12, 120, 129, 141, 143, 147, 149, 156–69 *passim*, 179, 187, 190, 192, 194, 200–7 *passim*, 215, 267–9, 278, 290–1, 296–8, 300, 302
influenza pandemic (1918–1919) 158, 204–7
integration 244
international relations 4, 6
International Sanitary Conferences 11, 60, 62, 66–8, 76n.77, 80, 93, 100, 144
International Sanitary Conventions 60, 106, 144
International Sanitary Council in Constantinople 89–91
interwar period 19
Islam, Islamic 34, 93, 187
  see also Muslims
isolation 8, 9, 17, 18, 21, 40, 41, 56, 59, 62, 64, 65, 69, 75n.61, 78,

108, 109, 110, 114, 118, 120,
121, 132, 141, 168, 169, 172,
173, 190, 270, 288
Israel 7, 15, 256–81 *passim*
Istanbul 34, 187, 188, 191, 192,
194, 252
see also Constantinople
Istria 63, 71n.12, 167
Italy 57, 64, 74n.59, 111, 288, 296,
300

Jackson, Mississippi 202
Jews 12, 15, 20, 81–2, 84, 159–68,
172–3
  east European 230, 264
  Ethiopian 265, 276, 277, 278,
  Israeli 256, 259, 263–7 *passim*,
  276, 283–5
  Nazi medicine and 183, 195
  new 263, 283
  see also Ashkenazi; Mizrachi;
  Ostjuden; Sefardim
Johns Hopkins University 211
Jupalnic (sunken village in
  Romania)
  quarantine of 38, 84

Kindertransport 14, 160–1
Klimoutz (village in Bukovina)
  115–19
Koch, R. (1843–1910) 62
Kogon, E. (1903–1987) 170, 173
Kolletis, I. (1773/74–1847), Greek
  Prime Minister 90–1
Kraków 81, 84, 171
Kriezis, A. (1796–1865), Greek
  Prime Minister 91
Kronstadt (town in Transylvania)
  see Braşov

Lampedusa 287, 297, 304, 308
Langermann, J. G. (1768–1832) 82

Langmuir, A. (1910–1993) 210–11,
213
LaPiere, R. T. (1899–1986) 208, 210
Latour, B. 5
Latvia 170
  see also Baltic states
lazarettos 7, 9, 10, 16–18, 37, 58–60,
  65, 67, 72n.19, 108–9, 129–151
  passim
  as archive 144
  as filtering apparatus 132
  as filtering instrument 129
  as multifunctional sites 132, 148
  expurgators in 130, 141–2, 145–8
  in specific regions
    Adriatic Sea 17, 72n.19, 108–9,
    131
    Dalmatia 142, 143
    Greece 141
    La Spezia 136
    Livorno 136
    Mahon 133
    Mallorca 136
    Malta 136, 139, 143, 150n.17
    Manoel Island 135, 139
    Mediterranean 153n.77, 190
    Naples 133
    Piraeus 138
    Red Sea 16
    Trieste 58–60, 65, 67, 72n.20,
    134
    Venice 146, 190
  see also quarantine, maritime
  production of medical-sanitary
    knowledge and 144
  see also detention; quarantine,
    maritime
League of Nations 158–9
  Health Organisation of 11
Le Bon, G. (1841–1931) 204
Lemberg/Lviv 84, 167
Lemkin, R. (1900–1959) 21, 160

leprosy 230
Lesvos 289, 305
Levant 10, 60, 62, 64, 89, 137
Lipovans (Old Believers) 115–19, 121
living conditions 63, 102, 105 266, 270
lockdown 10, 202
London 143, 155, 158, 178, 238
Lorinser, K. I. (1796–1853), Prussian medical officer 82–7, 89, 92–3
Lower Austria 37, 105, 111, 120
Lukowetz Lipoweny/Lukavtsi (town in Bukovina, now Ukraine) 118

Mahmud II (1785–1839), Ottoman sultan 88
malaria 167–9
Maria Theresa (1717–1780), female ruler of the Habsburg dominions 57
Marseilles 37, 146, 188, 189, 190
Marx, K. (1818–1883) 102
Mavrokordatos, A. (1791–1865), Greek Prime Minister 90
measles 112, 268, 278
Mecca
  pilgrimage and pilgrims to 11, 66–7, 93, 187–9, 189
  see also Hajj; Hajjis; Muslim pilgrims
medical examinations 137, 233, 240, 243, 249, 252n.13–255n.88 *passim*, 292, 306n.23
medicalisation 4, 5–6, 8, 16, 18, 32, 227
medical prevention 8, 75n.61
  see also *prevention*
medical screening 3, 7, 14–16, 19, 21, 156–7, 164–5, 167, 227, 232–3, 235–7, 239–41, 243, 245–7, 249–50, 292, 297, 302
Mediterranean 10–2, 13, 17, 70n.2, 72n.22, 78, 80, 83, 89, 91, 93, 108, 129, 179–82, 184–94, 287, 290, 294, 296–7, 302–3
Mehadia (town in Romania), quarantine of 38, 43
Mengele, J. (1911–1979) 20, 165–8
mental health 14, 159, 161, 164
mental illness *see* mental health
mercantilism, mercantilist policy 32, 57, 187–8
merchandise 59, 129–30, 137, 140, 142, 145–6, 148, 189
  see also goods
Metković 114, 121
miasma theory 13, 40, 46, 62, 73n.37, 78, 92, 144, 147–8, 154n.105, 184, 194
Middle East 11, 93, 256, 263–5, 284n.29
migrants 2–3, 6–8, 12–16, 21, 24n.23, 31, 155–9, 163, 186, 227–50, 256–77, 288–304
  labour 257, 261, 269, 276
  undocumented 8, 299, 301
  see also emigrants; immigrants
Mikołajczak, H. (1925–2018) 172
Miles, R. 295–6, 307
Minas F. X. (1790–1854), quarantine physician in Zemun 86
minorities, minority issues 14, 21, 159–60
Mitrowitz/(Sremska) Mitrovica 38, 84
Mizrachi 259, 263, 265, 266, 271, 275–6, 282
mobility
  see human mobility
modernity 215, 265

Moldavia 47, 80, 84, 87, 96n.30
Moltke, H. von (1800–1891) 81
Montenegro 67, 108
Mrugowsky, J. (1905–1948) 167, 170
Muslim pilgrims 11, 17, 70, 93, 187
　see also Hajjis; Mecca
Muslims 91, 138, 276

Napoleonic Wars 8, 80
national self-determination 19, 157–60
National Socialism *see* Nazi Germany
nation states 4–5, 8, 14, 158–9, 181, 185, 194, 209
Nazi Germany 19, 160–74, 210
neoquarantinism 65, 94, 107, 120, 186
　see also revision system
New Deal 157, 208
New Orleans 199, 203, 205
New York City 199, 203–7, 300
　see also Ellis Island
non-governmental organisations (NGOs) 21, 209
nuclear war 14, 200, 208–12

Office Internationale d'Hygiène Publique 11
'Orient' 11, 83, 188
Orientalism 190, 194, 258, 282n.12
　epidemiological 190
orientalist assertions 187
orientalist claims 190
orientalist logic 194
Ostjuden 264
Otto I (1815–1867), King of Greece 90–1
Ottoman Empire 10, 11, 34–5, 37, 42, 44, 47, 79, 80, 83–4, 86–93, 106, 159, 186, 187, 190–1, 264
　see also Turkey
Ottoman 'fatalism' 187, 190, 194

Ottomans 32, 38–9, 181, 187–8, 190–4
Ottoman territory 37, 181, 188–9, 191–2, 194
Ottoman world 43

Pacini, F. (1812–1883) 62
Palestine 12, 161, 256, 263–4, 274
Palmerston, (Viscount) H. (1784–1865), Secretary of State for Foreign Affairs (1846–1851) 90–1
Panama Canal 12
pan-American sanitary conferences 12
Panczova/Pančevo 38, 84, 86
pandemics 6, 14, 208, 215
　see also cholera, pandemics; COVID-19 pandemic; influenza pandemic (1918–1919)
panic 1, 13, 79, 92, 109, 169, 199–210, 212–17, 230, 242, 268, 287
　see also fear
Panzac, D. (1933–2012) 34
Paris 37, 60, 80, 93, 143
Parsons, T. (1902–1979) 23n.10
passengers 59, 64–5, 90, 132, 136–8, 141, 144–6, 148–9, 232, 237–8, 246
passports 31, 38–9, 41, 185–6
pathogens 2, 5, 9, 16, 20, 40, 156, 166, 167, 170–1, 211, 291, 292, 298, 300–1, 302, 303–4
　see also germs
pathology 164–6
peddling 68, 117–18, 121
penicillin 178–179, 195
Perl, J. (1847/8–1901), district physician in Bukovina 115–16, 119

Perponcher-Sedlnitzky, W.
        (1819–1893) 90
Pest 84
    see also Budapest
pesticides 5, 156–7, 163
Peterson, V. (1903–1983) 209
Pettenkofer, M. von (1818–1901)
        62–3, 65
physical contact 9–10, 40–1, 139,
        297, 302–3
physical disabilities 159, 161
pilgrims 107
    see also Muslim pilgrims
plague 8, 9, 10, 31, 32, 33–5, 37, 40,
        42, 45–48, 52n.50, 56, 57–8,
        60–1, 62, 78, 80, 81–3, 85–9,
        92–3, 96n.30, 106, 147, 184,
        187, 191–2, 199, 219n.40
    bubonic, 33–4, 42, 92
    Levantine 32
    Oriental 85
    prevention of 10, 33, 37, 58, 110
Poland 160–1
    Nazi invasion of 164
poliomyelitis 207, 268, 278
ports 7, 10–11, 32, 37, 56–9, 62, 69,
        70n.2, 74n.57, 80–1, 88–93,
        105, 108, 120, 137–8, 144,
        155–6, 161, 189, 199, 206,
        229–31, 233–8 *passim*, 241,
        243–6 *passim*, 250, 289, 296
postcolonial state 7, 15–16, 227,
        295, 304
poverty 15, 68, 76n.84, 102–3, 105,
        107, 111, 113, 120–1, 163,
        204–5, 219n.35, 266, 270, 275
Prague 82, 161
    see also cholera; disease
        prevention; epidemic
        prevention; plague,
        prevention of; sanitary
        prevention

prophylactics/prophylaxis 17, 56,
        60, 65, 68, 70, 129–31, 145,
        148, 288
Prussia 80–3, 88, 90, 92
Prut River 106
public health 2–11 *passim*, 13, 16,
        21, 32, 37, 41, 69, 113, 144,
        147, 169, 199–206 *passim*,
        211–16, 233, 235, 237, 241,
        243, 245–6, 268, 274, 290,
        292, 299
Pulvertaft, R. J. V. (1897–1990)
        178–80, 195n.3

quarantine 2, 3, 6, 7, 8–12, 13, 16,
        17, 19, 20, 31–5, 36–48, 56,
        59–62, 64–6, 67–70, 75n.66,
        78–94, 100, 129–32, 134–149
        passim, 149n.4, 150n.11–
        154n.102 *passim*, 180, 184–190,
        197n.20–198n.43
    Britain in 188, 230, 252n.8
    home 2
    mail and 130, 142–4, 148
    maritime 38, 59–60, 64–5,
        67, 69, 72n.22, 79–80,
        90–93
    refugee camps and 288
    refugees in Israel and 272
    terrestrial 31–48, 65, 74n.53,
        79–80, 82–88, 92–3, 106,
        109, 120
quarantine stations *see* quarantine,
        terrestrial

race 16, 164, 197, 282, 185,
        291, 292–3, 295, 306,
        307, 309
    biologisation and 295
    in Britain 247, 248, 254, 255
    disease and 186, 302
    in Israel 256, 275

relations in Britain 242–4, 248, 250
Select Committee on 244, 254
racialisation 16
  concept of 295–6
  disease argument and 291
  of migrants in Britain 228
racialism 293
  'post-racial' 293
racism 13, 16, 183, 194, 195n.8, 227, 287, 291–4, 301, 303–4, 306, 307, 309
  anti-Muslim 294
  biomedical perception of disease and 304
  colonial 294
  colour-blind 293
  cultural racism 304
  exceptional 294
  humanitarian 295
  in Israel 284, 286
  new racism 301, 303
  popular in Britain 231–2, 242, 244,
  rationalised 304
  'School without Racism' 294
  scientific 292
  secondary 304
  see also anti-racism; xenophobic attitudes
Ragusa 109
  see also Dubrovnik
railway 56, 59, 63–5, 105, 109–10, 120, 156, 158
Red Sea 11, 16, 93, 189
refugees 2–17 *passim*, 19, 21, 43, 160–1, 215–16
  in the European Union 287–91, 293, 295–304 *passim*
  in Israel 256–63, 265–78 *passim*, 280–1
  see also asylum seekers
revision system 94, 100–1

Rijeka (town in Croatia) 32, 58, 67
Robert Koch Institute (RKI) 166, 170, 171
Rockefeller Foundation 159
Roma 68, 159, 164–6, 168
  see also 'Gypsies'; Sinti and Roma
Romania 35, 84, 106, 109, 116–18, 121, 160, 165
Rothenturm *see* Turnu Roşu
Rush, B. (1745–1813) 203, 206
Russia/Russian Empire 47, 79, 81–2, 84, 87–8, 91–3, 96n.30, 106–7, 109, 115–18 *passim*, 121, 155–6, 158, 170
  Bolshevik Russia 158
  see also Soviet Union

San Bartolomeo (near Trieste) lazaretto 59–60, 67
sanitary cordon 32–4, 37, 42–8, 61, 64, 65, 74n.57, 79, 81–2, 85, 87–8, 89, 92, 106, 137, 181
sanitary prevention 79, 121
  see also prevention
Saramago, J. (1922–2010) 288
SARS *see* Severe Acute Respiratory Syndrome (SARS)
scarlet fever 107, 112
school inspections 205, 207
Schutzstaffel (SS) 20, 166–72
Second World War *see* World War II
security 6, 12, 14, 68, 79, 92, 136, 191, 195n.10, 271, 272, 277, 280, 287, 296, 297, 298
  border 272
  global 6, 308n.50
  health 6, 296, 297, 302
  regimes 292, 294, 302
  see also biosecurity
Sedgwick, W. (1855–1921) 205

Sefardim 264
Semlin *see* Zemun
sentinels 182–3, 192, 193–4, 195, 196, 198
Serbia 35, 82, 84, 87, 88
Sereth (district in Bukovina) *see* Siret
Severe Acute Respiratory Syndrome (SARS) 70, 215, 288, 304, 309
sexual diseases, sexually transmissible diseases 234, 264, 269
Sigmund, K. I. (1810–1883), Austrian medical professor 88
Sinti and Roma 162, 166
  see also Roma
Siret 115, 117–18
Skiathos 91
Slavonia 36, 38, 84, 105
smallpox 105, 107, 112–13, 115–19, 121–2, 234
smoking 212–13
smugglers, smuggling 45, 85, 92
Snow, J. (1813–1858) 62
social class(es) 17, 38, 76n.84, 101–3, 120, 137–9, 148, 186, 202, 206, 212, 256, 271
social distancing 2, 9, 94, 207, 216
South Sudan 257
Soviet Union 159–60, 167, 209
  see also Russia/Russian Empire
Spain 37, 199
Spalato/Split 108, 109, 110
Spanish flu *see* influenza pandemic (1918–1919)
spatial structures 4, 8–9, 13, 18, 32, 35, 39–40, 43, 59, 79, 88, 101–2, 114, 130–1, 180, 183–4, 186, 191, 194, 196n.18, 228
spatial turn 4

spotted fever *see* typhus (Fleckfieber)
SS *see* Schutzstaffel (SS)
Staff-Reitzenstein, H. von (1790–1867) 81–2
steamers, steamships 56, 67, 88, 105, 129, 145, 188
stigma, stigmatisation 19, 21, 68, 170, 257, 270–1, 302–3
Strasbourg 168
  Reichsuniversität Straßburg 171
Sublime Porte 46, 89–90, 187
Suczawa/Suceava 84, 109
Sudan 15, 257, 259, 261, 266–7, 278
  see also South Sudan
Suez Canal 12, 67, 76n.74, 76n.77, 93, 188
Sulina estuary *see* Danube River
surveillance 1–18 *passim*, 31, 33–4, 36, 38–9, 44, 46, 65, 111, 139, 168, 185–6, 189, 205, 209, 228–9, 233, 235–6, 240–1, 243, 246, 289–90, 294, 297
Syria 34, 306n.15

territorial state 10, 12, 32, 129
Thessaly 60, 92
Trachoma 157, 159
trade 38, 56–7, 80–1, 89, 92, 101, 106, 116–17, 121, 129, 139–40, 184, 188, 190–1
  free 9, 62, 75n.61, 92, 100, 187–8
  global 10, 80, 88
  restrictions 46, 78, 89
  routes 105, 119, 132, 188
  see also goods; merchandise
traffic 48, 100, 105–6, 108, 110–11, 116, 120
  cross-border 38, 88, 92, 106–7
  limitations 10, 120
Transylvania 33, 36–8, 42–3, 50n.20, 52n.49, 82–4, 87

travellers 17–18, 38, 41, 43–4, 77n.86, 78, 86, 109, 131–2, 136–41, 145, 298
Trieste 11, 32, 38, 56–9, 63–5, 67–9, 70n.2, 71n.12, 73n.37, 73n.39, 74n.57, 74n.59, 76n.72, 105, 108, 134, 167
Trump, D., President of the United States (2017–2021) 1, 216
tuberculosis (TB), 6, 166, 230, 232, 234, 237, 239, 240, 241, 245, 250, 251n.4, 252n.24, 254n.65, 255n.77, 267, 269, 278, 302, 308n.48
Turkey 44, 48, 58, 84, 137, 289
see also Ottoman Empire
Turkish Republic 159
Turks 68, 84, 91, 191
Turnu Roşu (mountain pass in Romania)
quarantine of 38, 43–4, 46, 53n.54, 83–4
typhoid fever 107, 112, 155–6, 172, 207
typhus (Fleckfieber) 11, 68, 107, 156, 158, 164, 166, 169–74, 230, 292
Britain, migration and 230
Mexican migrants in the United States 292
Nazi medical research and 179, 183, 184

UK Movement for the Care of Children from Germany *see* Kindertransport
Ukraine 20, 84, 158, 162, 170
United Kingdom (UK) 2, 7, 14, 15, 65, 100, 143, 145, 160, 188, 227–50 *passim*
United Nations (UN) 6, 209

United Nations Children's Fund (UNICEF) 290
United Nations High Commissioner for Refugees (UNHCR) 290
United States (US) 1, 12–14, 100, 155–162 *passim*, 199–224 *passim*, 232, 249, 292–3, 300
upper classes 101–3, 202
see also elites

vaccination 112, 115–19, 121, 158, 167–74, 205–6, 268, 269, 278
vaccines 5, 166–7, 169–74
vagabonds 68, 107
variola *see* smallpox
Venice 10, 37–8, 64, 146, 190
Vienna 36, 38–9, 43, 45, 84–5, 93, 103–6, 108–11, 115–20, 159, 161–2
Congress of Vienna (1815) 10
Virchow, R. (1821–1902) 2

Wallachia 47, 51n.32, 53n.54, 80–1, 83–4, 87–8, 96n.30
Wallerstein, I. (1930–2019) 101, 295
Walsh, R. (1772–1851), 43–4, 46, 53n.54, 83
Warsaw 164
welfare state 19, 156–61, 174, 235, 300
western medicine 56, 302–3
World Health Organisation (WHO) 13, 181, 193–4, 215, 290–1, 298
World War I 11, 19, 71n.14, 11, 155, 157–8
World War II 7, 14, 19, 174, 178, 200, 201, 210, 212, 214, 227, 231, 249

xenophobic attitudes 266, 268, 270, 271, 284, 291, 303
X-ray 237, 238, 241, 246, 267, 284n.41

yellow fever 9, 58, 60, 166, 202–3, 207
Yellowlees H. (1919–2006) 243, 254
Yellowlees Report 246–9, 254, 255

Zadar/Zara 105, 108–9, 114
Zbąszyń (town in Poland) 160
Zemun (town in Serbia)
 quarantine 38, 84–6, 89
Zsupanek *see* Jupalnic

EU authorised representative for GPSR:
Easy Access System Europe, Mustamäe tee 50,
10621 Tallinn, Estonia
gpsr.requests@easproject.com